D0301383

Revolutionary Lives

Revolutionary Lives

CONSTANCE AND CASIMIR MARKIEVICZ

Lauren Arrington

PRINCETON UNIVERSITY PRESS

Princeton & Oxford

Copyright © 2016 by Princeton University Press
Published by Princeton University Press, 41 William Street,
Princeton, New Jersey 08540
In the United Kingdom: Princeton University Press, 6 Oxford Street,
Woodstock, Oxfordshire OX20 1TW
press.princeton.edu
All Rights Reserved
ISBN 978-0-691-16124-2
British Library Cataloging-in-Publication Data is available
This book has been composed in
Garamond Premier Pro and Bauer Bodoni Std
Printed on acid-free paper. ∞
Printed in the United States of America
1 3 5 7 9 10 8 6 4 2

IN MEMORY OF SANDRA ELIZABETH FIELDS SEYMOUR,

WHO DEDICATED HER LIFE TO CARE FOR THE POOR,

AND IN HONOR OF MY MOTHER, RITA LONG

ARRINGTON, WHO CONTINUES TO SERVE THEM

Contents

Preface

The Rebel Countess and the Polish Irishman

THEIR STORY IS ONE OF INFLUENCE AND INDEPENDENCE, of art and the theater, of nation and empire. Constance Gore-Booth (1868–1927) grew up on an expansive estate in County Sligo, on the west coast of Ireland. Long before she made history as the first female member of Parliament to be elected to Westminster and as a leading figure in the Irish Revolution, she defied the conventions of her social class, riding with the men in the local hunt, smoking cigarettes, and dreaming of a bohemian life dedicated to art. In Paris she met Casimir Markievicz (1874–1932), the dashing Polish count who had also left a comfortable life on a large rural estate to forge a new life. When he wasn't carousing the streets of Montmartre where he and Constance met, he taught painting and exhibited his work alongside some of the most revolutionary figures of the European avant-garde. After Constance and Casimir were married, they moved to Dublin, which was in the midst of a rapid cultural transformation in which they became eager and important participants. The friendships that they formed through the city's amateur theaters and bohemian salons facilitated their politicization. Constance, already involved in the suffrage movement, began to take part in nationalist and anti-imperialist debates. Her creativity and prowess as a writer and public speaker resulted in her rapid rise to prominence in Irish political life. Conversations about Ireland's ambitions and its relationship to the British Empire provoked Casimir into thinking about his native Poland and its relationship to Russia. He was inspired to fight for the Russian Imperial Army on the Eastern Front in the First World War, while she was at the forefront of Irish Republicanism and fought in the 1916 Easter Rising, the Anglo Irish War (1920–1921) and the Irish Civil War (1922), activities for which she was imprisoned on numerous occasions.

Constance Markievicz is a controversial figure who is often either caricatured as ignorant, fickle, and bloodthirsty or canonized as a national hero, a Republican martyr, and an unwavering servant of the poor. For this reason, *Revolutionary Lives* tells the story of the Markieviczes from contemporary source material, including letters, diaries, newspaper articles, and contemporaneous state records. A return to these sources serves to correct the generalizations that continue to be asserted about her life, most of which draw from the polemical writings of W. B. Yeats, Sean O'Casey, and the novelist Sean O'Faolain, who published the first biography of Constance Markievicz in 1934. The source material used here also uncovers new information about Casimir's life: his role in the Parisian and Dublin avant-gardes, his political writing during the February Revolution of 1917, and the extremist anti-Jewish attitudes that he expressed after he left Dublin. This is a biography of two figures that were revolutionary in very different ways. It is also a study of the role of the artistic avant-garde in political radicalization; the way that nationalist and anti-imperialist discourses in Ireland borrowed from Polish, Egyptian, and Indian struggles for autonomy; and how paintings and plays were sometimes used to codify nationalist and anti-imperialist politics.

Revolutionary Lives would have never been completed without the enthusiasm and expertise of many people. Roy Foster first suggested the possibility of a double biography; Catriona Kelly offered invaluable advice on Russian archives and introduced me to Alexandra Kasatkina, who translated the articles from *Russkoye Slovo*; Nina Szymor translated Casimir's articles from *Rzeczpospolita*; Pat Quigley, the author of *The Polish Irishman*, has generously answered my questions; Pamela Cassidy and the Walsh-Cassidy family have kindly made the material in the Lissadell Collection available.

Several of the ideas articulated in this book were first tested out at seminars and conferences. I am grateful to John Kerrigan and the Cambridge Group for Irish Studies; Michal Lachman and the University of Lodz; Meg Harper and the University of Limerick; Christine Corton and the Humanities Society at Wolfson College, Cambridge; Noel Harvey and the Irish Association for Industrial Relations; Jenny Daly, Ben Murnane, Nicholas Grene, Eve Patten, Chris Morash, Tom Walker, and the English Department at Trinity College Dublin.

This project benefited immensely from conversations during my fellowship at Cambridge University's Centre for Research in the Arts Social Sciences and Humanities during Lent Term 2012; my thanks to the director Simon Goldhill and to the other visiting fellows, especially Rachel Havrelock and Wilson Jacob for exciting and enlightening discussions. Thanks also to the Institute of Irish Studies and the School of Histories, Languages and Cultures at the University of Liverpool for a semester of research leave during the fellowship.

I am indebted to many helpful archivists: Mary Broderick and Sandra McDermott at the National Library of Ireland; Liam O'Reilly at the Public Record Office of Northern Ireland; Malachy Gillen at the Sligo Public Library; Lee Russell at the Sydney Jones Library, University of Liverpool; Maree Rigney at the National Gallery of Ireland; Ken Bergin at the Glucksman Library, University of Limerick; Brian Kirby at the Capuchin Provincial Archives in Dublin; Anne-Marie Ryan at Kilmainham Jail; Krystyna Klejn-Pochorowska at the Biblioteka Narodowa, Poland; Jessica O'Donnell at the Dublin Municipal Gallery, the Hugh Lane.

Thanks also to Brendan Barrington, Guy Beiner, Richard Bourke, Niall Carson, Clara Cullen, Patricia Deevy, Marianne Elliott, Matt Kelly, Lucy McDiarmid, Lia Mills, Will Murphy, Ciaran O'Neill, Manus O'Riordan, Deirdre Serjeantson, Helen Shaw, Frank Shovlin, Anne Thompson, Sonja Tiernan, Diane Urquhart, and Maureen Waters for their advice and contributions. Ultán Gillen scrutinized the chapters on the revolutionary period; Corrina Connor's comments on early versions of the Dublin years were invaluable; and Caoimhe nic Dháibhéid, Frank Shovlin, and Kelly Sullivan read and commented on full drafts, for which I am much obliged. Thanks to the anonymous readers at Princeton University Press for their helpful comments, and to Ben Tate and Hannah Paul, with whom it is a pleasure to work.

I am ever grateful to my parents for their love and support, and to Ali Shah for providing retreat, companionship, and conversation.

Revolutionary Lives

Figure 1. Constance Gore-Booth and Althea Gyles in London, circa 1893. (Reproduced by the kind permission of the Deputy Keeper of Records, Public Record Office of Northern Ireland, D/4131/K/10/115.)

1

Origins

THE STUDIO IS CLUTTERED WITH BRUSHES AND EASELS, oils and watercolors. Her own paintings and the work of her friends hang haphazardly on the walls alongside prints torn from folios and tacked-up tapestries. In the corner, a low iron stove heats a kettle. Copper, iron, and enamel pots hang from a shelf that runs along the back. Constance Gore-Booth slouches, smoking: her elbow on the table, the ash of her cigarette hanging precariously over a neglected cup of coffee. The surface is littered with dirty cups and bits of paper. A single candle stuffed into the neck of a wine bottle serves as a centerpiece. Opposite, in high-collared, austere taffeta with leg-of-lamb sleeves, the artist Althea Gyles tilts her chin upward, looking defiantly at the photographer. Constance, wearing a spattered smock thrown carelessly over a shirt, unbuttoned and showing the soft indentation at her clavicle, looks away. A hint of a smile plays across her face. She has made it to London, the place she regarded as "the centre of the Universe!"[1]

Frustrated by a life in "isolation" in County Sligo on the west coast of Ireland, where she met "no people with ideas beyond our own happy little circle," Constance Gore-Booth longed to leave her family's estate, Lissadell, to study at the Slade School of Art. In 1892, at twenty-four years of age, she was anxious to "cut the family tie" and make a life of her own, and she believed that art was the "opening" she needed.[2] She had been born to a sense of adventure; her father, Sir Henry, was an Arctic explorer who was constantly setting sail from Sligo to regions unknown. Both Henry and Constance's mother, Georgina, encouraged their children's interests, giving Constance

[1] Constance de Markievicz, "Memories—Mr Arthur Griffith: The Sinn Féin Organisation," *Eire* (Aug. 18, 1923).

[2] Diary of Countess Markievicz (1892), National Museum of Ireland (NMI), HE.EW892.

Leabharlanna Poibli Chathair Bhaile Átha Cliath
Dublin City Public Libraries

free rein to pursue her passion and skill in horsemanship and even allowing her to ride with the men in the local hunts. Josslyn, just a year younger than Constance, was sent to school at Eton and treated to expensive private tutors in London before he joined the Royal Munster Fusiliers and settled briefly in Canada, later returning to assume his duties as heir.[3] Eva, two years younger than Constance and also a strong rider, accompanied her father on his travels to the West Indies and the United States and was supplied with endless books on English and German literature, poetry, philosophy, and history. Mabel, born in 1874, and their youngest sibling, Mordaunt, born in 1878, were equally indulged. Riding and painting helped to channel Constance's seemingly boundless energy, but boredom bred mischief. Not long before she left for London, she masterminded the theft of a neighbor's cow and calf and took inordinate delight in hearing the family "call 'Sucky Sucky' on the Sligo road til midnight!"[4] Many anecdotes would circulate after her death about Constance's kindness to the Gore-Booth family's tenants, but her transgression of the boundary between the Big House and the peasant cottage was mostly a matter of fun and would give rise to "enduring jokes about pigs in Irish parlours."[5]

Impatient with the pace of life, Constance was, on the whole, insensitive to her extraordinary privilege. Constance and Eva were sent with their governess on tour to the Continent, where they rowed on the Rhine, heard Wagner at Beyreuth, and studied painting and sculpture in Italy. As a family, the Gore-Booths attended the London season each year, staying at their pied-à-terre, 7 Buckingham Gate, where Constance had been born. In Sligo, Georgina arranged for the best tuition in drawing and painting, with lessons from the Irish painter Sarah Purser, who had recently returned from the Académie Julian in Paris, and from the Swedish artist Anna Nordgren. Georgina commissioned Purser to paint Constance and Eva, then aged twelve and ten, and Purser observed an aptitude and precocity in the elder sister and urged Georgina to cultivate her talent. None of this care and generosity was evident to Constance, who complained in her adolescent diary of her insufferable and "parsimonious family."[6]

The "whirl of excitement" of family theatricals provided some relief from the constraints of daily life, and Constance relished the attention lavished on her at dances at home and in London.[7] Beside a newspaper clipping that

[3] James, *The Gore-Booths of Lissadell*.
[4] Diary, April 16, 1892, NMI.
[5] Morrow, *Picnic in a Foreign Land*, 297.
[6] Diary, n.d. [May?] 1892, NMI.
[7] Ibid., Jan. 14, 1892.

praised her "fine style" during the Sligo Harriers' latest hunt, she pasted in her diary a gossipy article about a party given by Lady Jane Lindsay, where "Prince George accompanied his brother, and they both showed considerable discrimination in giving their early dances to Miss Gore-Booth, whose beauty was universally admired."[8] This was the future king against whom she would later demand insurrection. For the present, she thought simply: "What Vulgar People the Royalties must be—This is the conclusion I come to after going to the Victorian Exhibition—NO taste in anything & every family event birth & marriage being celebrated by an awful Daub by an incompetent painter."[9]

Seven years after Constance was presented at court during Queen Victoria's golden jubilee, she had yet to meet her match. At first she had longed for a lover—"even a married one"—but now she simply longed for freedom. She had been afraid of disappointment—"So many people begin with great promise, greater hope, & end in nothing but failure & the poor house or improper"—but she finally mustered the courage to make a break and convinced her "arrogant narrow conventional unreasonable mother & soft mild milk & water father" to send her to the Slade.[10]

London was a study in perspective. Constance had been born there and had spent months socializing under close scrutiny, but she could now negotiate the city on her own terms. She lived lavishly at Sloane Terrace on Sloan Square and had no qualms about offering a five-shilling reward should she happen to mislay her sketchbook—compensation that was equal to more than twenty pounds in today's money.[11] Despite her privileged existence, she began to notice the poor and working-class people living around her: catching in hasty lines the figure of a street hawker beside his cart and a young girl selling flowers; stopping to draw a portrait of a man, face shaded by a flat-cap, sitting on the steps of a grand terrace house, holding a baby wrapped in swaddling. The urban environment awakened her to the extreme economic disparity that had been masked by the Gore-Booths' patronage of their tenants in Sligo. Constance was drawn toward the bourgeois, non-Marxist socialism that was fashionable among London's artists, and she attended a lecture by Beatrice Webb on "Trades Unionism & Socialism" at the Essex Hall.[12]

---

[8] "County Sligo Harriers," *Sligo Independent*, Mar. 31, and untitled clipping, "The Oaks dance," Diary, NMI.

[9] Diary, Feb. 9, 1892, NMI.

[10] Ibid., n.d.

[11] Sketchbook, Lissadell Papers, Public Record Office of Northern Ireland (PRONI), D4131/K/11.

[12] Details noted in ibid.

Webb's theories about the organization of labor in London were in part inspired by cooperation, an economic model of which Constance was aware owing to its popularity in Ireland. In 1894 the Eton- and Oxford-educated Sir Horace Plunkett, third son of Lord Dunsany, founded the Irish Agricultural Organisation Society. The IAOS, or the cooperative movement as it was widely known, sought to increase the profits of small farmers by eliminating middlemen and enabling producers to sell their goods directly. Constance's father, Henry, and her brother, Josslyn, established the Drumcliff Creamery Cooperative Agricultural and Dairy Society in 1895; Georgina laid the foundation stone, and Constance and Eva dressed as dairymaids to pose for promotional photographs.[13] The local newspaper, the *Sligo Champion*, praised the family for its enthusiasm and exertions "to elevate and improve the condition of the Industrial Classes."[14] The Gore-Booths' support for the cooperative movement was an extension of Anglo-Irish patronage, the sense that it was the responsibility of landlords to educate and improve the lives of their tenants. In London Constance was curious about social reform and the lives of others, but she maintained an aristocratic distance.

Constance aspired to her tutor Alphonse Legros's motto, *summa ars est celare artem*: the highest art conceals the means by which it is achieved. She experimented with portraiture, drawing sketch after sketch of Legros with various permutations of his impressive moustache. In one daring drawing, he reclines across the page dressed in an undershirt and a splendid pair of striped bathing trunks.[15] She was most adept at drawing faces, sensitive to the emotion in a glance, the character of a nose. And, of course, she drew the horses that had been her lifeblood at Lissadell. Her faithful hunter Max bucks and gallops through her sketchbooks, rebellious at being left behind.

One of her closest friends in London was Althea Gyles, "a strange, red-haired girl," whom W. B. Yeats would later depict in his autobiographies as emaciated and neurotic.[16] Gyles was a fellow Irishwoman from a wealthy Waterford family, who had met Yeats through the Theosophical Society in Dublin. She was also a poet, and in one of Constance's sketchbooks, she scribbled a verse that anticipates in its meter and diction the short poem "Sympathy" for which Yeats would later write an introduction.[17] It may have

[13] Tiernan, *Eva Gore-Booth*, 22.

[14] Ibid.

[15] Sketchbook, PRONI, D4131/K/11.

[16] W. B. Yeats, *The Collected Works of W. B. Yeats*, vol. 9: *Early Articles and Reviews*, ed. Frayne and Marchaterre, 423–24.

[17] The poem reads, "Of all the names that he and I / On earth have called each other by / None have been best & none been worst / None sweeter [illegilble] than last nor first / But only one

been through Gyles that Constance Gore-Booth first met Yeats. He visited her in June 1893, not long after she arrived at the Slade, while she was staying with friends at 35 Bryanston Square West.[18] They continued to see each other throughout the summer of 1894, and that July he inscribed a copy of his new symbolic drama, *The Land of Heart's Desire*, to her.[19] Set "in the County of Sligo, and at a remote time," Yeats's play imagines a young countrywoman who neglects the expectations of her mother and the demands of the parish priest in favor of "a vague, mysterious world" where the wind laughs and the white waves dance. Yeats's imagery combines Irish folklore with occultist themes, which resonate heavily with the ideas of the Hermetic Order of the Golden Dawn into which he had been initiated in 1890.

Like Yeats, Althea Gyles had begun her experiments in mysticism with the Theosophical Society, but she had also moved on to the Golden Dawn, which was concerned with magical practice. Gyles collaborated with Yeats on his early volumes of poetry, drawing magically symbolist designs for *The Secret Rose* (1897), *Poems* (1899), and *The Wind among the Reeds* (1899).[20] Yeats encouraged Constance to join the Golden Dawn, and he persuaded a reluctant Moina Mathers—the wife of Samuel Liddell MacGregor Mathers, who founded the Order—to tell their fortunes. Yeats wrote to Constance:

> She at first refused absolutely on the ground that she had ceased to tell them at all except when she was certain that her doing so would do good, but after a moments thought said that if either you or Miss Gyles thought you were at a great crisis of any kind & would promise to consider carefully any advice she gave, she would devine on the matter. She would however only tell the fortune of the one whose affairs were at this crisis. If there fore you write to me that one of you feels it *of great importance* I will write & tell Mrs Mathers and she will arrange a meeting before she returns to Paris within the week. She is, despite her youth a very advanced Kabalist & always busy & very little of the world so you must grant to her these exacting conditions.[21]

The results of the audience—if it ever came about—were entirely secret.

---

name—Love." Sketchbook, PRONI, 4131/K/11. For Yeats's introduction, see *Collected Works*, 9:423–24.

[18] W. B. Yeats to Constance Gore-Booth [June 21, 1893], in *The Collected Letters of W. B. Yeats*, vol. 1: *1865–1895*, ed. Kelly and Domville, 357.

[19] W. B. Yeats to Augusta Gregory (June 9, 1902), in *The Collected Letters of W. B. Yeats*, vol. 3: *1901–1904*, ed. Kelly and Schuchard, 198.

[20] Fletcher, "Poet and Designer."

[21] W. B. Yeats to Constance Gore-Booth (June 28 [1894]), in *Collected Letters*, 1:393.

Yeats visited the Gore-Booths in Sligo at Christmas 1894, ostensibly as part of his project to collect folklore. He bragged to his sister Lily that despite the vogue for the subject among the gentry, "Folk lore was a new experience to them. They had not thought it existed." Constance's childhood sketchbooks bear out Yeats's supposition. She drew pictures of castles and ruins, but they sit in a generic rather than a discernibly Irish landscape and are indistinguishable from her drawings of scenes from *Romeo and Juliet* and the *Odyssey*, and the supernatural figures that she drew were mermaids, not fairies.[22] Despite the foreignness of the topic, the Gore-Booths were hospitable to the young Yeats and humored his obsessions. They took him to see their tenants, one of whom "poured out quantities of tales," much to Yeats's delight. On leaving Lissadell, he made sure "They have now got all my books—including a large paper copy of 'The Countess Kathleen.'"[23] He described the Gore-Booths as a "very pleasant, kindly, inflammable family. Ever ready to take up new ideas & new things." While Constance's father, Henry, thought "of nothing but the north pole," her brother Josslyn's politics had made a strong impression: "'theoretically' a homeruler & practically some kind of humanitarian, much troubled by the responsibility of his wealth & almost painfully conscious. . . . He is not however particularly clever & has not, I imagine, much will." Yeats was in terrific awe of Constance's grandmother, a Tory who was obsessed with horses, "an invalede" and "mostly invisable" but nonetheless ruling with "an iron claw."

The Gore-Booth matriarch's ghostly presence disguised from Yeats the fact that her husband, Robert, had also dabbled in spiritualism. Robert had held regular séances at Buckingham Gate in London that were led by the talented and tubercular medium Daniel Douglas Home, whose followers also included Elizabeth Barrett Browning, Mark Twain, Leo Tolstoy, and the Empress Eugenie.[24] Home was famous for his spontaneously playing accordion, which would strike up a tune as the lights began to flicker.[25] According to an officer in the local branch of the Royal Irish Constabulary, Samuel Waters, who participated in the séances at Lissadell, for Robert Gore-Booth these were not party tricks but serious psychic experiences. Waters remembered sitting around a table in the dark, the group's fingers touching to make a circle; the table moved, strange taps could be heard, but the replies from

[22] PRONI, D4131/K/11.

[23] W. B. Yeats to Susan Mary Yeats (Dec. 16 [1894]), in *Collected Letters*, 1:418.

[24] Tiernan, *Eva Gore-Booth*, 18.

[25] Oppenheim, *The Other World*, 10–16. Home's mediumship is enigmatic, since unlike other mediums he was willing to proceed under less than complete darkness.

the spirits were often "ridiculous, and some absolutely false."[26] When Robert's cousin was murdered during the 1868 election, Robert held séances in an attempt to identify the perpetrator, but of all the names spelled out by the spirits, none were of people who were present at the scene of the crime. This disappointment may have stymied the occultist enthusiasms of Robert's generation at Lissadell, but Constance's parents, Henry and Georgina, were both attracted to the positivistic mysticism that was popular at the end of the century.

Georgina Gore-Booth was a close friend of Frederic Myers, the founder of the Society for Psychical Research. Myers and his colleagues studied spiritual phenomena in an attempt to explain it scientifically and thereby—they hoped—rescue the immaterial world from the overbearing influence of Darwinism. For Henry and Georgina and some of the Gore-Booth siblings, the spirit world replicated the social hierarchies of this world. When a young Mordaunt saw the figure of the hall-boy John Blaney—who had died at his own home that morning—in Lissadell's kitchens, Myers suggested that "something" of or from Blaney had "reverted to well-known haunts," and perhaps "the dead boy waited to manifest until his young master reached a suitable spot."[27]

Constance's and Eva's spiritualism was of a different order. In the 1880s and 1890s socialism and occultism worked as elective affinities; spiritualist utopianism was entwined with a social utopianism in which societal change could be imagined outside of a Marxist economic paradigm. These ideas were typical of the literati who shifted between William Morris's house in Hammersmith and Madame Blavatsky's rooms in Holland Park.[28] Over the course of their lives, the politics of Yeats, Eva, and Constance would sharply diverge: Yeats would turn to Fascism, Constance to Bolshevism, while Eva's gaze would stay fixed on the dream of poets and utopians. Yet in the 1880s

[26] "Memoirs of S.A.W. Waters," PRONI, D4131/D/2 (1).

[27] Myers, "On Indications of Continued Terrene Knowledge."

[28] Beaumont, "Socialism and Occultism at the *Fin de Siècle*." Blavatsky, a Russian Ukrainian aristocrat, had been denounced as a charlatan by the Society for Psychical Research in 1885 and set up a theosophist circle soon afterward. Theosophists did not believe in miracles or magic but in the power of the individual soul, which they believed could transcend one's self and reach communion with the great "oversoul," the repository of divine wisdom. The theosophists' prohibition on magic is what caused Yeats to turn to the Hermetic Order of the Golden Dawn, which encouraged magical practice. The Golden Dawn had a Masonic structure; at the first level, apprentices studied the Kabbala, as mentioned in Yeats's letter to Constance about Moina Mathers. The second level, to which Yeats aspired, was the Ruby Rose and the Cross of Gold. This level involved the practice of magic in the form of tarot divination and even astral travel. The third level was occupied by the Secret Chiefs, who gave instruction from the other world; see Raine, *Yeats, the Tarot and the Golden Dawn*; and Harper, *Yeats's Golden Dawn*.

they were still very much of the same mind. When Yeats visited Lissadell again in 1895, the weather was freezing, so they arranged a skating party and "made coffey on the shore."[29] Perhaps it was on one of those evenings that, sitting around the fire, he attempted to divine their futures.

Eva's horoscope showed Taurus in the fifth house, confirming her artistic nature.[30] Saturn dominated the first, suggesting that work was central to her identity, and that her concern with responsibility meant that she frequently put others' needs ahead of her own. Uranus in the eighth house also suggested that she was a psychic sensitive. All these characteristics would be borne out through her relentless campaigning for suffrage and working-class women, her devotion to writing esoteric verse, and her telepathic communications with Constance during long years of separation. In drastic contrast to her sister, Constance's ego was ruled by the energy and aggression of Mars. Virgo in the eighth house indicated a compulsive nature, a constrained sexual life—and even susceptibility to abdominal disease. Just as striking is the presence of Uranus in her seventh house, the House of Partnership, which relates to cooperation of the self and society. There, Yeats found sudden upheaval, even revolution.

Yeats's friendship with Constance and Eva was potentially a courtship, although toward which of the sisters his fondness most gravitated is ambiguous, and he was master at the art of "flattering the confidante while inhibiting the development of a full love-affair."[31] His attempt to draw Constance into the Golden Dawn is particularly telling, since it was through the society that he cavorted with his other romantic interests, Althea Gyles, Florence Farr, and Maud Gonne. In 1895 Yeats wrote to his sister, Lily, about Eva's "delicate gazelle-like beauty [that] reflected a mind . . . subtle and distinguished," and the image of the gazelle recurred in his poem "In Memory of Eva Gore Booth and Con Markiewicz" (1927).[32] In his draft *Autobiography*, published posthumously as *Memoirs*, he wrote that Eva was "for a couple of happy weeks my close friend, and I told her of my unhappiness in love; indeed so close at once that I nearly said to her, as William Blake said to Catherine Boucher, 'You pity me, there I love you.' 'But no,' I thought, 'this house would never accept so penniless a suitor,' and besides I was still in love with that other."[33]

Yeats was wholly devoted to "that other," Maud Gonne; yet as Gonne was cast as his Helen, Constance was almost his Diana. He wrote of how Con-

[29] W. B. Yeats to Susan Mary Yeats (Mar. 3, [1895]), in *Collected Letters*, 1:447.
[30] The three horoscopes are held in the Lissadell Papers, PRONI.
[31] Foster, *W. B. Yeats*, 1:144.
[32] W. B. Yeats to Susan Mary Yeats (March 3, [1895]), in *Collected Letters*, 1:447.
[33] W. B. Yeats, *Memoirs*, 78.

stance "all through my later boyhood had been romantic to me," how thinking of her he had recalled more than once "Milton's lines: Bosomed deep in tufted trees, / Where perhaps some beauty lies, / The cynosure of neighbouring eyes," and how she "surprised me now at our first meeting by some small physical resemblance to Maud Gonne, though so much shorter and smaller, and by a very exact resemblance in voice."[34] In the April following their skating party, he wrote to her: "I hear you were rather bruised at the hunt the other day. I hope the rumour is wholly untrue. Sligo is always full of rumours & the slightest one about its wild huntswoman naturally & properly echoes from mountain to mountain."[35]

What emerged between Yeats and the Gore-Booth sisters was a relationship of mutual patronage. Eva sought in Yeats a literary mentor, while Constance was most interested in his celebrity. She asked him to collect autographs for her, and he obliged with the signatures of his fellow poets Richard le Gallienne, W. E. Henley, and Aubrey de Vere; Helen Patterson Allingham (painter and wife of the poet William Allingham); novelist Katherine Tynan Hinkson; as well as leading figures in the Irish Revival, John O'Leary, Standish O'Grady, Douglas Hyde (who signed in Gaelic script), and George Russell, whose prestige would later establish Constance and Casimir in Dublin's artistic elite.[36] Yeats used his network to connect Eva to "literary people," since she showed ability but needed discipline, "a proper respect for craftsmanship," which he thought "she must get in England."[37] These roles would shift, when in 1899 Constance became an important guarantor of the Irish Literary Theatre, Yeats's new project with Lady Augusta Gregory and her neighbor, the playwright Edward Martyn.[38]

In 1896 Eva fell ill with a respiratory illness and was sent to Bordighera, Italy, to convalesce. There she met the British suffrage campaigner Esther Roper, who became her lifelong partner. Roper worked for local organizations in her native Manchester as well as on a national level in England, and she inspired Eva to initiate a branch of the Irish Women's Suffrage and Local Government Association when Eva returned to Ireland later in the year.[39]

[34] Ibid. Donoghue notes Yeats's incorrect substitution of "deep" for Milton's "high" in the lines from "L'Allegro."

[35] W. B. Yeats to Constance Gore-Booth (April 8 [1895]), in *Collected Letters*, 1:461–62.

[36] Ibid.

[37] W. B. Yeats to Olivia Shakespear (April 12 [1895]), in *Collected Letters*, 1:463.

[38] W. B. Yeats to Editor of the *Irish People* (October 29, 1899), in *Collected Letters*, 2:458.

[39] For the circumstances of their meeting and for Roper's role in the Special Appeals Committee and as the secretary of the North of England Society for Women's Suffrage, see Tiernan, *Eva Gore-Booth*, 28–44. The Irish Women's Suffrage and Local Government Association was founded by the Quaker reformers Anna and Thomas Haslam in 1876; Quinlan, *Genteel Revolutionaries*.

Constance was ready for such an opportunity. In addition to public acts of rebellion—smoking conspicuously, leaving her family to study at the Slade—she expressed private frustrations about the relegation of women to a separate sphere. In her adolescent diary, she declared, "I have no God, nothing to worship & I feel the want, women are made to adore & sacrifice themselves." She demanded that she also deserved "something to live for, something to die for."[40] As she matured, this longing for a lover, "even a married one," was redirected into an ambition to change the social order.

Public reforms and private relationships inspired the Gore-Booth sisters' suffrage work. In addition to Esther's influence, their mother, Georgina, was a quietly sustaining influence. When Constance was very young, Georgina established a school of needlework for the women on the Lissadell estate. She taught crochet, embroidery, and darning and arranged for the women to sell their work, which provided them with an independent income.[41] In 1896 British and Irish suffragists believed that the United Kingdom was on the cusp of radical change. The Local Government Act of 1894 increased wealthy women's power in the public sphere, permitting those who met specific property qualifications to serve as Poor Law guardians. In Ireland the Dublin Women's Suffrage Association proclaimed that the act was a landmark in the women's movement: "There is nothing which has happened in our time that has imparted so powerful a stimulus . . . to our fellow countrywomen."[42] Provoked by Esther's work, Constance and Eva seized on this sense of promise.

Constance and Eva insisted that they were not going to settle for a mere extension of the vote but demand a complete parliamentary franchise. They organized a local committee of what would be just the third branch of the Irishwomen's Suffrage and Local Government Association in the country. On Christmas Eve, 1896, Constance was elected president; Eva, honorable secretary. Mabel served on the committee composed of local men and women. Despite support from both sexes, when the Gore-Booth sisters held an open meeting two days later, the building was "packed to the doors," mostly with men who had turned out in opposition.[43]

The sisters had prepared to meet their opponents with the full force of a rich and subversive discourse. Eva called on "Irishwomen to follow the example of the farmers at Drumcliff, and to insist . . . on taking their affairs

---

[40] Diary, Mar. 20, 1892, NMI.

[41] Tiernan, *Eva Gore-Booth*, 11.

[42] Quoted in Owens, *Social History of Women in Ireland*, 13.

[43] "Women's Suffrage Movement," *Sligo Champion*, Dec. 26, 1896.

into their own hands."[44] Her allusion had several possible interpretations, depending on the sympathies of the listener. Sligo farmers had recently asserted their independence through cooperation, but Sligo had also been central to the land agitation for which Constance and Eva had declared their support, riding to a meeting at Boyle where they stated unequivocally that "they were on the side of the people and against privilege."[45] Land agitation and women's suffrage were closely related because of the activities of the Ladies' Land League of 1881–82, when Irishwomen took control of the mass movement to liberate tenant farmers from the oppressive rents imposed by landlords.[46] Michael Davitt, the Land League's founder, held a meeting on the Gore-Booths' property in the autumn of 1879, when over eight thousand people assembled to hear his warnings of "impending famine and dire misfortune."[47] Davitt encouraged tenants to put their own family's needs first before giving anything to the landlord, and then only "give him what you can spare." Immediately after the meeting, Davitt was arrested on the charge of sedition and imprisoned in Sligo Jail, where he was subjected to a sensationalized trial before his release. The imprisonment of the leaders threatened to put an end to agitation, but Davitt encouraged prominent women, including Anna Parnell, the sister of Charles Stewart Parnell, to continue their work. The Ladies' Land League was dissolved after just one year, but it had a monumental legacy in women's exercise of political agency in the public sphere. While late Victorian Irish novelists, such as Emily Lawless, imaginatively conjoined the woman question and the land question, the Ladies' Land League was an actual political benchmark—not just for feminism but also for the partnership of feminism and nationalism. Most women in the Ladies' Land League were not suffragists since suffrage enjoyed a close relationship to a pro-imperialist, and even racist, position; nonetheless, the women in the league set a feminist precedent.[48] Later Constance would work in another women's organization, Cumann na mBan, alongside Jennie Wyse Power, when similar debates over the relationship of suffrage, the British Empire, and the Irish nation arose.

The Gore-Booths had a difficult history as landlords. Constance's grandfather, Robert, had left the management of Lissadell to an agent while he undertook his education at Westminster School and Queens College,

[44] Ibid.

[45] James, *Gore-Booths*, 203–4.

[46] Ward, "The Ladies' Land League, 1881–82," in *Unmanageable Revolutionaries*, 4–39; and Mulligan, "'By a Thousand Ingenious Feminine Devices.'"

[47] "Mr Parnell in Sligo," *Nation* (Nov. 29, 1879), quoted in Tiernan, *Eva Gore-Booth*, 14.

[48] Ward, "Gendering the Union." For a similar relationship between the Ladies' Land League and the Ladies' Committee for the Patriotic Children's Treat, see Pašeta, *Irish Nationalist Women*, 35–37.

Cambridge. His absenteeism led to a great deal of suffering; the Royal Commission for Inquiring into the Condition of the Poorer Classes in Ireland reported in 1836, "Nothing could exceed the miserable appearance of the tenantry, living, for the most part, in wretched small cabins, clustered together without deserving the name villages" and subsisting on an illicit trade in whisky.[49] Robert's improvements to the estate were also misguided. He consolidated small farms in order to clear large tracts, which displaced many tenants; in his munificence, he offered to send them to North America. During the famine of the 1840s, Robert redressed some measure of wrong by setting up a mill for grinding corn to distribute to the poor and by using his investments in England to concentrate his finances in the Sligo economy.[50] On the whole, Robert managed Lissadell in an attitude of fear. During the election of 1868—the year that his cousin, Captain King, was murdered and the year that Constance was born—Robert put the house in a "state of defence": sandbagging the windows, mounting guns on the roof, cutting down trees around the house, and sending out mounted patrols from the household servants and male family members to cooperate with the police.[51] Henry's attitude was not exactly antithetical to his father's. He spent months away from Lissadell on his Arctic excursions, "drawn by some magnetic power towards the north," but he responded positively to the land agitations.[52] Henry reduced rents on his estate to the most recent valuation and lowered them below their market value when tenants were suffering from particularly difficult conditions. In this way Henry and Georgina's philanthropic attitude toward their tenants laid the foundations for Constance and Eva's social activism.

Amid the Christmas evergreen that decorated the meeting hall, the Gore-Booth sisters hung banners proclaiming revolutionary slogans that illustrate a nexus of ideas at play among Irish nationalism, feminism, and abolitionism. One banner brandished Lord Byron's line, "Who would be free, themselves must strike the blow," words that Frederick Douglass adopted in his abolitionist essays and speeches in which he addressed the emancipation of Irish Catholics in conjunction with the emancipation of black slaves.[53] There was even a hint of republicanism. The battle cry of the American Revolution—"No taxation without representation"—was proclaimed alongside the demand for "liberality, justice, equality."[54]

---

[49] Quoted in Tiernan, *Eva Gore-Booth*, 3.
[50] Thomas Kilgallon, "Memories," PRONI, D4131/D/2 (1); and Tiernan, *Eva Gore-Booth*, 7.
[51] Kilgallon, "Memories."
[52] Yeats, *Collected Letters*, 1:418–19n4.
[53] Douglass, "Men of Color, to Arms!"
[54] "Women's Suffrage Movement," *Sligo Champion*, Dec. 26, 1896.

Constance proved to be a natural public speaker, addressing the crowd with remarkable confidence. She announced that she intended to dispel the "wild gossip" that was circulating about suffrage: "that it will cause women to ape the other sex, to adopt their clothes, copy their manners and peculiarities, that it will cause women to neglect their homes and duties, and worst of all, prevent the majority marrying. (oh.) Of course this may be true; 'Pigs might fly,' as the old prophecy says, 'but they are not likely birds' (laughter)."[55] For Constance, twenty-eight years old and unmarried, with horsemanship that exceeded the abilities of most men in County Sligo, to claim that suffrage was not a threat to masculinity may have seemed tenuous. She nonetheless carried her audience through politically deft turns of argument. She claimed that Ireland—"our country"—had been at the forefront of the fight for liberty but was now "so far behind England" in the struggle to emancipate such a large portion of its population. She asked, rhetorically, "if women are so incompetent," why had there never been an outcry against "our woman Queen?" Such a blatant appeal to reason was grounded in her reading of John Stuart Mill, whose "The Subjection of Women" (1869) she quoted to her audience. (There is a connection to the land question here, too. Mill's stepdaughter, Helen Taylor, was a radical suffragist and served as president of the Ladies' Land League of Great Britain and attended demonstrations in Ireland.[56]) Constance reminded her listeners that it had been a generation—thirty years—since Mill and Disraeli supported suffrage in the British Parliament. She complemented reason with feeling, concluding with emotive religious rhetoric that would characterize her propaganda throughout her life: "Many of our ablest teachers are gone, they saw the Promised Land from the mountain top, then died like Moses in the wilderness, having had their glimpse of the land of Canaan, dim and faint in the distance."

In these early days of political activity, it was easy to put campaigning aside for family and fun. The short winter days were spent on hunting and shooting parties, and amateur theatricals and concerts filled the evenings. The year culminated in the annual ball, which kept Lissadell alit until five o'clock on Christmas morning. The family's gruff but beloved butler, Kilgallon, described the festivities: sideboards crowded with a boar's head sporting an orange in its mouth, "game pies, boned turkeys, roast turkeys, ham, round spiced beef," washed down with an "unthinkable" quantity of booze: "whiskey and wine. Port and Madeira, champagne of the best vintage."[57]

---

[55] Ibid.
[56] Ward, "Imperial Feminism," 82. Taylor advocated land nationalization in Britain.
[57] Kilgallon, "Memories."

The holiday spirit lapsed into an austere January, when Constance spoke about suffrage to the Sligo branch of the Women's Temperance Union. In the little schoolroom attached to the Congregational Church, she professed her full support of abstention, as a "woman who realized her position in the world." After a round of applause replete with waving handkerchiefs, the teetotalers elected Constance Gore-Booth the president of the North Sligo Women's Suffrage Association.[58] Constance proved that she was willing to do what was necessary politically, but she privately mocked asceticism. With her course at the Slade finished, she could not countenance a permanent return to Irish country life. Eva moved to Manchester, and Constance embarked for Paris to try once again for a life dedicated to art.

[58] "Miss Gore-Booth on Women's Suffrage," *Sligo Independent*, Jan. 30, 1897.

Figure 2. Casimir and Constance Markievicz in Paris, circa 1899. (Reproduced by the kind permission of the Deputy Keeper of Records, Public Record Office of Northern Ireland, D/4131/K10/111.)

2

##

Bohemia

AT THE HEART OF FIN DE SIÈCLE EUROPE, IRISH SEPARATISM
was gaining force, but Constance Gore-Booth never met Maud Gonne, who
was publishing the radical newspaper *L'Irlande Libre*.[1] She was moving in
different circles in the metropolitan avant-garde. Paul Henry, one of the
most famous Irish artists of the twentieth century, remembered parties with
" '*The* Gore Booth,' as we called her," and the annual bacchanalia that was the
student ball at the Moulin Rouge. For Constance's first year at the Académie
Julian, the theme was the Inquisition, and the young artists were tasked with
designing costumes for "a couple of hundred Trappist monks in their white
habits. A gruesome collection of racks, thumbscrews and other instruments
of torture"; it was a "huge success."[2]

Alongside the Irish revelers were the Poles, who had gravitated to Paris
in the 1880s following the first wave of foreign students, mostly Americans and Britons, who aspired to learn this new "Parisian quality" at the
École des Beaux-Arts.[3] In 1890, at least eleven important Polish modernists were there.[4] Yet not all the novateurs, jeunes, or indépendants, as they
were described—for they had yet to identify collectively as an avant-garde—

---

[1] Gonne later wrote to Stanislaus Markievicz that she had "no information" about Constance's
Paris days: "I was not much there when she was working at Julian's Academy. I was working for
evicted tenants in the Land War, & preparing the '98 Centenary." PRONI, D4131/K/8.

[2] Henry, *An Irish Portrait*, 18.

[3] Cottington, "Formation of the Avant-Garde," 601.

[4] These were Teodor Axentowicz (1882–1895), Józef Czajkowski (1891–1894), Stanislaw
Debicki (1890–1891), Konstanty Laszczka (1891–1896), Ludwik de Laveaux (1889–1894), Józef
Mehoffer (1891–1896), Józef Pankiewicz (1889–1890), Wladislaw Podkowinski (1889–1890),
Jan Stanislawski (1885–1895), Leon Wyczólkowski (1889), and Stanislaw Wyspianski (1891–
1894); see Cavanaugh, *Out Looking In*, 42.

were modernists, and neither were all bohemian novateurs.[5] Bohemianism was reliant on the bourgeoisie, both as an aesthetic Other and as a material means. Private incomes enabled middle-class people, particularly men, to live for art's sake. In the late nineteenth century the bourgeoning independence of bourgeois women made them an important new market for Parisian academies. Although they would not be permitted to enter the École des Beaux Arts until 1897, Rudolphe Julian's academy was open to both sexes, but women paid higher fees and were taught in separate studios from the men. This segregation was Julian's concession to bourgeois families who were as concerned about "mixed classes" as they were with the mixing of the sexes.[6] The first of Julian's women's ateliers, at 27 Galerie Montmartre in the passage des Panoramas, became so full that by 1895 he expanded into rooms in the nearby rue Vivienne. In 1888 a new women's studio was opened on the rue du Faubourg Saint-Honoré, in the fashionable eighth arrondissement near the Champs-Élyssées. There Constance Gore-Booth studied in an environment no less rigorous than that of the men, some of whom were taught by Casimir Markievicz across the river, in Julian's studios in the rue du Dragon.

Casimir had come to Paris from Kiev, where he had studied—and utterly failed at—law. Inattentive to endless rote learning, which he felt created "a vacuum in his brain," he applied himself to portraiture and to learning the traditional techniques of Polish landscape painting.[7] As in some early Irish modernist painting, in Polish landscape painting, rural scenes codified the idea of the Polish nation and could simultaneously express romantic and subversive ideas. While there was certainly a Parisian influence on Polish painting, this was not overly determinate; rather, Polish modern artists were developing stylistic innovations that complemented the Paris scene.[8] Casimir's training in Kiev accelerated his success in Paris, where he, like Constance, sought like-minded people. Unlike Constance, however, Casimir did not travel unaccompanied. During his time in Kiev, he had fallen in love with Jadwiga Splawa Neyman, a fair-haired, hazel-eyed twenty-something, who followed him to Paris on the pretense of studying music. They moved in together, living on Casimir's allowance of two hundred francs a month from the Markievicz family, who gave him the money alongside a large dose of disapproval. Out of obligation or convenience, Casimir and Jadwiga married, living first in a hotel and then in rooms in the rue St. Placide, west of the

[5] Cottington, "Formation of the Avant-Garde," 607.

[6] Fehrer, "Women at the Académie Julian in Paris."

[7] The phrase comes from Markievicz's later semiautobiographical short story; see Quigley, *Polish Irishman*, 11.

[8] Cavanaugh, *Out Looking In*, 125–29.

Luxembourg Gardens, before moving to a better address in the rue Bona-parte, off the boulevard Saint-Germain. There their first son, Stanislaus, was born, on July 22, 1896.[9]

Soon after Stanislaus's birth, Casimir left Paris for St. Petersburg to un-dertake his military service in the Russian Army. This was compulsory for all men of twenty-one years of age throughout the empire, with varying lengths of service depending on the level of education each man had received. The elite, who were university educated and had fluency in the Russian language, were required to serve only one year of active duty. Graduates of second-ary or higher education could also enlist voluntarily, which enabled them to enjoy greater freedoms, such as living outside the barracks. After their year of compulsory service, these men were granted a commission and served as officers during the remainder of their service.

The Markieviczes, like the Gore-Booths, were upper-class landowners who were settled in disputed territory. Their expansive estate, Zywotowka, stretched over the fecund plains of western Ukraine, nominally Poland but also considered as part of Russia. Caught between two empires, the landed elite in eastern Galicia believed that their best future did not rest in the hands of Austria-Hungary, which had a policy of supporting the under-classes, particularly white-collar workers, in order to enforce a sense of loy-alty. The elite was courted by Russia, which saw the landed class as an impor-tant ally in its anti-Austro-Hungarian policy.[10] Importantly, despite having fluency in the Russian language and professing an allegiance to Russian po-litical structures, many of these families, including the Markieviczes, were *Russianized* but not *Russified*. Essentially, they were Poles whose affinity to Russia was driven by opportunism.

Despite his voluntary enlistment, Casimir was not an army man. After a year of service, he returned from St. Petersburg to the prestigious École des Beaux Arts and to the apartment that he shared, for the moment, with Jad-wiga. Admission to the Beaux Arts was competitive and its standards exact-ing (Rodin and Vuillard famously failed its entrance exam), but its aesthetic had become far too conventional for Casimir's tastes. None of his surviving paintings suggest that he was interested in such radical experiments as poin-tillism or Cloisonnism, but he embraced the Indépendants' rejection of the staid selection process of the Salon. The Indépendants rebelled against the academy by putting their work directly on public view. Cézanne, Gauguin, Toulouse-Lautrec, Seurat, and Pissarro had founded the Indépendants, and

---

[9] Quigley, *Polish Irishman*, 13.
[10] Leslie, *The History of Poland since 1863*, 96–98.

they selected Casimir's oil paintings and portraits for the exhibitions of 1896, 1897, and 1898. They saw in his work a revolutionary use of color. Most of Casimir's paintings survive only in black-and-white reproductions from catalogs, which disguise his remarkable use of strange shades, such as the purple sky of *Landscape Study*, which now hangs in the Dublin City Gallery, the Hugh Lane.

In addition to his use of color, the fluidity of Casimir's brushstrokes exemplifies what Roger Fry would later describe as postimpressionism, although Casimir would disavow the categorization. One of the paintings in his first exhibition for the Indépendants was *The Travelling Beggar*, which by its title evokes one of Manet's preoccupations.[11] There is also a strong pre-Raphaelite influence in Casimir's depiction of human figures, such as in his allegorical painting *Amour*, which was also exhibited under the titles *St. John's Eve* and *Russian Legend*. The painting depicts a nude man lying on the forest floor, his body covered by a nymph who shelters him from the towering sinister trees.[12] The luminescent quality of the male figure's body is similar to Millais's *Ophelia* or Rossetti's *Dante's Dream*. Casimir's portrait *Constance in White* from 1899 (retitled *The Artist's Wife* after their marriage) similarly evokes a pre-Raphaelite influence. Constance stands in profile on a tall canvas, which exaggerates her long throat and slender arms, and on her left hand is the ring she wore as a symbol of her marriage to art. Casimir's most triumphant piece for the Indépendents was the triptych *Bread*, which was exhibited in 1898. On the left panel, *Sowing with Seed* depicts a solitary figure, seed-sack on his back, walking away from the viewer down a plowed furrow toward the horizon. The right panel, *Harvesting*, depicts a woman standing with her head bowed, scythe in hand, between tall sheaves of wheat. In the center the steaming *Loaf of Bread* is exalted on a pristine white cloth, behind which the plain wall of the cottage is broken by a small square window, a crucifix, and the vague lines of a painting that suggests a landscape of standing sheaves. This secular triptych subverts the orthodoxy of religious art and proclaims the sanctity of the everyday in accordance with Pissarro's line, "Let us, rather, be artists, and we will be able to experience everything, even a *paysage* without being *paysan*."[13]

At some point during 1898, Casimir and Jadwiga began to live separately. In Paris he had developed a reputation as a bit of a cad, but there are suggestions that Jadwiga was also unfaithful. Their relationship was already

---

[11] See, e.g., *Beggar with a Duffle Coat (Philosopher)* (1867), now at the Art Institute of Chicago.

[12] According to the legend that *Amour* depicts, true love is promised to the person who picks a rare fern, but any display of emotion on finding that love will be met with immediate death.

[13] House, "Framing the Landscape."

disintegrating when a second son, Ryszard, was born. According to a later account by Stanislaus, who would have been too young to remember the details well at all, Jadwiga fell ill with consumption, and Casimir sent her and both children to live with her parents in Ukraine. Shortly afterward, she and the baby succumbed to illness. This became the official story in the Markievicz family. However, another account in a more reliable but incredibly sparse Russian police report suggests that Jadwiga went into labor on the train to Ukraine and developed peritonitis, and she and the baby died soon after arriving home. Neither story gives any suggestion that Casimir made the journey back to Zywotowka, even briefly. Instead, Stanislaus stayed on at the Markievicz estate in the care of his grandmother, while Casimir began life again as a boulevardier.[14]

It is unclear whether it was before or after Jadwiga left Paris that a Polish art student, Janina Flamm, who had recently married the British landscape painter Eric Forbes-Robertson, took Constance to a party that changed the course of her life. There she met and danced with the aspiring writer Stefan Krzywoszewski, who had dined earlier that evening with Casimir Markievicz on cheap steak, undoubtedly *cheval*. When Casimir arrived he found the atmosphere full of

> noise, crowd, indescribable squealing. Dancing in a way unknown to any ballet school are Africans, Indians, maharajas, Apacheans, monks with hoods on their heads, medieval knights, bullfighters, Florentine masters, Empire ladies, odalisques, Columbines, all sorts of nymphs and goddesses of different types. Lanterns are glimmering, confetti is in the air, the orchestra is playing loudly. . . . It's hot; the smell of perfume is everywhere, so the smell of art studios, fresh paint and sweat. Champagne is popping somewhere. I'll go and have a look.[15]

Krzywoszewski, dancing with Constance (whom he described as "this living Rossetti or Burne-Jones"), introduced her to Casimir as soon as he passed by, remarking, "You will be well matched in height and bearing," before withdrawing to watch them chat "animatedly," "outstanding in the lively, dancing crowd."[16] They were, as Constance later wrote home to Josslyn, "great pals and comrades ever since."[17] Eva and Esther Roper met Casimir on one of

[14] Quigley, *Polish Irishman*, 14–16.
[15] Casimir Markievicz, "Letters from Ireland," *Rzeczpospolita* 252 (n.d. [1922]): n.p. My thanks to Nina Szymor for translating this series of articles.
[16] Quoted in Quigley, *Polish Irishman*, 19.
[17] Constance Gore-Booth to Josslyn Gore-Booth (n.d.), PRONI, D4131/K/1.

their visits to Paris, but Constance waited much later to introduce him to her family officially.

One of the reasons for her delay was the sudden death in January 1900 of her father from complications arising from a severe bout of influenza. Henry was susceptible to lung disorders after years spent exposed to the Arctic air. He and Georgina first sought out the arid climate of South Africa, but they had been driven home by the Boer War. They soon left Ireland again, this time for St. Moritz in the Swiss Alps, where they hoped the dry cold would ease the strain on his lungs, but there he died suddenly and possibly wrongfully. Josslyn's daughter, Aideen, later wrote that Henry was administered an overdose of chloroform from the clinician who was treating him.[18] Constance almost certainly made the journey from Paris to St. Moritz, but there is no surviving correspondence with her family until her letters to Josslyn on black-bordered stationery, announcing her engagement.

Con and Casi, as they called each other, spent their days cycling around the city, smoking in the cafés, talking, painting, and partying—often outrageously in fancy dress in the cobbled streets of Montmartre. Their easy companionship quickened when Casimir received news of Jadwiga's and Ryszard's deaths. The British novelist Violet Hunt—lover of Somerset Maugham and H. G. Wells—remembered meeting Constance and Casimir at a restaurant in the boulevard Montparnasse. "Teuf-teuf," as Constance's fellow students called her, came up to the table where Hunt was dining with a friend. With her tawny hair "worn *a la Mérode* over her ears and under her sailor hat," a pink blouse "very much open at the collar," and a face full of "boyish frankishness and camaraderie," she

> ordered an exiguous lunch and sat down. All the rapins looked at all the other rapins as if all the rapins were in love with her. I have heard that they were. One of them rose from his distant seat and offered her a light from his cigarette. When the handsome Byronic figure had gone back to his place she whispered to me: "I didn't introduce my friend. He is a genius, only very poor, and that makes him shy. He is a Polish Count. His name is Casimir Markievicz."[19]

Whether Casimir was in fact a count was a major concern for Josslyn, who immediately enlisted the British ambassador to the Russian Empire, Sir Charles Scott, to find out whether he was the caliber of person "the young lady's friends would like to see her marry." Scott in turn contacted Count

[18] James, *Gore-Booths*, 93–94.
[19] Quoted in ibid., 139.

Muravieff, the imperial Russian foreign minister, who enlisted State Councilor Rachkovsky, a member of the secret police, to spy on them. Rachkovsky reported that "Without right" Casimir had taken the title of count: "Poland has never had a Count of that name." He suggested that the Markieviczes may have insalubriously purchased their title at the Vatican or from the Austro-Hungarians. During the investigation, Casimir's finances were also called into question; Rachkovsky reported, "one knows that he spends a lot of money" keeping up his reputation as a "Bon Vivant," entertaining fellow art students, drinking "a great deal of champagne," hiring musicians, playing "billiards and cards" and so "passionately given to gambling that he allowed himself to lose his prized bicycle."[20] With those qualifications, Rachkovsky surmised, "there is nothing with which to reproach him."

Josslyn, hardly relieved, felt as the family heir a deep sense of responsibility for his sister. In an attempt to regain some measure of control over her behavior, he kept a tight hold on her finances, tacitly refusing to send her a checkbook and thereby unintentionally putting Constance behind in her rent. With just three francs left, she wrote with uncharacteristic pleading to ask him to send £10 that she might pay her landlord, buy paints and canvasses, and pay £2 owed to her color-mixer.[21] When she heard nothing in reply, she tried good humor: "I hope to goodness we don't go into chancery, I gather if that is the case one's grandchildren may possibly receive 6d one-selve ne'er a sou." To assuage whatever panic the mention of grandchildren might have induced, she added, "of course we wont have children, I think it would be really wicked on this money we may possibly have. At the best we shall only just be able to live & work at our painting."[22]

Josslyn sought council from the Gore-Booth family's friend Violet Bryce, the wife of the Viscount James Bryce who was serving as MP for Aberdeen South and would later hold the post of chief secretary for Ireland.[23] Constance and Casimir had spent part of the winter of 1899–1900 with the Bryces and had left Violet with the impression that there was not "the smallest chance of his making her happy." She warned Josslyn that she suspected Casimir of being a fortune hunter. She had first met him in Paris, and when prompted by the rumors circulating about Constance and Casimir, she had

---

[20] "Mrs Markievicz I Presume?," *Irish Times* April 4, 1994, 10. Josslyn Gore-Booth, at Constance's advice, also contacted the Department of the Heraldry in St. Petersburg, which confirmed that Casimir Markievicz had been "accorded the dignity of Hereditary Noble" and had the right to be included in the genealogy of the nobility; PRONI, D4131/K/1 (96).

[21] Constance to Josslyn Gore-Booth (n.d.), ibid. (22).

[22] Ibid. [received April 28, 1900] (25).

[23] James Bryce served as chief secretary from 1905 to 1907.

asked him rather bluntly whether or not he intended to propose: "he told me he had no intention whatever of doing so" since Constance was more of a "'Comrade' and more of a man than a woman." However, Casimir would be willing to choose her over anyone else if there were "sufficient money to help him in his art."[24] Bryce worried that she had overstepped her place and had perhaps "pitted" herself "against an unscrupulous man and a woman who is desperately in love & who would sacrifice anything—friendship and her chance of happiness in life to acquire her desire." She offered to do whatever possible to prevent Constance from making a miserable mistake but also promised Josslyn that she would say nothing further if "the thing is inevitable."

The "thing" was. Constance was sensitive to her family's concerns but had firmly resolved to marry: "I hope you all wont mind because its a foreigner, but, I'm awfully fond of him & he is not like a Frenchman, much more like a fellow countryman."[25] Even so, she wished he were an Englishman for her family's sake, since she worried that the marriage risked "putting a barrier" between herself and her family and might make her "an alien & a stranger." Bryce's warning prompted Josslyn to caution Constance that Casimir might have ignoble motives, but Constance leapt to his defense. She had every intention to "keep control" of her own finances and would take full advantage of the Married Women's Property Act, which gave her, not her husband, the right to her inheritance. She wanted nothing from the Markievicz family in terms of a dowry, but she was careful to let Josslyn know that this was not because Casimir was penniless. She expected that Casimir would come into his inheritance of £160 a year within four years, would inherit the family estate on his mother's death, and was in any case entitled to a house in the meantime, with "servants horses everything."[26] But new money meant very little to Josslyn. What mattered was the Markievicz title. As Constance was in the midst of trying to explain, Casimir came into the room and declared: "[I am the] son of a count whose family has been on a certain property for 7 generations," which Constance relayed promptly in her letter. Exasperated and a little embarrassed, she turned the tables. Since the Markieviczes were "very proud & don't care a bit about money but would like to be sure I am 'noblesse,'" she asked Josslyn to send an official statement about their own family's title. While Casimir's family, unlike her own, was willing to take her at her word, she would "like them to have no doubts."

[24] Violet Bryce to Josslyn Gore Booth (May 20, 1900), PRONI, D4131/K/1.
[25] Constance to Josslyn Gore-Booth (n.d.), ibid. (1).
[26] Ibid. (3).

Lest Josslyn hear the gossip from someone else, Constance decided to be forthcoming about Casimir's disaster of a previous marriage. She wrote quickly, relishing the scenario that Casimir had woven:

> He is a widower & has a child which is with his mother. He married very young & was most unhappy, his wife deceived him, & there was a great scandal, her lover tried to kill her, they tell me he [Casimir] behaved wonderfully and was awfully good to her, when she was deserted ill & brokenhearted he took her back & looked after her. She died of consumption a year ago.[27]

That concluded the matter, as far as she was concerned. As for her own marriage, she believed that ceremonies were "a great bother" and weddings had always seemed to be "the acme of disagreeable for the bride . . . so barbarous and public." If they must have a wedding at all, she thought that London would be "less of a show" than Dublin or Lissadell. Whatever was decided about the venue, the date should be either May or later in the year in order not to disrupt their plans to spend the summer painting together. They might marry immediately or else go home to Lissadell, where they could be carefully chaperoned in order to avoid any scandal. In either case, she demanded that they must be together. Josslyn was eager to postpone the inevitable and urged her to come home for a month to see her family alone. Constance refused. Apart, she and Casimir would only be "wretched and not work"; they must paint, "start something serious or get married at once, so as to not waste time."[28]

In her letters home, she continued to offer reassurances that Casimir was of sound character, had excellent "relations with Russia," and was emphatically not involved in Polish nationalism: "he hates politics & has never meddled in any plots or belonged to any political societies." In fact, she told Josslyn, he exhibited in Paris as a Russian and not a Polish painter: "This is all of grave importance, as if a man is known to be Political & Patriotic he is liable to be seized & sent to Siberia on the merest suspicion."[29] As she wrote, she began to feel more and more angry at what she felt was Josslyn's impertinence: "I don't recognize that you or anyone else has any more *right* to make enquiries & ask questions than I should if you were in a similar position."[30] She qualified—"Don't think I don't appreciate your affection & interest &

[27] Ibid.
[28] Ibid. (10).
[29] Ibid.
[30] Ibid.

fully realize the bother of it for you"—but she had left for Paris precisely to get out from under that sort of paternalism.

In early May Casimir's mother, Marya, traveled to Paris to meet Constance, and they "got on very well."[31] On her return to Zywotowka, she sent her blessing and told Constance that she now looked upon her as a granddaughter.[32] Constance relayed all this to Josslyn, who could only relent. She returned to Lissadell at the beginning of the summer, with Casimir triumphantly in tow. The family was still in mourning for Henry, so the house was quiet, but the long evenings were brightened by the garrulous Pole. Casimir was shocked by the persistently wet summer weather and paced the hall continually. Georgina, frustrated by his visible boredom, sent him to the window to check the weather, which he dolefully pronounced to be "raining, rainin' like blue hell."[33] Insuppressible, he set to work painting the dining room, caricaturing the family and its servants in frescoes that were so adored they survive to this day.

Casimir stayed at Lissadell until July, when he left for Zywotowka. A late summer visit to Ukraine would become an annual ritual, but in 1900 there was the added imperative of gathering assorted documents and endorsements that were necessary before his marriage to Constance could take place. Josslyn sought advice from the registrar general at Charlemont House in London, since there were complications due to Constance and Casimir's differences in nationality as well as their families' religions. The registrar advised that the marriage of foreigners to "English subjects" was at the discretion of the foreign state.[34] The Russian Consulate General confirmed that the imperial government would recognize marriages between Catholics and Protestants, as long as there was a Catholic ceremony.[35] This was anathema to the Gore-Booths and impossible for Constance, who was a Protestant by birth and an atheist by disposition: "the R.C.s wont give their consent to mixed marriages unless you promise them the children as well as being married in their Church *only*."[36] The registrar's office offered further advice that for their marriage to be legal in Britain and Ireland, it must occur in the presence of a registrar or in a Protestant ("i.e., *Established*") church. Afterward the couple could present their documents to the Russian Embassy, where the marriage

---

[31] Ibid. [received May 8, 1900] (32).

[32] Madame de Markievicz (Marya Markiewicwa) to Constance Gore-Booth (n.d.), ibid. (25). The letter is in Polish, translated into French by Casimir's brother.

[33] Quigley, *Polish Irishman*, 40.

[34] Registrar General to Josslyn Gore-Booth (July 19, 1900), PRONI D/4131/K/1 (5).

[35] Russian Consulate General to Josslyn Gore-Booth (July 28, 1900), PRONI D/4131/K/1.

[36] Constance Gore-Booth to Josslyn Gore-Booth (n.d. [received Sept. 11, 1900]), ibid. (2).

would be registered to prevent future complications. To Constance, this was "a choice of two evils":

1) Marriage recognized by Rome with PAPISH Babies OR
2) Marriage *not* recognized by Rome and ones Babies ones own.
   I choose the latter.[37]

When the date was set for September 29 at St. Marylebone's Church in London, the legal details were far from settled. Even on the day itself, Josslyn would receive a legal opinion from a Russian lawyer who confirmed that despite the Markievicz family's insistence on a Catholic wedding, a marriage in England in a Protestant church would be sufficient; yet any female children must be brought up in their mother's religion and male children in their father's.[38]

The marriage settlement included a clause that ensured Constance's independence, both in determining the faith of any children that would result from the marriage and by stipulating that she should "not in any way be or become subject to Russian or Polish law."[39] Casimir also gave the Gore-Booths written assurance that Catholic rites would be administered privately elsewhere, possibly in Paris, but he and Constance eventually decided against a Catholic ceremony. To register the same marriage twice—at the Russian Consulate in London and in a Catholic church—would give rise to far too many complications. In any case, Constance told Josslyn, "If R.C.s by any chance found out [about a Protestant service] it would be much worse for his family than if we are not married."[40] Despite Josslyn's early doubts about Casimir's suitability and the logistical and legal wrangling over the ceremony, Casimir's visit to Lissadell had won him over. In the midst of tedious letters about the wedding, Josslyn sent his future brother-in-law news of his latest pigeon shoot, to which Casimir "egaculated 'Chasse incrofable'!"[41]

In the end, Constance and Casimir were married three times: at the Russian Legation in London, at the Marylebone registry office, and at St. Mary's Church, Marylebone, which was their official ceremony. Regardless of Constance's private resistance to any fuss, she and Casimir complied with most social expectations. Eva, who was at first unsure whether she should even attend ("that is to say if I can waddle under the wad of fat put on during the

---

[37] Constance Gore-Booth to Josslyn Gore-Booth (Sept. 12, 1900), PRONI, D/4131/K/1.

[38] Translation of Legal Opinion from Russian Lawyer (n.d. [received Sept. 29, 1900]), ibid.

[39] Copy of Marriage Settlement of Constance Georgine Gore Booth and Casimir Joseph Dunin de Markievicz (Rooper & Wately), PRONI D/4131/K/1.

[40] Constance to Josslyn Gore-Booth (n.d. [received Oct. 13, 1900]), ibid. (89).

[41] Ibid.

rest cure"), was amused at the thought of the "Bomb bursting."[42] But there was no explosion. Instead, the day was a model of propriety, with Eva and Mabel attired in dark purple satin, frilled fichus collarettes, and matching hats. The other two bridesmaids, the *Irish Times* reported, "Miss Mansfield and Miss Mildred Grenfell," wore "green gowns to compliment the Irish connection."[43] Constance wore white duchesse satin, with a lace and chiffon bodice, and a full court train made of silver brocade, with orange blossoms arranged at the corners. She carried a bouquet of exotics, tied with white satin streamers. Her jewelry attracted as much attention as her dress: "a very massive pearl necklace, and a splendid diamond crescent and pendant, the gift of Lady Gore-Booth."[44] Casimir was regarded as looking every bit the "Polish noble" in his "Russian dress": the traditional court uniform of black tunic with gold braid on the collar and cuffs, white trousers, a rapier, and a tricorn hat.[45] Josslyn "gave her away," but there was subtle resistance to convention in the omission of the word "obey" from the ceremony, which was conducted by the Lissadell clergyman Frederick Sheridan Le Fanu.[46] After a reception at 41 Devonshire Place, the newlyweds left—ostensibly—for their honeymoon in France. Unbeknownst to the official guests who waved them off, they hopped off the train before it left London and spent the evening carousing with their bohemian friends who had come from Paris for the party but had *not* been invited to the church.[47]

Constance and Casimir left London a few days later and spent three weeks cycling around Normandy before returning to Paris. Their change in circumstances afforded them new luxuries: a studio, a four-room apartment at 17 rue Campaigne Première near the famous cemetery of Montparnasse, and a servant named Josephine.[48] Casimir secured a number of lucrative commissions for portraits, including one from Lady Westmacott, Caroline Elizabeth, who was married to the English sculptor Richard Westmacott the younger. She later remembered Constance's "hospitality & generosity" during their "happy times" in Montparnasse.[49] Relieved of financial worries, Constance and Casimir traveled frequently: to London in December for Mabel's marriage to Percy Foster, then on to Nice for Christmas, and back again to Paris, where Constance sat for the portrait artist Boleslaw von

[42] Eva Gore-Booth to Constance Gore-Booth (n.d.), ibid. (45).
[43] "Fashionable Marriage," *Irish Times*, Oct. 1, 1900, 7.
[44] Ibid.
[45] "Society Gossip," *Irish Times*, Oct. 20, 1900, 3; and Quigley, *Polish Irishman*, 46.
[46] F. Sheridan Le Fanu was the nephew of the gothic writer Joseph Sheridan Le Fanu.
[47] Quigley, *Polish Irishman*, 46.
[48] Ibid., 47.
[49] Lady Westmacott to Casimir Dunin Markievicz (July 18, 1927), PRONI, D4131/K/9.

Szankowski, who had studied in Krakow and Munich and was a student in Paris of Jean-Paul Laurens.[50]

Their life together as artists and vagabonds was soon interrupted by the arrival of a daughter. In the summer of 1901, the Markieviczes made the journey back to Lissadell to live quietly until the baby's birth. They resumed their old routine of walking and painting, but instead of riding there was croquet on the lawn, much to Constance's impatience.[51] Maeve Alyss was born in the early hours of November 13, 1901.[52] The name was replete with symbolism. Maeve, the mythological queen whose tomb lay at the summit of Knocknarea, reflected their attachment to the Sligo landscape, while Alyss honored their mutual friend in Paris, an Englishwoman with whom Casimir had a brief affair before she married someone else and he proposed to Constance.[53] This private cipher was a quiet mark of unconventionality on a child who would be sacrificed to family expectations. She was christened as a Protestant on a cold morning in January 1902 by the same clergyman who had conducted their marriage ceremony. Casimir, despite his best efforts to fit in, felt wholly out of place, and his name on the baptismal certificate read, "Cassimir de Markie."[54]

Constance and Casimir soon left Lissadell—and Maeve—to return to their Paris life. What seemed to outsiders to be the neglect of their daughter was, in fact, quite conventional behavior among the aristocracy. Maud Gonne later defended Constance against accusations of being a "neglectful mother": "Nothing could be falser than that, but she was so unselfish she sacrificed everything for Ireland, & in this case did what she thought was best for her child."[55] In fact, Constance's commitment to the cause of Ireland was still years in the distance. In 1901 she and Casimir were motivated by their plans to travel, to paint, and to continue to live beyond the bounds of family expectation.

In the summer of 1902, they traveled together to Zywotowka. It was Constance's first visit to Ukraine, and she was surprised to find after journeying through Berlin, Warsaw, and Kiev to the tiny local station of Oratow that Casimir's home was so much like her own. Situated in a large, enclosed park, a two-story manor house presided over a village of thatched cottages,

---

[50] Szankowski's portrait, produced later as a postcard, was presented by Stanislaus to the Dublin Municipal Gallery, the Hugh Lane, after Casimir's death.

[51] PRONI, D4131/K/10.

[52] Scoular, *Maeve de Markievicz*, 9.

[53] Quigley, *Polish Irishman*, 22–23.

[54] Ibid., 48–49.

[55] Maud Gonne MacBride to Stanislaus Markievicz (May 14 [1931/1941]), PRONI D4131/K/8.

full of peasants who spoke a different language from that of their landlords and worshipped in a different church (Orthodox rather than Catholic). The emancipation of the serfs in 1861 had not been followed by a drive for peasant proprietorship; unlike in Ireland, where the most radical voices in the Land League demanded land nationalization, in eastern Galicia peasant grievances were not about landownership but about taxation and infrastructure, such as the maintenance of communal roads.[56] However, there were other points of similarity, including the Polish gentry's organization of the Galician Agricultural Society, which promoted education, the improvement of farming practices, and cooperation in ways that were very similar to the cooperative movement in Ireland. The Markievicz family's account of its own history is, unsurprisingly, that of benevolent landlords. Yet Casimir seems to have been less sensitive than Constance to the conditions of the people living on his family's estate. In one letter to Eva, Constance describes riding past a drunken peasant who was passed out by the side of the road; she wanted to stop to help, but Casimir insisted that they ride on since there was nothing to be done.[57]

Photographs from their visit show Casimir's family wearing what could easily be taken for Edwardian costume. The women wear white, high-necked blouses with long sleeves and broaches at the throat; the children stand in stiff sailor suits. (Constance, however, was the only woman to wear a hat, a voluminous, ostrich-plumed thing that required her to sit slightly apart from the rest.) She discovered that, like her own family, the Markieviczes enjoyed fancy dress, which often took the form of imitating an idealized version of the peasantry. Just as she and Eva had dressed as dairymaids from the local cooperative creamery, at Zywotowka she donned the full white skirt, embroidered blouse, and dark sash of a Ukrainian peasant woman and posed for photographs drawing water from a well and standing barefoot beneath the trees.

This display of primitivism is very different from her depictions of the peasantry in her paintings from the trip. Casimir had a studio built in the park so that he and Constance could paint undisturbed. He focused on landscapes: poppies and gladioli lining the avenue to the house; rough cottages clustered in muddy plots. Constance, always more interested in people, painted *Russian Harvest*, which depicts a peasant woman in a dark blue dress and white apron sitting in the center of a field. A swathe of yellow suggests a haystack behind her; greens and blues evoke the expansive landscape beyond.

[56] Hryniuk, "Polish Lords and Ukrainian Peasants," 122–23.
[57] Quigley, *Polish Irishman*, 52.

The focus of her study is this single figure, her eyes half-closed, mouth thin and downturned, hands resting on her knees, too tired to unpack the lunch that is tied up in a kerchief set on the ground beside her. There is a similar sympathy in *The Conscript*, which Stanislaus would later regard as her "best Ukrainian picture."[58] A boy sits between his parents at their simple table. He stares ahead, toward the viewer, his shoulders hunched, perhaps resigned to his fate. To his right, his father leans forward, one arm on the table, the other supporting his head. Light from the window falls across his mother's face. Her glassy gaze betrays a sadness that is only given further expression in her work-worn hand that droops from the table toward her lap. None of the figures look at one another. The back wall of their cottage is crowded with paintings, suggesting an aesthetic sophistication that may be intended to compound the sense of injustice that the painting's title condemns. Here are cultured, working people, subject to the will of an empire that demands the sacrifice of their sons. Constance began to put these sympathies into practice. As she and Casimir were leaving Ukraine, they pretended that a young boy, Janko, was their servant so he could flee the country and escape conscription. It was probably for his sake that she shouted "*Moskal swinja!*" (Muscovite pig!) at a policeman as the train was leaving the station.[59]

They returned to Paris briefly in the autumn before spending Christmas 1902 with the Gore-Booths at Lissadell, when Georgina offered them the gift of a house in the fashionable south Dublin suburb of Rathgar. It was a tempting proposition. They had enjoyed spending time with Stanislaus at Zywotowka and now imagined life as a family of four in Dublin, where Casimir's reputation among the artists returning from the Continent was sure to guarantee lucrative commissions. By summer it was settled. They traveled to Zywotowka again to collect Stanislaus from a reluctant Marja, sent for Maeve who was still at Lissadell, and moved together into St. Mary's, which would soon be the nexus of a new revolution.

[58] Stanislaus Dunin-Markievicz, "Constance de Markievicz," *Irish Press*, Jan. 26, 1938.
[59] Ibid.

Figure 3. Casimir Markievicz in Brittany, August 1899. (Lissadell Collection.)

Figure 4. Constance Markievicz's *The Conscript* (1903), signed "Con Gore-Booth." (Reproduced by the kind permission of the Deputy Keeper of Records, Public Record Office of Northern Ireland, D/4131/K/10/114.)

Figure 5. Constance Markievicz dressed as a Ukrainian peasant on a visit to Zywotowka. (Reproduced by the kind permission of the Deputy Keeper of Records, Public Record Office of Northern Ireland, D/4131/K/10/119.)

3

——

The Politics of Art

WHEN THE NEWLY WED CASIMIR AND CONSTANCE MARKI-
evicz moved to Dublin in 1903, the Irish Revival was well underway. The
fin de siècle had seen the rise of the new evangelism of the Cooperative
Movement, the Gaelic League, the Gaelic Athletic Association, a flurry of
little magazines and newspapers, and the springing up of amateur dramatic
groups. Despite the prolific activity of the amateur scene, Ireland's most visionary writers and artists were restless. The painter and mystic George Russell ("AE") looked forward to the Markieviczes' arrival. He wrote to his fellow artist Sarah Purser:

> The Gore-Booth girl who is married to the Polish Count with the un-
> spellable name is going to settle near Dublin about summertime. As
> they are both clever it will help to create an art atmosphere. We might
> get the materials for a revolt, a new Irish Art Club. I feel some desper-
> ate schism or earthquaking revolution is required to wake up Dublin
> in art matters.[1]

He was unprepared, perhaps, for just how "earthquaking" the couple's presence would be. For Russell, they promised the vibrancy of Paris and the
exoticism of eastern Europe, but they would embody a passion and unconventionality that would be difficult for even the most bohemian elements
of Dublin society to accommodate. When Russell wrote to Constance's
brother, Josslyn Gore-Booth, the next year to inform him of his progress on

[1] George Russell to Sarah Purser (Mar. 5, 1902) in Denson, ed. *Letters from AE*, 38–40. Russell
(1867–1935) was a nationalist, mystic, poet, painter, and economic theorist. He is best known as
the fulcrum of the Dublin Theosophical Society and as editor of the *Irish Homestead*, which was
central to the development of cooperative enterprise in Ireland.

a painting (probably *Children Seated among Sand Dunes*), he added, "Will you please ask Lady Gore Booth what I am to do about her picture. Madame Markievicz has stolen it and the only thing I can think of is to sneak into St Marys [*sic*] with a crowbar and when I think of Cassy I rather get nervous about the proceedings."[2]

When Constance Gore-Booth swept off to Paris to live in a student hovel, she eschewed the expectations of the previous generation and the conventions of Dublin Castle society. On her return to Dublin—as Countess Markievicz—she reintegrated easily into the Castle set. They were living, as Sylvia Townshend Warner later described it, in "a narrow society, gay and assured, with the gaiety and assurance of those who live habitually on the slopes of a volcano."[3] In the first Drawing Room of the season at Dublin Castle, Casimir was part of the "General Circle" while Constance joined the "Private Entrée."[4] The newspapers gave extensive reports on her public appearances. At Dublin's Horse Show Week, where the elite paraded themselves alongside the thoroughbreds, the *Irish Times* reported, "Dame Fashion" flaunted itself: "Muslin and voile were the most popular fabrics . . . lace was the favourite trimming, and it is gratifying to record that Irish lace held its own. . . . The Countess Markievicz wore a black voile inserted with lace, and a leghorn hat with bows and strings of pale pink satin."[5] Even then there was a sense of unease about the excesses of the South Dublin suburb of Ballsbridge:

> its air of gaiety, its wonderful medley of nationalities, personalities, and the generally happy inconsequence which seems to infect peer and peasant alike, which invariably gives strangers a somewhat mistaken idea of "the most distressful country" and its inhabitants. For example, someone remarked audibly yesterday, "Well, if all one hears is true, there must be a lot of poverty walking around here; but, upon my word, they look more like a lot of millionaires out for an airing!"[6]

Constance Markievicz was not fully awakened to these issues of class and nationality. Later, at Lady Aberdeen's Irish Lace Ball in 1910, she embraced the fashion of supporting Irish industry, wearing a gown of emerald green chiffon over silk, which was "entirely veiled with beautiful Limerick lace, caught with black velvet rosettes, and finished off with a black velvet

[2] George Russell to Josslyn Gore-Booth (Sept. 14, 1904), PRONI, D4131/K/3.
[3] Warner, "Countess Markievicz," 124.
[4] "Drawing Room at Dublin Castle," *Weekly Irish Times*, Feb. 20, 1904, 22.
[5] "Social Aspect of Horse Show Week," *Irish Times*, Aug. 25, 1904, 10.
[6] Ibid.

sache."[7] As a member of the nationalist women's group the Daughters of Ireland, which she joined in 1908, she would mock such superficial shows of allegiance.

Despite their prominence at upper-class social occasions, Casimir and Constance were more at home among the city's avant-garde, and it was through their association with Russell and Purser that they began to move in more radical circles. In late summer 1903 Russell organized an exhibition of *Young Irish Artists*, in which he included Casimir and Constance along with a new generation of painters: Dorothy Elvery, Frida Perrott (who had recently won prizes at the Royal Hibernian Academy), Lily Williams, Beatrice Elvery, and Estella Solomons.[8] Constance exhibited twenty-seven paintings, while Casimir presented twenty-four, almost all of which were scenes from "Poland."[9]

A larger exhibition was held during Horse Show Week in August 1904 on the theme of *Pictures of Two Countries* and consisted solely of paintings by the Markieviczes and Russell. The exhibition illustrated the extent to which Constance's work was influenced by her travels with Casimir to Zywotowka, while his work also demonstrated his new associations in Ireland. His landscapes from the park surrounding his family's estate and scenes of peasants and cottages complemented his paintings of the countryside surrounding Lissadell and his depictions of peasant life in the west of Ireland. Few of Casimir's or Constance's paintings from this exhibition survive in public galleries, but *The Cottage*, reproduced in the *Irish Review* in 1914, and *Landscape Study*, now in the Dublin City Gallery, with their skeletal trees and desolate landscapes suggest the kind of codification of the national question to which Irish audiences were conditioned by the aesthetics of the Irish Revival of the late nineteenth century. In plays, poems, and paintings, peasants were understood to symbolize the essence of the national character. The titles of

[7] "Irish Lace Ball at Dublin Castle," ibid., Mar. 6, 1907, 8.

[8] "Royal Hibernian Academy," *Weekly Irish Times*, June 27, 1903, 1. Dorothy Elvery Kay (1886–1964) was a portrait artist, figure painter, and illustrator. She studied at the Dublin Metropolitan School of Art and the Royal Hibernian Academy before emigrating to South Africa in 1917, where she had a prolific career, serving as an official war artist during the Second World War. Frida Perrott (1899–1946) painted landscapes, portraits, and still lifes and exhibited at the Royal Hibernian Academy until late in life. Lily Williams (1874–1940) was a portrait and figure painter and exhibited at the Royal Hibernian Academy annually from 1904 to 1939. Her pastel portrait of Padraic Colum hangs in the Abbey Theatre, Dublin. Beatrice Elvery (later Lady Glenavy, 1881–1970), sister to Dorothy, was a painter, sculptor, and stained glass artist. She published her memoir, *Today We Will Only Gossip*, in 1964. Estella Solomons (1882–1968) was a landscape painter, etcher, and portrait artist. Her subjects included W. B. Yeats and the IRA chief of staff Frank Aiken. The Elvery sisters and Estella Solomons studied in Paris together at Colarossi's studio in 1904.

[9] Snoddy, "Constance Gore-Booth," in *Dictionary of Irish Artists*, 149.

Casimir's paintings from *Pictures of Two Countries* reinforce this interpretation: *Sunset in the Village* and *Polish Nocturne* symbolize a dormant nation, waiting for its moment to awaken. *Sunrise on the Steppes* provides a contrasting optimism, looking eastward, perhaps to Russia. Most telling, perhaps, of all Casimir's paintings is *A Village of Tolstoy*, which not only invokes Russia's most famous writer but reminded his audience of an aristocrat who denounced the inhumanity of imperialism. While Casimir was in Paris, he had been eager to portray himself as a Russian painter, but that identity—with its imperial connotations—was no longer useful to him. In Dublin he was emphatically a Pole. He might be a count, but that gave him a certain mystique among the bohemians; his position as a landlord in an occupied territory was occluded in the public perception of him as one of Europe's subject peoples.

The vogue for the peasantry and the exoticism of the Markieviczes' eastern European connections generated much interest in Constance's *The Conscript*, which she had painted during their most recent trip to Zywotowka: so much attention, in fact, that it was able to carry the remarkable sale price of £150.[10] Her depiction of a young peasant boy on the verge of conscription into the imperial army lent itself to perceptions of an analogous relationship of Ireland to Britain. Yet this affinity was available but not overt, so the Markieviczes' paintings had the widest possible audience: the upper-class establishment; middle-class "cultural nationalists" who enjoyed artistic pursuits that were distinctly Irish but were not attached to a particular political program; and radical separatists, as evident in Thomas MacDonagh's possession of Casimir's *The Cottage*.[11] In its reviews of the Markieviczes' exhibitions, the *Irish Times* muted the potential political content of their work. Although Casimir was described as "frank and fearless," his painting *Near Ballinahinch* was cast as "a poetical and harmonious treatment of a hillside, on which the sheep browse peacefully beside the rath of some forgotten chieftain."[12] The technical skill of both Constance and Casimir was praised; her work showed

---

[10] "Pictures of Two Countries," *Irish Times*, Aug. 24, 1904, 3; and catalog, *Pictures of Two Countries*, National Library of Ireland (NLI), IR 70841 P1.

[11] MacDonagh was a member of the Irish Republic Brotherhood, which had a longstanding affinity with Polish nationalism. See Matthew Kelly, "Irish Nationalist Opinion and the British Empire." *The Cottage*, from a 1905 exhibition with Russell, Percy Gethin, and Constance Markievicz, was in MacDonagh's possession in 1914 when it was reproduced in the *Irish Review*, which MacDonagh edited. MacDonaugh was a poet, won the Dublin Feis Ceoil for his lyrics to the cantata *The Exodus*, and in 1908 founded with Patrick Pearse the nationalist boys' school, St. Enda's. He was a signatory of the Proclamation of the Republic and would be executed in 1916 for his role in the Easter Rising.

[12] "Pictures at the Leinster Hall," *Irish Times*, Aug. 26, 1907, 6.

a "delicate appreciation of the subtle and fleeting effects of light" in contrast to Casimir's "vividness" and "unrestrained utterances."

George Russell's ambition to stir things up was coming to fruition. John B. Yeats was incensed by the audacity of the upstarts, perhaps out of a deep anxiety that Casimir's talent would threaten his hard-won commissions for portraits. Although they shared a friendship with George Russell, Sarah Purser, and George Moore, Yeats believed that he and Casimir Markievicz had antithetical aesthetics. As he wrote to Rosa Butt, the daughter of the Home Ruler Isaac, "I take great interest in the person I paint. Portrait painting with me is friendship or it might be hatred, but I must have a real personal interest in whom I paint, whereas other painters, even the very best, only think about the painting. . . . That's why my *work is interesting*."[13] His judgments on Markievicz were scathing. The elder Yeats wrote cattily to his eldest son, W. B.: "I saw to-day Count Markevitch. N[athaniel] Hone had bought one of his pictures . . . he says he has seen too many pictures, and that when he paints he looks at his painting not at what he paints: he says he has faculty but no brains and that he is a stupid man."[14] Although W. B. Yeats continued to correspond politely with "My dear Countess Markievicz," he remarked in passing to Lady Gregory, "I saw Madam Macrovitch (Con Gore Booth)'s work. . . . It is not good enough."[15] But the Yeatses could do little to suppress the Markieviczes' popularity; Gregory's nephew, Hugh Lane, purchased several of their paintings from "Pictures of Two Countries," including a large portrait by Casimir of George Russell, which he planned to feature in his campaign for a new gallery in Dublin.

Lane was a philanthropist and astute collector, whose death in 1915 aboard the *Lusitania* would provoke a long battle between the National Gallery in London and the Irish government over the ownership of his collection. He hoped to give Ireland a gallery of modern art much as his aunt, Lady Augusta Gregory, and W. B. Yeats hoped to give it a modern theater. The new gallery would be founded on purchases from the estate of Scottish

---

[13] John B. Yeats to Rosa Butt (Jan. 20, 1917), quoted in William M. Murphy, "John Butler Yeats," 14. For a detailed discussion of Yeats's style, see White, *John Butler Yeats and the Irish Renaissance*.

[14] John Butler Yeats to W. B. Yeats (Aug. 30, 1907) in Hone, ed., *J. B. Yeats*, 101. Landscape artist Nathaniel Hone (1831–1917) was resident in France for seventeen years and traveled as far afield as Turkey, Greece, and Egypt for his subjects. Sarah Purser organized an exhibition of Hone's and John B. Yeats's paintings in 1901. George Moore commented with characteristic vitriol in the catalog for that exhibition that Hone's "painting is somewhat abstract. It is not so vivacious as a Frenchman's. It is, perhaps, a little apathetic, the painting of a man who lives in a flat country where life is easy and indolent."

[15] W. B. Yeats to "Countess Markievicz" ([Nov. 19?, 1904]), and Yeats to Gregory (Nov. 22, 1904), in Yeats, *Collected Letters*, 3:675.

railway baron James Staats Forbes, which consisted of over four thousand pictures and drawings, valued at over £220,000 in 1904.[16] Lane had been promised first refusal of paintings from the collection, but that was contingent on the pictures having a suitable home. His campaign for a gallery was launched with an exhibition at the Royal Hibernian Academy that featured paintings from the Staats Forbes collection as well as pieces borrowed from the Duran Ruel Galleries in Paris and the private collections of Lane and his friends. The Dublin intelligentsia supported the plans with full force, yet while the idea of a gallery was widely endorsed, the emphasis on Continental art irritated some nationalists. Surprisingly, Arthur Griffith (who was generally amenable to any European model so long as it could be compared favorably to the British) opposed Lane's campaign—perhaps because of the collection's Scottish provenance. The isolationist mentality of the most extreme nationalists was articulated in the *United Irishman*'s assertion that any "creditable Irish school of painting" would not be developed through "slavish imitation of a foreign school."[17]

Casimir attempted to solve the perceived conflict of nationalist and internationalist interests, suggesting in a letter to the *Irish Times* that a building might be procured along the lines of the Petit Palais (Musée de Beaux-Arts de la Ville de Paris). Such a space could be used to display the Staats Forbes collection and then be given to the municipality.[18] It was a sensible solution, and an exhibition and accompanying lecture series was held at the Royal Hibernian Academy to raise funds and generate publicity. The exhibition opened in December 1904 with George Moore—according to himself, "the only one in Dublin who knew Manet, Monet, Sisley, Renoir, [and] Pissarro"— giving his *Personal Reminiscences of Modern Painters*.[19] Casimir, whose portrait of Russell hung prominently on the staircase, took the chair and addressed the audience in French. It was possibly a tacit endorsement of Moore's Parisian reflections, perhaps a challenge to isolationist nationalists, but more likely a cover for his lack of fluency in English. Casimir's choice of language would not go far in the way of winning over the wider Dublin public, but neither would Moore's repudiation of the idea of a gallery as a nationalist endeavor, or his insistence that its benefit would be to "send art students to France in search of education." Despite Moore's controversial

---

[16] O'Byrne, *Hugh Lane*, 60–87. The Staats Forbes collection would eventually become part of the collection of the Dublin City Gallery, the Hugh Lane.

[17] Quoted in Boylan, *All Cultivated People*, 6–7.

[18] C Drinin [*sic*] Markievicz, letter to the editor, *Irish Times*, Nov. 24, 1904, 7.

[19] Moore, *Hail and Farewell!*, 529; "Mr. George Moore's Lecture," *Irish Times*, Dec. 7, 1904, 7.

lecture, no objection was recorded, and the cognoscenti unanimously adopted W. B. Yeats's vote of thanks to the lecturer.

Constance and Casimir were prominent figures throughout the fundraising campaign. The day after Moore's lecture, they hosted a tea with the undersecretary for Ireland, Sir Anthony MacDonnell.[20] Constance made the most of her society connections, serving as secretary for a Ladies' Picture League (over which Gregory presided), organizing subscriptions from leading novelists including Violet Martin ("Martin Ross" of Somerville and Ross) and Emily Lawless.[21] Constance and Casimir pledged over £5 of their own money and persuaded Josslyn to subscribe £10; it would be one of the few causes on which the siblings would agree. Lane's campaign brought together people whose politics would soon sharply diverge: George, the Prince of Wales, sponsored the purchase of a Corot for the collection, and the chair of the Committee of Management for the fundraising exhibition was Alderman Tom Kelly. Kelly had joined Sinn Féin at its founding, and he would be a close ally of Constance Markievicz during protests at the visit to Dublin of the same George (now King George V) in 1911.[22]

But in 1905 Constance and Casimir were still keeping company with the ruling class. In February they attended a ball in honor of the Prince of Wales at the Royal Hospital in Kilmainham (now the Irish Museum of Modern Art), followed by the first Drawing Room of the season at Dublin Castle, and a dinner hosted by the lord lieutenant of Ireland, the British monarchy's official representative in the country.[23] Following on from their support of the municipal gallery, they continued to establish themselves as patrons and not just of the arts. In addition to serving on the committee of the Art Union of Ireland, Constance was on the executive that organized a ball in aid of the establishment of a fund for a club for the British Army and Navy Veterans' Association.[24] Through the Irish Fencing Club, which he founded, Casimir created a strong network of potential clients; he secured the services of Monsieur Charles Daine, formerly *maitre d'armes* at Biarritz and

[20] O'Byrne, *Hugh Lane*, 77.

[21] Frazier, *George Moore*, 339; Boylan, *All Cultivated People*, 7; O'Byrne, *Hugh Lane*, 77. Emily Lawless (1945–1913), who occasionally wrote under the pen name Edith Lytton, was a prolific writer, best known for her collection of poems, *With the Wild Geese* (1902), and her novel about the Land War in Ireland, *Hurrish* (1886); Standlee, *Irish Women Novelists*, 25–64.

[22] For a discussion of the scope of support for the gallery, see Cullen, "The Lane Bequest." Tom Kelly would later be imprisoned in Kilmainham and Richmond jails after the Easter Rising and in Wormwood Scrubs in 1919. He was elected lord mayor of Dublin in January 1920.

[23] "Ball at the Royal Hospital," Feb. 4, 1905, 13; "Dublin Castle Season," *Weekly Irish Times*, Feb. 11, 1905, 4; and "Viceregal Court," ibid., Mar. 4, 1905, 8.

[24] "Art Union of Ireland," *Irish Times*, Feb. 6, 1905, 10; "Coming Events," ibid., May 11, 1905, 8; and "Army and Navy Veterans' Association," *Weekly Irish Times*, Dec. 2, 1905, 13.

professor to the previous lord lieutenant of Ireland, and gained an important commission for Daine's portrait.[25] Casimir took sittings from his new acquaintances in Dublin Castle society, including a commission from the lord chief justice, Lord O'Brien of Kilfenora, whom Markievicz painted in regalia standing three-quarter length, which the *Irish Times* remarked was "characteristic and dignified."[26]

For about five years Constance and Casimir moved in multiple and sometimes politically opposing spheres: among the imperial elite and amid the artists and writers who would in retrospect be seen as leading figures in the Irish Revival. Operating at its ideal, the revival wove separate political and religious strands together in common cultural pursuits, creating a "cultural fusion" that the historian F.S.L. Lyons later argued was doomed unless the "Anglo-Irish" were prepared to turn "their backs completely on the tradition that bred them."[27] This is, of course, exactly what Constance Markievicz eventually did. Yet during the Markieviczes' first years together in Dublin, their involvement in the avant-garde art world laid the foundations for her radicalization. Painting was just one aspect of this revolutionary culture; the theater was equally essential. However, these new amateur dramatic groups, several of which evolved into professional companies, were not all politically radical. Drama was no more the province of Sinn Féin than it was of the aristocracy.

The Markieviczes' debut on the Dublin theater scene came in early 1905 in a series of dramatic recitals by Elizabeth Young, who appeared under the stage name Violet Mervyn and hired the Abbey Theatre for her productions. Publicity for the production referred to the "Comtesse and Count Markievicz," who returned for a second performance where they appeared alongside the Viscountess Ikerrin (married to the seventh Earl of Carrick) and Captain Otway Cuffe, member of the Gaelic League, the organization that was the cornerstone of the revival.[28] This was not an "Irish" evening, as the *Irish Times* was quick to comment: "The pretty theatre founded for the National Theatre Company is, we see, not to be entirely given up to the Celtic drama."[29] Yet even at a performance that featured such a trifling entertainment as *In the Wood*, "a comedietta," there was potential for nationally

[25] "Irish Fencing Club," *Irish Times*, Mar. 24, 1906, 7. Casimir's portrait of the fencing master was printed in the *Irish Review*.

[26] Untitled, *Irish Times*, Jan. 3, 1906, 7.

[27] Lyons, *Culture and Anarchy in Ireland*, 82–83.

[28] The Viscountess Ikerrin was Ellen Rosemand Mary Lindsay, wife of Charles Ernest Alfred Somerset Butler, the seventh Earl of Carrick. Cuffe was elected lord mayor of Kilkenny in 1912.

[29] "The Abbey Theatre," *Irish Times*, Jan. 28, 1905, 7.

minded overtones. At the conclusion of the play one night, Casimir sang two Polish songs, one of which was "Poland's Prayer for Freedom," which provoked an enthusiastic response from the audience, who, like the audience for his paintings, interpreted his song as a codification of the Irish nation.[30]

Critics and historians have been hesitant to ascribe any politics to Casimir Markievcz's artistic pursuits. Certainly, his role as the Pirate King in *The Pirates of Penzance* went a long way in discrediting the seriousness of his theater work.[31] As trivial as some of his subjects may seem, through the theater both Casimir and Constance became more politically conscious and more involved in national affairs. In the spring of 1908, Casimir organized the Independent Dramatic Company, a professional troupe that would stage plays at the Abbey and Gaiety theaters and would draw the attention of the national press. His first production was of his own play, *Seymour's Redemption*, which was staged as a fundraiser for the purchase of a Corot for the municipal gallery.[32]

Seymour's Redemption is about a successful MP, Walter Seymour, who has made a politically expedient marriage and sacrificed his true love. In the first act the young lovers are reacquainted, and with his passions ignited, Seymour makes revolutionary speeches in Parliament, "brimful of ideas on free love, the abolition of marriage," and relief for the unemployed.[33] To preserve Seymour's career, his political adviser, Morley, demands an end to the relationship, and Mrs. Seymour attempts to alleviate the consequent depression by bringing her husband his lover. The play ends with Seymour's lover's return and the couple's reunification in defiance of marriage law. Reviews in the Dublin press were understandably lukewarm and unanimously praised the acting over the play itself. The *Manchester Guardian* found much to fault in the play but described "its author [as] a man of intellect and imagination who, if he will only practise patience, is bound to produce interesting

[30] Ibid.

[31] The production was a charity performance for the Institutions for the Industrious Blind. Constance Markievicz also performed in productions for charity; she took the lead in James Duncan's *The Last Patient*, staged in November 1907 to raise funds for a new national school in Drumcondra. See "'Old Ireland' Bazaar," *Irish Times*, Nov. 21, 1907, 7.

[32] MJ, "The Theatre in Ireland," *Manchester Guardian*, Mar. 10, 1908, 14. The debate over a gallery for modern art had been sidelined into a discussion of the legitimacy of an "early Corot" that Lane had hung in the Harcourt Street exhibition and had selected for the new gallery. In response to the controversy, the Prince of Wales transferred his name from the contested Corot to a landscape by Henri-Joseph Harpignies, leaving the Art Union of Ireland to sponsor the Corot. The "Corot" was later determined to be a copy of a Meszoly, and the gallery's detractors attempted to use the controversy to undermine Lane's credibility. Hutchinson, "Sir Hugh Lane and the Gift of the Prince of Wales."

[33] J. H. Cox, "A Problem Play / at the Abbey Theatre," *Irish Independent*, Mar. 10, 1908, 4.

plays."[34] The *Guardian* also suggested that *Seymour's Redemption* was particularly welcome since "the Irish public" wanted "relief from peasant plays," which needed to be complemented by "a really socially intellectual relief from time to time."

W. B. Yeats was predictably incensed. When the Abbey Theatre's magazine, *Samhain*, reemerged in winter 1908, it included a virulent attack on the Independent Dramatic Company and a personal assault against "Count Markiewicz."[35] The little magazine had not been published since 1906, when, in objection to Yeats's restructuring of the company, some of the Abbey players had seceded and formed the explicitly democratic and national Theatre of Ireland. *Samhain's* reappearance in 1908 demonstrates the extent to which Casimir's Independent Dramatic Company and other new companies were rivaling the Abbey. Yeats's attack was provoked in part by rumors that Markievicz and the Theatre of Ireland were joining forces. The insult was compounded since both companies had hired the Abbey for their productions. Or, as Yeats put it, "I asked our company to give up two of our Saturday performances that we might give the Independent Theatre and the Theatre of Ireland the most popular days."[36] While Yeats exempted "one or two of the players" who "had a gift for acting," *Seymour's Redemption* was described in *Samhain* as "lamentable" and the IDC as "not finer at its finest moments and much worse at every other moment than a third-rate touring company": "Count Markiewicz [is] struggling with the difficulties of a strange language and strange circumstance. . . . Such adventures can do nothing but injury to the drama in Ireland."[37] Public vitriol descended into petty gossip. Casimir alleged that Yeats attended a "God Save the King" dinner at the Corinthian Club, and Yeats accused Casimir of "hiss[ing] at me . . . at the conclusion of *Deirdre*."[38]

Nevertheless, in December 1908 Yeats sullenly agreed to hire out the Abbey to the Independent Dramatic Company and the Theatre of Ireland for a joint production of Casimir's new play, *The Dilettante*, and a new one-act farce, co-written with Nora FitzPatrick, *Home, Sweet Home*. The *Irish*

---

[34] MJ, "The Theatre in Ireland," *Manchester Guardian*, Mar. 10, 1908, 14.

[35] Casimir Markievicz had annoyed Yeats—not only by setting up the Independent Dramatic Company but also by inflaming an antagonism between Yeats and the playwright, Padraic Colum. Yeats wrote privately to Lady Gregory: "that liar Markievich told him that I had prevented or tried to prevent them from asking him to the Mrs Campbell supper, on the grounds that he had not the dress clothes." W. B. Yeats to Gregory [Oct. 17, 1908], in *Collected Letters of W. B. Yeats*, acc. 975.

[36] "Samhain: 1908—Events," in *The Collected Works of W. B. Yeats*, vol. 8: *The Irish Dramatic Movement*, ed. Fitzgerald and Finneran, 201.

[37] Ibid.

[38] Foster, *Yeats*, 1:375.

Times did its best to straddle the Yeats and Markievicz camps in its review—
"The microbe of drama has infected nearly everybody in Dublin. It is as in-
fectious as influenza"—but then went on to say that Markievicz had "written several plays in Polish, which were performed with considerable success
in his own country" and that "with increased knowledge of English he has
made immense progress." *The Dilettante* was judged to be "a very great advance upon 'Seymour's Redemption' . . . a novel subject, treated with much
originality."[39]

It was unanimously agreed that Constance's acting was completely over
the top. In *The Dilettante*, a society farce set in a shooting lodge in Scotland,
she played Lady Althea Dering, who professes her love to Archibald Longhurst, a man who is not her husband. Lord Dering dies entr'acte, presenting an opportunity for Lady Althea and Longhurst to be together—were it
not for Longhurst's involvement with the daughter of the family steward,
Ella Watt, played by Máire nic Shuibhlaigh. In a delicately handled turn of
events, avoided by the reviews, Lady Althea discovers that Ella's integrity has
been compromised. The women strike up a friendship and turn against the
caddish Longhurst, who, it emerges, is more interested anyhow in his discovery of a lost Gainsborough, for which he pays a bargain price of £50. The
Irish Independent found "something unsavoury about the whole proceeding"
and recognized an Ibsenite theme but complained, "In thesis-drama, it is a
serious blemish to have no revelation of the thesis."[40] The importance of art
in the play has caused some critics to interpret Longhurst as a cipher for Casimir and suggest that Markievicz was not interested in his own marriage.
If *The Dilettante* is in any way an allusion to real life, it is in its reflection
of Constance's commitment to female friendships, a conviction that she enacted outside the theater in her campaign for suffrage and in her growing
connections with the nationalist movement.

Nic Shuibhlaigh, who had left the Abbey for the Theatre of Ireland during Yeats's restructuring of the company, was one of the most important
influences on Constance.[41] Unlike Constance, she was from a politically
radical family. The daughter of a typesetter who had worked for the Irish
Republican Brotherhood (IRB), she joined the Gaelic League soon after it

---

[39] "Count Markievicz's New Play," *Irish Times*, Dec. 3, 1908, 6.

[40] J. H. Cox, "Two New Plays," *Irish Independent*, Dec. 4, 1908, 4.

[41] Nic Shuibhlaigh returned to the Abbey for financial reasons in 1910. She also played under
the name "Marie Walker" and was one of the most popular actresses at the Abbey (starring, for
example, as Nora in Synge's *The Shadow of the Glen*), and she was the star performer of the Theatre
of Ireland. Pašeta notes that nic Shuibhlaigh was the first Irish actress to Hibernicize her name; see
Irish Nationalist Women, 38.

was organized and was a founding member of the Daughters of Ireland, a group for nationalist women that Maud Gonne founded in 1900.[42] One of the Daughters' first activities was the establishment of a "Patriotic Children's Treat" as an alternative to the celebrations to mark Queen Victoria's jubilee. The society also staged *tableaux vivant* as part of its propaganda; nic Shuibhlaigh acted in these alongside her work for the Theatre of Ireland. She and Constance both played in the Theatre of Ireland's production of George Russell's *Deirdre* in 1907, and they grew even closer during rehearsals for *The Dilettante*.

Casimir Markievicz was also building a circle of more radical associates. Through the Dublin theaters, he met Seumas O'Kelly, a poet and playwright whose work appeared prominently in the pages of the nationalist newspaper *Sinn Féin*. Markievicz and O'Kelly collaborated on the one-act play *Lustre*, which takes cues from J. M. Synge's *Riders to the Sea*. In Markievicz and O'Kelly's play, however, rather than being devastated by forces of nature as in Synge's drama, the matriarch has lost her children to mechanization, industrialization, and gritty urban life.[43] One of her boys, "distant and dark in his ways like his father's people," was maimed at a railway crossing; another "got swallowed up in Glasgow," and her daughter disappeared "on the streets of New York." Her sole surviving son, Jimmy, embodies the rupture between past and present. His preoccupation with materialism, manifested in his attempt to claim his legacy (a "lustre jug") at any cost, causes the death of his mother, an old woman who easily stands as a symbol for Ireland. *Lustre* was a much more successful play than any of Markievicz's solo efforts, undoubtedly because of O'Kelly's skill but also because the form of a peasant play set in the west of Ireland was a genre familiar to Dublin audiences. This rural peasant drama could accommodate the type of political engagement that underlies, albeit less successfully, Casimir's other plays.

Casimir also planned a program of masterpieces of European modern drama, plays in Irish, and the best of modern Irish drama in English. He was uninterested in staging the patriotic plays that the most artistically conservative nationalists in Sinn Féin preferred. Nevertheless, the Markieviczes' close ties to influential people such as nic Shuibhlaigh, O'Kelly, and George Russell put them in good favor, and the party newspaper, *Sinn Féin*, heralded the Independent Dramatic Company as the new alternative to the Abbey Theatre, which it considered to be a vulgar, unnational institution.[44]

---

[42] Clarke, "Máire nic Shuibhlaigh."

[43] The exact dates for *Lustre* are unknown; Saul suggests composition in 1907–1909. O'Kelly, *Lustre*; and Saul, *Seumas O'Kelly*.

[44] Garach, "The Theatre of Ireland," *Sinn Féin*, Dec. 7, 1907, 3.

Stanislaus later wrote that these early years in Dublin represented "the transitory period for Madame; contact with the men and women who were planning for the freedom of Ireland moulded her thought, and by 1908 she had made the bold resolution that her place was among them."[45]

Despite their intention to make St. Mary's a family home, it proved impossible for Constance and Casimir to provide the children with the life they wished for them. In 1907 they sent Stanislaus to Mount St. Benedict's boarding school in Gorey, County Wexford, possibly under nic Shuibhlaigh's guidance, since the school "attracted the children of nationalist intellectuals."[46] The next year Maeve was sent to Sligo. For a decade she would live with her grandmother at Ardeevin, near Lissadell, which was now the home of Josslyn and his wife, Mary. Molly, as she was affectionately known, and their grandmother "Gaga," were loved dearly by both children and would be important sources of comfort in the coming years.

[45] Count Stanislaus Dunin-Markievicz, "Madame de Markiewicz, Last Memories," *Kerryman*, Christmas number (Dec. 1938): 21.
[46] Foster, *Vivid Faces*, 34.

Figure 6. Casimir and Constance Markievicz with Constance's cousin Madeline Wynne, at a Dublin Castle Ball, St. Patrick's Day, 1908. (Reproduced by the kind permission of the Deputy Keeper of Records, Public Record Office of Northern Ireland, D/4131/K/9/p25.)

Figure 7. Casimir Markievicz's *Landscape Study*. (Dublin City Gallery, the Hugh Lane.)

Figure 8. Constance Markievicz's *Woman Knitting*. (Lissadell Collection.)

4

———

Suffrage, Nationalism, and the Daughters of Ireland

THE CULTURAL ACTIVITIES OF THE IRISH REVIVAL RADI-
calized Constance Markievicz, but suffrage was her first introduction to political activism. Twelve years after the Gore-Booth sisters led the inaugural
meeting of the Sligo branch of the Irish Women's Suffrage and Local Government Association, they were working together again. In England, Eva
and Esther campaigned vigorously against the Licensing Bill, which threatened the livelihoods of working women because a subclause to the bill
made a public house's license conditional on the business not employing
women. Constance traveled from Dublin to Manchester to help lead a rally
co-organized by the Barmaid's Political Defence League and Manchester
suffragists.

The demonstration was carefully orchestrated, scheduled for April 22 to
coincide with a major electioneering campaign by Liberals and Conservatives. The Irish in Manchester were supporting the incumbent MP Winston
Churchill, who had crossed the floor from the Conservatives to the Liberals
and was embarking on a radical program that showed great promise. The Irish
in Britain believed, as the *Guardian* reported, that Churchill "had helped
to give self-government and manhood suffrage to the Transvaal, and they
looked forward hopefully for some such measure for their own country."[1]
However, suffragists opposed both Liberal and Conservative candidates.
Eva Gore-Booth protested that the Liberals were dismissive of female activists, and she urged the crowd to "say by their votes at the election that it
was not a minor matter to take away the livelihood of 100,000 respectable,

---

[1] "Midnight Electioneering," *Manchester Guardian*, April 23, 1908, 10.

hard-working women."[2] Constance gave a rousing speech and, in a show of defiance against gender norms, drove the wagon that served as a platform for the speakers.

She took the reins again at a mass meeting of suffragists and women's trade unions in London, driving the four-in-hand carriage that led the procession from King's Cross through Holborn and all the way to Trafalgar Square. Standing on top of the carriage in order to speak to the huge crowd that had filled the square, Eva and Constance both addressed working-class women's politics ("the industrial aspect of suffrage"). The newspapers commended Constance for her articulateness; the *Irish Times*'s report on the rally ended with a premonitory aside: "as in most other political agitations, the voice of Ireland was not silent."[3]

The year 1908 is widely regarded as a critical one in the development of Constance Markievicz's political identity. One writer even claims it as the year that Constance met the IRB man Bulmer Hobson, who "took her in hand and launched her into the nationalist world."[4] However, as the Markieviczes' cultural pursuits have shown, the "nationalist world" was not a separate sphere of Dublin society but was integrated with other radical political spheres, including socialism, suffrage, and vegetarianism.[5] Constance's dedication to suffrage, her sense of identity as an Irishwoman, and the friendships that she formed with nationalist artists and performers during her first years back in Dublin combined to effect a new form of political commitment.

She was attracted to the Irish nationalist women's organization Inghinidhe na hÉireann, the Daughters of Ireland, because of her work for suffrage with Eva and her friendship with Máire nic Shuibhlaigh, one of the Daughters' founders. Constance arrived at her first meeting straight from a function at Dublin Castle, wearing a blue velvet ball gown and diamonds in her hair.[6] The outfit and her cut-glass English accent made a striking impression on the other women, some finding her glamorous, others immediately classifying her as an outsider. Her gregariousness did much to win them over, as did her political experience in Britain. In August 1908, the month after the mass meeting of suffragists in London, the Daughters stepped up the campaign to attract Irish nationalist suffragists to the policy of parliamentary abstention. These were the exact tactics that Eva Gore-Booth and

[2] Ibid.

[3] "London Correspondence," *Irish Times*, June 15, 1908, 6; "Lancashire Suffragists," *Manchester Guardian*, June 15, 1908.

[4] Hay, *Bulmer Hobson*, 77.

[5] Foster, *Vivid Faces*.

[6] Hayes, ed., *The Years Flew By*, 42–43.

Esther Roper had advocated in Manchester. On August 29 *Sinn Féin* published a front-page notice on behalf of the Daughters that announced "plans for organising the women of Ireland and bringing them into close touch with the National movement." The phrasing of the advertisement suggests that women—the "majority" of whom were "thoughtless and apathetic regarding Ireland's future"—would be brought in line with a "National movement" in which men set the benchmark.[7] This auxiliary role of women, implicitly established in the early work of the Daughters of Ireland, would ultimately drive Constance Markievicz away from the nationalist women's organization and into the more egalitarian Citizen Army.

Yet, for the present, Constance was a vocal and important contributor to the women's nationalist movement. With Helena Molony, she set about publicizing the Daughters through a "women's journal—conducted on Nationalist lines." *Bean na hÉireann* (Woman of Ireland) made an immediate impact on Dublin's lively periodical culture.[8] Molony edited the journal and Markievicz designed the masthead, which featured the revivalist tropes of a woman in traditional dress and the sunburst, an image that would also be used by the Irish labor movement and would be replicated in the masthead of the labor movement's newspaper, the *Irish Worker*, as well as the later Republican newspapers.

Women's suffrage was the most important debate that the Daughters of Ireland had to confront. Moderates and conservatives within Sinn Féin were uninterested in the suffrage question, but they nonetheless borrowed British suffragists' opposition to parliamentary politics to reinforce their evolving policy of parliamentary abstention. The affinity between the two movements was so strong that the party organ, *Sinn Féin*, repeated comments by the militant British suffragist Christabel Pankhurst, who pointed to the Irish Parliamentary Party as an example of "political inefficiency" that held fast to the same political strategies that had failed to push the Home Rule Bill through Westminster.[9] When the inaugural issue of *Bean na hÉireann* was published in November 1908, *Sinn Féin* wished it success:

> The women of Ireland do not ask for votes, for the men of Ireland have no parliament for them to use it in. They are therefore not "Suffragettes;" but they ask to have a voice and influence in matters concerning

[7] "Inghinidhe na hEireann," *Sinn Féin*, Aug. 29, 1908, 1.

[8] Pašeta discusses the foundational role of *Bean na hÉireann* as the "backbone of every political campaign in which Irish women were involved in this period"; Pašeta, *Irish Nationalist Women*, 9–10, 33–45.

[9] "The Women Suffragists and the Irish Parliamentarians," *Sinn Féin*, Sept. 5, 1908, 2.

the economic welfare of their country in the industries and the arts, the health and the wealth of Ireland; and, above all, in the education of their children.[10]

Both *Sinn Féin* and *Bean na hÉireann* were implicitly writing against the newly organized Irish Women's Franchise League (IWFL).

The IWFL was founded in November 1908, following on the heels of the Daughters of Ireland's renewed campaign to organize nationalist women. Indeed, the IWFL may have even been founded in response to the Daughters' initiative. Unlike the Daughters of Ireland, however, the IWFL was open to an array of political persuasions—from unionists to all schools of Irish nationalists. Even some members of Sinn Féin joined the organization. Markievicz, however, fundamentally disagreed with the principles of the IWFL since she believed that it was against the Sinn Féin party line, which she fully embraced. Again, Máire nic Shuibhlaigh was an important influence on Markievicz's politics; nic Shuibhlaigh's adamant support for parliamentary abstention was cited in debates on suffrage in *Bean na hÉireann* as being even more radical than majority opinion within the Daughters of Ireland.[11]

Just as a shared vision of women's role in national life united the Daughters of Ireland, suffrage threatened to divide the group. Like Constance Markievicz, Jennie Wyse Power had campaigned for the Irish Women's Suffrage and Local Government Association at the turn of the century, but she now argued that the IWFL's demands were not contradictory to the tenets of Sinn Féin.[12] Perhaps surprisingly, the inveterate nationalist Maud Gonne and the founder of Sinn Féin, Arthur Griffith, agreed with Wyse Power.[13] Debates about Sinn Féin's position on suffrage filled the pages of *Bean na hÉireann* and spilled over into the *Irish Nation and the Irish Peasant*.[14] "Firín" (probably the pseudonym of Bulmer Hobson) challenged Wyse Power's position and argued that although he had sympathy with "the Suffragettes of England," just as "Hyndman, Shaw . . . and others on behalf of the race,"

[10] "Bean na hEireann," ibid., Nov. 14, 1908, 1.

[11] Editorial, *Bean na hÉireann* (April 1909): 8–9.

[12] Wyse Power and Markievicz would also disagree on their ideas of a republic; Wyse Power was elected to the Seanad (the Irish Senate) in 1922, while Markievicz and other Republicans would object to the Senate as undemocratic.

[13] Gonne had refused W. B. Yeats's persistent proposal of marriage on the basis that he was insufficiently passionate in his nationalism and married instead the abusive John MacBride. She was a close friend of Hanna Sheehy-Skeffington, who founded the IWFL, a friendship that may have influenced Gonne's position. Ward mentions the IWFL briefly in her biography, *Maud Gonne*, 163.

[14] The *Irish Nation and the Irish Peasant* was edited by William Patrick Ryan and addressed social questions within nationalism. It ceased publication in 1910, and Ryan moved to London where he became assistant editor of the *Daily Herald*.

Irish women must focus immediately on "the salvation of Ireland and the Irish people."[15] Both Wyse Power, writing as "the editor for December" of *Bean na hÉireann*, and Maud Gonne ("M.G.") replied to Firín's provocation: Wyse Power protested that women did not have any real "political power" in Ireland, and Gonne argued that women's suffrage was not a party question.[16]

Eight weeks later the *Nation and Peasant* reported a split in the Daughters of Ireland: Markievicz and Molony were singled out as being "strongly opposed" to seeking the vote from "the Westminster Parliament."[17] Markievicz published a long letter of explanation in *Sinn Féin* in which she discussed her reasons for opposing the IWFL, which, she emphasized, had derived from the British Women's Social and Political Union: "Their propaganda is excellent—from any foreign woman's standpoint—but we contend that over here we are differently situated to Englishwomen and the women of other countries, and that a propaganda readymade from over the sea, and bearing the hall mark of an English agitation, does not entirely suit our needs."[18] The similarity between the IWFL's and British suffragists' propaganda would be especially clear to Markievicz, since she had distributed British suffrage pamphlets at rallies in Manchester and London, a point that she astutely ignored. Her idea that "we" Irish were different from "Englishwomen and the women of other countries" is not such a drastic shift as it may seem at first. The Gore-Booths were proud landlords who maintained close ties to England but nonetheless identified as Irish. This latent identity was activated through friendships, public debates, and the zeitgeist of revivalist Dublin.

Markievicz thought if Irish women were to support the IWFL, its foremost demand must not be the vote but "a Parliament to be represented in." She asked, how could Irish women claim that "the possession of a vote will in itself raise the status of women" if "the national heroes of Ireland are felons and convicts; men who were just as much without a vote as we are ourselves"? Those last words, "we ourselves," echo the "ourselves alone" of Sinn Féin and reflect a clever propagandist tactic that Markievicz would hone as she became more deeply entrenched in nationalist discourse. Griffith and Wyse Power attempted to argue, rather semantically, that the phrase " 'We demand the vote on the same terms as it is, or may be, extended to men' does not mention an English Parliament, and therefore does not mean it!" Markievicz retorted: To which gates were suffragists chaining themselves? And into which

[15] Firín, "Sinn Féin and the Suffragettes," *Irish Nation and the Irish Peasant,* Jan. 9, 1909, 7.
[16] "The Editor for December," "Bean na h-Eireann," ibid., Jan. 30, 1909, 3; and "M.G.," "Sinn Féin and the Suffragettes," ibid., Jan. 30, 1909, 8.
[17] "On the People's Service," ibid., Mar. 20, 1908, 8.
[18] "Irishwomen and the Suffrage," *Sinn Féin*, March 27, 1909, 4.

parliament were suffragists attempting to force entry? Westminster. She let fire the rhetoric that would characterize her propaganda in the coming years:

> Let Irishwomen who are not admitted to the rights of British citizens rather glory in the fact and organise over here and join with those men who believe in Liberty in making Ireland ungovernable; let them fan the flame of Rebellion and Revolution, helping to intensify the aspirations of the whole people in the councils of their nation, that England daily more harassed and perplexed through the effects of her iniquitous foreign policy, towards free nations and towards nations subjected by her, will have to capitulate and accede to their demands.[19]

This attack on Griffith—leader of the Sinn Féin Party and editor of its newspaper—borrowed heavily from the writings of Theobald Wolfe Tone, allusions that were ignored in *Sinn Féin*'s postscript to the article that argued that Markievicz had not proven how the IWFL violated the principles of the party. Gonne published a response to the article that effectively outed Markievicz as "Maca," the pen name she used in *Bean na hÉireann*; Gonne argued that if Irishwomen were to be politically effective, "they have got to come down out of the clouds, eschew high-flown remarks about martyrs and deathless renown, and get votes."[20]

By April 1909 *Bean na hÉireann* had managed to reach a degree of consensus:

> We do not "refuse to join the woman's Franchise movement" . . . but we decline to join with Parliamentarians and Unionists in trying to force a bill through Westminster. We prefer to try and organise a woman's movement on Sinn Féin lines, or on lines even broader still. Freedom for our Nation and the complete removal of all disabilities to our sex will be our battle cry.[21]

The debates over the suffrage question illustrate just how far and how quickly Markievicz's idea of Sinn Féin exceeded the politics of the party's leaders. She expressed a vision for the nation that rejected the authority of a foreign government and embraced "the whole people of Ireland": the basis for her concept of the republic and her bourgeoning anti-imperialism.

---

[19] Ibid.

[20] Maud Gonne, "Nationalist Women and the Clouds," *Irish Nation and the Irish Peasant*, Mar. 27, 1909, 5. Markievicz also signs in autograph "C de M" the article "Free Women in a Free nation" by "Maca" in *Bean na hÉireann* (n.d. [Mar. 1909]), 8–10, NLI IR, 3996 B15. The first pages of this issue are missing, but the date March 1909 can be inferred as the next issue in NLI's holdings is April 1909.

[21] Editorial, *Bean na hÉireann* (April 1909): 8–9.

5

Women's Work?

WHEN CONSTANCE MARKIEVICZ WAS INVITED TO GIVE A lecture to the Students' National Literary Society in 1909, her opponents expected her to address the suffrage question. Instead, she focused on the primacy of national sovereignty. Previously, in an article for *Sinn Féin*, she had compared the Irish people to "Indians, Egyptians, or any other unfortunate race that is groaning under British injustice." She now looked to Poland for her comparison:

> In Ireland the women seem to have taken less part in public life, and to have had less share in the struggle for liberty, than in other nations. In Russia, among the people who are working to overthrow the tyrannical and unjust government of the Czar and his officials, and in Poland where, to be a nationalist, men and women must take their lives in their hands, women work as comrades, shoulder to shoulder with their men.[1]

The historical connections between Ireland and Poland, long emphasized by the Irish Republican Brotherhood, were now clear to her. This understanding may have been facilitated by nationalists' enthusiasm for the Markieviczes' paintings on Polish subjects. Her increasing acquaintance with the IRB member Bulmer Hobson, who moved from Belfast to Dublin in 1907, also gave her a more thorough knowledge of the history of the IRB.

Importantly, Markievicz's lecture to the literary society reveals that she did not see Russia's role in Poland and British imperialism in Ireland as a simple analogy of national oppression. Rather, she used the imperialist contexts

[1] Markievicz, *Women, Ideals and the Nation.*

as a way of exploring the relationship between the emancipation of women and the emancipation of the nation. For example, she referred to the imprisonment of women in St. Petersburg: "Many a woman has been incarcerated in the dungeons under St Peter and St Paul." She also used an extended trope of religious affiliation to imply that suffrage was integral to Irish nationalism just as Catholicism was central to Polish national identity: "a Pole of the Orthodox religion would even now be regarded with suspicion in Poland and could not possibly enter any Polish National Movement."[2] Her implication was that nationalists who were not suffragists—and suffragists who were not nationalists—should be regarded with suspicion: Irish suffragists must also be Irish nationalists, since national sovereignty and female emancipation went hand in hand. The subtext encoded in her argument about religious identity and political alignment seems obscure now, but to her audience—living in the midst of fraught debates over the place of suffrage in the national campaign—her meaning was clear. During the questions after the lecture, a representative of the IWFL provocatively argued that the vote was the most important political weapon and should be granted by the British government first. Hobson rose in Markievicz's defense and blamed sexual inequality in Ireland on "Anglicisation," which, he argued, had destroyed an ancient egalitarian society. He hoped that Irishwomen "would not commit the same political blunder as the men, and go begging to England to give them votes."[3]

Markievicz's speech to the National Literary Society was reprinted in three installments in the *Irish Nation and the Irish Peasant* throughout the month of April.[4] She was clearly conscious that she was contesting the majority of Sinn Féin. In the party newspaper, an anonymous article titled "Irishwomen's Duties" had asserted that there was no time to be wasted "suffragetting" and arguing: "If we must contend let it be in seeing who'll be the most Irish."[5] Markievicz published a rejoinder in the *Nation and Peasant* in which she conceded that women who lived by the national ideal "will know that for Ireland's sake she must make her home life beautiful and ideal too."[6] However, in her lecture to Dublin's Drumcondra and Glasnevin branch of Sinn Féin in May, Markievicz went further, arguing that while there was a great deal of national work to carry out in the home, "she would rather see

[2] Ibid., 6.

[3] "On the People's Service," *Irish Nation and the Irish Peasant*, April 3, 1909, 5.

[4] "Irishwomen's Duty at the Present Time," ibid., April 20, 1909, 3; April 17, 1909, 3; and April 24, 1909, 3.

[5] "Irishwomen's Duties," *Sinn Féin*, Feb. 27, 1909, 4.

[6] Maca, "Irish Women's Duty—a Rejoinder," *Irish Nation and the Irish Peasant*, May 15, 1909, 5.

women working for the nation as comrades with men, each according to her own abilities in power."[7]

It was at the Drumcondra and Glasnevin Sinn Féin meeting that Constance Markievicz initiated her plans for a scouting movement in Ireland. Robert Baden-Powell's *Scouting for Boys* (1908), which launched the scouting movement in Britain, typified the way in which children—particularly boys—across Europe were being indoctrinated into the imperial project. The lord lieutenant of Ireland, Lord Aberdeen, whose parties at Dublin Castle the Markieviczes had reveled in, patronized the British Scout movement, which Constance thought was outrageous. She believed that a boys' brigade organized on Irish nationalist lines could subvert the British Army's recruitment drive in Ireland. In this way the founding ethos of what would become the Fianna Éireann was very similar to the impetus behind the revitalization of the Daughters of Ireland: a separate national organization to preoccupy Irish people who might otherwise be swept up in British concerns. Irish girls were already being informally incorporated into the nationalist movement through the activities organized by the Daughters: in June they made a pilgrimage to Bodenstown Churchyard in County Kildare to pay homage at the grave of Wolfe Tone, hero of 1798. Now it was time to rally Irish boys. The July issue of *Bean na hÉireann* announced the founding of the Red Branch Knights, which would be the genesis of the Fianna.

Although Hobson was at the Sinn Féin meeting where Markievicz discussed her plans, he does not seem to have been involved in the early stages of organizing the scouts. Constance first thought of approaching the schoolmaster of St. Andrew's National School on Brunswick Street, William O'Neill, for assistance. However, Tom Clarke, who organized the Irish Republican Brotherhood (IRB) covertly from his sweetshop on Parnell Street, advised her that since "she was a non-Catholic," O'Neill would probably suspect her of "proselytism."[8] Clarke suggested that she ask his and Hobson's close friend in the IRB, Seán McGarry, to accompany her and vouch for her credentials.[9] Together they recruited a handful of boys with which to begin the movement.

---

[7] "Irishwomen in the Nation: Lecture by Countess Markievicz in Drumcondra," ibid., May 22, 1909, 7.

[8] Marnie Hay, "The Foundation and Development of Na Fianna Éireann," 55. Clarke is often referred to as "the father of the revolution." He was the first to sign the 1916 Proclamation and was executed by firing squad on May 3, 1916.

[9] McGarry was imprisoned in Lewes Jail after the Easter Rising. He was elected president of the Supreme Council of the IRB in November 1917.

Constance Markievicz and Helena Molony, along with O'Neill, McGarry, and another IRB man, Patrick McCartan, attempted to design a program to teach scouting, signaling, and drilling techniques to the boys. The result was chaotic. According to Markievicz's first biographer, Seán O'Faolain, their single achievement was the depletion of Casimir Markievicz's whiskey supply. When Constance became aware of Hobson's previous attempt to combine physical culture with militant nationalism by way of a hurling club in Belfast, she invited him to help guide the experiment.

Unsurprisingly, Arthur Griffith was unsupportive of the new scouts. This may be, in part, a legacy of Griffith's and Markievicz's disagreements over suffrage. But his primary opposition was to her commitment to physical force separatism. The question of militancy, and to what degree Irish nationalists' resistance to the British government should be expressed, was dividing Sinn Féin, and from the very beginning the militant ethos of the scout troop was clear. *Bean na hÉireann* unambiguously declared that with the boys' troop "the promoters hope to make the nucleus of a National Volunteer Army."[10] The advertisement for the scouts that the organizers placed in the *Nation and Peasant* was more moderate in tone to prevent potential participants from being excluded owing to debates within Sinn Féin: the troop would be "managed by the boys themselves on non-party lines," and "any boy in Dublin who wishes to work for the independence of Ireland" was invited to take part.[11]

The group was renamed Na Fianna Éireann as a memorial to Hobson's Belfast boys, and he chaired the first meeting and was appointed as the scouts' first president. A young Gaelic Leaguer, Pádraig Ó Riain, was elected as treasurer on the executive council, and Constance Markievicz was voted in as an honorable secretary, although not without some controversy.[12] On one hand, Markievicz's sex was perceived to be important for securing the trust of hesitant parents, who might see her as a mother figure. On the other hand, she came up against the chauvinism that was intrinsic to the IRB as a whole. Some boys protested that she and Molony should not even be allowed in the hall during Fianna meetings.[13] A similar misogyny would be articulated later by many members of the Irish Volunteers and even within the ranks of the Irish Transport and General Workers' Union (ITGWU).

[10] Editorial, *Bean na hÉireann* (July 1909): 8.

[11] "National Boys," *Irish Nation and the Irish Peasant*, Aug. 14, 1909, 8.

[12] Markievicz and Patrick Walk were co–honorable secretaries alongside nine others, including Helena Molony and Con Colbert, who would be executed for his part in the Easter Rising.

[13] Helena Molony, statement, National Archives of Ireland (NAI), Bureau of Military History (BMH), WS 391.

Markievicz soon won over the majority of the boys. When Hobson was forced to return to Belfast, she was elected president of the Fianna and was kept in the post after his return in 1911.[14] The early meetings of the scouts were educational lectures, often on the subject of Irish history. Patrick McCartan spoke on "The Boy Heroes of '98" and included the story of Willie Nelson, a boy of sixteen years of age who was hanged for his part in that rising.[15] McCartan emphasized the nonsectarianism of the 1798 rebellion and gave it currency for boys who had been too young to remember or participate in the centenary commemorations in 1898. McCartan evangelized, "Tis true the revolution did not give us, as it aimed, a republic; but it did give us a republican spirit, which has never since died, nor, please God, will ever be killed—not even by tuberculosis." Robert Emmet, who had been just a boy when he first made contact with the United Irishmen, was given as an example on which members of the Fianna should model themselves. With Emmet's energy and determination, McCartan enthused, he had "snatched the glowing embers of the revolution and kindled them into fire." A lecture by Seamus Deakin in the following month on "A Boy's National Duty" was more tempered, urging the boys to moral scrupulousness—"No Fianna ever lied"—and recommending that they be an example to their schoolmates.[16]

The Fianna quickly gained momentum, and several troops (*sluaighte*) were organized within district councils, which were part of a central council (*ard-choisde*) that was governed by the congress (*ard-fheis*).[17] Drilling practice was organized for every Tuesday and Thursday; Irish language and Irish history classes were held weekly on Wednesdays; and regular cultural events were planned to educate the boys and to raise funds for the scouts. At a fundraising concert in the Fianna Hall, rented rooms at 34 Camden Street, in November, Markievicz gave a lecture on "The Women of '98": a strong choice of topic for an audience that had initially resisted her involvement with the scouts.

These educational activities were complemented by a strong physical culture; drilling and signaling exercises alternated with leisure pursuits, following Baden-Powell's model for teaching military techniques to children. Markievicz took her troop on a three-day camping trip to the Dublin Moun-

[14] Hay, "Na Fianna Éireann," 58.

[15] "Na Fianna Eireann," *Irish Nation and the Irish Peasant*, Oct. 16, 1909, 8. In 1798 the revolutionary organization the United Irishmen, inspired by Enlightenment ideals and sparked by the American and French Revolutions, staged a rebellion with the support of the French. Bad luck and bad weather delayed the French Navy, and the British won. Leaders of 1798, of which Wolfe Tone and Robert Emmet are most prominent, became canonized as national martyrs.

[16] "Na Fianna Eireann," *Irish Nation and the Irish Peasant*, Nov. 13, 1909, 8.

[17] Hay, "Na Fianna Éireann," 57.

tains, where, as one member of the Fianna reported to *Bean na hÉireann*, "the damp evenings were passed quickly with the singing of Irish songs and talks of Irish heroes."[18] Yet the goal of the Fianna was more transparent than Baden-Powell's imperialist project: these boys were "the recruits for the future armies of Ireland." When Rosamond Jacob visited Molony and the Markieviczes in Dublin, she commented on how the Fianna were constantly coming and going. One afternoon, two "big Fianna boys" came to tea and stayed until ten o'clock at night. Their conversation ranged from "whether the old [mythical] Fianna or the '98 men" were the best examples for the "youth of Ireland" to "the question of sport." Jacob was alarmed by "Madame's frightful callous talk about shooting birds—starlings included. . . . Madame is a bloodthirsty sportswoman, was brought up so, and the boys seem the same in theory." She judged, "Now if some humane person had charge of the Fianna, what a lot of good might be done."[19]

Bean na hÉireann had begun as a women's magazine concerned with issues that directly affected women: suffrage, campaigns for Irish-made goods, and other topics related to the domestic sphere. Through its support of the Fianna—an organization for children and thereby considered to be appropriate territory for women—the magazine entered into major theoretical debates about the nature and goals of Irish nationalism. Rather than beginning with its usual piece of short fiction, *Bean na hÉireann* opened its September issue with the first of a two-part anonymous article, "Physical Force." The essay took Arthur Griffith to task for his proposal of an Austro-Hungarian model for the government of Ireland, in which Britain and Ireland would be granted equal status under the monarch.[20] "Physical Force" argued that Prussia, vital to the "rebirth of Hungary," was now "The German Empire." Ireland should not be drawn into the imperial war that seemed imminent; rather, Ireland should join forces with other oppressed nations, such as India and Egypt, in their fight against imperialism. The second installment of "Physical Force" focused on the way in which boys' and girls' brigades and the Territorial Army in Britain were being used to recruit for the army. The same had to be done in Ireland: "Learn to discipline and be disciplined, learn to shoot, learn to march, learn to scout, learn to give up all for Ireland."[21] The rhetoric is very similar to Constance Markievicz's articles for the Fianna, and the imagery used in the article included the sunburst, "flickering on the

---

[18] "One of the Fianna" and "Na Fianna Éireann," *Bean na hÉireann* (September 1909): 8–9 and (October 1909): 8–9.

[19] Rosamond Jacob Diary, July 30, 1911, NLI, MS 32,582/22.

[20] See Griffith, *The Resurrection of Hungary*.

[21] "Physical Force: The Writing on the Wall," *Bean na hÉireann* (Oct. 1909): 3–4.

skyline at last," which may indicate that she was the author, although the article could just as plausibly have been written by another of Griffith's antagonists, such as Hobson or Molony.

Casimir was also writing for *Bean na hÉireann*, although not about Poland and not under his real name. Using the pseudonym Seamus Cassidy, he published short stories in the December 1909 and January 1910 editions. Both were terrible, and only the first, "After '48," is of any interest. The story is set in a Paris hospital, where Brian—who has fled Ireland by "crossing the channel in a fishing smack"—lies dying. With his friend Dermod, he awaits the proofs of his political pamphlet, which will be his "Christmas gift to Ireland." The crude syntax belies Casmir's struggle to learn English: "I will take with me to Ireland many thousands of my pamphlets. . . . I will go among the people from house to house and distribute it. I shall see my country at last."[22] The plot is just as roughly constructed as the sentences. With a final "shriek" of "Revolution," Brian falls back on the pillows, exhausted, just as a printer's boy delivers the papers. Brian dies, and "outside the bells break into a peal, gaily announcing that hope was born for Christianity, but not for Ireland."

Scholars have contested the authorship of "Woman with a Garden" in *Bean na hÉireann*, but this series was also written by Constance Markievicz.[23] It regularly featured practical gardening advice alongside humorous, sometimes violent suggestions for ridding the metaphorical garden of its imperialist infestations. The column is frequently signed "Armid," and Sidney Gifford Czira much later recalled that Markievicz wrote under the names "Maca" and "Armid" for *Bean na hÉireann*. In fact, an article by Armid in the January 1909 copy of *Bean na hÉireann* held by the National Library of Ireland is signed in manuscript, "C de M," in Constance's distinctive hand.[24] Helena Molony, the journal's editor, later attributed the column to Maud Gonne, and it is possible that Markievicz and Gonne shared authorship and perhaps even a pseudonym. Yet "Woman with a Garden" also hints strongly at Markievicz in its prose style and its choice of subject.

In the November 1909 issue, "Woman with a Garden" refers to Polish history and has a strong resemblance to Constance's *Woman, Ideals, and the Nation*. Looking out at "a pale green gold oak tree," the author cast her mind

---

[22] Seamus Cassidy, "After '48," ibid. (Dec. 1909): 9–10. The other story, "A Bunch of Violets," deals with the romantic trials of a Parisian law student, who, bored by "his Roman burden," is lured to a garret by beautiful music, which he discovers is played by a lupus-afflicted woman with a "wound" on her "wretched" face; Seamus Cassidy, "A Bunch of Violets," ibid. (Jan. 1910): 3–5. This was the last story Seamus Cassidy published in *Bean na hÉireann*.

[23] For a note on the contested authorship, see Weihman "National Treasures and Nationalist Gardens," 361.

[24] NLI, IR 3996 B15.

to Ireland's long battle for liberty and the struggle of "Ireland's sister in misfortune, Poland," the nation for which the oak tree was an emblem. She wrote that in the "Polish Revolution" of 1830, young boys—cadets from the military school in Warsaw—took command of regiments of enlisted men who refused to obey Russian orders. She mentioned the Polish military leader Jan Zygmunt Skrzynecki as a specific example of incompetence among a group of generals who were too busy quarreling among themselves to launch a successful revolution.[25] This event is particularly resonant because the Russian-Polish War is also known as the Cadet Revolution, which encapsulates Constance Markievicz's vision for the Irish scouts. She cautioned that the Polish War had ended in failure and "a few more names to add to the list of martyred heroes," solely because of the rifts in nationalist leadership.[26] This was a thinly veiled warning to Sinn Féin.

At a meeting of the Sinn Féin executive council in December, Constance Markievicz was among the majority who voted against the party's proposed departure from its policy of parliamentary abstention.[27] She had been marginalized within the party because of her militant abstentionist stance, but she was now proving to be at the vanguard of the nationalist movement. She found that all her experience organizing social events, charity fundraisers, and even art exhibitions could be put into service for the nation. The aristocracy had patronized Irish craftsmanship—as at Lady Aberdeen's Irish Lace Ball—but Sinn Féin mocked that woolly breed of cultural nationalism. The purchase of Irish-made goods was imperative, not just as a display of national affinity but as a practical means of promoting the national economy, stemming the tide of emigration, and diminishing reliance on "aid from foreigners."[28]

The Markieviczes' involvement in Dublin theatricals was also becoming more political. Since its founding, the Daughters of Ireland had produced tableaux vivant, including the premiere of Yeats and Gregory's one-act play *Cathleen ni Houlihan*.[29] Constance was excited to take to the boards again alongside Helena Molony and Máire nic Shuibhlaigh. The Daughters' productions usually depicted scenes from Irish legends, particularly those involving female heroes. The mythical Deirdre was frequently featured, famous

[25] Jan Zygmunt Skrzynecki was commander in chief of the November Uprising of 1830–1831 in the Russian-Polish War.

[26] "Woman with a Garden," *Bean na hÉireann* (Nov. 1909): 8.

[27] Kelly, *The Fenian Ideal and Irish Nationalism*, 186. Hobson and Dublin city councillor P. T. Daly also voted against a departure from abstention.

[28] "Aonach: Irish Christmas Market," *Irish Times*, Dec. 10, 1909, 5.

[29] In 1902 Inghinidhe na hÉireann coproduced the play, which became the benchmark for the Abbey Theatre's later productions.

for being the most beautiful woman in Ireland, who took her fate into her own hands and pursued the man she loved rather than the man she was decreed to marry. In this way, the characters chosen for the Daughters' early tableaux were identifiably nationalist but essentially romantic figures. By Samhain (the harvest festival) of 1909, the Daughters' productions were more provocative, making pointed accusations against Britain and the Irish servants of imperialism. A caricatured statue of the ubiquitous emblem of empire, Queen Victoria, was staged as "Britannia seated on a throne of moneybags." She held a scepter shaped like a skeleton in one hand and a skull in the other and was surrounded by, as *Bean na hÉireann* described it, "tame snakes and tax-gatherers": "recruiting sergeants, police and detectives."[30] These same collaborators would be the targets of Constance Markievicz's extensive campaign of propaganda and intimidation in which she would enlist the Fianna.

[30] Editorial Notes, *Bean na hÉireann* (Nov. 1909): 8.

6

Conversion

ANTI-IMPERIALIST DISCOURSE IN IRELAND WAS BECOMING increasingly reflective of socialist ideas, which were on the rise in Dublin. This was not the arts-and-crafts socialism that characterized the cooperative enterprises of the 1890s but a radical socialism that was due to the influence of the labor leaders James Larkin and James Connolly. Larkin organized the Irish Transport and General Workers' Union at the end of 1908, but the labor movement lacked a party-political affiliation. He had a separatist ethos in establishing an Irish union for Irish workers, but his party politics were still tied to the English-based Independent Labour Party.[1] Alongside the organization of an all-Ireland union, James Connolly envisaged an all-Ireland labor party that would accommodate workers "irrespective of creed or race."[2] The manifesto of the society was not issued until Connolly returned to Ireland from New York, where he worked as a labor organizer from 1903 to 1910. Even from abroad, his message was powerful: Irish socialists responded to his call in his Irish American newspaper, *The Harp*, and a reinvigorated Socialist Party of Ireland (SPI) was launched at a public meeting in Dublin in September 1909.

The following month, Fred Ryan, secretary of the new party, gave a lecture to the Drumcondra branch of Sinn Féin on "Socialism and Nationality" at which Constance Markievicz was present. Ryan suggested that there were three models of nationality: romantic, capitalistic, and social democratic. Socialism, he argued, was not opposed to nationalism but "deepened our

[1] Greaves, *The Irish Transport and General Workers' Union*, 53.
[2] Connolly, "Socialist Party of Ireland: Its Aims and Methods," in Connolly, *Collected Works*, 1:472–73.

conception of the true ideal of nationality."[3] His speech implicitly addressed the Irish Parliamentary Party's antagonism to the independent labor movement in Ireland, which was perceived to pose a threat to the Home Rule program.[4] Parliamentary nationalists and socialists had long been at odds. In the *Workers' Republic* of 1898, Connolly had argued that politicians who sought only Home Rule—"for mere changes within the Constitution"— were "political hucksters seeking a good price for the votes they offer as wares."[5] Reflecting Connolly's teaching, Ryan rejected the dependence on the "capitalist or landlord class" that was implicit in the campaign for parliamentary reform. He argued, "The exploiting classes never fought for Irish freedom."[6] When Constance Markievicz proposed the vote of thanks to Ryan, she declared herself "converted by Mr. Ryan's remarks. The only difficulty was as to how Socialism was to be worked."[7]

Constance had encountered Fabian socialism in London while she studied at the Slade. Her sketches and drawings from that time reflect a degree of class consciousness, which developed in her observations of the relationships between peasants and landlords at Zywotowka and at her own family's estate, Lissadell. She became more politically aware through Eva and Esther's campaigns for working-class women in England, which culminated in the "conversion" that she experienced in Dublin.

Her interest in socialism may have also been sparked by her frustration with the more conservative views within Sinn Féin. The manifesto of the Socialist Party of Ireland asserted that socialism would suffocate within Sinn Féin, and a new party was required: "old political organisations will die out and new ones must arise to take their place; old party rallying cries and watchwords are destined to become obsolete and meaningless."[8] Some socialists would remain within Sinn Féin, but P. T. Daly left the party at the end of 1909 to join the SPI, and Hobson joined the Belfast branch of the SPI when Connolly founded it in August 1910.[9] *Bean na hÉireann* took the Connolly line. In its January 1910 issue, it posed "A Question for Irish Socialists": "what keeps the working man subservient?" The answer was the

---

[3] "Seanchuc na nDaoine," *Irish Nation and the Irish Peasant*, Nov. 27, 1909, 8.

[4] Greaves, *Irish Transport and General Workers' Union*, 46.

[5] "Parnellism and Labour," in Connolly, *Collected Works*, i, 347–48.

[6] Ibid.

[7] "Seanchuc na nDaoine," *Irish Nation and the Irish Peasant*, Nov. 27, 1909, 8.

[8] "Socialist Party of Ireland," in Connolly, *Collected Works*, i, 472–73. The exact date of the composition of the manifesto is uncertain. It was written in 1910 or early 1911.

[9] Greaves, *Irish Transport and General Workers' Union*, 53. Connolly praised P. T. Daly, an old Fenian, for his receptiveness to the new politics. See "Harp Strings," *The Harp* (June 1908), in *James Connolly*, ed. Ó Cathasaigh.

lack of education provided by the unnational "National schools," a problem that proved "the main cause of all the misfortunes of Irish workers cannot be found in the fact that we are not a free people." Connolly had long argued that social ills should be regarded as the product of British imperialism, and *Bean na hÉireann* now followed suit.[10] On October 1, 1910, after a torchlight procession by the Irish Transport and General Workers' Union and the Socialist Party of Ireland to celebrate Larkin's release from prison, Markievicz gave a speech in which she reasserted this argument: "all Ireland's troubles were due to the English connection."[11]

All of Constance Markievicz's preoccupations—suffrage, antisectarianism, national emancipation, and the mobilization of Ireland's youth—came to the fore in Casimir Markievicz's new play, *The Memory of the Dead*, a historical drama set during the rising of 1798 when the Irish and the French joined forces to launch a rebellion against British rule in the country. The play takes its title from a famous ballad by John Kells Ingram and also repeats a famous line, "The French are landing at Killala," from Yeats and Gregory's play *Cathleen ni Houlihan*, which Constance later credited with keeping her spirits up during her imprisonment after the 1916 Rising.

The Memory of the Dead opens with Colonel Charort (J. M. Carré) coming to the Doyle family's cottage to request a guide to Donegal, where he is to meet Napper Tandy, an actual historical figure who helped to plan the 1798 Rising from abroad.[12] All the able-bodied young men have already left the village to join the fight, so Norah Doyle (played by Constance) disguises herself in men's clothing and volunteers. Along the way, Charort and Norah meet a wounded soldier, Norah's former suitor, James McGowan, and she stays behind to care for him while Charort goes ahead to meet Norah's husband, Dermod O'Dowd. The final act of the play is set a year later. Norah assumes that she has been widowed, since O'Dowd never returned from battle; the townspeople speculate that he is a traitor, but Norah refuses to lose faith. When O'Dowd returns to the village disguised as a tramp, he is unrecognized by the family. Brought inside the cottage, he overhears speculations about his loyalty. He rises to leave, dejected, but British soldiers have surrounded the house. O'Dowd is recognized by the Doyles the moment

---

[10] Donncad ua hAnnagáin, "A Question for Irish Socialists," *Bean na hÉireann* (Jan. 1910): 13–14, 14.

[11] Larkin had been charged with conspiracy and imprisoned after funds raised to support the ITGWU in Cork were applied to union action elsewhere. See Greaves, *Irish Transport and General Workers' Union*, 54.

[12] Napper Tandy was instrumental in planning the rebellion. In Paris with Wolfe Tone at the beginning of the year, he organized the collaboration with the French, sailed from Dunkirk on a French corvette, and landed off the coast of Donegal in September 1798.

before he is shot, and Norah is arrested as she attempts to prevent the British soldiers from taking his body. She declares,

> My husband, you have not died in vain. For I swear by your innocent blood, shed for your country, by your unknown deeds, by your patriot's heart, and by your love of me—my husband. I swear that I will bring up your child to take your place, to live as you lived, to die as you died—a hero for our country; and I know that there will be thousands of others who will keep sacred in their hearts your memory and your love for your country, and on that love they will rebuild Ireland free!

Given her past performances, Constance was perfectly suited for such melodramatic speech.

But the melodrama has a serious function too. Typically a subversive drama, here it is used to express both the ambitions of the nation and the role of women in their realization. *The Memory of the Dead* emphasizes the necessity of a united front, of action over oratory, and of gender equality within nationalism, epitomized in Norah's line, "If there are men in Ireland ready to die for their country, there are just as many women."[13] As its plot indicates, like *Women, Ideals, and the Nation* and Constance's columns for *Bean na hÉireann*, *The Memory of the Dead* posed a challenge to Sinn Féin, which had been distracted from its principal aims by internal debates over militarism, parliamentary abstention, and the role of women in the national movement. *Bean na hÉireann* applauded the return of melodrama to the Dublin stage and deemed it "refreshing" after J. M. Synge's controversial *The Playboy of the Western World*, "to see a man shouldering a pike, and go out to fight the English, and to see a woman send him. We want more plays of that style in [the] Ireland of to-day—rousing, Nationalist plays. Art, not for art's sake, but for Ireland's. We want to see stimulating action, and heroic deeds."[14] Tellingly, *Bean na hÉireann*'s review emphasized the conventional role of women as educators and motivators, not participants. While Norah takes an active role in the rebellion, serving as Charort's guide, she does so while disguised as a man. Importantly, she also embodies the dominant ideal of women's maternal, nurturing role as she cares for the wounded James Mc-Gowan and promises to teach her child how to live and die as a patriot. In

[13] *Memory of the Dead*, act 2, scene 1, 45.

[14] Delia Cahill, "'The Memory of the Dead': Thoughts from the Gallery," *Bean na hÉireann* (Aug. 1910): 10. The *Playboy* riots are one of the most famous moments in Irish theater history; some leading nationalists, including Maud Gonne and Arthur Griffith, denounced Synge's play as antinationalistic, and some critics went so far as to say that the play's brief mention of undergarments ("shifts") was a "slur on Irish womanhood."

this way, *The Memory of the Dead* explores the possibilities for women in the national struggle but reinforces the dominant gender politics of Irish nationalists and the wider social status quo—so much so that Maud Gonne's estranged husband, John MacBride, supported it.[15]

The Special Branch of the Royal Irish Constabulary, a paramilitary surveillance police force operating from Dublin Castle that was formed in 1883 to combat the rise of the Irish Republican Brotherhood, was tipped off about the radical potential for *The Memory of the Dead* when Bulmer Hobson—under close surveillance—encouraged the Fianna to attend Casimir Markievicz's new play. *The Memory of the Dead* was returning to Dublin after successful performances in Roscommon, Castlerea, and Westport, where it had been "supported by the extremists."[16] These "extremists" included a host of town and county sporting and cultural organizations, which had strong links with the IRB. For example, the Castlebar program for the play was signed by the presidents or secretaries of the County Mayo GAA, the Connacht Council GAA, the Castlebar Gaelic League, the local branch of the United Irish League, the Town Tenants' League, the Irish National Foresters, and the Castlebar branch of the Celtic Literary Society, who all called for the audience to "Support the Men and Women who are not ashamed of Ireland and Her Cause."[17]

Reviews in the provincial press drew attention to Constance's performance, describing her as the sister of "Sir Jocelyn Gore Booth, Bart," doubtlessly to his chagrin. Her acting was described as "best when she found herself in well nigh hopeless misery, and one could see with what heart and soul she threw herself into the piece, and how she raised inquisitive, appealing eyes—it seemed to the audience as if to say, 'See you the lesson of it all'."[18] The play's warm reception in local newspapers illustrates the disjuncture between the power structures of the capital and the rural West. On its production in Dublin, the *Irish Independent* dismissed it as a "little melodrama," unintelligent, with long speeches that had "too much of the 'die for Ireland' note in them."[19] The *Irish Times* was—unsurprisingly—even more hostile, describing the audience as "volatile in its enthusiasms" and suggesting that the author's sympathies were with "the insurgents."[20]

---

[15] Constance Markievicz wrote to MacBride, "Thanks for interesting your friends in 'The Memory of the Dead.' We got great help & support from them both in Castlebar & Westport" (n.d.), NLI, MS 26,77.

[16] *Précis of Reports Relative to Secret Societies* (1911–1912), National Archives (UK) CO94/13.

[17] Scrapbook, PRONI, D4131/K/8.

[18] Unidentified clippings, ibid.

[19] Jacques, "A Drama of '98," *Irish Independent*, April 15, 1910, 6.

[20] "New Play by Count Markievicz," *Irish Times*, April 15, 1910, 3.

But *The Memory of the Dead* goes further than simply using the Rising of 1798 as a cipher for contemporary Irish separatism. Casimir Markievicz also uses Ireland as an allegory for his native country. A review of the Castlebar production of the play noted that at the conclusion, when Casimir thanked the audience for their warm reception, "he added pathetically that when he was writing it he was, perhaps, thinking of his own Beloved Poland."[21] *The Memory of the Dead*'s emphasis on unity was relevant to divisions in Poland as well as within Sinn Féin. The recent Russo-Japanese War had caused a decline in Polish industry and a corresponding increase in unemployment, which in turn led Polish political parties to escalate their demands to the Russian government. Armed revolutionary societies were organized at both ends of the political spectrum: the Union of Active Struggle by the socialists and the Polish Army by the nationalists. In Poland, as in Ireland, political divisions within the national movement impeded progress in the movement for sovereignty.[22] It is difficult to gauge the degree of Casimir's participation in Polish politics during his years in Dublin, but he made annual visits home to Zywotowka, including a trip in June 1910 just after *The Memory of the Dead* was produced.

Casimir later disavowed any knowledge of Constance's participation in militant Irish separatism, but in 1910 they were implicated equally in the national struggle. When *The Memory of the Dead* was produced in spring 1911 by an amateur company at the Kilkenny Theatre, the *Kilkenny People* commented,

> The Count and Countess are now active leaders of the Nationalist propaganda in Dublin and strenuous opponents of the policy that would represent Irish men and women as the loyal slaves of a foreign power. Coming from Poland, whose sad history has so much in common with Ireland's, Count Markievicz's love of liberty was "bred in the bone" and his passion for freedom and hatred of the yoke of the foreigner, whether exercised in Warsaw or in Dublin Castle, found its affinity in and is heartily reciprocated by the beautiful young Irishwoman whom he met for the first time when both of them were art students in Paris.[23]

The glamour of their story was seductive, but the nuances of their very different visions for the nation would emerge as Constance's attitude toward empire and her practice of socialism became more clearly defined.

[21] Scrapbook, PRONI, D4131/K/8.

[22] This allegorical use of Ireland laid the foundations for Casimir Markievicz's later pamphlet *Irlandiya*, published after the February Revolution of 1918, discussed further below.

[23] Scrapbook, PRONI, D4131/K/8.

After their Dublin production of *The Memory of the Dead*, while Casimir was away at Zywotowka, Constance moved out of their house in Rathgar and took the lease on a rambling estate, Belcamp Park, in the northern Dublin suburb of Raheny. Inspired by James Connolly's focus on the nineteenth-century Utopian experiment at Ralahine in his book *Labour in Irish History*, she and Hobson intended to found a commune.[24] In 1832 the Irish landowner and grandfather to the Gifford sisters, Arthur Vandaleur, was inspired by the English socialist Robert Owen to transform his estate in County Clare into a cooperative community. Connolly knew of Vandaleur through E. T. Craig's book *The Irish Land & Labour Question* (1882), which made a case for cooperation as a means of radically reorganizing society, rather than replicating the system of patronage that structured rural society.[25] Craig contested the inexorable focus on political "remedies" when "the chief want of Ireland is the Social Organisation of Industry":

> Had all the land and buildings belonged to the people, had all other estates in Ireland been conducted on the same principles, and the industries of the country, also so organised, had each of them appointed delegates to confer on the business of the country at some common centre as Dublin, the framework and basis of a free Ireland would have been realised.[26]

Connolly attributed the "downfall" of Ralahine to Britain's refusal "to recognise the right of such a community to hold a lease or act as tenants." The end of utopianism was imperialism.

On Connolly's recommendation, Hobson and Constance Markievicz read Craig's book and together with Helena Molony tried to coax the Fianna into the role of part-time communards. Their efforts fell just short of disaster. A camp for the boys that was scheduled for the August bank holiday Monday was spontaneously extended for the entire weekend when the troops arrived early on the Friday. Markievicz scrambled to organize activities and with some relief took the group on a route march to Coolock Chapel for mass on Sunday morning. *Bean na hÉireann*'s reports gave no

---

[24] Haverty gives the date as 1910, whereas Hay (based on O'Faolain and Marreco) states that they moved to Ralahine at the end of 1909. For Ralahine, see "An Irish Utopia," in Connolly, *Labour in Irish History*, 83–95.

[25] For example, Craig argues that in Competitive Co-operation and Co-operative Partnerships, "capital takes all the profits from industry . . . the more equitable principal of Mutual Co-operation, which secures the full reward of toil by sharing the profits arising from labour," is the "principle of justice." Craig, *The Irish Land & Labour Question*, n.p.

[26] Craig, *History of Ralahine*, n.p.; and Connolly, *Labour in Irish History*, 94.

indication of the unraveling chaos and commented not on the socialist enterprise but on the "thorough Irish national atmosphere."[27]

The commune was not an unmitigated failure, since the recreational activities of the boys paid dividends as the Fianna membership continued to increase. A new branch was established at Beresford Place in January 1910 under the auspices of the North Dock branch of Sinn Féin, followed by three more new branches at John Street, James's Street, and Sandwith Street and even an international branch in Glasgow.[28] At Beresford Place, Con Colbert, who was one of Patrick Pearse's students at the militant-minded, religiously devout boys' school St. Enda's, studied British Army manuals to learn tactics and instructed the boys in drilling techniques, while Markievicz continued to lead at Fianna headquarters and organized similar training sessions on scouting, cartography, and route marching.[29] She also continued to emphasize cultural events as a means of providing edifying entertainment and attracting new members, while she surreptitiously used concerts and similar events as a way to involve the young girls of Daughters of Ireland in the scouts. *Bean na hÉireann* rather optimistically predicted that the Fianna were "taking the little cailín [girls] in hand too. . . . Now that the Countess de Markievicz has kindled the flame" of organization.[30]

Although girls were never fully integrated into the Fianna, the boys' acceptance of Markievicz as a leader is confirmed by her presiding at the first annual Fianna conference at the end of August 1910. She further aligned the scouts with Sinn Féin policy, leading the adoption of a constitution and new rules, which prohibited any Fianna from taking part in parliamentary or municipal elections. This was the same policy of absolute abstention from British politics that she and Hobson had fought for in the pages of *Bean na hÉireann* and the *Nation and Peasant*. She also reaffirmed their militant separatist ambitions: these boys "were the pioneers of what she hoped would be the National Army of Ireland."[31]

Her sex may have seemed to offer, from the point of view of the IRB leadership, a reassuring female presence to ease the minds of parents who were hesitant to enlist their children. But the only gendered role Markievicz assumed was that of the Róisín Dubh, the black rose that codified a patriot's love for the nation. In a lecture to the Fianna on "Love of Country," extracts

[27] "Na Fianna hÉireann," *Bean na hÉireann* (Sept. 1910): 11–12.
[28] Ibid. (Aug. 1910): 10.
[29] Ibid. (Feb. 1910): 6. For Colbert's education, see Foster, *Vivid Faces*, 128; for Colbert's study of British military tactics, see Townshend, *Easter 1916*, 39.
[30] C. Ua. S., "na Fianna hÉireann," *Bean na hÉireann* (April 1910): 10.
[31] "Na Fianna hÉireann," ibid. (Sept. 1910): 11–12.

of which were printed in *Bean na hÉireann*, Markievicz used florid rhetoric to extol the virtues of self-sacrifice. She began by proposing that "he who loves a country that is enslaved and in the power of her enemies has nothing to gain and all to lose by his love," and then proceeded to build an argument that surpassed the simple heroic stories on which the Fianna's cultural curriculum had been based.[32] She fused religious metaphor with national mythology, invoking Patrick Pearse's doctrine at St. Enda's. As the death of Christ had created Christianity, Markievicz argued that martyrdom would make Ireland strong. To go to battle and to live would be good fortune; to go to battle and to die would be heroic:

> [You might be] one of the lucky ones who will triumph with her [Ireland], or you may be one of the blessed ones who will die in the fight. Give yourself to the struggle without considering what your own fate will be, make up your mind to win Ireland's freedom as Tone and Emmet did, and go on the right way, fearless of consequences, that leads to liberty.

The urgency she invoked was evangelical: "Dark Rosaleen is whispering to you now; she knows that the chance she has waited for so long is coming to her, and she wants you to make ready to win back her crown and her royal robes for her."[33]

Markievicz's propaganda disguises the sophistication of her anti-imperialist thought, which was increasingly nuanced. Speaking to the Central Branch of Sinn Féin in November 1910, she offered a subtler perspective on British Army recruits than may have been expected. Reflecting James Connolly's service in the British Army as a teenager, she argued that recruits fell into three classes: those who were obviously pro-British; those who were looking for adventure; and finally the "workers whom economic circumstances drive into it." She argued that Sinn Féin must fight for increased wages and a better standard of living if they were serious about driving down recruitment for the army. The men who were most susceptible to British recruitment tactics were agricultural laborers and unskilled urban workers. There must be "a vigorous national campaign with regard to the conditions affecting the lives of these men."[34]

[32] Constance de Markievicz, "Love of Country," ibid. (Oct. 1910): 8–10. For Pearse's rhetoric, see, e.g., his passion play, performed by the students of St. Enda's at Easter 1911, in Trotter, *Ireland's National Theaters*, 138. Desmond Ryan later wrote of the production: "The Man is crucified as the Nation, and the Soul moves slowly, falteringly, towards the redemption."

[33] Markievicz, "Love of Country," 10.

[34] "Countess Markievicz and Anti-Enlisting," *Irish Nation and the Irish Peasant*, Nov. 26, 1910, 2.

She complemented her drive for an economic policy with a children's crusade. During the winter of 1910, the Fianna boys were kept busy with a program of wrestling, singlesticks, and boxing. Troops organized hurling and Gaelic football teams, giving a uniquely Irish identity to the scouts.[35] Two hundred Fianna marched to the tune of the Irish war pipes in the Gaelic League's annual procession, and when they were not embarking on public displays of militarism in Dublin, the boys assembled at a farm in Scholarstown on the outskirts of the city to compete against one another in maneuvers held under the guise of "defend the citadel."[36] When King George V visited Ireland in the summer of 1911, Constance Markievicz deployed the Fianna in a covert anti-imperialist propaganda campaign. The British Special Branch began to pay closer attention:

> On 9th July she came to the Camp [in the Dublin Mountains] with two strangers from Dublin. They scattered leaflets along the road from Dundrum to the Camp. The purport of these leaflets was that Ireland would never regain her legislature as long as men and women of Ireland stand in the streets of Dublin to cheer the King of England and crawl to those who oppress and rob them. On the 10th the Countess with about 30 of the Boy Scouts took up position in Fitzsimmons Wood, a place close to the route to be traversed by Their Majesties en route to Leopardstown. Shortly before Their Majesties were to pass Sandyford Village, one of the Scouts was observed there with his pockets full of the leaflets already referred to, but seeing his movements were observed he returned to Camp without distributing any leaflets.[37]

The Fianna remained peripheral and protected, but Markievicz now undertook a militant engagement against the imperial forces. She began with the police.

---

[35] The "revival" (or invention) of the Irish sports hurling and Gaelic football was central to the development of a mass culture that reflected a uniquely Irish identity and characterizes the period known as the Irish Revival. See Mandle, "The I.R.B. and the Beginnings of the Gaelic Athletic Association"; and Cronin, *Sport and Nationalism in Ireland*.

[36] "Na Fianna hÉireann," *Bean na hÉireann* (Nov. 1910): 11.

[37] Report on "Prominent Suspects and Suspicious Strangers" (July 1911), NA, CO 904/13.

7

Physical Force

IN JANUARY 1911 CONSTANCE MARKIEVICZ PUBLISHED AN article in *Bean na hÉireann* on "The Police and the Nation" in which she urged "Irish Nationalists" to pursue "a campaign of exterminating the police." While she did not advocate "a wholesale massacre," she argued that public opinion must turn against these protectors of capital and agents of empire. The change should be premeditated but must not seem so: "When opportunity offers let a strong blow be struck as if the striking were a spontaneous, unpremeditated outburst.... Those who strike must be prepared to risk the consequences, but the risk is well worth taking."[1] Markievicz's ideas can be traced to Bulmer Hobson's argument in favor of "defensive warfare," expressed as early as 1900 in the *United Irishman*:

> The underlying principle of it [i.e., defensive warfare] is that whereas the traditional method, the attack, proceeded upon the basis of an enemy being in possession of the country, and aimed at retaking it from its hands, the aggressive defence proceeds upon the basis of the people being in possession of the country, treats the enemy as an invading force, thrown upon him the necessity of crushing out the popular centres of resistance[,] the necessity, practically of reconquering the whole country.[2]

In 1909 Hobson published his pamphlet *Defensive Warfare: A Handbook for Irish Nationalists*, which was an extension of earlier articles like this one. In light of Hobson's policy, Markievicz's attack on the police is in line with

---

[1] C., "The Police and the Nation," *Bean na hÉireann* (Jan. 1911): 6–7.
[2] Quoted in Kelly, *Fenian Ideal*, 135; see also Hay, *Bulmer Hobson*, 76.

other nationalist, anti-imperialist activity, since she argued that conquering the police—the agents of British imperialism—was a step necessary to claiming Ireland for its people.

Markievicz had been in Paris when the Daughters of Ireland protested Edward VII's visit to Ireland in 1903, but at the next royal visit—as recently elected vice president of the Daughters—she was at the center of the action. At a Sinn Féin meeting in late March 1911, Alderman Tom Kelly proposed a motion that "Nationalists of all sections of Dublin" petition members of Dublin Corporation to refuse to welcome King George V in order to accurately represent the "nationalist position." Markievicz voiced her support for Kelly's motion and called on the "women of Ireland" to refuse the king welcome.[3] In a further show of support for Kelly, she attended a meeting of Dublin Corporation at the beginning of April, at which a resolution on women's suffrage was considered. That resolution proposed that owing to the delay of the suffrage bill in Parliament, Dublin Corporation should send its members to petition Westminster. In keeping with the Sinn Féin policy of abstention, Kelly proposed an amendment to eliminate all references to a petition to Parliament. At the same time, he made his support for suffrage clear: sending the lord mayor and other civic officers to London would be "a waste of money." This comment provoked a woman in the gallery, obviously ignorant of divisions in Sinn Féin, to shout, "Where are you looking for your home rule from?"[4] Further discussion was postponed, as the meeting descended into chaos.

At the end of April, under police guard, the Dublin Chamber of Commerce hosted a public meeting to formalize the response to the royal visit. To open the meeting, the president of the Chamber of Commerce, John Mooney, proposed a resolution that "a Citizens Committee be formed for the purpose of arranging a suitable welcome and preparing and presenting a loyal address to the Most Gracious Majesties the King and Queen on their approaching visit to Dublin." When the lord chief justice seconded the resolution, the socialist and feminist agitator Francis Sheehy Skeffington rose from his seat in the hall and proposed that the word "not" be inserted after the word "be." He argued wryly that ignoring the visit was the best compromise to satisfy both loyal supporters and nationalist objectors. Seán Milroy—a future minister in the Irish Free State—stood to second Sheehy Skeffington's motion, while the chairman, the Earl of Mayo, attempted to maintain order over cries of "Hear, hear" and "Put him out!" In an effort to

---

[3] "Sinn Féiners and the King," *Weekly Irish Times*, April 1, 1911, 14.
[4] "Dublin Corporation," ibid., April 8, 1911, 13.

silence the dissenters, Mayo called a vote on Sheehy Skeffington's amendment; thirty-six supported it while "some hundreds" voted against. But that was merely the first stage of the protest. The objectors continued to heckle the speakers, interjecting cries of "He is not our Sovereign" and "Give us the names of the Irish traitors." Constance Markievicz rose from the crowd to propose another amendment, which brought the meeting to boiling point: the word "Unionist" should precede the word "citizens." Uproar ensued and the rest of her speech was lost, but the *Irish Times* reported that "she continued to speak and gesticulate wildly for some considerable period."[5] The meeting ended with Lord Iveagh, Dublin businessman William Martin Murphy, and the provost of Trinity College speaking in favor of the king's welcome, while a voice declared over the crowd that the interrupters "had not spoken on behalf of any considerable body of Nationalists."

Markievicz and her fellow protestors were undaunted. On June 22 they held a meeting on the steps of the Customs House to oppose the celebration of the coronation, which was taking place that day at Westminster Abbey. John MacBride opened the meeting by declaring that the people present were not assembled in the name of socialism, republicanism, or the monarchy but were united by a love for Ireland. Nor were they there to denounce England or its king.[6] Rather, he argued, they were assembled to assert that no king had the right to rule a country against the opinion of the majority of its people. MacBride suggested that the king's visit to Dublin was part of a recruiting strategy, similar to Victoria's visit to the Irish capital during the Boer War. IRB man Patrick McCartan followed MacBride, arguing more vehemently that Ireland should ally itself with Germany, England's greatest enemy. Markievicz then took the platform to assert an anti-imperialist feminist agenda: "The women of Ireland were just as keen for the independence of the country as the men, and they were prepared equally to sacrifice their lives on its behalf." At that instant, a firework was discharged from a boat in the Liffey. Seizing the opportunity, she continued, "In Dublin at this moment our enemies are firing rockets to sound our slavery." Speeches from Arthur Griffith and Tom Kelly followed, and the meeting concluded with the singing of "A Nation Once Again" and the burning of a Union Jack.

Flag burning became a regular occurrence at protests. On July 4, the night before the city council was scheduled to vote on the king's welcome, an open-air meeting under the auspices of the United National Societies was held at Foster Place. This was an umbrella organization that incorporated

[5] "Royal Visit to Dublin," *Irish Times*, April 28, 1911, 7–8.
[6] "Anti-Coronation Meeting in Dublin," ibid., June 23, 1911, 11.

nationalists and socialists from across the political spectrum who assembled to demonstrate against the lord mayor Alderman Farrell and the majority of Dublin Corporation's support for the royal visit.[7] They organized a sarcastic display of small green flags that were trimmed with black ribbon, "In memory of the dead patriotism of Alderman Farrell." Dissenters from within the corporation attended, including J. J. Kelly, who chaired the meeting. Sean MacDermott, Seán Milroy, Francis Sheehy Skeffington, and Helena Molony all spoke in support of McDermott's resolution that the corporation refuse to acknowledge the visit, and every speaker argued that the corporation's decision was unrepresentative of the sentiment of the Irish people. Molony indicted not only the lord mayor but also the Dublin public who were so apathetic about the future of their country to elect him in the first place.[8]

As the speeches drew to a close, Markievicz attempted to set fire to a Union Jack. The superintendent of police, accompanied by several constables, seized the flag, at which point—according to the *Irish Times*—the protest became violent.[9] Markievicz was "hustled along for some distance" by the crowd, moving swiftly to evade the police. They drove through the city from Dame Street to Smithfield, where Markievicz, standing on the wagon, was "received with loud cheers." She argued that the police had captured the flag "not because they were more numerous but because they were better organised." She urged Irish people to become better trained and better organized so that when fighting the police, "they would learn how to fight the soldiers. (Cheers) In Ireland nothing was to be got from England except by force."[10] Another Union Jack was torn apart and flung among the crowd, where pieces of it were burned. Markievicz and the leaders of the crowd moved on again from Smithfield toward the Mansion House on Dame Street, with the assembled public following behind. At the corner of Grafton and Nassau Streets, Helena Molony threw two stones from the wagon, allegedly at the head of a police inspector. If she was aiming, she missed, and the stones ricocheted off a shop window, where pictures of the newly crowned monarch and his queen were displayed. The police moved in. They formed a cordon to prevent the crowd from following, and there were several scuffles between the crowd and the officers. When the wagon arrived at the Mansion House, Molony (described in the *Irish Times* as the editor of *Bean na hÉireann*) and James Pike (previously of the newspaper the *Nation*) were arrested.

[7] "Other Meetings, Exciting Incidents," ibid., July 5, 1911, 9A.
[8] "Royal Visit to Dublin," *Weekly Irish Times*, July 8, 1911, 4.
[9] Ibid.
[10] "Other Meetings, Exciting Incidents," *Irish Times*, July 5, 1911, 9A.

A protest against the lord mayor was held outside City Hall the following day. Police protection was called in by the councilors in favor of the royal visit, not only to protect the municipal property but also to prevent dissenters from entering the municipal buildings, which were—by law—freely accessible to the public. Once more, Markievicz refused to be daunted. She scaled the wall that surrounded the buildings and was caught by a friendly city councilor who was waiting for her on the other side. She ran up the steps of City Hall before she was grabbed by several constables and ejected back into the crowd. Molony, who had been released on bail, followed her lead and was subjected to the same treatment. At that point, councilors opposed to the lord mayor's royalism started to arrive. Once inside the chamber, they protested that they had been abused by "the hirelings of Dublin Castle." These claims were dismissed, and the lord mayor adjourned the meeting on the basis that attendance was inadequate to reach a quorum.[11] The meeting continued, unofficially, with the councilors who remained denouncing the lord mayor's policies.

On the same day as the demonstration outside City Hall, Constance Markievicz was an important witness in the trials of the protestors arrested on the night of July 4. First to be charged was James McArdle, whose alleged crimes were burning a flag and assaulting two police officers. When she was called for the defense, Markievicz stated that the flag had been in her possession. Asked if McArdle had anything to do with the burning of it, she claimed that she had "never seen him in her life."[12] Molony's charges were less severe since the arresting sergeant stated that she did not seem to be aiming at the police but rather at the photo of the monarchs in the shop window. When Markievicz was asked to give a statement in Molony's defense, she exhibited a similar fit of blindness: "she did not see Molony throw a single missile." The charges against Pike were disorderly conduct, the use of profane language, and threatening to "do away with the Lord Mayor." While Molony testified that she had heard Pike accuse the police of brutality but that he did not encourage the crowd to break the cordon, Markievicz—now afflicted by deafness as well—denied hearing Pike use any profane language or "raise his voice at all or gesticulate."

Surprisingly, the credibility of the women's testimony was never questioned during the trial. The judge declared that while Pike had indubitably acted as charged, this did not mean that "the ladies were not telling the truth. They were telling what happened when they were there." Even so, Markievicz's

---

[11] "Lord Mayor and the Royal Visit," ibid., July 6, 1911, 5.
[12] "Disturbances in Dublin Streets," ibid.

defense of McArdle was ineffective, and he was sentenced to one month's imprisonment with hard labor. Since Molony refused to swear that she had not thrown stones at the police, she was given the option of paying a fine or undergoing a month's imprisonment. She refused to pay. When McArdle attempted to say good-bye to her, he was caught by the throat by a constable who was then—in a rare stroke of justice—charged with assault.[13]

The Socialist Party of Ireland hosted a united demonstration in solidarity with Molony and McArdle. Over one thousand people were present to protest the lord mayor's actions and the pair's imprisonment. J. J. Kelly—declaring himself neither a member of the SPI nor of the Daughters of Ireland—proposed a resolution expressing admiration for their actions, and he was seconded by Alderman Tom Kelly and supported by Constance Markievicz, Sean MacDermott, and Bulmer Hobson.[14] Not only would violence against the police now be endorsed, the police—as officers of the crown—would not be petitioned for their early release. Constance, now confident in her convictions, wrote unreservedly to Josslyn:

> While for the quiet poor a Royal Visit means a drunken & immoral orgy; the town filled with drunken & immoral soldiers & sailors, their pockets full of money, utterly undisciplined & bent on amusing themselves, these fellows in their gay uniforms with their talk of foreign Courts have no difficulty in making themselves popular & corrupting boys & girls alike. One gets so furious at this sort of thing being forced on a city against its will, & one wonders so why a king comes at all, if—to do safely—he has to bring an army & a navy from England, & of police from the country.[15]

Nonetheless, she attempted to reassure him about the sensational newspaper reports on her activities: "Everything here has subsided again, & Dublin is its usual peaceful self; & we are all praying that King George will not come again for many a long day. Even if I were not a nationalist I should object to Kings visits, for they but bring out the worst qualities of people."[16]

Any reassurance Josslyn found was short lived. The very next week, presiding over a meeting of the Socialist Party of Ireland, Constance was arrested. She was standing in for Walter Carpenter, secretary of the SPI, who had been imprisoned for making seditious remarks about the king. Francis

---

[13] Ibid.

[14] "The Imprisonment of Miss Moloney," *Irish Times*, July 10, 1911, 15.

[15] Constance Markievicz to Josslyn Gore-Booth (n.d. [received July 24, 1911]), PRONI, D4131/K/3.

[16] Ibid.

Sheehy Skeffington and Helena Molony both spoke in his support. In her speech, Molony used the same phrase for which Carpenter had been arrested: "King George was the descendant of one of the worst scoundrels in Europe."[17] The police moved to arrest her, but Markievicz sprang into action; as the newspapers put it, she repelled the constable "by means of her foot." For this practical demonstration of her new doctrine of physical force, Markievicz was also taken into custody.[18]

Francis Sheehy Skeffington and Jennie Wyse Power were among the friends who accompanied Molony and Markievicz to the police court. The official charge against Molony was "using language calculated to provoke a breach of the peace." The charge against Markievicz was more serious: she was alleged to have kicked one constable twice in the chest and kicked another in the left leg while throwing gravel in his face. Markievicz argued that it was in fact the police who had acted violently against *her*, and the protestors had peacefully "joined hands" in an effort to prevent them from mounting the truck. She raised a countercharge of assault and testified that she

> thought Constable Smyth (226 C) was going to trip her up, and she moved back a little, and put her hand on his shoulders to prevent him catching her. Then another policeman tried to do the same thing. They were all in a row in front of her. Then one got behind, and she was bustled and pulled down among the whole lot of the policemen. Constables had her by the two hands the whole time. She might have touched the constable with her feet when she was tilted back, but she did not strike him deliberately. There was not the slightest truth in the statement that she had thrown gravel. She would not throw sand nor gravel in any man's face![19]

When the verdict was delivered on August 12, the charges against Molony and Markievicz were proven, but no conviction was handed down. The judge explained that when "it is only a trifling assault, or the person is charged for the first time," he reserved the right to dismiss the defendant with a caution. The judge stated explicitly that the verdict against Molony was made "in consideration of her sex," and the same was certainly true of Markievicz's case. Although unacknowledged, the question of class certainly factored into the judge's decision. These two considerations—her class and her sex—were to Markievicz infuriatingly chauvinistic condescension and would haunt

[17] "Attack on the King," *Irish Times*, Aug. 7, 1911, 5; and "Police Court Proceedings," ibid., Aug. 12, 1911, 5.

[18] "Attack on the King," 5.

[19] "Prosecuting Socialist Agitators," *Irish Times*, Aug. 12, 1911, 5.

her in the future. So would her unwillingness to accept responsibility for committing an act of violence against a policeman.

Josslyn learned of Constance's arrest through a report in the *Sligo Champion*. He wrote to her immediately, concerned first for her well-being and second for the degree of her involvement. She replied, "It never struck me that anyone would believe the charge against me, so I'm writing to tell you what really happened."[20] Her account of the events begins as an attempt to defuse family tensions. She told Josslyn that Helena Molony "got muddled in her speech & gave the impression that she was joking to abuse the King." When the police rushed the truck, Constance claimed that she had "stepped over in front of her [Molony] so that in case they were violent, I would be able to save her a bit, she is so delicate." She had "stepped back" when a policeman tried to grab her ankle, and she "reached forward & pushed him back." She was adamant that she neither kicked him nor threw sand: "I did nothing to warrant my arrest." She told Josslyn that they had engaged counsel, and she had been advised to raise a countercharge:

> Unless they are able to get a great number to perjure themselves, or unless some fool—wishing to make a heroine of me—lies about what I did, I must win. The nationalists are very keen that the question of Freedom of Speech & of the Police interrupting meetings without the authority to do so should be fought. They say that the whole thing was illegal from the Police point of view, but of course, its hard to fight the police, as they are such liars & the men who employ them do not know what truth & honour is.

She concluded, "Everyone has been awfully kind & sympathetic, but it's a great bore & worry." There was more boredom and worry in store.

---

[20] Constance Markievicz to Josslyn Gore-Booth (n.d. [received Aug. 10, 1911]), PRONI, D4131/K/3.

8

Social Realism

AFTER THE FAILURE OF BELCAMP PARK, CONSTANCE AND Casimir lived for a short time in a makeshift commune with Helena Molony at 15 Lower Mount Street. When the Quaker, vegetarian, and Irish language enthusiast Rosamond Jacob came to visit from Waterford in summer 1911, she was struck by the bohemian atmosphere: no carpets on the floors, paintings by Constance and Casimir scattered everywhere, a parlor full of books,

> mostly Irish historical, and a human skull, very brown & old, said to be Asiatic, on a cupboard, and a bronze bust of Emmet higher up on the cupboard, and portraits of Emmet, Tone, Russell, Mitchell and Grattan on the chimneypiece, besides a couple of little Russian ikons. There is a sort of sofa too that gives the impression of consisting of a pile of feather beds with a big piece of canvas, or something like canvas, over it & cushions on top, extremely comfortable.[1]

Jacob was in awe of Constance's style and commented at length on her extravagant outfits: "Madame" appeared at breakfast one morning garbed in "a white alpaca coat down to her knees, long pink stockings and high heeled shoes."[2] Other days, she dressed more simply in a "narrow, high-waisted grey linen dress," but she still sported "very swagger shoes." Even more shocking was Constance's habit of punctuating her conversation with "damn & my God every now and then" in her "very tory accent."[3]

By the next spring, the Markieviczes and Molony were living in a rented house on Leinster Road. They acquired a carpet, lost the bronze bust of

[1] Rosamond Jacob Diary, July 28, 1911, NLI, MS 32,582 (22).
[2] Ibid., Aug. 4, 1911.
[3] Ibid., July 28, 1911.

Emmet, and existed in a chaos of theatrical properties, books, papers, and a great deal of dust.[4] Constance and Helena spent time together at Constance's cottage in the Dublin Mountains, while Casimir stayed occasionally at the Arts Club or lodged with James and Ellen Duncan at 44 St. Stephen's Green, where he was at the time of the 1911 census. The widow May Manders, just two years younger than Casimir, also boarded there, but if there was an affair, it had little effect on Constance and Casimir's amicable relationship. Constance's friends often found that it was Casimir who greeted them at the door at Leinster Road, and the couple continued to attend parties together, teasing each other good-naturedly about how long it took to get ready. Jacob looked on bemused one evening as Constance—dressing for a dinner party—got distracted by a catalog with "a suit of tights and tunic that was just what she wanted for a fancy dress ball at the Arts Club" and stopped everything to measure the length of her leg so she could order the costume immediately (thirty inches: "very poor," Casimir joked). She then lost and found her gloves, and Constance and Casimir were finally out the door at a quarter to nine, leaving Molony and Jacob behind to while away the evening.[5] Molony was at times resentful of their relationship, telling Jacob quite bluntly on one occasion that "the Count... does not really bother about this country at all"; it was Constance who "inspired all the Memory of the Dead"; and his conversation was a "mixture of childishness & wickedness."[6] Jacob observed astutely that Molony "prefers women and Madame prefers men."[7]

Molony emphasized Constance's and Casimir's differences, but the Markieviczes continued to have a great deal in common, not least of which were their ideas about art and the theater. At an exhibition with George Russell, Paul and Grace Henry, and Frances Baker at the Leinster Lecture Hall in autumn 1911, Casimir displayed his triptych, *Bread*, which had first been exhibited in the Indépendant Salon in Paris. The painting was described at length in the *Irish Times*, which seasoned its review with more than a pinch of sarcasm:

> In the right panel is an idealised Sower delicately walking, tight-rope fashion, on a furrow edge. In the right-hand panel, a reverent maiden stands rapt before some corn sheaves lit by the evening glow. The central panel displays a kind of altar-table with what looks like a coiled cat,

---

[4] Ibid., May 7, 1912 (23).
[5] Ibid., Mar. 16, 1913 (24).
[6] Ibid.
[7] Ibid., Aug. 4 [*recte* 3], 1911 (22).

veiled in clouds of incense upon it. The intelligent observer corrects his vision, and concludes that the mysterious object is a glorified cottage loaf in the odour of sanctity. The sentiment of the work speaks for itself. The quality of its execution is appropriate.[8]

The style of *Bread* is similar to that of a painting by Constance from this period in which a woman sits knitting by a window; raw wool, ready for carding, lies on the sill beside her. The tone of these paintings seems less like primitivism and more like social realism, especially in light of the Markievoczes' experiments on the Dublin stage.

Casimir's newly organized Independent Dramatic Company produced George Birmingham's *Eleanor's Enterprise* at the Gaiety Theatre in December 1911, with "Countess Constance de Markievicz" playing the lead role as the rebellious "Girton girl" Eleanor Maxwell. There were familiar faces in the rest of the cast, too: George Nesbitt, Violet Mervyn, Helena Molony, and Seán Connolly. Birmingham's farce deals with the serious problem of the dire poverty affecting rural people in the west of Ireland. Rejecting the ideals of the peasant play, popular at the Abbey Theatre, Birmingham confronts the often ignored question of social class in the country in a plot that satirizes a landlord's superficial attempt to improve the conditions of the tenants on his estate. The *Irish Independent* commented that the "Countess Markievicz can win hearts on the stage, as she can off it. She was not even self-conscious in her duel with two policemen—her friends the enemy."[9]

Casimir alternated the performance of *Eleanor's Enterprise* at the Gaiety with his own new play, *Rival Stars*. His farce also dealt with social questions: the conflict between the life of the aesthete and the life of the activist, as embodied in his characters, the English artist Robert Willis and his wife, Dagna: "his friends are all Bohemians of the musical comedy type. Dagna prefers the society of a Socialistic and Jewish journalist."[10] The *Irish Times* was condescending and dismissive, not just of Markievicz's experiment but of the class issues underlying it:

> Count Markievicz evidently wrote "Rival Stars" with great enjoyment, and it was acted in the same spirit. Dramatically, the fault of the piece is want of consistency. . . . Just as the summer crop of strikes may be attributed largely to the excessive heat, so in the strained excitement attending Robert Ellis's artist life in Paris, things happened which

[8] "The Five Artists / Pictures at Leinster Hall," *Irish Times*, Oct. 16, 1911, 7. *Bread* was not listed in the exhibition catalog.

[9] Ibid.

[10] "Gaiety Theatre / Production of "Rival Stars," *Freeman's Journal*, Dec. 13, 1911, 10.

bore a less tragical complexion when a cold douche in the form of a solicitor coming to negotiate a separation allowance precipitated the heat-fog of misunderstanding, which had arisen between Robert Ellis and Dagna.[11]

All accounts of the play suggest that it is weak dramatically, and the reviews provide scant evidence for a deeper understanding of its subject. Several of Constance Markievicz's biographers have interpreted *Rival Stars* as a simple autobiographical articulation of the Markieviczes' alleged marital discord, but this reading is too simplistic when the nuances of Constance and Casimir's relationship, and their continued work together, are taken into account.

Briefly, they formed an alliance with Edward Martyn, who—like Constance—had fallen out with the Abbey Theatre's directors, W. B. Yeats and Lady Gregory, over their refusal to take a strong nationalistic line. In late January 1912, under the aegis of the short-lived Independent Theatre Company, Casimir produced Martyn's *Grangecolman*, about an aristocratic Irish suffragist, and Eva Gore-Booth's *Unseen Kings*, which takes its plot from the Cuchulain myths but focuses on the "prophetess" Niamh.[12] Martyn soon left to establish with Thomas MacDonagh and Joseph Plunkett the Irish Theatre at Hardwicke Street, while Casimir disbanded the Independent Theatre Company in order to establish a new company that would be dedicated to producing Continental drama.

His first production in this vein was Alexander Ostrovsky's *The Storm*, a play that may have inspired *Rival Stars* since Ostrovsky dealt with the conflict between spiritualism and art (personified in the character Katerina) and the anti-aesthetic commercialism of the merchant class, characterized in Katerina's husband's family, the Kabanovs.[13] Seeking refuge from her vulgarly capitalist in-laws, Katerina takes a lover, Boris, but when the affair is discovered, Boris goes off to China and Katarina throws herself into the Volga. The melodramatic plot contrasts with the "very realistic" set that Casimir painted for the production, and the *Freeman's Journal* focused on describing Ostrovsky as "a realist": "And between the Realism of Russian artists and Naturalism in its conventional French sense, there is a world of difference. Ostrovsky's Realism is selective; he does not employ incident merely because it is accurate, only because it is significant."[14] Constance and Casimir

---

[11] "Gaiety Theatre / Count Markievicz's New Play," *Irish Times*, Dec. 13, 1911, 7.

[12] Nolan, "Edward Martyn's Struggle for an Irish National Theater"; Martyn, *Grangecolman*; Gore-Booth, *Unseen Kings*, 41.

[13] Beasley, "The Art of Ostrovsky."

[14] Hayes, *Years Flew By*, 31; "Ostrovsky," *Freeman's Journal*, Feb. 20, 1911, 8.

attempted to explain the Russian aesthetic to Dublin audiences in the co-written article "Taste in Drama." They contrasted the Irish sensibility with "the taste of the British public," which they mocked for its fascination with the freakish "giants, dwarfs, human apes, etc." that were common to panto-mime. Alongside these theatrical exaggerations, they cast the vulgarities of "post impressionists in Art," again suggesting a turn to a realist aesthetic.[15] For Casimir, it was social realism; for Constance, it was socialist—although her theory and practice of socialism were, and would remain, embryonic.

Constance and Casimir's different emphases coalesced in the production of Shaw's *The Devil's Disciple* under the aegis of the Dublin Repertory Theatre. Shaw wrote his play on the eve of the 1798 centenary, but he used the American Revolution as his setting because it was, as Holroyd argues, "culturally equivalent to modern Ireland."[16] Shaw's protagonist, the roguish Dick Dudgeon, is arrested by British soldiers when he is mistaken for a Presbyterian minister called Anderson who is suspected of revolutionary activity. Dudgeon goes along with the mistaken identity in order to protect Anderson, and the experience of his imprisonment transforms the rake into a hero. Explicitly, Shaw's target is Puritanism, but reviews of the play also focused on the issue of national independence.[17] As an extreme experiment with realism—and delighted with the inevitable frisson it would cause—Casimir emphasized the politics of Shaw's play by casting Trinity College students as the British soldiers and boys from the Fianna as the mob.[18]

The Devil's Disciple is just one example of how Molony's claim that Casimir was unconcerned with Ireland is an exaggeration. Both Markieviczes also took part in the Gaelic League's Oireachtas, or gathering, in the summer of 1911. Casimir displayed paintings in an exhibition that was dedicated exclusively to "Irish modern art," indicating his acceptance within Dublin's nationalist avant-garde.[19] Constance played an ancient Irish queen in the Oireachtas pageant, dressed in "a lovely pale blue velvet gown that flowed after by the yard & had great loose hanging sleeves." (Her outfit for the party afterward, "a black velvet Empire dress, very low & with short little sleeves and a salmon pink gauze double sort of scarf with gold fringe, & a necklace, & a gilt spangled headdress," seemed a little overblown.[20]) Yet to emphasize the Markieviczes' commonalities is not to eliminate their

[15] Scrapbook, PRONI, D4131/K/9.
[16] Holroyd, *Bernard Shaw*, 396.
[17] The Gaiety Theatre," *Freeman's Journal*, May 13, 1913, 2.
[18] Marreco, *The Rebel Countess*, 149.
[19] "The Oireachtas," *Weekly Irish Times*, Aug. 7, 1911, 5.
[20] Rosamond Jacob Diary, Aug. 2, 1911, NLI, MS 32,582 (22).

differences. Casimir's interest in Ireland was always mediated by his under-standing of Polish nationality, and it was always second to his aesthetic and commercial interests. After the production of *The Devil's Disciple*, he left Dublin for his annual visit home. He was feted at a dinner at the Dolphin Hotel on May 19 and presented with a gold matchbox in gratitude for his service to the Dublin Repertory Theatre and the Gaiety, perhaps on the sus-picion that he might be leaving Dublin for good.[21] But he returned in Au-gust, when his relationship with the management of the Gaiety would be very different, and Dublin would be changed utterly.

[21] "Count Markievicz/Honoured by Dublin Friends," *Irish Independent*, May 21, 1913.

9

The Beginning

IN THE SUMMER OF 1913 DUBLIN ERUPTED IN A VIOLENT battle between capital and labor, a fight that would prove to be a cornerstone of the Irish struggle for independence. The progenitor of the dispute was the most powerful businessman in the city, William Martin Murphy. Terrified of the effects of the reforms advocated by the rapidly expanding Irish Transport and General Workers' Union, which now had over ten thousand members, Murphy organized a meeting of three hundred of the capital's employers who were afraid that a reduction of the seventeen-hour workday would severely affect profits. Their solution was to summarily dismiss any employees who were ITGWU members. Murphy led the charge, firing more than three hundred workers from the United Tramways Corporation in fewer than two weeks. The tramway workers responded with a strike, and the industrial dispute quickly escalated as the Dublin Employers' Federation refused work to any member of the ITGWU. The Dublin Lockout had begun.

The industrial dispute also became a battleground for contesting Ireland's relationship to the British Empire. The mortality rate in Dublin was equal to that of Calcutta, with Irish wages steadily falling behind inflation and the rise in wages in Britain.[1] The British government's seeming indifference to the plight of Irish workers led James Connolly to declare at a meeting on Friday, August 29, that "he did not recognise the authority of the British Government in Ireland, and refused to be bound" by it.[2] Connolly was promptly arrested. The police also sought to arrest the ITGWU's founder, James Larkin, but Larkin outfoxed them and went on the run. After grandly

---

[1] Yeates, *Lockout*, 31.

[2] F. Sheehy Skeffington, "More Evidence of Brutal Repressive Methods," *Manchester Guardian*, Sept. 1, 1913, 7.

proclaiming that "dead or alive" he would address the people of Dublin on Sackville Street on Sunday, he disappeared from public view.[3]

He was hiding at the Markieviczes' residence, Surrey House. Constance had first become involved in the ITGWU through a campaign to expand the union's membership to women. The call for a union of women workers had been issued by *Bean na hÉireann* as early as January 1910, which marked the beginning of the regular "Labour Notes" column by "A Worker." Until the weekly labor newspaper, the *Irish Worker*, was founded in spring 1911, "Labour Notes" was the forum for reports on major debates within the labor movement and occasions of industrial action. *Bean na hÉireann* fully supported James Larkin's establishment of an independent federation of Irish labor, the Irish Transport and General Workers' Union, and James Connolly's advocacy of an independent Irish Labour Party. However, it criticized labor's reluctance to incorporate women fully into the movement: "While generally admitting the needs of the unorganised female worker the male members of the wage-earners looked with suspicion on their sister slaves, and are seemingly loath to offer any practical help."[4]

In response to the marginalization of women, Delia Larkin, James's sister, moved to Dublin from Liverpool in summer 1911 to begin organizing a women's union that would form a subset of the ITGWU. Her "Women Workers' Column," published weekly in the *Irish Worker*, put domestic labor and work outside the home on equal footing: "the women-workers have an opportunity of doing away with these cliques, a union has been started for them, which takes in all classes of workers and will therefore enable these different sections of workers to meet."[5] The "Countess Markievicz" spoke at a mass meeting to launch the new union, saying, "Friends, I am very glad Mr. Larkin asked me to come here and address you. Without organisation you can do nothing, and the purpose of this meeting is to form you into an army of fighters. You will all, I hope, join this union: by doing so you will be doing a good day's work, not only for yourselves, but for Ireland."[6] The industrial unrest of summer 1913 provided the occasion to enlist the union's "army of fighters" in the larger struggle.

Riots exploded across Dublin. Protestors threw stones and bottles at police, who retaliated with "baton charge after baton charge."[7] Casimir Markievicz made his way home through the pandemonium to find Jim Larkin

---

[3] "Grave Labour Riots in Dublin," *Irish Times*, Sept. 1, 1913, 5.

[4] "Labour Notes," *Bean na hÉireann* (April 1910): 10.

[5] D. L., "Women Workers' Column," *Irish Worker*, Sept. 2, 1911, 2.

[6] "Women Workers' Union: Great Meeting in Antient Concert Rooms," ibid., Sept. 1911, 3.

[7] "Grave Labour Riots in Dublin."

hiding at Surrey House under the protection of Constance, Helena Molony, and Nellie Gifford.[8] According to Dublin legend, Casimir was co-opted immediately into the labor struggle and lent Larkin his own top hat and frock coat to wear as a disguise for his reappearance the next day. Masquerading as the deaf old Mr. Donnelly and his niece, Larkin and Gifford entered the Murphy-owned Imperial Hotel on Sackville Street while Casimir and Constance waited in the street, where a crowd was quickly gathering. When Larkin emerged triumphantly onto the balcony, Constance called out, "Three cheers for Larkin," drawing the attention of the police, who forced her carriage into a side street. The disturbance attracted more people to the scene in time for Larkin to declare that "he had made good his promise" before he was taken into police custody.[9]

When a window in the Murphy-owned Clery's Department Store across the street was broken, the tense atmosphere provoked the police—hot-blooded after the violence of the night before—to draw their batons and charge the crowd. Constance, standing near the door of the Imperial Hotel, managed to shake Larkin's hand as the police escorted him away, saying "Good-bye, good luck," before she was punched in the face by a Dublin Metropolitan Police inspector.[10] She later recounted the events, emphasizing the brutality against women and children and the drunkenness that she would argue characterized agents of the British Empire:

> I reeled against another policeman, who pulled me about, tearing all the buttons off my blouse, and tearing it out all around my waist. He then threw me back into the middle of the street, where all the police had begun to run, several of them kicking and hitting me as they passed. . . . I saw a woman trying to get out of the way. She was struck from behind by a policeman with his baton. As she fell her hat slipped over her face and I saw her hair was grey. . . . I saw a barefooted boy with papers hunted and hit about the shoulders as he ran away. . . . I noticed that the policemen who struck me smelt very strongly of stout, and that they all seemed very excited.[11]

[8] Nellie Gifford worked alongside Markievicz, Madeleine Ffrench-Mullen, and Kathleen Lynn to feed children during the Lockout; she was sister to the political cartoonist Grace Gifford, who married Joseph Plunkett at Kilmainham Gaol on the eve of Plunkett's execution after the Easter Rising; and Murial Gifford, who married Thomas MacDonagh, also executed in 1916.

[9] Yeates, *Lockout*, 64; "Comedy Turns to Tragedy," *Manchester Guardian*, Sept. 1, 1913, 7. Also see "Grave Labour Riots in Dublin." Yeates gives Larkin's words as "I am here today in accordance with my promise." *Lockout*, 63.

[10] Yeates, *Lockout*, 65–66.

[11] Quoted in Nevin, ed., *1913*, 34–35.

Another policeman struck Markievicz across the face with a baton before she was pulled to safety inside a house in Sackville Place.[12]

The *Irish Times*'s report relayed the events in a blithe tone of faux objectivity—"the police had to disperse [the crowd] by means of baton charges"—in contrast to the sympathetic *Manchester Guardian*, which had itself been born out of the Peterloo Massacre of 1819.[13] Under the headline "Wild Bludgeoning by Police," the *Guardian* reported that two men were dead and more than two hundred had received treatment in hospital. Irish socialist Francis Sheehy Skeffington suggested in his report to the *Guardian* that the violence had been selective: "well-known people . . . [were] carefully left untouched, but the workingmen present were truncheoned severely," along with several women, including "Countess Markiewicz."[14] Sheehy Skeffington's version of the events was supported by the observations of other reporters who described the crowd as peaceful.[15]

Casimir immediately protested the police brutality in a letter to the *Irish Times* in which he cast himself "as an impartial witness."[16] He argued that the violence "was equalled only, perhaps, by the Bloody Sunday events in St Petersburg." Markievicz's analogy was quickly adopted in contemporary discourse, and the events of September 1, 1913, became the touchstone for future occurrences of police brutality in Ireland. Markievicz wrote emotively:

> Round the corner of Prince's street I saw a young man pursued by a huge policeman, knocked down, and then, whilst bleeding on the ground, batoned and kicked not only by this policeman, but by his colleagues, lusting for slaughter. I saw many batoned people lying on the ground senseless and bleeding. Women, old and young, were not spared, but were knocked down and trampled on. When the police had satisfied the bloodthirsty pursuit, the terror-stricken people and we, the passers by, [timorously] sought shelter in the doorways, but the baton was still used freely. It was a complete triumph for the Metropolitan Police. . . . It was indeed a great day for the baton and the physical

[12] Yeates, *Lockout*, 65–66.

[13] "Grave Labour Riots in Dublin"; and "Fierce Fighting in Dublin," *Manchester Guardian*, Sept. 1, 1913, 7. On August 16, 1819, the British cavalry charged a crowd of over sixty thousand citizens who were assembled in St. Peter's Field, Manchester, to demand parliamentary reform.

[14] Markievicz's victimization was the subject of a short column below Sheehy Skeffington's. "A Correspondent" contributed "Countess Markievicz Struck with Truncheon" and noted that "Miss Constance Gore" was "well known to Manchester electors." See *Manchester Guardian*, Sept. 1, 1913, 7.

[15] Sheehy Skeffington, "More Evidence of Brutal Repressive Methods."

[16] Casimir Dunin Markievicz, "The Conduct of the Police," Letter to the Editor, *Irish Times*, Sept. 1, 1913, 7.

training of the Dublin Metropolitan Police. They overshadowed Cossacks and bashi-bazocks [*recte* Bashi-bazouks]. Indeed, a Bloody Sunday for Ireland. Photographs taken by the *Freeman's* representatives would bear irrefutable testimony to the truth of my statements. I at once sought out Sir James Dougherty [the undersecretary for Ireland], and told him what I had witnessed. I have also informed the foreign Press. No human being could be silent after what I saw. These acts of uncalled for and inhuman cruelty must be punished, and the public should insist on a sworn inquiry.[17]

Markievicz's language reveals as much about his eastern European politics as it does about the situation in Ireland. Importantly, at Bloody Sunday 1905, when the Russian state massacred workers who proceeded to the Winter Palace in St. Petersburg to demand civil liberties, the workers' protest was neither socialist nor antimonarchist.[18] This is crucial for understanding Casimir's later engagement with Russian politics. His reference to Bashi-bazouks, a disparaging term for irregular soldiers who served in the Ottoman Army, sheds light on his decision to produce François Coppée's *For the Crown* at the Gaiety Theatre the previous year and may be a clue to his decision to travel to the Balkans in the autumn of 1913. The derogatory term "Cossacks" had a very specific relevance to Ireland's Bloody Sunday, as the Dublin Metropolitan Police, who took direction from Dublin Castle, were perceived as imperial agents. In addition to adopting the phrase "Bloody Sunday," the *Irish Worker* also co-opted the term "Cossacks"; the following week, Delia Larkin wrote, "The drunken Cossacks may do their share by taking the life and the employers their share by locking out the workers, hoping to break their spirit; but not all the combined forces will make the workers deviate one inch from the path of progress they have taken."[19]

The *Irish Times* attacked Markievicz's claims of impartiality, defended the police, and referred to the industrial dispute as a strike rather than a lockout.[20] A letter to the Murphy-owned *Irish Independent* went further:

It is quite easy to understand the chagrin and disappointment of Count Markievicz . . . at the intervention of the police to prevent him and his friends from posing on their self-erected stage in O'Connell Street, when we hear that the entire properties, including the luggage,

---

[17] Ibid.
[18] Ascher, *The Revolution of 1905*, 26–27.
[19] Delia Larkin, "W. and R. Jacob's and Co., Ltd. Charge," *Irish Worker*, Sept. 6, 1913, 2.
[20] "The Dublin Riots," *Irish Times*, Sept. 1, 1913, 4.

tall hat, frock coat, and even the "niece, Miss Donnelly," were provided by his near relatives.[21]

Casimir retorted, "Surely you may spare me your inverted commas 'as an impartial witness.'"[22] He insisted that he had "no interest whatever"' in the industrial dispute and that he was in Sackville Street "merely as a representative of the foreign Press." He even claimed, "As a foreigner and an artist, standing outside the politics of any country—and I have lived in Ireland for ten years without taking any part in politics—I took no part in demonstrating my sympathy with either side in this dispute."[23] Markievicz's insistence on objectivity contradicts his extensive involvement in the politics of cultural life. The Lane pictures and the subjects of his own paintings and plays had been the vehicle for his political expression during his decade in Dublin. In the following months, he would risk the success of his dramatic company, which had been built through ten years of hard work, to profess his unequivocal support for Constance and the Irish labor movement.

Casimir's Dublin Repertory Theatre planned to revive *Eleanor's Enterprise* for the autumn 1913 program. However, his outspokenness at the atrocities of Bloody Sunday destroyed his good relationship with the management of the Gaiety Theatre and led to the play's cancellation. The chairman of the Gaiety, David Telford, objected to Constance reprising her role as Eleanor, "owing to the high feeling which prevails in the city at the present moment, and owing to the prominent part which the Countess has taken in the labour disputes."[24] Casimir's business partner, Edward Ashley, agreed with Telford and privately told him that he had already protested against "Countess Markievicz appearing at all in our productions," but Casimir had refused "to see

[21] "Count Markievicz and the Police," *Irish Independent*, Sept. 8, 1913, 6.

[22] Casimir Dunin Markievicz, Letter to the Editor, "Conduct of the Police," *Irish Times*, Sept. 2, 1913, 7.

[23] Stanislaus Markievicz's depiction of his father also distances Casimir from the politics of the Irish workers' protests. Yet this may be as much a product of Stanislaus's politics as Casimir's posturing. In his unpublished biography of Constance, Stanislaus wrote, "Many years later in Poland, my father told me how she insisted on going to that meeting of Larkin's which ended in a baton charge by the police, when 500 people were injured and 50 constables. Casimir had just returned from the Ukraine, where he had gone, as a well-informed writer has said rather wittily, 'to earn his year's income'; at all events, fearing there would be trouble, he decided to accompany his self-willed lifepartner. They arrived in the midst of it, just as the police were about to charge the crowd." Stanislaus Markievicz, TS, "Life of Constance Markievicz," NLI, MS 44,619.

[24] (Copy) D. Telford to Edward Ashley (Sept. 25, 1913), reprinted in *Freeman's Journal*, Nov. 13, 1913, 9. Also see "Count Markievicz and the Repertory Theatre," *Evening Irish Times*, Nov. 13, 1913, 9, in Hogan, Burnham, and Poteet, *The Rise of the Realists*, 299. The articles are signed variously "Duinin Marckievicz," "Dumir Markievisz," and "Dumir Markievicz." See *Freeman's Journal*, Nov. 14, 1913, 5.

that his attitude and that of his wife is only calculated to do the Repertory Theatre movement irreparable injury."[25] Ashley sent Telford's letter to Casimir, enclosing a copy of his own reply and apologetically insisting "that Madame's attitude, however well intentioned, has already done our movement very great injury."[26] Casimir promptly resigned and stated unequivocally that it was the vital responsibility of the company to be engaged with Dublin politics. He wrote to Ashley, "I am convinced that your policy must be fatal to the interests of the Repertory Theatre movement, as well as insulting to the other people of this city."[27]

Casimir's opinions about the necessity for theater to be political are expressed more subtly in his painting, but politics are evident there too. Fewer than two weeks after Bloody Sunday, the Markieviczes held their final collaborative exhibition with George Russell. The title of the exhibition, *Irish Artists "at Home,"* suggests both a sense of Irish nationality (in which Casimir was co-opted) and the avant-garde's departure from conventional academic display. Like the Parisian Indépendants, the Irish avant-garde brought the private salon into public view. The *Irish Times*, omitted any reference to the Markieviczes' recent political statements but gave Russell top billing.[28] The atmosphere was that of "Upper Bohemia," with the Yeats sisters, the flaneur and Abbey playwright Lennox Robinson, actress Elizabeth Young, playwright Edward Martyn, poet Padraig Colum, and the theosophist and future militant Republican Ella Young all turning out.[29]

Casimir's paintings were described at length in the *Irish Times*, which characterized the work as of the "impressionist type"—a summation that Casimir probably found irksome, in light of his denunciation of the postimpressionist aesthetic and his turn to social realism:

> "The Cornfield" is an embodiment of the impression produced on the eye by a mass of growing corn, depending not on the realisation of it stalk by stalk, but speaking of the rich glow of colour, and the rustling of the ears of grain. "Ploughing" again gives us the spirit of the

[25] (Copy) A. E. Ashley to Telford (Sept. 26, 1913), reprinted in *Freeman's Journal*, Nov. 13, 1913, 9.

[26] (Copy) A. E. Ashley to Casimir Markievicz (Sept. 26, 1913), reprinted in ibid.

[27] (Copy) Dumir Markievicz to A. E. Ashley (Oct. 1913), reprinted in ibid., Nov. 13, 1913, 9.

[28] "Irish Artists 'at Home': Mr George Russell's Pictures," *Irish Times*, Sept. 15, 1913, 9.

[29] Ella Young (1867–1956) was a protégé of Russell's; a theosophist, poet, and scholar of Celtic mythology, she hid pistols, ammunition, and Thompson submachine guns for the Republicans during the Irish Civil War, after which she emigrated to the United States to take up a post in Celtic Studies at the University of California at Berkeley, where she delivered her lectures while dressed in flowing purple Druidic robes. See Murphy, *Ella Young, Irish Mystic and Rebel*; and Starr, *Golden Dreams*, 234–26.

rude toil and struggle necessary to gain the fruits of the earth, the impression being conveyed primarily by the line of animals strung out at length. One cannot recall without having given particular notice whether the plough is drawn by horses or by oxen, but the impression of patient endeavour remains, and a breath from the wide country is felt instinctively. From "The Park" one gains the impression of quiet restfulness and stateliness. This atmosphere is also well conveyed in the tree studies.

Markievicz continued to work from a tradition of fin de siècle Polish art that imbued landscape painting with symbols that evoked national preoccupations. *Ploughing* is very similar to Ferdynand Ruszczyc's *The Earth* of 1898, a plein air composition of a bowed figure whipping his oxen across a hill beneath an expansive, stormy sky.[30] Irish and Polish art of the period glorified the rural landscape and the agricultural laborer, reifying the peasant as an emblem of the nation. In addition to these nationalist sympathies, Casimir's recent work also reflects his newfound social conscience. His portrait of a chimney sweep, the *Irish Times* commented, "conveys rather the mental attributes of the subject than his actual facial characteristics." This observation suggests that aspects of Casimir's work can be situated in the genre of working-class impressionism, which blends academic and impressionist techniques but engages with social questions in "Emile Zola fashion."[31] Like Zola, Markievicz moved in bourgeois social circles while challenging bourgeois values in his art; however, Markievicz would never have the financial security nor the inclination to depart fully from bourgeois patronage.

Casimir made an annual trip from Dublin to Zywotowka. When he left Ireland in autumn 1913, however, it was not for Zywotowka but for Durazzo (now Durrës), an ancient port city on the Adriatic. His motivations are unclear. With the Dublin Repertory Theatre's contract at the Gaiety canceled, he may have simply had little to do, so the prospect of traveling to the Balkans may have appealed to his sense of adventure. The First Balkan War had drawn to a close in May, with a German, Prince William of Wied, selected by the imperial powers as a puppet ruler for the newly established and severely unstable state of Albania.[32] The timing of Markievicz's visit has led to wild speculation. In his memoirs, Casimir's friend Mieczyslaw Fijałkowski

[30] Ruszczyc (1879–1930), *The Earth* (1898), National Museum, Warsaw. See Charazinska and Kossowski, eds., *Fin de Siècle Polish Art*, viii.

[31] Swanson, "Naturalist Working-Class Tradition, 1870s–1917," in *Soviet Impressionist Painting*, 48.

[32] Hall, *The Balkan Wars 1912–1913*, 131.

suggests that Markievicz was a drinking companion of Wied's; in an even more sensational sketch, later published in *Kurier Warszawski*, another friend, Kornel Makuszynski, incriminates Casimir in an imperial plot:

> It would be surprising if such a strange and insane event would take place without the participation of a Pole. Markievicz turns up in Albania and helps to establish Wied on the throne of that gay and belligerent kingdom. Maybe he reckoned slyly that the brave Albanians would chase the skinny Wied away and the mighty-looking Pole might be called to found a new Albanian dynasty.[33]

Makuszynski goes on to connect the deposal of Wied with Casimir's decision to leave the country, but the parallel is too convenient. While Markievicz enjoyed the company of the wealthy and powerful, there is little in his life to suggest that he either sought or was capable of political leadership.

Back in Dublin, the cultural conservative D. P. Moran and the founder of Sinn Féin Arthur Griffith condemned "the sway of socialist doctrines" as another aspect of the Anglicization of Irish life.[34] In the coming years, debates over whether the ITGWU was a socialist organization would divide the union membership, but from the Lockout until the suppression of the *Irish Worker* in 1915, socialist discourse was prominent. In contrast to Moran's and Griffith's conservatism, the Dublin avant-garde published letters in support of the locked-out workers in the *Irish Worker*. George Russell's "To the Masters of Dublin" was published in October, and a host of correspondence in support of the ITGWU followed, from writers as predictable as Maud Gonne and as unexpected as W. B. Yeats.[35] In her letter to the paper, Constance reflected on Larkin's imprisonment in terms that were explicitly socialist: he was "in jail for championing the poor against the rich, the oppressed against the oppressor."[36] She launched an attack on the British government in which all of its agents—including civil servants—were cast as capitalist imperialists:

> Under the flag of "Capitalism" you find the British Crown with all its minions, its judges, magistrates, inspectors, spies, police. . . . The case was tried by his enemies, his accusers, the "just" judge a capitalist . . . all the craft and cunning of trained police witnesses, and of Castle

---

[33] Quoted in Quigley, *Polish Irishman*, 155.
[34] John Hutchinson, quoted in Oikarinen, *A Dream of Liberty*, 79.
[35] Yeats's letter was probably motivated by the opportunity to resume his long campaign against Murphy, who had refused to support the plans for a municipal gallery in Dublin.
[36] Madame Markeivicz, "In Jail," *Irish Worker*, Nov. 1, 1913, 2.

note-takers; the whole power of Capitalism and English rule were ranged against the man, Jim Larkin.[37]

As in her earliest political speeches in support of women's suffrage, she rapidly shifted register, moving from socialist rhetoric to a nationalist discourse of religious martyrdom. She described Larkin as a Christ-like figure: "All honest men and women must love, respect, and honour him; all true hearts must be prepared to follow him." The tone that she uses here for a working-class audience is identical to the pedagogical tone of her articles for the Fianna: "Jim is in jail for us; what sacrifices can we make for Jim? What offering of work and self sacrifice can we lay at his feet?"[38] In a poem for the *Irish Worker*, published under the pseudonym "Maca," Markievicz similarly describes Larkin as a savior: "We found in Jim, a heart ablaze, / To break down unjust laws."[39] The poem's title, "Who Fears to Wear the Blood Red Badge," invoked the ballad "Who Fears to Speak of '98" and could be sung to the same tune. Markievicz's use of socialist, Christian, and Irish republican tropes in her writing for the *Irish Worker* illustrates the various components of her political thought and the way that she was able to manipulate different discourses in her propaganda.

Constance Markievicz and Delia Larkin, both of whom were criticized by conservative nationalists, who characterized them as outsiders and do-gooders, directed the response of the Irish Women Workers' Union (IWWU) to the Lockout. Markievicz and Larkin led a large contingent from the IWWU in a ten-thousand-strong march through Dublin in mid-October; on a more practical level, they organized a soup kitchen in Liberty Hall for the locked-out workers and their families, feeding over three thousand people each day.[40] Despite the efficacy of Markievicz's work, which was acknowledged by the British Trade Unions Council, Sean O'Casey later caricatured her posing for pictures "in a spotless bib and tucker, standing in the steam, a gigantic ladle in her hand."[41] Markievicz's less prominent activism suggests that she used the privileges of her social status to the benefit of her comrades. She stood bail for Dora Montefiore and Lucille Rand when they were arrested as a result of their campaign to send the children of Dublin's

---

[37] Ibid.

[38] Ibid.

[39] "Maca," "Who Fears to Wear the Blood Red Badge," *Irish Worker*, Oct. 11, 1913, in Oikarinen, *A Dream of Liberty*, 77; also see Van Voris, *Constance Markievicz in the Cause of Ireland*, 362.

[40] "Mr Larkin, Dictator," *Irish Independent*, Oct. 17, 1913, 5; Yeates, *Lockout*, 191.

[41] Yeates, *Lockout*, 191, 322; O'Casey, *Drums under the Window*, 211–12.

locked-out workers to socialist families in England.[42] She similarly vouched for the alibi of locked-out IWWU members Annie Kavanagh and Kathleen Sheffield, who were charged with "a breach of the peace." On that occasion the judge was hesitant to contradict a woman of Markievicz's social class, commenting merely that "he did not disbelieve the testimony of the Countess Markievicz and the other ladies, but it was quite possible they were mistaken as to the time."[43]

The victimization of unionized women workers during the Lockout drew the attention of suffragists in Ireland and Britain to the Irish labor movement. In turn, James Connolly, Constance Markievicz, and Hanna Sheehy Skeffington increased their support of the Irishwomen's Franchise League, attending a meeting of the league on November 11. In his speech, Connolly advocated the militant tactics used by some suffragists, and he intimated the forthcoming mobilization of the Irish Citizen Army: "he had never yet heard of a militant action which he was not prepared fully and heartily to endorse."[44] Connolly's and Markievicz's endorsement of the IWFL—an organization that Markievicz had previously vehemently opposed—is one example of the Irish Left's attempts to unite trade unionists, suffragists, and nationalists in opposition to the Third Home Rule Bill. (Britain's entry into the First World War the following year and the subsequent threat of conscription in Ireland would provide the catalyst for the change that they sought.) The devolved parliament that the bill described was unsatisfactory for radical separatists, and Britain's failure to address the demands of Irish suffrage, labor, and a vocal—and militant—socialist minority further radicalized the political Left in the country. Home Rule would also radicalize Irish Unionists, particularly those of northeastern Ulster, who organized a militia—the Ulster Volunteers—and threatened to fight the British state for the right to remain in the Union. This set a precedent for the organization of arms-bearing militias in Ireland.

Markievicz stood at Connolly's side at a rally organized to greet Jim Larkin on his release from Mountjoy Prison on November 13. She proclaimed that the occasion was "the proudest moment of my life, to be associated with the workers of Dublin when their great and noble leader has been

[42] McDiarmid, "Hunger and Hysteria: The 'Save the Dublin Kiddies' Campaign, October–November 1913," in *The Irish Art of Controversy*, 124–25; Yeates, *Lockout*, 365.

[43] "Provocative Language," *Freeman's Journal*, Nov. 12, 1913, 10.

[44] "Irish Women's Franchise League," *Irish Citizen*, Nov. 16, 1913, 210. Murphy notes that Connolly adopted the suffragists' "most famous prison tactic," the hunger strike, to effect his release from a three-month sentence to Mountjoy in September 1913; his daughter, Ina Heron, later recalled him saying, "What was good enough for the suffragettes to use . . . is good enough for us." See Murphy, *Political Imprisonment and the Irish*, 30.

released."[45] Although Markievicz and Connolly were both willing to praise Larkin publicly, Connolly found Larkin's cult of personality irksome and complained privately to William O'Brien of what Greaves describes as "Larkin's thirst for admiration."[46] He used the occasion of Larkin's release to lay the foundation for the new militant campaign: "Why should we not drill men in Dublin as well as in Ulster? . . . I say nothing about arms at present. When we want them, we know where to find them."[47] He declared that the workers were "in a state of war" and when collecting their strike pay from Liberty Hall should provide their name and address so that they could be informed "when and where you have to attend for training."

R. M. Fox's orthodox history of the Irish Citizen Army (ICA) locates the establishment of the group in October 1913 and describes it as "a strike force" that was later formally organized as an army under Captain Jack White and James Connolly.[48] White had served in the Boer War after training as a cadet at Sandhurst, and Connolly had served in the British Army as an enlisted man, so the two were well equipped to organize Dublin's workers into a rank-and-file citizens' militia. White was also prominent in the citizens' peace committee that was organized after Bloody Sunday, and it was at a meeting of the committee in the rooms of Reverend R. M. Gwynn at Trinity College that he secured the initial funding to equip the workers with boots and staves.

On March 13, 1914, a skirmish occurred between the ICA and the Dublin Metropolitan Police. Constance Markievicz was among four hundred unemployed men and women who marched from Beresford Place, armed with staves and carrying banners proclaiming "Victimised" and posters reading "Better die fighting than starving." On their way to the Mansion House, they were stopped on Eden Quay when a mail van blocked their procession. According to the *Irish Times*, White attempted to hit the driver of the van and "made one or two strokes with a heavy knob-ended stick at a policeman who was near the head of the horse." When a police inspector attempted to arrest him, White allegedly swung his stick at the policeman, making contact at the same time that he was "hit heavily upon the head by a man behind and stunned." The workers, rushing to protect White, were attacked by the po-

---

[45] Yeates, *Lockout*, 395–96. See "Meeting at Beresford Place," *Freeman's Journal*, Nov. 14, 1913, 8; and *Irish Times*, Nov. 14, 1913.

[46] Greaves, *Irish Transport and General Workers' Union*, 91.

[47] Yeates, *Lockout*, 395–96. See "Meeting at Beresford Place"; and *Irish Times*, Nov. 14, 1913.

[48] Fox, *History of the Irish Citizen Army*, 42.

lice. White was taken to Store Street Police Station, and Markievicz, "feeling herself then the 'only friend he had,'" accompanied him.[49]

White was released on bail and tried the following day. The charges against him were assaulting the mail van driver, assaulting a DMP inspector, resisting arrest, "calling on the crowd to rescue him from the custody of the police," and striking a DMP sergeant as he was taken into the station. Markievicz, her friend the actress Elizabeth Young, and "two other ladies" stood as White's defense, with Francis Sheehy Skeffington serving as his counsel. Markievicz's testimony was vivid: a team of horses had broken into the workers' procession, and "she saw then what looked like a football scrimmage. . . . A man fell at her feet, and a policeman hit him when he was down." He was "more or less a football in the hands of the police, going from one to the other." When White addressed the court, he told "the people that it was their duty not to starve without some form of energetic and drastic protest."[50] Professing to be an "Irish Nationalist," he nonetheless "believed that while the workers in Dublin were strong and down-trodden, and bullied by a Cossack police force, it was a waste of breath to talk about a free Ireland." In the end, White's charges against the police provided enough leverage for the prosecution to agree to enter a *nolle prosequi* and to apologize for the treatment that White "undoubtedly did receive."[51]

After the confrontation with police on March 13, the Citizen Army was reconstituted under a more formal structure. An Army Council was established with White as its chair and six vice-chairs, including Constance Markievicz, who also served as co-treasurer.[52] Her prominence in the leadership of the ICA reflects her central role in the army's reorganization. She and Connolly drew up the new constitution, which adopted two important strains of discourse: Wolfe Tone's eighteenth-century republicanism and the nineteenth-century revolutionary James Fintan Lalor's doctrine of national ownership. Lalor's essay "The Rights of Ireland," published in the *Irish Felon*, declared:

> The entire ownership of Ireland, moral and material, up to the sun and down to the centre, is vested of right in the people of Ireland; that they, and none but they are the land-owners and law-markers of this

[49] "UnEmployed and the Police: Fracas on Eden Quay," *Weekly Irish Times*, Mar. 21, 1914, 5.

[50] "Captain White and the Police," *Irish Times*, April 4, 1914, 12.

[51] "Charge against Captain White Extraordinary Result," ibid., April 9, 1914, 6.

[52] Other members of the Army Council were Jim Larkin, P. T. Daly, William Partridge, Thomas Foran, and Francis Sheehy Skeffington; Sean O'Casey was elected secretary, and Markievicz shared the post of treasurer with Richard Brannigan.

island . . . that the entire soil of a country belongs of right to the entire people of that country, and is the rightful property, not of any one class, but of the nation at large.[53]

Lalor's claim is repeated, verbatim, in the ICA's new constitution: "the first and last principle of the Citizen Army is the avowal that the ownership of Ireland moral and material is vested of right in the people of Ireland." The presence of Wolfe Tone in the ICA's constitution is equally strong; one of the militia's aims was "to sink all differences of birth, property, and creed under the common noun of the Irish People."[54] Both of these ambitions would be echoed in the Proclamation of the Republic issued just three years later. The ICA constitution made it clear that the workers were not engaged solely in an Irish struggle. Just as the Citizen Army stood for "the absolute Unity of Irish Nationhood," it also supported "the rights and liberties of the democracies of all nations."

The ICA was a small, leftist faction of the many local volunteering organizations that were provoked by the formation of the Ulster Volunteers, who were opposed to Home Rule. These local nationalist militias were dedicated to fighting for Home Rule and were eventually organized as the Irish Volunteers under the umbrella of the Irish Parliamentary Party.[55] This vampirism vexed Sinn Féin, which was committed to parliamentary abstention; antiparliamentary militants instead drilled as part of the secret society of the Irish Republican Brotherhood, members of which were nonetheless represented on the councils of the Irish Volunteers.[56] In the same way that the IRB used the larger, officially endorsed Irish Volunteers as a means of accomplishing its aims, the leadership of the Citizen Army sought to establish links with the Volunteers.

This was a controversial maneuver. For one, hostility between the Volunteers and the Citizen Army was palpable. The Volunteers refused to grant the ICA permission to use its halls when indoor drilling was preferable to outdoor drilling in Croydon Park, so the ICA was restricted to using the auditorium in Liberty Hall and the small hall in Camden Street where the Fianna held its meetings.[57] Furthermore, there was open concern that the ICA's affiliation with the Volunteers would subvert the aims of the Citizen Army. Sean O'Casey, who would later write a bitter anti-Connolly his-

---

[53] Lalor, *The Writings of James Fintan Lalor*, 67–68.
[54] "Citizen Army," *Irish Worker*, Mar. 28, 1914, 2.
[55] McConnel, *The Irish Parliamentary Party and the Third Home Rule Crisis*, 284–95.
[56] Foster, *Modern Ireland 1600–1972*, 468.
[57] Fox, *Citizen Army*, 68.

tory of the ICA, wrote prolific anti-Volunteer articles for the *Irish Worker* in May 1914. In one front-page essay, he named principal organizers of the movement, including the O'Rahilly and John (Eoin) MacNeill: "What have these ever done for the working classes? What could they do, seeing they know nothing of poverty, wage-slavery, and the awful day-by-day struggle to maintain the vitality to perform additional prodigies of production for the rich and idle."[58]

O'Casey also included in his condemnation the women of the newly formed Cumann na mBan (Irishwomen's Council), which defined its role as to assist in arming and equipping the Volunteers.[59] (O'Casey pleaded sarcastically, "May we ask does Madame O'Rahilly ever look at the ghosts flitting about the slums or feel the pulse of the remnants of humanity flung by Capitalism in a decayed heap in the different Sanatoria of Ireland?") Markievicz had attended the inaugural public meeting of Cumann na mBan, at which she encouraged the women to avoid party politics to ensure the widest base of support.[60] The aims of the new organization, as declared in Agnes O'Farrelly's opening address, were "to give our allegiance and support to the men who are fighting the cause of Ireland," which cast women in a subordinate role. Crucially, O'Farrelly allowed for an actively militant role in future: "It is not ours to undertake physically and directly the defence of the nation except in a last extremity and in the direct stress of war."[61] The potential for women to actually fight was essential for Markievicz's support of the organization; she was willing to put her concerns about women's auxiliary role aside, albeit briefly, since she believed that the women's organization was important to uniting Irish separatists.

At the end of May 1914, Cumann na mBan incorporated the Daughters of Ireland, mirroring the collaboration of the Volunteers, the IRB, and the Citizen Army. In the wake of the Volunteer split, Cumann na mBan became more radical; most of its members concentrated on nursing care and first-aid,

[58] Sean O. Cathasaigh, "Right about Turn: Wage Slaves in the Volunteers," *Irish Worker*, May 9, 1914, 1.

[59] Cumann an mBan held its first public meeting at 4:00 PM on April 2, 1914, in Wynn's Hotel on Lower Abbey Street. Both the location and the timing of the meeting are evidence of the council's middle-class constituency. Cumann an mBan's vision of itself as a supportive organization secondary to the men of the Irish Volunteers provoked objection from suffragists, including Hanna Sheehy Skeffington.

[60] *Freeman's Journal*, April 3, 1914, in McCarthy, *Cumann na mBan and the Irish Revolution*, 19–20.

[61] Inaugural address by Agnes O'Farrelly, *Irish Volunteer*, April 18, 1914, quoted in Oikarinen, *A Dream of Liberty*, 85.

but its most extreme elements began weapons training.[62] O'Casey demanded that Markievicz resign from either Cumann na mBan or the ICA; he insisted that she could not be a member of both, since the organizations had, in his view, conflicting aims. Markievicz refused, and the ICA passed a vote of confidence in her favor, pushing O'Casey to the margins.[63]

Rising international tensions, which would lead to Britain's declaration of war on Germany on August 4, 1914, facilitated Irish radicals' importation of arms from the Continent. The gunrunning to the seaside village of Howth, north of Dublin, in July 1914 was an intimation of what could be accomplished by collaboration between the Irish Volunteers, the IRB., and the Citizen Army. The Ulster Volunteers had provided a model for importing weapons; in late April 1914 they landed twenty-five thousand rifles and three million rounds of ammunition, which had been purchased in Germany. A few weeks afterward, the English-born Irish Home Ruler Erskine Childers (author of the premonitory *Riddle of the Sands*) and the Shakespeare scholar and Irish Volunteer Darrell Figgis traveled to Germany, where they purchased fifteen hundred Mauser rifles for the Irish Volunteers.[64] Unlike their anti–Home Rule antagonists who operated under cover of darkness, the Irish Volunteers planned to ferry the arms over on the *Kelpie*, a boat owned by Conor O'Brien, and Childers's yacht, the *Asgard*, and land them in broad daylight. In the end, publicity was their greatest achievement, since a scant twenty-five thousand rounds of ammunition were brought ashore, and the guns themselves proved obsolete.[65]

The gunrunning at Howth coincided with the Fianna convention in Dublin, with delegates from across the country attending, including Connolly's daughters Ina and Nora, who traveled down from Belfast. The "jolly little fellows," as Constance described them to Hanna Sheehy Skeffington, were armed with wooden batons—possibly borrowed from the ICA's arsenal—

---

[62] McCarthy, *Cumann na mBan*, 47.

[63] Fox, *Citizen Army*, 73.

[64] Darrell Figgis (1882–1925) began his career entrenched in the culture of the British Empire: he was a tea-buyer at London and Calcutta. He then turned to literature and divided his time between London and Achill Island, off the west coast of Ireland. He joined the Irish Volunteers on its London committee. After the 1916 Rising, he was arrested and imprisoned in England, which initiated a series of releases and rearrests. He served as honorary secretary of Sinn Féin and edited the newspaper *The Republic*. In addition to Irish Revivalist poetry, political essays, and histories, he published studies of Shakespeare (1911) and William Blake (1925) and a posthumous edition of Milton's *Comus* (1926). A supporter of the treaty with Britain, Figgis helped to draft the constitution for the Irish Free State that followed. He was murdered in a Bloomsbury boarding house in October 1925 during what historian F. X. Martin has described as "an unsavoury law-case in London." See Martin, ed., *Howth Gun-Running*, 28.

[65] Foster, *Modern Ireland*, 469; and Foster, *Vivid Faces*, 204–6.

and sent to guard the entrance to the pier at Howth, while rifles were packed into motorcars and the Fianna's trek-cart.[66] The King's Own Scottish Borderers and police sent from Dublin Castle attempted to blockade the road, but the Irish Volunteers ignored the order to halt. Blank rounds were fired at the Volunteers, and the police charged to seize their arms. The rear guard of the Volunteers held their position to face the military, while the frontline dispersed into small parties, which made their way back to the city.

The subsequent tragedy was unanticipated, but in light of Bloody Sunday it is hardly surprising. As the humiliated British military marched back into Dublin, they were heckled by crowds. One observer, recently discharged from the Inniskilling Fusiliers, reported that youngsters threw stones at the soldiers, and it was then that he

> heard the officer, a young man, give the order to load. . . . I tried to get a couple of women and a girl out the way. I got the little girl clear, and the women lay down on the pavement. I saw the soldiers load their rifles with ball cartridge. They seemed to be very excited. They were within ten yards of me, and I saw one man fire. He re-loaded, and as he put in his second cartridge he pointed his rifle downwards without taking aim. He pulled the trigger, and I was shot in the leg.[67]

Three civilians were killed: Mary Duffy and Patrick Quinn, both fifty years old, and James Brennan, just nineteen. Thirty-eight others were injured.

The government's response to what became known as the Bachelor's Walk Massacre was stern and expedient; the chief of the Dublin Metropolitan Police was immediately forced to resign. Nonetheless, the spontaneous shooting was interpreted widely as a manifestation of a sinister policy toward Irish nationalists. The *Irish Independent* quoted the *Daily Chronicle's* summation: "For the Nationalist there is the bullet and the baton; for the Orangeman there is the freedom to do as he pleases amid the enthusiastic plaudits of the Tory Party in Ireland and in Great Britain."[68]

The morning after the shooting, Fianna captain Joe Robinson delivered a cache of rifles to Constance Markievicz's cottage in the Dublin Mountains. In her memoir, Nora Connolly recalls receiving a warning from a sympathetic neighbor, who saw the delivery arrive and knew it would arouse the

[66] C de M to Mrs Skeffington (n.d.), NLI, MS 22670; and Pádraig Ó Riain, "Sealed Orders: The Part the Fianna Played at Howth," in Martin, *Howth Gun-Running*, 157.

[67] "Bachelor's Walk Scene," *Irish Independent*, July 29, 1914, 5. Another report stated, "There was no provocation beyond the usual hostile display of a crowd who had no desire to try conclusions with fixed bayonets"; see "Deadly Onslaught," ibid., July 27, 1914, 5.

[68] Quoted in "Bachelor's Walk Scene."

suspicions of a police sergeant who lived nearby. "Nono," Nora Connolly's autobiographical persona, recounts that she went to Dublin to seek advice from Liam Mellows, who suggested that the rifles be returned to Dublin in a taxi.[69] She gleefully remembers spending the day "sitting on rifles" to camouflage the guns as they were dispersed across the city. Those days were more tragic than her childish delight allows. Lyons remarks in his account of Bachelor's Walk, "Had it not been that Europe was then moving almost hour by hour closer to war, this terrible end to the episode might well have led to an explosion in Dublin."[70]

Instead of insurrection, there was commemoration. The Markievicz house in Leinster Road became the center for planning the public funeral for the victims of the atrocity. It was a major event, with a procession on a scale that rivaled the numbers who turned out for royal visits. Constance directed the Fianna in making wreaths with flowers donated from local florists, and a requiem mass was planned for the Pro-Cathedral on July 29.[71] The Irish Volunteers took credit for organizing the event—publicizing in the newspapers their plans to parade at 5 o'clock in the afternoon from the Custom House—but their schedule was usurped by the widespread support for the victims. "Tens of thousands" gathered outside the cathedral to observe the removal of the remains and to join the long procession to Glasnevin Cemetery. By 5 PM the crowd made the streets almost impassable.[72] The *Freeman's Journal* remarked, "The composition of the cortege was even more striking than its dimensions": the Volunteers "muster[ed] in their thousands" alongside "trades and labour bodies of the city. . . . Professional and commercial men, civic dignitaries, clergymen, tradesmen and labourers, rich and poor, and persons of different religious persuasions. . . . A common sorrow broke down all barriers of class and creed."[73]

As news of Bachelor's Walk spread around the country, the ranks of the Irish Volunteers swelled. A cohesive separatist movement may have seemed at hand, but any unity was brief and was shattered by compromises within the Volunteers. While the Howth gunrunning was being planned, the Irish Parliamentary Party had maneuvered itself to have greater control over the Irish Volunteers and had gone so far as to demand larger representation on the central committee. This was largely due to Home Rule politicians' sense

---

[69] Fox, *Citizen Army*, 78–79; and O'Brien, *James Connolly*, 183–84.
[70] Lyons, *Ireland since the Famine*, 327.
[71] O'Brien, *James Connolly*, 186.
[72] "Public Funeral Today," *Irish Independent*, July 29, 1914, 5.
[73] "Impressive Cortege," *Freeman's Journal*, July 30, 1914, 7.

that they needed the power of a militia behind them to match the Ulster Volunteers, who provided Unionists with the threat of armed struggle. Bulmer Hobson supported the Irish Volunteers' concession to the Irish Parliamentary Party's demands. To Markievicz, this was a great betrayal by a man she had considered her friend and comrade. Their relationship would never recover, and it would set Hobson apart from the majority of radical nationalists.

The Citizen Army immediately distanced itself from the leadership and strategy of the Irish Volunteers. On August 1 "Citizen Army Notes" in the *Irish Worker* upbraided the Volunteers in Markievicz's characteristic tone:

> Surely it was a gross error of judgement to send of all the ammunition without at least serving out a few rounds to picked men. The spectacle of men marching home with rifles and no ammunition was deplorable, and if the officers had confidence in the men it should not have happened. We pity the rank and file.... But we are unable to excuse men in uniform coming home on "Murder Murphy's" scab trams after discarding their rifles. These same trams were used only a few hours previous to bring out to Howth the military and police sent by Dublin Castle to disarm the men.
>
> Surely we Irish workers have short memories. Only a few months ago several of our comrades were brutally murdered by Murphy's police, and we now cheer the hooligans because two of them refused to obey orders, whether from funk or otherwise.
>
> Bravo Boy Scouts, you at least gave a good account of ourselves, it was grand to see several wounded boys being assisted home by their comrades, and not on Murphy's trams, or the ambulance which was offered and refused because it was contaminated by one of the military.... Europe is in a flame and England is likely to be embroiled at any moment. Ireland is armed from north to south, and if our manly but mistaken brothers in the north would only join with us there would be an end of foreign rule in our dear land.
>
> May that time come soon and sudden.[74]

Markievicz conceded that there were "great possibilities" in the Irish Volunteer movement, but she argued that the Citizen Army was "the only armed force in Ireland to-day standing for the rights of the worker and the complete independence of our country." She advised readers that if rifles were not available, "revolvers are cheap, handy and effective and very suitable in

[74] "Citizen Army Notes," *Irish Worker*, Aug. 1, 1914, 2.

sudden emergencies"; whatever the means, "get arms, anyhow or anywhere, BUT GET THEM."[75]

The rumblings of a European war made the gulf dividing separatist nationalists who abstained from parliamentary politics and those who adhered to parliamentarianism deeper and more perceptible. The Irish Volunteers had provided a firm anchor for the minority IRB and Citizen Army, but this security was persistently destabilized by divisions within the majority group. The Irish Volunteers were ultimately split by the Irish Parliamentary Party leader John Redmond's speech at Woodenbridge, County Wicklow, on September 20 when he pledged the Irish Volunteers to support Britain's war and to fight "wherever the firing-line extends." Within days, Redmond's supporters took the name of "National Volunteers," marking them out from the minority who remained under the name of the Irish Volunteers and who returned to the IRB's militant separatist principles that had preceded the parliamentarian takeover.[76]

Markievicz immediately aligned the Fianna with the Irish Volunteers. In an address to the annual Fianna congress in October, she proclaimed that "theirs was the first military organisation which had for its ideal the complete independence of Ireland" and that "they would never put Home Rule or any other measure of an English Parliament as the ideal of Irish Nationality." Borrowing directly from Wolfe Tone, she argued that the British Empire was "the never-failing source of all our political evils." In the *Fianna Handbook*, she set out a creative history of anti-imperialism.[77] Practical lessons in first aid, signaling, and drilling were prefaced by an introduction that invoked the mythical Cathleen ni Houlihan's demand "to give her all, to give themselves."[78] Markievicz presented the Fianna with a pantheon of anti-imperialist role models, including Joan of Arc, the Manchester Martyrs (three IRB men hanged in 1867 for killing a policeman), and the misspelled "Madar Lal Dingra" (Madan Lal Dhingra), who in 1909 assassinated Sir Curzon Wyllie for the cause of Indian independence. Wyllie was a civil servant, working as aide-de-camp to the secretary of state for India, but both Dhingra and Markievicz believed that those in the service of the empire were culpable, regardless of their rank.

---

[75] Ibid.

[76] Figures estimate the National Volunteers at 150,000, while the Irish Volunteers stood at anywhere between 3,000 and 10,000 men. The majority held by the National Volunteers was soon overturned, as militant abstentionist separatism thrived. See Foster, *Modern Ireland*, 472–73.

[77] "National Boy Scouts Convention," *Irish Volunteer*, Oct. 10, 1914, 16.

[78] *Fianna Handbook* (Dublin, n.d. [1914]), 6.

Under the protection of an armed guard of the Irish Volunteers, a mass meeting was held on November 16 in front of the memorial arch at St. Stephen's Green that commemorated Irish soldiers killed in the Boer War. The symbolism was clear: Irish nationalists should never again fight for the British Empire. The platform was shared by the leadership of the Irish Volunteers and the Citizen Army. Irish Volunteer and future Sinn Féin teachta Dála (minister to the Dáil, the Irish parliament) Sean Milroy declared, "They must all join either the Volunteers or the Citizen Army to be prepared for the day of reckoning, which was much nearer than many of them imagined." Constance Markievicz was one of the final speakers. Importantly, on this occasion, she did not identify herself with the Citizen Army but with Cumann na mBan; she "announced that the members of her society, the women of Ireland, were learning how to shoot, so that they might help to resist conscription."[79] Markievicz's affiliation with the ICA had not slackened, but she believed that it was essential that Cumann na mBan be openly aligned with the Irish Volunteers in the wake of the Volunteer split.[80]

A rousing speech from Connolly concluded the rally. In a rebuttal of Redmond, he pledged the Irish soldiers fighting at the front to the protection of the Irish people:

> If the police or the military were let loose on the citizens of Dublin . . . before the week was over it would be known to every soldier serving at the front—(applause)—and when it was known that they were being slaughtered in Dublin, the next time that the Dublin Fusiliers were sent to cover the retreat of the British, the Dublin Fusiliers would forget to follow the British. (Applause)[81]

In fact, the Royal Dublin Fusiliers would turn their weapons against Connolly and the Volunteers just two years later, but this would have seemed like an impossible scenario from the vantage point of the militant separatists who were gathered at the gates of the green. The Citizen Army, Cumann na mBan, and the Irish Volunteers proclaimed they were acting on behalf of the

---

[79] "Dismissal of Government Employe[e]: Violent Speeches in Dublin," *Irish Times*, Nov. 16, 1914, 9.

[80] Privately, Cumann na mBan also split over the First World War; the antiwar faction ceased to use the dual-language name Cumann na mBan/Council of Women and operated only under the Irish-language name. Its members drafted a new manifesto, which was published in the October 17 edition of the *Irish Worker*, denouncing John Redmond and stating its object to "advance the cause of Irish liberty." See "Manifesto from Cumann na mBan," *Irish Worker*, Oct. 17, 1914, 3.

[81] "Dismissal of Government Employe[e]: Violent Speeches in Dublin," *Irish Times*, Nov. 16, 1914, 9.

Irish people: "On the motion of Mr. Connolly, the crowd pledged themselves as fighters for Ireland, and never to rest until they were privileged to see Ireland a free and independent republic among the nations." "A Nation Once Again" was sung in benediction, and the Volunteers fired shots into the air. All the while, the police stood guard, silently watching.[82]

The British Empire struggled to feed its war machine. Low recruitment figures for Ireland and the prominence of antirecruiting propaganda in leftist and nationalist newspapers led to questions in Parliament about Ireland. The chief secretary for Ireland, Augustine Birrell, responded with warnings to the most radical newspapers, including *Sinn Féin*, the *Irish Worker*, and the *Irish Volunteer*. Birrell threatened that if they were found to publish material "likely to cause disaffection," their presses would be seized and destroyed by the police acting with the authority of the Defence of the Realm Act and under the direct control of the military.[83] In reply to the government's caution, the Irish Volunteers and the Citizen Army held another joint protest.

Despite heavy rainfall, on December 6 crowds began gathering around noon at Beresford Place, outside Liberty Hall. At 1 PM, members of the Citizen Army entered the hall carrying rifles and took up posts on the roof. By 2.30 PM, approximately five hundred people were present, many of whom were dressed in the uniform of the Irish Volunteers. Antirecruiting leaflets were distributed throughout the crowd. Standing on a chair that served as an improvised platform for the speakers, Connolly declared that Dublin was under "martial law" and would be subject to "military bullies who would be absolutely ignorant of the law and of evidence." Markievicz, standing beside Milroy, declared "any Irishman who joined the British Army" would be regarded as "a traitor to his country." She pledged herself ready, "though only a woman . . . to fight with the men with her back to the last wall fighting for Ireland."[84]

---

[82] Ibid.
[83] "Seditious Papers in Ireland: Action by Military Authorities," *Irish Times*, Dec. 4, 1914, 4.
[84] "Seditious Papers in Dublin: Protest against Their Suppression," ibid., Dec. 7, 1914, 6.

10

===

The Markieviczes at War

CASIMIR MARKIEVICZ WAS IN WARSAW AT THE OUTBREAK of the First World War, working at the Polish Theatre. The threat of a German invasion of Warsaw prompted Arnold Szyfman, the founder and director of the theatre who was from the Austrian part of partitioned Poland, to take the actors on tour to Kiev, which seemed more secure, and Casimir returned to Zywotowka. At the conclusion of Szyfman's tour, Casimir invited him to stay at the Markievicz estate, rather than return to Warsaw. Szyfman later recalled being met at the station in Koziatywa by an "impeccably dressed" Casimir who drove "a gleaming horsetrap." It was, according to Szyfman's account, a halcyon time. Mornings began with bird-hunting excursions, which were followed by opulent breakfasts of meats, fish, and cheeses, and copious amounts of vodka. Undisturbed by news of the war, Casimir spent his afternoons painting in the grounds of the estate.[1]

All of that changed when the czar, Grand Duke Nicholas II, promised Poland freedom in return for Polish allegiance to the Russian Empire:

> A century and a half ago, the living body of Poland was torn in pieces; but her soul did not die. It was kept alive by a hope for the resurrection of the Polish nation and for its fraternal union with Great Russia.
>
> The Russian Army brings you the blessed news of that union. May the frontiers that cut across the Polish nation be erased.

---

[1] Quigley, *Polish Irishman*, 156.

> May the Polish nation be joined in one under the sceptre of the Russian Emperor. Under that sceptre Poland will be reborn, free in her own faith, language, and self-rule.[2]

The landed class in eastern Galicia—the Polish-settled Ukraine—believed that the protection of Russia ensured their future in the region. Casimir's decision to enlist in the Russian Army was therefore typical of his social class. He later told the newspaper *Russkoye Slovo*, "After the proclamation to the Polish made by the Supreme Commander-in-Chief I considered it necessary to join the Russian army."[3] Neither in 1914 nor in the revolutionary period to follow would Markievicz's national politics extend to anti-imperialism. His analogy of Bloody Sunday, 1905, and September 1, 1913, was based on an accurate understanding of the St. Petersburg protest: it was not a socialist event. Although Casimir expressed sympathy with the Dublin working class, the political elements of his aesthetic were nationalist and suffragist, not anti-imperialist. Therefore his imperial service was not a departure from his Irish politics but an extension of them.

At the age of fifty-two, he was suited to a place in the ratnik—an irregular army, similar to a home guard—which comprised men ineligible for the regular army or who had special benefits due to their family's status. Casimir volunteered for the lowest rank in the 12 Achtyrski Regiment of Hussars, and in late September 1914 the *Irish Times* reported that he was serving in Austria.[4] In fact, he was in Austrian Poland (Galicia), a subtlety for which the *Irish Times* would have little sympathy. Under the leadership of General Aleksei Brusilov, Markievicz fought in the Russian Army's arduous campaign in the Carpathians, which lasted through the winter of 1914–15. Brusilov later praised the stamina of his men, who "had spent the winter in the mountains up to their necks in snow and at the mercy of cruel frosts," repelling bayonet charges by day and conducting counterattacks at night to conserve their poor supply of munitions, hampered further by inadequate railway links.[5]

The details of Casimir's war are unclear. He may have been fighting when Nicholas II visited the southwestern region of the Eastern Front in April, or

---

[2] Quoted in Davies, *God's Playground*, 2:382–83. Davies notes that despite the manifesto being distributed in Polish, the posters on which it was printed showed the Polish flag in an upside-down position, which significantly impeded the manifesto's effectiveness.

[3] "Ireland: Constance Markievicz," *Russkoye Slovo*, April 16 [May 9], 1916, 2. My thanks to Alexandra Kasatkina for her translation of all articles from *Russkoye Slovo*.

[4] "Count Markievicz," *Irish Times*, Sept. 29, 1914, 6; and "Count Markievicz," *Weekly Irish Times*, Oct. 3, 1914, 5.

[5] Brusilov, *A Soldier's Note-book*, 122–23.

he may have already sustained injuries from the exploding shell that left him partially deaf, with a wound to his side and left arm. Given the conditions under which the men fought, O'Faolain's account of Casimir lying for nearly twelve hours in the snow is not improbable.[6] Eventually recognized by a fellow soldier, he was carried to the nearest railway line, where he waited for hours for a passing train. He was finally transported in a cattle wagon, full of soldiers afflicted by cholera, for the 150-mile journey to the field hospital in Lwów, where he was diagnosed with typhus. A letter to Constance, quoted in O'Faolain's biography, conveys his good-humored misery:

My Darling,

I am not a bit sure that this will get to Dublin at all, as it seems that the Germans are playing lots of dirty tricks in the Irish Sea. However I am glad to tell you that I am much better and in a week's time I am going to be sent to [illegible] for a couple of months.

I am still very weak, especially my legs can hardly support my weight. My rib is almost covered up with new skin and I feel much less shaky although I am still very def [sic] and one has to yell at me. Gradually I am recovering the use of my left arm. Now fare you well my darling. Burn this as it is supposed to be covered with typhus bacillus and wash your hands. Best love to all yours.

Dunin Markievicz[7]

Decorated with the St. George Cross for bravery, Casimir returned to Zywotowka, where he wrote to Dublin asking Constance to send Stanislaus to join him.[8] He later told *Russkoye Slovo* that he wanted Stanislaus to fulfill his "compulsory military service."[9]

The Dublin Lockout had left Constance so deeply in debt that she had to ask her brother Josslyn for the fare for Stanislaus's return. She promised that she would be able to pay him back since she could live more frugally with Stanislaus gone: "while he was here it was nothing but money, money, money."[10] Constance's further reassurance, "Casi will send money when Stas

[6] Quigley, *Polish Irishman*, 162.

[7] O'Faolain, *Constance Markievicz*, 264.

[8] Quigley, *Polish Irishman*, 160.

[9] Casimir gives these reasons in "Ireland: Constance Markievicz." His letter to Constance is the subject of a letter from Constance Markievicz to Josslyn Gore-Booth (n.d. [received June 13, 1915]), PRONI, D4131/K/3.

[10] Constance Markievicz to Josslyn Gore-Booth (n.d. [received June 13, 1915]), ibid.

arrives," did nothing to assuage Josslyn's doubts—and with good reason. Casimir had borrowed £100 against the lease of St, Mary's and had repaid the money but never returned the lease document to Josslyn. Constance vowed that she would repay the bills that she had let slip during the Lockout—£151 was owed to the grocer, the dentist, the chemist (including the cost of Stanislaus's spectacles), and the vet for her dog, Poppet. She admitted, "For the moment, I'm in an awful hole." Stanislaus had needed "clothes & odds & ends of things, & Russian lessons," but now she would be able to return to living week by week, as she had lived before the Lockout: "it's the only way to keep out of debt for unbusiness like people with small incomes."

Stanislaus later wrote that Easter 1915 was the last time "we were all together."[11] In this "all," he did not include his father but referred instead to Constance and his half-sister Maeve, who would soon be sent back to Lissadell to live with her grandmother and a governess, where she would be conscripted by Georgina Gore-Booth into the Children's Effort in Support of War Work. The entire Gore-Booth family, except for Constance and Eva, was committed in some degree to supporting the imperial war. Josslyn gave his full support to the British recruiting effort. In a speech in 1914 at a public meeting in the village of Ballymote, twenty miles to the south of Lissadell House in County Sligo, he used what influence he still possessed:

> I urge you to join up that we may be free—fighting that we may be spared the horrors which have overtaken Belgium, Northern France, Poland and Serbia. And what of Ballymote?
>
> I had the honour of owning this town once, and now, by means of British credit, the ownership of this place is being gradually vested in the occupiers. You have done with landlords. I was very sorry to lose you as tenants, but I expect you are glad to get rid of me as landlord. You have won the land, you are winning the houses in the villages, you have won the trust of British Democracy. You know that in the future when the military pact in Germany is broken you come into your own.
>
> I too know something of the German idea of liberty, and I can assure you that, bad and all as the landlord was, Clanrickard himself was not a patch on what the Germans would be. No doubt I will be told that Ballymote has done well, and perhaps it has, but it is a fact that there are still 7,225 recruitable men now left in Sligo. It is our duty to try to get them to realise that Germany will not admit she is beaten until the last ounce has been thrown into the scale.[12]

---

[11] TS, Stanislaus Markievicz, Life of Constance Markeivicz (part 2), NLI, MS 44,619.
[12] "Lissadell during World War One," Lissadell Collection.

At Lissadell he turned the estate's machine workshop over to the British War Office and manufactured munitions. By 1916 he was sending shell bases to the Woolwich Arsenal in England; by 1917 the Lissadell factory was delivering orders for seven thousand plates weekly.

Stanislaus's journey to Russia was difficult: first by boat across the North Sea to Norway, then overland across the Scandinavian Peninsula, and finally across the Baltic to St. Petersburg, where he arrived in June 1915. He was immediately conscripted in the Russian Navy but was permitted a brief visit to Zywotowka, where he traveled by military and Red Cross trains. He arrived to find that the first years of the war had in fact been very good for the Markievicz family estate. Profits from the sale of horses facilitated some petit-empire building; the house had been extensively remodeled to include "a grand porch flanked by pillars."[13] None of the wealth had been appointed to Casimir's debts in Ireland, which were creating increasing financial discomfort for Constance and prompted a rare tetchy remark in a letter to Eva: "Someone said, 'the more I know men, the more I love my dog,' and I think I rather agree. Dogs don't lie."[14]

By October Stanislaus was back in the renamed Petrograd for training. He found speaking Russian difficult since it had become mixed with his Polish, but his fluency in English meant that he was put to work as an interpreter and correspondent. He was posted with the Russian Volunteer Fleet in Archangel on the bleak coast of the White Sea, a crucial port where good translators were essential for the cooperation of Russian and British fleets.[15] This also made it a strategic target for the Germans. December in the Arctic was brutal compared to relatively temperate Ireland. Winter set in rapidly, freezing Russian ships into place before they sank under pressure from the ice. Stanislaus was immediately homesick for Ireland, but the home that he remembered had been turned upside down.

For Irish separatists, England's difficulty was Ireland's opportunity. Constance churned out propaganda, carefully crafting her writing for her respective audiences. For the Citizen Army, whose de facto newspaper was the *Workers' Republic*, she wrote anti-imperialist doggerel to reinforce the ICA's collaboration with the Irish Volunteers: "When the enemy scattered and down and out / Bows low to our crowned Queen, / When our blood-stained swords have set Ireland free / And hoisted the flag of green."[16] The

---

[13] Quigley, *Polish Irishman*, 164.

[14] Roper, ed., *The Prison Letters of Countess Markievicz*, 169.

[15] ALS "Staskow'" to Josslyn Gore-Booth (August 17–30, 1916), PRONI, D/4131/K/13 (1); and Greger, *The Russian Fleet*, 40–41.

[16] "Maca," "To the Citizen Army," *Workers' Republic*, June 26, 1915, 1.

imagery is stereotypical but important nonetheless. The flag is not the blue Starry Plough, the symbol of the ITGWU, or—for that matter—the red flag of communism; Markievicz envisions the victorious symbol as the green flag of the Volunteers. This is an anticipation of the actual replacement of the Starry Plough by the green flag in the week prior to the 1916 Rising. Equally, though less noticeably, important is Markievicz's publication of the poem under the pseudonym "Maca." Not only is this an identifiably female name, it is the same pseudonym under which she previously published prosuffrage essays in *Bean na hÉireann.* The female authorship encodes the sexual equality espoused by the Citizen Army, expressed more directly in the poem's lines, "When comrade by comrade we / stand on the day." (Importantly, the Volunteers did *not* share the ICA's gender politics.)

James Connolly and Constance Markievicz both believed that Irish suffragists possessed the militant tactics that were necessary for revolution. Constance worked extensively to convince the suffragists of the necessity of Irish separatism. She took a prominent role in several Irish Women's Franchise League events, including the Daffodil Fete, a festival of tableaux, short plays, and recitations that propagandized suffrage. Several of Constance's friends from the theater, Máire nic Shuibhlaigh, Marie Perolz, and Elizabeth Young, also took part.[17] (Nic Shuibhlaigh and Perolz would be two of Constance's most trusted friends during the revolution.) One of the most successful performances of the fete was a series of tableaux depicting the life of Joan of Arc, who was an icon for militant suffragists in Britain.[18] Markievicz played "Joan in Full Armour" in three scenes, including Joan in her prison cell and Joan "leading on a group of Irishwomen who had been to prison for the cause, [all] the while they . . . sang the Women's Marseillaise," the lyrics of which were written for Emmeline and Christabel Pankhurst's Women's Social and Political Union of Great Britain.[19] In her study of Markievicz, Oikarinen argues that "Markievicz in a way replaced the essentially Irish figure of Cathleen ni Houlihan with the international figure of Joan of Arc"

[17] Nic Shuibhlaigh and Perolz costarred in a one-act play, *The Prodigal Daughter,* which may have been Henry Pettit and Augustus Harris's *An Up-to-Date Sporting Drama Entitled The Prodigal Daughter* (1892). In April 1916, when Special Branch forbade Markievicz to travel to Tralee, where she was to deliver a lecture on the "Fenian Rising of 1867," Marie Perolz, who was similar in stature and bearing to Markievicz, traveled instead; her impersonation fooled the police, who followed her on the train and to her hotel; Markievicz took delight in recounting the episode.

[18] Oikarinen notes the importance of Joan to Emmeline Pankhurst, Emile Gavison, and Elsie Howey; Joan was also co-opted by feminists and nationalists in Finland; see Oikarinen, *A Dream of Liberty,* 57; for other uses to which the persona of Joan has been put, see Warner, *Joan of Arc.*

[19] "Suffragist Fete in Dublin," *Irish Citizen,* May 2, 1914, 396. The lyrics to the "Women's Marseillaise" were printed in the WSPU's newspaper, *Votes for Women,* Jan. 28, 1909, 294.

and in doing so "broadened and reshaped the image of Ireland itself."[20] In fact, Cathleen ni Houlihan remained part of Markievicz's discourse, but her use of Joan in her essays for the *Irish Citizen* and work for the IWFL was undoubtedly calculated to attract women from a wide spectrum of society to militant separatism. Yet the relationship that Markievicz cultivated with the IWFL was not purely utilitarian; she firmly believed that an independent Ireland would guarantee the equality of the sexes.

In a speech to the league on "The Future of Irishwomen," reprinted in the *Irish Citizen* at the end of October 1915, Markievicz used vignettes from Irish history to illustrate a historical precedent for women taking an active role in the national movement; she drew from the mythology of the "warrior queens" of ancient Ireland, from a new folklore about the role of Irish women in 1798, and the short-lived but nonetheless important activities of the Ladies' Land League. She argued that women's auxiliary committees—such as Cumann na mBan—"demoralise women, set them up in separate camps, and deprive them of all initiative and independence. Women are left to rely on sex charm, or intrigue and backstairs influence." She urged women to reject impractical fashions, absurd fantasies, and to be willing to arm themselves:

> Dress suitably in short skirt and strong boots, leave your jewels and gold wands in the bank, and buy a revolver. Don't trust to your "feminine charm" and your capacity for getting on the soft side of men, but take up your responsibilities and be prepared to go your own way depending for safety on your own courage, your own truth, and your own common sense, and not on the problematic chivalry of the men you may meet on the way.[21]

Here, too, Markievicz is borrowing from the wider discourse of suffrage but also from her private relationships. Eva Gore-Booth's poem "Comrades," published in the *Egyptian Pillar* (1907), cautions women not to trust men, no matter how sympathetic they seem, with their quest for justice. By 1907 Gore-Booth's suffrage poetry was less agitational and more esoteric; "Comrades" concludes, "only the gods in heaven are true enough to be just."[22]

Markievicz sought justice in this world, not the next, but she nonetheless shared some of Eva's esoteric ideas about gender. In "The Future of Irishwomen," she argued that the "masculine side of women's souls" must be brought out, "as well as the feminine side of men's souls." This is a theosophical idea: the belief in the duality of humanity; the apparent differences

---

[20] Oikarinen, *A Dream of Liberty*, 58.
[21] "The Future of Irishwomen," *Irish Citizen*, Oct. 23, 1915, 137.
[22] "Comrades," in Gore-Booth, *The Egyptian Pillar*, 32.

between men and women were a result of their reflecting the same cosmic essence, which comprised both masculine and feminine elements.[23] Between her early occultist pursuits with Eva and the 1916 Rising, Markievicz leaves little record of any spiritual preoccupations. Nevertheless, the theosophical approach to gender, which was important to several prominent suffragists, underpins her idea about the flexibility of women's roles in the private and public sphere.

This is illustrated in two series of articles that Markievicz wrote for the *Irish Citizen* in 1915: "The Women of '98" and "Experience of a Woman Patrol in Dublin." "Women of '98" was published under her full name, Constance de Markievicz, and recounts both the "active," by which she meant militant, and "passive" (auxiliary) roles of women in the 1798 Rising. Wolfe Tone's writings and the memory of 1798 were foundational to Markievicz's political thought, but '98 became even more important as nationalist separatists' anxieties about northeastern Ulster increased with the consolidating effect the war had on Ulster Unionists.[24] Markievicz emphasized the heroism of Betsey Grey, killed in the Battle of Ballinahinch in County Down, and Susey Toole, who fought with Joseph Holt in the Wicklow Mountains.[25] In addition to the unity of women across the island, she implicitly advocated a unity of social classes, describing how well-educated women and peasants both fought alongside the men. Throughout the series, Markievicz argued that the "rebel ranks" respected women, in contrast to the treatment they received at the hands of the British Army.

"Experience of a Woman Patrol in Dublin," which appeared with the byline "C.M.," was far more moderated and seems calculated to appeal to the middle-class philanthropists among the *Citizen*'s readership. These articles emphasize the disparity between social classes in Ireland rather than their unity. Markievicz describes walking a nightly "beat" from 9:30 to 11:30 around the north of the city center, from Sackville Street—"one great low saloon"—to Alexandra Basin, "and through the many dirty laneways that run between the main thoroughfares."[26] She writes about the dire conditions in which the working-class lived, conditions that had only worsened after the Lockout. Children roamed the streets, and whole families lived in one-room tenement houses, where there could "be little attempt at decency, let alone comfort or cleanliness.... Many factory girls I know do not care to go

---

[23] These theosophical ideas are also present in the Irish suffragist and theosophist Charlotte Despard's "The Case of Women's Suffrage"; see Dixon, *Divine Feminism*, 182.

[24] Laffan, *The Partition of Ireland*, 49.

[25] "Women of Ninety-Eight," *Irish Citizen*, Nov. 13, 1915, 161.

[26] C.M., "Experience of a Woman Patrol in Dublin," ibid., Oct. 9, 1915, 122.

to their homes till bedtime, so they frequent the streets."²⁷ Despite the relatively temperate tone, the series remained clearly anti-imperialist. First and foremost, a citizen assumes responsibility for policing her district—an implicit condemnation of the ineffectuality of the Dublin Metropolitan Police, whom radicals perceived to be imperialist collaborators. Markievicz took a swipe at the "foreign men" who encouraged women to debase themselves, but she also blamed the women who supported the British war effort rather than improve the desperate conditions at home. Women were "dying to make munitions, wait on the wounded soldiers, drive motors, etc. etc. Why should not some of them come forward to help cure this open sore that has been in their midst all their lives."²⁸

The ITGWU's antagonists from the Lockout, including William Martin Murphy, not only were profiting from the war through exports but also had pledged to support Britain by supplying the names of male employees of military age who were considered "dispensable," in the event that conscription was imposed in Ireland.²⁹ Connolly and Markievicz perceived an immediate threat to the working class. Their concerns were amplified by reports from the British suffragist Sylvia Pankhurst, who wrote an article for the *Workers' Republic*, "Conscription Applied to Industry," in which she warned that the National Register in Britain made it possible to track down any man. All men in state employment were ordered to enlist or be dismissed, while private employers were also "asked to bring the same economic pressures to bear."³⁰ Connolly employed the term "economic conscription" to refer to the imposition of enlistment through economic imperatives. At the beginning of December 1915, the Dublin Trades Council passed a resolution agreeing that the "question was one of immediate and pressing importance and affected them all," not just members of the Irish Volunteers or the ICA.³¹

In November 1915 Delia Larkin was forced out of the ITGWU. The previous year she had been involved in a severe dispute with the ITGWU leadership over the IWWU's expenditure, including her purchase of a piano for use by the union's choir and dramatic society.³² These tensions may have provoked her dismissal during Connolly's rationalization of the union's various

²⁷ Ibid.; and "Experience of a Woman Patrol in Dublin," *Irish Citizen*, Dec. 4, 1915, 182.
²⁸ C.M., "Experience of a Woman Patrol," *Irish Citizen*, Oct. 23, 1915, 137.
²⁹ "Enlist or Starve," *Workers' Republic*, Nov. 27, 1915, 4. "Is This Conscription" included a copy of a circular from the Department of Recruiting for Ireland that directed employers in Ireland to provide the number of military age who were employed and the benefits that each employer was prepared to grant employees who volunteered for active service, *Workers' Republic*, Dec. 18, 1915, 4.
³⁰ Sylvia Pankhurst, "Conscription Applied to Industry," ibid., Nov. 27, 1915, 5.
³¹ "Dublin Trades Council," ibid., Dec. 4, 1915, 3.
³² Greaves, *Irish Transport and General Workers' Union*, 135.

activities in order to reduce debts and replenish the union's coffers.[33] Jim Larkin had left for the United States in autumn 1914, and William O'Brien suspected that Larkin hoped the union would be poorly managed in his absence, so "he could come back and show how to put it right."[34] Connolly—as acting general secretary of the ITGWU and commandant of the Irish Citizen Army—was under extreme pressure to ensure that the union was working effectively. However, there may have been more personal motives at play; Anne Matthews suggests that Delia Larkin's role gave Jim Larkin a de facto presence in the union and that Connolly's dismissal of her completed his takeover of the ITGWU leadership.[35] Helena Molony took Delia Larkin's place as general secretary of the Irish Women's Workers' Union. She would assist Kathleen Lynn in commanding the new Citizen Army Women's Ambulance Corps.

To involve the Irish Women Workers' Union in the Citizen Army, in late October 1915 Connolly initiated a medical corps that would "be attached to the citizen army." The language here is important since it does not suggest an auxiliary role for the women workers. Rather than "assist," the ambulance corps would be "attached to" the militia. Connolly hoped that the corps would create "a body of women who will be as efficient in their particular subjects as the Citizen Army are in theirs."[36] Initially, recruitment to the corps was targeted at girls, providing a culturally normative way for them to participate in militant activities. Markievicz wrote propaganda to assist in recruitment of women to the union, although she privileged a full-fledged militant role. In her essay "Conscription and Women Workers," published in the *Workers' Republic* in December, she declared:

> A decent woman ought to kill herself rather than submit to a foreign invader. If she has not that much pluck; if she won't die to preserve her own honour, why should anyone else trouble about the matter?... Buy a revolver and shoot any man, Jew or German, South Irish Horse or Connaught Ranger, patriotic employer or bullying foreman, whoever he may be, who attempts to injure you. Keep your last bullet for yourself, and don't whine about men protecting you.[37]

[33] Matthews, *Irish Citizen Army*, 52–54.
[34] Graves, *Irish Transport and General Workers' Union*, 136.
[35] Matthews, *Irish Citizen Army*, 15.
[36] Quoted in ibid., 62; Matthews argues that the ambulance corps was an auxiliary association and that Connolly's language reflects his belief that "women should act in a support role to the men."
[37] "Irish Citizen Army," *Workers' Republic*, Dec. 18, 1915, 8; see Anderson, *James Connolly and the Irish Left*, 24, for the argument that Connolly was the author of this column. If Anderson is

She wrote in the same register as in "The Future of Irishwomen" for the *Irish Citizen*, but now the language of self-sacrifice that she had preached for years to the boys of Fianna Éireann was directed toward adult women. In fewer than six months, the Rising would test their willingness to die for the Republic.

In mid-January 1916 the IRB military council—a secret society within a secret society—met to determine a date for the Rising.[38] The battle cries of the *Workers' Republic* provoked the Volunteer leadership to meet Connolly and ascertain his plans. Despite opposition from the Volunteers' chief of staff, Eoin MacNeill, Patrick Pearse, Éamonn Ceannt, Joseph Plunkett, Tom Clarke, Seán MacDermott, and Connolly agreed that Easter was optimal.[39] The utmost secrecy of their meeting meant that Connolly told no one of his whereabouts; his sudden disappearance led to wild rumors that he had been kidnapped.[40] Markievicz thought that Connolly may have been arrested; she told her fellow trade unionist William O'Brien that Connolly, Michael Mallin, and she had agreed that if any of them were taken into police custody, the others would mobilize the ICA immediately and launch an insurrection.[41] Much to everyone's relief, Connolly returned before Markievicz and Mallin mustered their troops.

Just three months before the Rising, the Dublin Metropolitan Police realized that Constance Markievicz's frequent public appearances on behalf of the Fianna, Cumann na mBan, and the Dublin workers signified that she was a key player in the revolutionary movement. On January 22, 1916, the *Workers' Republic* published an open letter from Markievicz to Francis Sheehy Skeffington in which she accepted his challenge to a debate on the merits of war.[42] Sheehy Skeffington supported American entrepreneur Henry Ford's peace crusades, but Markievicz pledged that she would not welcome peace until "the British Empire had been smashed."[43] The same evening that the article was published, the Dublin Metropolitan Police raided Surrey House and seized a printing press and "a number of leaflets of an

---

correct, then Connolly borrowed from Markievicz's rhetoric. Her polarizing use of "Jew or German" here does not reflect anti-Jewish attitudes but rather widespread perceptions that the German national and Jewish religious identities were oppositional.

[38] Townshend, *Easter 1916*, 122.

[39] Townshend relates Diarmid Lynch's account that the "1915 Easter manoeuvres 'furnished the basis for a solution.'" Ibid., 118.

[40] See ibid., 119.

[41] Hughes, *Michael Mallin*, 108.

[42] Constance de Markeivicz, Letter to the Editor, *Workers' Republic*, Jan. 22, 1916, 1.

[43] For the crusades, see Lewis, *The Public Image of Henry Ford*, 78–92.

anti-British character."[44] Connolly reported in the *Workers' Republic* that the raid on Markievicz's home was just one raid of a series across the city and suburbs:

> A body of about forty plain clothes men armed with revolvers and under the command of a District Inspector rushed this house about 8 p.m. They apparently expected trouble, for in addition to the extraordinarily large force of police . . . a picked body of soldiers were detained in Portobello Barracks close by in order to aid the police in slaughtering the inhabitants of the house should resistance be offered.[45]

In fact, the only people at home were a few Fianna boys and girls, who seized their chance to heckle the police with renditions of "The Peeler and the Goat," "Watch on the Rhine," "The Saxon's on the Run," and "A Nation Once Again." Connolly took delight in relaying the encounter, but his report concluded on a serious note: the Irish Volunteers had mobilized immediately—the most successful swift mobilization yet attempted—"And that is significant. Is it not?"

Either before this police raid or after the Rising, Markievicz's housekeeper stashed away at least one incriminating piece of evidence: Markievicz's study of Emmett's plans for the 1803 Rising, which she sketched out in a Polish notebook. Markievicz identified four points of attack—the Pigeon House, Dublin Castle, the Artillery Barracks at Island Bridge, and Cork Street Barracks—and three "points of cheque"—the old Custom House, Mary Street Barracks, and the Corner House on Capel Street—and she noted two lines of defense, along Beresford Street North and Merchant's Quay South.[46] Of these, only Dublin Castle would be occupied during the 1916 Rising, but her plans nonetheless illustrate Emmett's influence on her strategy and political thought. She noted plans to position troops in case the army attempted different routes. These may have been notes for a lecture to the Fianna, since she jotted "new branch," "prize," Emmet," "Discipline," "Be prepared," "wait & watch," "Content to do what you *can*," and "*Little things*."

Plans for the insurrection intensified rapidly. The regular "Irish Citizen Army" column in the *Workers' Republic* was replaced by first-aid instructions on the treatment of broken bones and hemorrhages. The Irish Workers' Cooperative store on Eden Quay began to advertise "The 'Irish Freedom' First-Aid Outfit," which at 6½ pence included bandages, iodine, and anti-

[44] "Irish Questions/Police Raid in Dublin," *Irish Times*, Jan. 28, 1916, 5.
[45] "The Dublin Raids," *Workers' Republic*, Jan. 29, 1916, 1.
[46] Constance Markievicz's Plans for the Rising, Lissadell Collection.

septic dressing.[47] In February a series of mobilization orders were issued in the *Workers' Republic*, which openly stated that the ICA would assemble in uniform and full equipment at a specified day and time under the direct command of the commandant, Connolly.[48]

A large-scale mobilization of the ICA was launched on St. Patrick's Day, 1916. Armed and unarmed members, including the bicycle corps, the Fianna under the direction of Markievicz, and the women's ambulance corps that was led on this occasion by Helena Molony, were ordered to assemble at 11:00 AM in full equipment, with haversacking and one day's rations.[49] Accompanied by the ITGWU pipers' band, named for the nineteenth-century revolutionary James Fintan Lalor, the ICA embarked on a seventeen-mile march from Liberty Hall, along the north quays, right through the city center: down Grafton Street, through St. Stephen's Green, and out to the south Dublin suburb, Rathdrum, where they attracted the notice of the local police.[50] From there they turned to the southeast and marched toward the coast. Near rural Booterstown, they practiced combat maneuvers, disturbing only "an unsuspecting donkey innocently making its appearance" as they shouldered their weapons, "bayonets flashing."[51] On their return to the city, the militia halted at St. Stephen's Green, and a bugle sounded. This may have been an attempt to attract maximum attention in a busy park on a public holiday; it may also have signaled that the green would be one of the sites of occupation at Easter under the command of Mallin and Markievicz.

Accounts of Markievicz's militancy in the *Workers' Republic* are simultaneously affectionate and jestful. The day after the St. Patrick's day route march, "Our good friend and true, 'the Countess,'" was described as having turned out fully armed, "so much so that the casual onlooker might readily be pardoned for mistaking her for the representative of an enterprising firm of small arms manufacturers."[52] Similarly, reporting on a police raid of the Workers' Cooperative shop at Eden Quay, the *Workers' Republic* reported that when the second wave of police arrived, "the Countess amongst others was lovingly toying with a large automatic, whilst a number of rifles were peeping round the corner."[53] These accounts illustrate Markievicz's exceptional position in the ICA and ITGWU. Other women belonged to the

---

[47] "Irish Citizen Army," *Workers' Republic*, Jan. 29, 1916, 8.

[48] "ICA," ibid., Feb. 12, 1916, 8.

[49] Ibid., Mar. 18, 1916, 8. Kathleen Lynn was the appointed leader of the ambulance corps; see Matthews, *Citizen Army*, 63.

[50] "St Patrick's Day Manoeuvres of the I.C.A.," *Workers' Republic*, April 1, 1916, 6.

[51] Ibid.

[52] Ibid.

[53] ICA column, "A Call to Arms," ibid., 8.

Citizen Army Women's Ambulance Corps, to which the ICA membership list referred as the Women's Section ICA.[54] The articles also demonstrate the dominant perception of Markievicz as anomalous within the ICA; even though the entire Citizen Army turned out fully armed, only Markievicz's weapons were subjected to comment. These sometimes humorous and sometimes sexualized depictions of Markievicz by her comrades had a lasting effect, shaping both popular memory and historical accounts of her character.

Markievicz's propaganda, which is often taken at face value, also had a profound effect on her legacy. But her writing was part of a large corpus of work intended to prepare the ICA mentally. Her "Hymn on the Battlefield," "dedicated to the Citizen Army" and published in the *Workers' Republic* in November 1915, declared "Tone is our battle-cry, Emmet inspires us / Those who for freedom fall never shall die."[55] With its prominent Christian iconography and vision of martyrdom, there is nothing in the hymn to differentiate it from Volunteer propaganda.

The week prior to the Easter Rising, Connolly announced that the ICA's flag that flew over Liberty Hall would be replaced by the green flag of the Volunteers. He organized an expansive display to draw attention to the symbolic act.[56] The ICA and the Fianna assembled in front of Liberty Hall to witness the changing of the colors. Flanked by Michael Mallin on his left and Markievicz on his right, Connolly presented the new flag and "pledged his hearers to give their lives if necessary to keep the Irish Flag Flying."[57] The same week, Connolly's play, *Under Which Flag?*, was staged by the Irish Workers' Dramatic Company.[58] It was a propaganda piece, urging its audience to remain loyal in moments of crisis. Propagandistic poetry also appeared with increasing frequency in the *Workers' Republic*. On April 15, just nine days before the Rising, Markievicz's "The Call" appeared under her own name rather than a pseudonym. The poem, composed of cliché, is constructed to induce a sense of urgency, demanding "To arms! For the day has come" and "Choose now, 'tis the time to decide." She concludes with an assertion of solidarity: "We answer the call with a ringing cheer / With fixed bayonets we stand; / We are ready and steady without a fear / To die for our native land."[59] The image of the bayonets here and the flashing bayonets described in the *Workers' Repub-*

[54] Matthews, *Citizen Army*, 63.

[55] Constance de Markievicz, "Hymn on the Battlefield. Dedicated to the Citizen Army," *Workers' Republic*, Nov. 13, 1915, reprinted as Crofts, arr., *A Battle Hymn*.

[56] "Notes on the Front: the Irish Flag," *Workers' Republic*, April 8, 1916, 1.

[57] "Labour and Ireland," ibid., April 27, 1916, 4.

[58] F.S.S. "Under Which Flag?," ibid., April 8, 1916, 6; and Ó Ceallaigh Ritschel, "James Connolly's *Under Which Flag*, 1916."

[59] C. de Markievicz, "The Call," *Workers' Republic*, April 15, 1916, 8.

lic are examples of the way that cultural memory of past risings constructed visions for the present and future. In 1916 petrol bombs, rifles and pistols were the weapons of the revolutionaries, but bayonets were the signifiers of rebellion.

On Good Friday, Connolly issued the mobilization orders that were to go into effect the moment that the rebellion began.[60] The day was replete with the symbolism of self-sacrifice, but—more pragmatically—it was a public holiday, which enabled members of the ICA to assemble freely at Liberty Hall. William O'Brien later recalled interrupting a meeting that morning between Mallin, Markievicz, and Connolly; he learned later, from Michael Mallin's brother Dan, that they had been considering plans to occupy St. Stephen's Green.[61] Whether the military council ever intended to take the green has been subject to much debate, and Dan Mallin's statement to O'Brien may have been a belated attempt to justify his brother's rather inglorious legacy. Historians continue to puzzle over the logic behind the rebels' occupation of sites across Dublin. In his history of the Rising, McGarry asks, "Why were positions of negligible military value, such as St Stephen's Green, seized?"[62] Close study of the ICA's route marches, documented in the *Workers' Republic*, shows that the green was an important site prior to the Rising; it was the principal public space in the city center, a transportation hub, and full of imperial iconography, from the gate commemorating the Boer War to the equestrian statue of George II at its center.[63] These facts support a reading of the Rising as a symbolic event, but as Peter Hart notes, this does not exclude "some military rationale," no matter how obscure.[64]

Easter weekend was spent preparing rations and manufacturing ammunition at Liberty Hall. Most of Saturday was dedicated to the preparation of homemade bombs, later described by one participant as "like oil-cans through the neck of which a galvanized iron tube went down. The fuse passed through this . . . it was blue and red. You lit the blue end, and when it burned to the red, you threw it."[65] These munitions, however rudimentary, became even more vital when the Aud, transporting German rifles and ammunition destined for the rebels, was scuttled in Cork harbor.[66] Another factor contributing to the sense of the Rising as ill-fated was Eoin MacNeill's

[60] Fox, *Citizen Army*, 137.
[61] Foy and Barton, *Easter Rising*, 88.
[62] McGarry, *The Rising*, 120.
[63] For possible strategic reasons for taking the green, see Townshend, *Easter 1916*, 166.
[64] Hart, "The Fenians and the International Revolutionary Tradition," 199.
[65] Eyewitness account by Peter Wilson, Cathal O'Shannon Papers, Irish Labour History Society (ILHS), MSS19/COS 109.
[66] For a vivid discussion of the affair, see Townshend, *Easter 1916*, 125–29.

countermanding order, issued in the *Sunday Independent*.[67] MacNeill called off the rising, canceling "all parades, marches, or other movements of Irish Volunteers."[68] The Volunteer leadership, including Patrick Pearse, delayed action, but many of the rank-and-file ignored (or were unaware of) MacNeill's command and began assembling on Sunday according to plan. Chaos ensued, as some Volunteers were convinced to return home only after receiving orders from Thomas MacDonagh and Éamon de Valera confirming the delay.[69]

The Proclamation of the Republic had already been signed and was being printed on the presses of the *Workers' Republic* at Liberty Hall. Townshend describes Markievicz threatening to shoot MacNeill the next time she saw him and acting with "typical reckless impetuosity" as she "grabbed one of the first copies off the press and rushed out to declaim it to the passers-by in Lower Abbey Street."[70] The caricature ignores Connolly and Markievicz's plans to proceed with a Rising whatever the cost. Although Connolly refrained from launching a full-scale rebellion on Sunday, he took the ICA on a route march through the city that afternoon. From Liberty Hall, they marched across the Liffey at Butt Bridge, over to College Green, down Grafton Street, and west along York Street by the College of Surgeons. In his history of the ICA, Fox writes that the ICA turned right onto Great George's Street, which would have taken them past the eastern perimeter of Dublin Castle. Citizen Army member Rosie Hackett recalled that the march proceeded to Jacob's Biscuit Factory, in which case the soldiers would have turned left, marching south along Aungier Street before turning right onto Bishop's Street and returning to Liberty Hall perhaps via Bride Street, flanking the Castle on its western perimeter. Hackett remembers, "As we came to each of these places that were taken afterwards, the bugle sounded. We did not know it at the time but, as each place was taken afterwards, we thoroughly understood what that route march was for."[71]

When the ICA returned to Liberty Hall, tea was served, and an evening's entertainment was organized to pass the time. Michael Mallin's grandly titled (four-piece) Workers' Orchestra gave a concert, and there may have been a play, since Hackett remarked in a later statement that "Sean Grogan was head of the dramatic group."[72] The men spent the night in the hall, but

---

[67] For the "dramatic effects" of MacNeill's countermand, see ibid., 142–43.
[68] Ibid., 139.
[69] Ibid., 140.
[70] Ibid., 138.
[71] NAI Bureau of Military History Witness Statement (BMH WS) 546 (Rosie Hackett).
[72] Hughes, *Michael Mallin*, 119; and BMH WS 546 (Rosie Hackett).

the women—including Markievicz, Hackett, and Kathleen Lynn—were instructed to stay at the home of Jennie Wyse Power, who had been elected president of Cumann na mBan in 1915 and was a veteran of the Ladies' Land League, the IWFL, and the Daughters of Ireland.[73] Prior to the Rising, Markievicz was at the periphery of the Cumann na mBan executive, but the experience of the Rising changed her relationship to the organization and with Wyse Power. When Jennie's elder sister Maire died in summer 1916, Markievicz wrote a note of affectionate sympathy from Aylesbury Jail, sending her love; it was a letter that Jennie would treasure for the rest of her life.[74]

On Monday morning, Markievicz and Lynn were whisked to Liberty Hall, where they joined the assembling militia. Of the estimated 300 members of the Citizen Army, 220 fought in Easter Week.[75] Proportionately, this reflected the strengths of the ICA's leadership compared to the abysmal turnout of the Volunteers, some units of which mobilized less than twenty-five per cent of their battalions.[76] At 11:45 AM on Easter Monday, the order was sounded to fall in, and a column of about forty of the ICA set off from Liberty Hall, marching to College Green under the leadership of Seán Connolly. Their destination was Dublin Castle, a location with symbolic and practical significance.[77] The secrecy of the military council and the executions of the leaders of the Rising mean that very little of the strategy of the insurrection is clear. In their history, Foy and Barton indicate James Connolly had instructed Seán Connolly to secure Ship Street Barracks and Dublin Castle by taking the buildings overlooking them and thus preventing any movement of British troops.[78] More recently, McGarry states that the "small Citizen Army raiding party [had] orders to occupy the adjacent City Hall building."[79] Markievicz and Lynn arrived by car in time to see Seán Connolly shoot an unarmed Dublin Metropolitan Police constable who was the only guard on duty at the castle gate.[80] Markievicz later described the scene that followed as one of "wild excitement."[81] The shooting was met with startlingly

[73] BMH WS 357 (Dr. Kathleen Lynn); for Wyse Power, see McCarthy, *Cumann na mBan*, 20, 33.

[74] O'Neill, *From Parnell to de Valera*, 88–89.

[75] Foy and Barton, *Easter Rising*, 75. McGarry gives the figure as 219 citing Donal Nevin's *James Connolly* (Dublin, 2006), 731; see McGarry, *The Rising*, 127.

[76] McGarry, *The Rising*, 127.

[77] Townshend notes that the Castle was "the symbolic—and indeed actual—seat of British rule in Ireland," *Easter 1916*, 162.

[78] Foy and Barton, *Easter Rising*, 73.

[79] McGarry, *The Rising*, 141.

[80] Townshend, *Easter 1916*, 162–63.

[81] "Women in the Fight," in McHugh, *Dublin 1916*, 123. After the ICA secured the guardhouse, they did not proceed to take the castle but retreated to the rooftop of City Hall, which stood

mild retaliation as a single army officer, Major Ivor Price, charged into the yard with his revolver.[82] Stranger still, the ICA retreated, as Seán Connolly ordered the occupation of City Hall and the premises of the *Daily Express* across the road. Kathleen Lynn stayed behind to give medical support to the ICA, and Markievicz drove onward to St. Stephen's Green.

There she rendezvoused with Michael Mallin, who had led a contingent of ICA, Cumann na mBan, and Fianna from Liberty Hall. On reaching the green, a section under the command of Richard McCormick continued to Harcourt Street Station while Mallin's section demanded the keys to the green from a baffled gardener and proceeded to evict the civilians from the park. This was a far from peaceful process, as the ICA commandeered civilian vehicles to construct barricades in the street. One man who attempted to dislodge his truck from a barricade near the Shelbourne Hotel was shot.[83] Although most accounts of the Rising describe the role of Cumann na mBan at the green as being restricted to administering first aid, Markievicz later commented, "Some of the girls had revolvers and with these they sallied forth and held up bread-vans."[84]

Armed patrols of the ICA stood guard at the railings on the north side of the green (adjacent to Grafton Street, Dawson and Kildare Streets, and Merrion Row), while Mallin put others to work digging trenches. This was a tragic mistake in tactics, digging in to defend a twenty-two-acre flatland surrounded by tall buildings from which British snipers would have the advantage over the entire green.[85] The decision was a product of Mallin's imperial training; he had perfected the art of trench digging during his British Army service in India. The devastating consequences of such tactics in an urban war occurred to neither him nor Markievicz, whom he instructed to supervise the digging. She described it as "exciting work," as she walked "round and round the Green, reporting back if anything was wanted, or tackling any sniper who was particularly objectionable."[86]

---

adjacent to the castle to the east. There, Connolly became the first casualty among the rebels. He was shot once in the arm and a second time, fatally, by a British sniper. See Foy and Barton, *Easter Rising*, 73–76.

[82] Townshend, *Easter 1916*, 163.

[83] Ibid., 165.

[84] Constance de Markievicz, *Cumann na mBan*, 2.10 (Easter 1926), in *In Their Own Voice*, ed. Ward, 73–76.

[85] The main sites for the trenches were the four entrances to the park, where the gates were blockaded with any available materials, including park benches and commandeered motorcars; Foy and Barton, *Easter Rising*, 82.

[86] "Women in the Fight," 123.

The headquarters for the rebellion was the General Post Office (GPO) on Sackville Street, where James Connolly—now commandant general of the Dublin Division of the combined ICA and Volunteers—was stationed with other members of the IRB military council, Volunteers, Cumann na mBan, and a few of the ICA.[87] By some accounts, the leaders intended to have Dublin Castle as their base, but the failure of the ICA to take control of the castle precipitated a change in plans.[88] Nonetheless, the GPO was "an impressive stage" for what Townshend describes as "key symbolic acts."[89] The tricolor flew from one corner of the building, with its green, white, and orange signifying a united national republican movement.[90] Opposite flew a makeshift green banner, with a gold harp and gold letters declaring the "Irish Republic." According to one apocryphal account, Markievicz fashioned the flag out of a spare bedspread and used gold paint thinned with yellow mustard, fetched from the kitchen of Surrey House by one of the Fianna, for the lettering.[91] (Similarly, it is rumored that the flag, now displayed in the Irish War Museum in Collins' Barracks, has a missing piece—not a casualty of battle but of a vicious tug-of-war with Constance's dog, Poppet.)

Outside the GPO, Pearse read the Proclamation of the Republic, which declared that "supported by her exiled children in America and by gallant allies in Europe," the Irish Republican Brotherhood, the Volunteers, and Irish Citizen Army jointly proclaimed "the right of the people of Ireland to the ownership of Ireland, and to the unfettered control of Irish destinies, to be sovereign and indefeasible." The proclamation guaranteed religious and civil liberty, equal rights, and equal opportunities to all citizens. The phrasing unambiguously grants suffrage to Irishwomen in the new Republic. Yet the degree to which the proclamation was a socialist document continues to be debated. The declaration of ownership by the people was ambiguous enough to satisfy both leftists and centrists, as was the Republic's "resolve to pursue

[87] Winifred Carney, a member of the Belfast branch of Cumann na mBan, was a trade unionist and prior to the Rising acted as James Connolly's secretary. She was the only woman in the GPO at the outbreak of the Rising, but by the end of the week she was joined by over thirty other women, not all of whom were members of Cumann na mBan. See McCarthy, *Cumann na mBan*, 58, 60–61.

[88] Townshend, *Easter Rising*, 100.

[89] Ibid., 159.

[90] The Irish tricolor was introduced during the 1848 Rising and by 1916 was "the generally accepted symbol of the republican movement"; ibid.

[91] NLI, MS 18,463. The memory seems particularly fanciful since MacKay writes that "with the Countess' consent, [James Connolly] sent Sean Connolly over to the G.P.O. with the Green Flag, so that Padraig Pearse could fly it from the roof." In fact, James Connolly was with Pearse at the GPO, and Seán Connolly was fighting for his life on Dame Street. An image of the flag is also available at http://www.nli.ie/1916/pan0659.jpgfjb06_JF__The_Rising_FJ_06_JF_02_FJ_full.html.

the happiness and prosperity of the whole nation and of all its parts, cherishing all the children of the nation equally." While the proclamation ensured religious equality, it also invoked "the protection of the Most High God," which satisfied Pearse's religiosity and would have the (perhaps) unintended consequence of enshrining Catholic values in the future state. The precise structure of the new Republic was undetermined, and until an elected national government could take its place, the signatories claimed the right to administer both the civil and military affairs of the Republic.

Through Monday afternoon, Mallin and Markievicz concentrated on keeping up morale, patrolling the green and monitoring their troops' preparations. Since it was a holiday, many of the surrounding buildings were empty, including the Shelbourne Hotel, which was one of the tallest buildings in the vicinity. Mallin sent out sharpshooters to take up positions in houses and businesses in the adjacent streets, but he ignored the Shelbourne, which would prove to be another crucial mistake. In response to a rumor that the College of Surgeons, which flanked the western side of the green, held a cache of rifles belonging to Trinity College's Officer Training Corps, Mallin sent Markievicz along with an ICA squadron under the command of Frank Robbins on a reconnaissance operation. A hasty search failed to unearth the guns, but Mallin instructed that the building be captured anyhow. He sent a supply of bombs from the green and ordered Robbins's crew to take up positions on the roof.[92]

After the college was secure, Markievicz returned to the green, where she was in charge of the western perimeter and oversaw the commandeering of passing traffic. The response from civilians was incredulous, especially from the families of British Army servicemen, who taunted the rebels, interfered with the construction of barricades, and stopped traffic before it reached the green in order to divert the drivers onto another route. One gentleman, W. Hopkins Ashmore, was captured by the rebels as he returned to Dublin from a weekend in the country. Soon after the Rising, he reported to the *Irish Times* that "Countess Markievicz, who was attired in male uniform and armed with an automatic pistol, was profuse in her apologies to the prisoners. She explained that their detention had to be enforced for the cause of the Irish Republic."[93] This measured, rational communication with civilians is very different from depictions of Markievicz's behavior in one of the most controversial events of the Rising: the shooting of the unarmed police constable, Michael Lahiff.

[92] Foy and Barton, *Easter Rising*, 82.
[93] "[...] Inside," *Weekly Irish Times*, April 29, 1916, 3.

By the afternoon of the first day of the Rising, six policemen had been shot, two fatally, and at least two whom were unarmed.[94] Seán Connolly had killed the unarmed constable who stood guard at Dublin Castle, but it is Markievicz's shooting of an unarmed policeman at St. Stephen's Green that has plagued the public imagination. One witness, the district nurse Geraldine Fitzgerald, recorded in her diary that she saw the shooting as she was returning from duty to the nurse's home, which was located at the southwest corner of St. Stephen's Green.[95] She describes the scene:

> A lady in a green uniform, the same as the men were wearing (breeches, slouch hat with green feathers etc.) the feathers were the only feminine feature in her appearance, holding a revolver in one hand and a cigarette in the other, was standing on the footpath giving orders to the men. We recognized her as the Countess de Markievicz—such a specimen of womanhood. There were other women, similarly attired, inside the Park, walking about and bringing drinks of water to the men. We had only been looking out a few minutes when we saw a policeman walking down the path from Harcourt Street. He had only gone a short way when we heard a shot and then saw him fall forward on his face. The Countess ran triumphantly into the Green saying "I got him" and some of the rebels shook her by the hand and seemed to congratulate her.[96]

Fitzgerald gives details of Lahiff's wounds: he had been "shot in the lung, close to the heart and was bleeding profusely. A doctor arrived at the same time as we did."[97] Lahiff was sent to hospital, where he died a half hour after admission. The death certificate attributed the cause to "a bullet through both lungs and left arm."[98] In his recent history of the Rising, McGarry cites Max Caulfield's history, which reports that Lahiff was shot three times in the head.[99] Such circulation of factual inaccuracies exacerbates the confusion surrounding the event, and Markievicz's insistent denial that she did not shoot a policeman further obscures the truth. Seven months later, in November 1916, Constance told Eva "how she held a revolver at a policeman's chest but *could* not shoot when it came to the point" because "she recognised him & had known him before"; however, she recalled that she may have "hit one

[94] McGarry, *The Rising*, 137.
[95] Matthews, *Citizen Army*, 95.
[96] Geraldine Fitzgerald, extract from diary in Castle File no. 84 (Constance Markievicz), NA, WO 35/207.
[97] Quoted in Matthews, *Citizen Army*, 96.
[98] Ibid.
[99] McGarry, *The Rising*, 137.

in the arm as he jumped."[100] It appears that by "shot" Markievicz understood "killed." Lahiff did not die at the scene, so Markievicz had no way of knowing that what appeared to be a wound to the arm had been fatal.

The first night at the green seemed to pass uneventfully. Markievicz spent the night stretched out in Kathleen Lynn's car, while the men hunkered down in their trenches and the other women sheltered in the summerhouse. During the short summer night, British troops moved quietly in to occupy the Hibernian United Services Club and the Shelbourne. Snipers stood at every window, and a machine-gunner manned the roof, waiting for dawn. At 4:00 AM on Tuesday, machine-gun fire mowed through Mallin's trenches. Supporting fire from British troops who were barricaded behind sandbags at Merrion Row blanketed the north side of the green, where most of the ICA was positioned. The ICA troops were quick to take cover in the shrubbery, an untenable position that they managed to hold for over four hours. It was not until 8:00 AM that Mallin ordered a retreat to the southwest corner of the green, where the park met Harcourt and Cuffe Streets. From there, he began to evacuate the ICA troops and hostages to the College of Surgeons, which was still held by Robbins. Amid flying gravel, the women and children were the first to dash across the perimeter road, but the wounded had to be smuggled through the hedges and hustled across to York Street.[101] Even in tumult, there was civility: both sides agreed a brief ceasefire twice a day to allow the park keeper to feed the ducks.[102]

The lecture rooms in the College of Surgeons were converted into a dormitory, a recreation room, a dining room, and an infirmary. The headquarters was established on the first floor, where Markievicz and Robbins took charge while Mallin made a last attempt to defend the barricades at the northwest corner of the green.[103] He was soon driven back to the college, where the ICA attempted to mount a bombing campaign on the British Army's positions, but they only succeeded in killing teenager Fred Ryan and wounding Markievicz's friend, Margaret Skinnider.[104] The insurgents at the college were supplied by fifteen-year-old Mary McLoughlin with ammunition from the GPO, but they were more concerned with food than with bullets.[105] Among the kitchen's scant provisions, Nellie Gifford managed to find a bag of oats

---

[100] Eva Gore-Booth to Josslyn Gore-Booth (n.d. [received Nov. 23, 1916]), PRONI, D/4131/K/5/13.

[101] Foy and Barton, *Easter Rising*, 87.

[102] Hughes, *Michal Mallin*, 149.

[103] Foy and Barton, *Easter Rising*, 90.

[104] "Women in the Fight," 125.

[105] Hughes, *Michael Mallin*, 151; Townshend, *Easter 1916*, 168.

and made "pot after pot of the most delicious porridge," which Markievicz credited with keeping them going. As the days wore on, communication between the rebel posts became more difficult. In the evenings the garrison at the College of Surgeons passed the time with singing and also prayer. It was here that Constance Markievicz converted to Catholicism.

Markievicz was not the only high-profile Irish Protestant to convert to Catholicism in 1916, although in her mind she was converting not from Protestantism but from atheism. Roger Casement, secretly baptized as a Catholic by his mother but raised as a Protestant, converted to Catholicism during his imprisonment in London after the Easter Rising, just weeks prior to his execution for treason.[106] Casement had been arrested in Kerry after his failed attempt to land arms from Germany and was taken to London. During his interrogation, he was asked, "When did you become a nationalist?," to which he replied, "I have been a nationalist all my life but not so extreme." The next question is telling: "But your father was a Protestant?" Casement's response: "I am now—or was."[107] Casement had begun to distance himself from Protestantism in 1913, when he returned to Ireland after three decades of humanitarian work in Africa and South America. In Belfast, he saw Catholics relegated to unemployment and poverty solely on the basis of their religion, while "no single clergyman of the Irish Protestant Church has said one word against this cruel and wicked conduct." Orange parades and marches by the Ulster Volunteers were to Casement demonstrations of how the "Orange Ascendancy gang" "exploited" Presbyterians as well as "Papishes," an extremism that morphed Catholic attempts to win civil rights into sectarian struggle.[108] While Casement's process of conversion was long and was a product of protracted deliberation, Markievicz decided suddenly to convert, during the battle at the College of Surgeons.[109] In her study of Markievicz, Oikarinen describes the conversion as a "final touch, in a way, the creation of an 'ideal' Irish rebel."[110] This is certainly one aspect of her motivation, but conversion was also an expression of solidarity, provoked by experiences similar to Casement's and a sense of estrangement from what

[106] His conversion was a long process, but Casement publicly identified as a Protestant until, on June 29, 1916, he registered at Pentonville Prison as a Catholic. In Brixton Prison, where he was incarcerated after his initial imprisonment in the Tower of London, Casement had taken instruction in Catholicism but expressed reservations: "I don't want to jump, or rush or do anything hastily just because my time is short. It must be my deliberate act, unwavering and confirmed by all my intelligence." Quoted in Ó Síocháin, *Roger Casement*, 474.

[107] Ibid., 442.

[108] Ibid., 359.

[109] "Events of Easter Week," *Catholic Bulletin* (Feb. 1917): 130.

[110] Oikarinen, *A Dream of Liberty*, 100.

Markievicz and Casement both perceived as the values of the Ascendancy class.[111] Grace Gifford, fiancé of Joseph Plunkett, converted just prior to the Rising, on 7 April 1916.[112] These conversions would contribute to the increasing identification of Sinn Féin as a Catholic organization. (When Albinia Brodrick, sister to Lord Midleton, joined Sinn Féin and Gaelicized her name to Gobnait ní Brudair, Rosamond Jacob commented to Hanna Sheehy Skeffington, "I'm in a fright now for fear she may turn Catholic herself, like Casement and Madame de Markievicz. I do dislike to have things look as if no one could be a Sinn Féiner without being a Catholic."[113])

On Wednesday, martial law was declared. Four eighteen-pounder field guns had been transported into Trinity College, and an armed yacht, the HMS *Helga*, which had been on antisubmarine duty in the Irish Sea, began shelling Liberty Hall.[114] Eighteen-pounders roughly entrenched in Tara Street started firing as well, and soon the ITGWU headquarters was "reduced to a burnt-out shell."[115] Markievicz and Mallin prepared for a direct attack on the College of Surgeons and began transferring the wounded to local hospitals, storing grenades along the staircase in preparation for a last stand, and even contemplating retreating into the Dublin hillsides to fight a guerrilla war.[116] Markievicz's comrades at the college remembered her as exhibiting a cheerful resolve. Liam Ó Brian recalled that she wished for bayonets or "some stabbing instrument for action at close quarters," to which Mallin quipped, smiling, "You are very blood-thirsty."[117]

Somehow, in the midst of battle, the Easter edition of the *Workers' Republic* was issued. A poem by Markievicz, "Our Faith," took the place of the regular ICA column and appears to have been written in the midst of battle, as the fate of the rebels grew clear. It begins by asserting a collective willingness to die, "Be the chances nothing at all," and names Tone and Emmet as exemplars of the correct conduct under such circumstances.[118] She reminds the fighters to trust their commandant:

> Our Leader we trust, for we know full well
> Our honour is safe in his hands;

---

[111] Ibid. Oikarinen cites Boyce (1995), who argues that the Rising was a rebellion by Catholics for Catholics.

[112] "Events of Easter Week," *Catholic Bulletin* (Feb. 1917): 127.

[113] Quoted in Laffan, *The Resurrection of Ireland*, 192–93.

[114] Townshend, *Easter 1916*, 191.

[115] Ibid.

[116] Ibid., 251.

[117] Foy and Barton, *Easter Rising*, 93; and Hughes, *Michael Mallin*, 148.

[118] C. de Markievicz, "Our Faith," *Workers' Republic*, April 27, 1916, 8.

Each Comrade would follow his pal to Hell
Fulfilling friendships' demands
So we're waiting till "Somebody" gives us the word
That send[s] us to Freedom or death;
As freemen defiant we'd sooner fall
Than be slaves to our dying breath.

On Sunday morning, news came that Pearse and Connolly had signed the surrender. Pearse's nurse, Elizabeth O'Farrell, arrived at the College of Surgeons in the company of Major de Courcey Wheeler of the British Army. Mallin was upstairs resting, so Markievicz was the first to see the order. She was, O'Farrell remembered, "very much surprised."[119] This is very different from Frank Robbins's recollection that the college was suffused in an "atmosphere of gloom."[120] After waking Mallin in order to consult him privately, Markievicz accepted the instructions for surrender. Rosie Hackett recalled seeing her soon afterward:

[She was] sitting on the stairs with her head in her hands. She was very worried but did not say anything. I just passed in as usual, and she only looked at me, but I knew that there was something wrong. Mr Mallin went round, shaking hands with all of us. I was coming down the stairs when I met him. He took my hand and did not speak. He was terribly pale.[121]

Despite resistance from the rank-and-file of the ICA, Mallin was intent that they obey the orders of Connolly, their commanding officer, and Markievicz agreed. She was nonetheless shocked by the turn of events and kept repeating, "I trust Connolly, I trust Connolly."[122]

The *Irish Times* gave a sensational account of the evacuated College of Surgeons in which the anatomy room, which the rebels had converted into a makeshift mortuary, was depicted as a gothic tableau: "Slabs for bodies being made of old House of Lords benches removed from the Examination Hall. A rude crucifix, composed of black metal coffin breastplates, the central plate bearing the letters 'R.I.P.,' was affixed to the wall."[123] The newspaper took particular delight in mocking Markievicz, describing the caretakers' quarters—"It was here that Countess Markievicz slept"—in extensive detail,

[119] Foy and Barton, *Easter Rising*, 94.
[120] Townshend, *Easter 1916*, 251.
[121] Foy and Barton, *Easter Rising*, 94.
[122] Ibid., 95.
[123] "Inside the Royal College of Surgeons: After the Rebels Left," *Weekly Irish Times*, May 20, 1916, 11.

including the remnants of the sickly sweets, smuggled from Jacob's, that had nourished the ICA in the absence of proper food: "she and the others seem to have had a partiality for chocolates and other similar articles, many broken packages of sweetstuffs being left behind."[124] In the Saturday edition of the *Irish Times*, a Mrs. Nelson offered reflections on Markievicz's character: "connected with some of the noblest families in England, she appears to have cut herself completely adrift and to have consorted with a class of persons of a kind very different from those with which she was associated in early youth." Then again, Nelson insisted, Markievicz had never been quite normal: "always a constant source of trouble and anxiety to her people owing to her eccentricity . . . always peculiar about her religion and was a student of occult science. In her early youth she went in for spirit-rapping and table turning, and later is said to have had a room for her spiritual exercises, the shelves of which contained many human skulls."[125] The discovery of the mortuary in the college appeared to confirm such caricatures, which were compounded by Markievicz's theatrical sensibilities.

Although there were some female combatants in the ICA, such as Rosie Hackett, who was stationed with Markievicz in the College of Surgeons, most women worked as couriers during the Rising, carrying communications and supplies between the various posts and administering first aid. Although the women of Cumann na mBan were not officially armed by the organization, some carried weapons, and there are reports that women in some of the garrisons relieved snipers and loaded rifles.[126] In the same diary entry in which Geraldine Fitzgerald records Markievicz's shooting of Michael Lahiff, she notes seeing a woman at St. Stephen's Green hold up a milk cart: she "ran out, pointed a bayonet at them and compelled them to give her one of the cans which she took into the Park and returned to them empty."[127] However, the overall lack of visibility of women in the fight served to increase Markievicz's celebrity. The former Anglo-Irish debutante, actress, and artist was caricatured as having undergone a drastic transformation. The *Daily Mail* and the *Irish Times* depicted her appearing to surrender looking like an overgrown leprechaun, "dressed entirely in green, including green shoes. She walked up to the officer, and, saluting, took out her revolver, which she kissed affectionately, and then handed it up."[128] This image captivated the public imagination. When Lady Gregory visited Dublin in the autumn, she

---

[124] Ibid.
[125] "[. . .] Work in Ireland," *Irish Times*, April 29, 1916, 9.
[126] McCarthy, *Cumann na mBan*, 64.
[127] NA, WO 35/207.
[128] "Surrender of the Countess Markievicz," *Irish Times*, May 2, 1916, 3.

remarked, "Dublin cynicism has passed away and was inventing beautiful, instead of derisive, fables. They told me that Madame Markiewicz had kissed her revolver."[129]

With astonishing insouciance, de Courcey Wheeler offered Markievicz a lift to the barracks in his car. She refused and insisted on accompanying Mallin and the rank-and-file. As de Courcey Wheeler later reported at Markievicz's court martial, she "said she preferred to march with her men as she was second in command."[130] Pelted with cries of "shoot the traitors" and "bayonet the bastards," what remained of Mallin's garrison marched the five kilometers westward to Inchicore. Along the way, he and Markievicz debated whether they would be shot or hanged.[131]

---

[129] Smythe, ed. *Seventy Years*, 549.
[130] NA, HO 144/1580/316818 (16).
[131] Foy and Barton, *Easter Rising*, 96.

11

===

War and Family Life

MARKIEVICZ'S ROLE IN THE RISING—AND HER FATE AFTER-ward—were the subject of international gossip, from the United States to Russia. In Dublin, Diarmid Coffey's mother, Jane, recorded hearing "all kinds of rumours, of Germans having organized this, of its being mainly the Citizen Army, Connolly & Con Markiewicz, of both of them being shot, & those that are taken prisoner [that] Con fired the first shot & killed a policeman."[1] For a while it was widely believed that Markievicz was being held prisoner in Dublin Castle. In fact, she was at Richmond Barracks, which was used as a "clearing house" for the men and women who were taken into custody in Dublin and other parts of the country.[2] Nearly 3,500 men and 79 women were arrested after the Rising, but owing to anxieties that blanket detention would increase disaffection, 1,500 men were released almost immediately.[3] Most of the women were also let go, dismissed by General Sir John Maxwell as "silly little girls" who had been enamored with the glamor of the battle or so crazed by poverty they had not known what they were doing. The blanket arrests led even the *Freeman's Journal*, a strong antagonist to Sinn Féin, to criticize the British military's actions to the extent that the newspaper was threatened under the Defence of the Realm Act.[4]

What to do with the prisoners was a matter of intense debate between the British War Office, the Home Office, and the British government in Ireland.

[1] Account of the Rising by Jane Coffey (April 27, 1916), Coffey/Trench Papers, NLI, MS 46,315/4.
[2] Murphy, *Political Imprisonment*, 56; Townshend, *Easter 1916*, 275.
[3] Townshend, *Easter 1916*, 275–76.
[4] Ibid., 276.

A central question, and one that would be key to Markievicz's treatment during this and subsequent imprisonments, was how to deal with Irish people who were—in spite of their own ambitions—British citizens.[5] Despite reservations that elements of the Defense of the Realm Regulations risked violating civil liberties, it was determined that Sinn Féin's connections with Germany, through the gunrunning at Howth, Casement's failed arms-landing, and the reference to "our gallant allies in Europe" in the Proclamation of the Republic were enough to classify the rebels as having "hostile origins or associations."[6] Disregarding the British government's advice not to deal with the prisoners under martial law, Maxwell tried the leaders of the Rising, or those he believed to be in positions of leadership, by courts martial.[7] Eight men were executed in just three days. These included four signatories of the proclamation, Patrick Pearse, Tom Clarke, Thomas MacDonagh, and Joseph Plunkett, but also MacDonagh's vice-commandant, Maud Gonne's estranged husband John MacBride; twenty-five-year-old Fianna veteran and commandant of the Dublin First Battalion, Ned Daly; MacDonagh's second-in-command, Michael Hanrahan; and Willie Pearse, aide-de-camp to his brother, Patrick, at the GPO. The rapidity of the executions and the questionable execution of Willie Pearse prompted strong cautions from the British prime minister, Herbert Henry Asquith, that large-scale executions would only increase disaffection and "sow the seeds of lasting trouble in Ireland."[8]

Nevertheless, the killings proceeded apace, demonstrating, as Townshend has argued, "how completely the civil government in Ireland had been superseded by the military."[9] Constance Markievicz, the only woman to face court martial, fully expected to receive the death penalty. However, before her trial, Asquith told Maxwell explicitly that "no sentence of death on any woman, including Countess Markievitz should be confirmed and carried out without reference to the Field-Marshal Commanding in Chief and himself."[10] Markievicz and her friend in the Fianna Con Colbert were among thirty-six prisoners to be tried on May 4, with Michael Mallin following on May 5, and James Connolly—who was taken from hospital to the barracks

---

[5] Ibid., 278.

[6] Ibid., 277–78.

[7] Ibid., 278.

[8] Willie Pearse's death sentence was based on hearsay evidence from an officer from the Inniskilling Fusiliers who was held captive in the GPO and testified, "I know that William Pearce was an officer but do not know his rank." Ibid., 280, 282.

[9] Ibid., 281.

[10] Quoted in ibid., 279.

for court martial—on May 6.[11] The prisoners faced a "Preliminary Examination" by the military, which Markievicz thought "was in reality a dress rehearsal for the soldiers." A statement from Piaras Béaslaí, Ned Daly's vice-commandant, confirms that the first examination was "the frame up."[12] This preliminary trial may have been an interpretation of the *Manual of Military Law*, which governed field general courts martial, which "stipulated that the accused must be present when the summary evidence was being taken from prosecution witnesses after he [the accused] was remanded—in order to give him 'notice of the charge he will meet' at his trial."[13] Under the field general courts martial, the accused did not automatically have the right to legal counsel, and legal counsel was denied to the accused during the trial.[14]

Markievicz claimed that during the preliminary examination, she was given the opportunity to respond to two testimonies. She agreed that the first, by de Courcey Wheeler to whom she surrendered, was "the truth." The second testimony, by a pageboy at the University Club who maintained that he saw her fire a shot into the second-floor window of the club, was false. Markievicz argued that if the boy had been standing where he claimed, then he would not have been able to see the clock to know the exact time of day (since he did not possess a watch), nor would he have been able to see the bullet strike the building. After presenting this rebuttal, she was sent outside to wait for an hour in a car before she was brought back into the barracks for the official court martial. The boy testified again, eliminating the discrepancies that Markievicz had identified in his statement.[15] During the official court martial, she was not allowed to comment on discrepancies between the "two trials," which limited the effectiveness of her cross-examination. She wrote, "I had done nothing I was ashamed of but that little liar made me sick. No notice was taken of this. I said it various times."[16]

All the leaders of the Rising, including Markievicz, were charged with taking part "in an armed rebellion and in the waging of war against His Majesty the King," which was "calculated to be prejudicial to the Defence of the Realm and being done with the intention and for the purpose of assisting the enemy." When the charge was read out, Markievicz interjected, "Do you mean the Germans? I didn't help them for I couldn't." The officers were so surprised by her candor that they agreed her plea could be listed as

[11] Ibid.
[12] Court Martial Proceedings, "Constance Markievicz's Statement," PRONI, D4131/K/4 (1).
[13] Barton, *Secret Court Martial Records*, 36.
[14] Ibid., 46.
[15] NA, HO 144/1580 /316818 (16).
[16] Court Martial Proceedings, "Constance Markievicz's Statement," PRONI, D4131/K/4 (1).

"not guilty," although she did not dispute her role in the Rising.[17] Connolly, MacDermott, Mallin, and Markievicz faced an additional charge of attempting "to cause disaffection among the civilian population."[18] She was the only person to be convicted on this offense, to which she pled guilty with typical swagger: "I always talked sedition." The account of her statements and behavior in this copy of the Court Martial Proceedings, held in the Public Record Office of Northern Ireland, differ substantially from the Home Office's official record of the trial, which states that she concluded her defense by saying, "I went out to fight for Ireland's freedom and it doesn't matter what happens to me. I did what I thought was right and I stand by it."[19]

The Court Martial Proceedings in PRONI and the Home Office records differ not only from each other but also from a famous account given of Markievicz's court martial by W. E. Wylie, a king's counsel and member of the Territorial Army who served in the Trinity College Officer Training Corps during the Rising. Wylie was appointed assistant provost-marshal during the Rising and assisted with administering the surrender and with guarding and sorting prisoners, and he prosecuted at the courts martial.[20] His attitude toward female prisoners prior to the courts martial smacks of machismo; he referred to them as "the girls" and wrote, "I chased them all off home except the four [Madeleine Ffrench Mullen, Kathleen Lynn, Helena Molony, and Winifred Carney] and often wondered what happened to them afterwards or did any of them remember the gallant Second Lieutenant."[21] This attitude certainly influenced his account of Markievicz's behavior, which is unquestioningly quoted by the historian León Ó Broin, who writes that the military officials

> quite expected [that Markievicz] would make a scene and throw things at the judge and counsel. "In fact," said Wylie, "I saw the General getting out his revolver and putting it on the table beside him. But he needn't have troubled, for she curled up completely. 'I am only a woman,' she cried, 'and you cannot shoot a woman. You must not shoot a woman.' She never stopped moaning the whole time she was in the courtroom. . . . I think we all felt slightly disgusted," Wylie declared. "She had been preaching to a lot of silly boys, death and glory,

[17] Ibid.

[18] NA, HO 144/1580 /316818 (16). Foy and Barton state that only Connolly, MacDermott, and Mallin faced this charge.

[19] Ibid.

[20] Ó Broin, *W. E. Wylie.*

[21] Quoted in ibid., 36.

Leabharlanna Poiblí Chathair Bhaile Átha Cliath

die for your country, etc., and yet she was literally crawling. I won't say any more, it revolts me still."[22]

This account exhibits the resentment that many British officials held toward Markievicz. In an inquiry into the rebellion at the end of May, the head of the Dublin Metropolitan Police remarked that it was "a serious state of affairs to have the peace of the city endangered by a gang of roughs with rifles and bayonets at large at that time of night, with a female like the Countess Markievicz in charge."[23] Similarly—even before the court martial—General Maxwell expressed his belief that she was "blood guilty and dangerous . . . a woman who has forfeited the privileges of her sex," and so did the viceroy, Lord French, who wrote to Maxwell, "Personally I agree with you—she ought to be shot."[24]

Rumors about Markievicz's supposedly indecorous and cowardly behavior circulated among the Dublin elite. The daughter of the provost of Trinity College, Elsie Mahaffy, repeated it in her diary: "She utterly broke down, cried and sobbed and tried to incite pity in General Blackaddar [*recte* Maxwell]: it was a terrible scene—the gaunt wreck of a once lovely lady."[25] This image was an attractive one for a political elite who believed that Markievicz had betrayed the values of her class; one could not be a revolutionary *and* a lady.

Not all the leaders of the Rising exhibited the resolve that Markievicz expressed during her trial. Michael Mallin disavowed the part he played in the Rising and offered incriminating evidence about Markievicz's role:

> I had no command in the Citizen Army. I was never taken into the confidence of James Connolly. I was under the impression that we were going out for manoeuvres on Sunday, but something altered the arrangement and the manoeuvres were postponed till Monday. I had verbal instruction from James Connolly to take 36 men to St Stephen's Green and to report to the Volunteer officer there. Shortly after my arrival at St Stephen's Green, the firing started and the Countess of Markievicz [*sic*] ordered me to take command of the men. As I had been so long associated with them, I felt I could not leave them and from that

---

[22] Ibid., 27. In his history of the court martial proceedings, Barton describes Wylie's account as "patently inaccurate"and that it "reflected deep-rooted sexual prejudice and rank misogyny"; Townshend quibbles that Wylie's "motive is obscure"; see Townshend, *Easter 1916*, 286; and Barton, *Secret Court Martial Records*, 97–99.

[23] "Rebellion Inquiry," *Irish Times*, May 26, 1916, 7.

[24] Foy and Barton, *Easter Rising*, 325.

[25] Quoted in Townshend, *Easter 1916*, 286.

time I joined the rebellion. I made it my business to save all the officers and civilians who were brought into Stephen's Green. I have explicit orders to the men to make no offensive movement. I prevented them attacking the Shelbourne Hotel.[26]

Mallin was one of just three people who called witnesses in their defense during the courts martial; the others were John MacBride and Éamon Ceannt.[27] Markievicz refused to call a witness because she believed that it would endanger her comrades. It is unlikely that she ever discovered Mallin's betrayal, but if she did, his statement did not lessen her affection for him. At his execution, she would be wrought with concern for his widow, and long after the Rising, she would wear Mallin's cast-off Citizen Army uniform.

Verdicts were not presented at courts martial but were read out to each prisoner once he or she was interned in Kilmainham Gaol. There, Markievicz learned she had been sentenced to "death by being shot," but the court recommended "the prisoner to mercy solely & only on account of her sex." That her sex would preclude her from sharing the fate of her comrades was a biting insult to all that she had fought for, and would continue to fight for, over the next decade. It was not clear to Constance's friends and family that her sentence was commuted. Eva, in England and eager for news, half-wished that a British tabloid's erroneous report that Markievicz's dead body had been found in Stephen's Green were true: "so much worse does it seem to the human mind to be executed coldly & deliberately at a certain hour by the clock, than to be killed in the hurry and excitement of battle."[28] George Russell wrote to Eva coldly expressing his hope that the British would impart penal servitude instead: "My heart is too heavy to write more."[29] He wrote again, afraid that he had appeared "inhuman": "This is a terrible time for you and all Constances friends. I have friends shot on both side[s], and Dublin will never be the same again to me."[30]

Over one thousand people were killed or severely wounded in the Rising, but Markievicz expressed no regrets. She later said, "If we failed to win, so did the English."[31] Her resolve was strengthened by her imprisonment after

---

[26] Foy and Barton, *Easter Rising*, 299; and Barton, *Secret Court Martial Records*, 278. Only the last of these statements is true, since after Skinnider was wounded in a trial bombing run, Mallin refused to permit an attempt to bomb the Shelbourne.

[27] Foy and Barton, *Easter Rising*, 297.

[28] Holograph account by Eva Gore-Booth of visit to Dublin after Easter Rising; Newspaper Cuttings Book, NLI, MS 21,815; CA/BV/1 (1).

[29] George Russell to Eva Gore Booth (May 6, 1916), PRONI, D/4131/L/12.

[30] Ibid. ([Wednesday] 1916).

[31] "Women in the Fight," 125.

the Rising. Kilmainham Gaol had been closed in 1911 but hastily reopened as a military prison when the world war broke out. It was a dark place. Tom Clarke's widow, Kathleen, remembered the smell of damp and the faint, eerie light emitted by candles stuck inside jam jars.[32] Most of the cells had no furniture, so the prisoners slept on sacks or ground sheets that were laid on the floor; slop buckets served as latrines, and the inmates were poorly fed. Ned Daly's family remembered seeing him curled up in his cell, reduced to eating dog biscuits.[33] Prisoners were moved frequently between cells; those whose death sentences were confirmed by Maxwell were transferred to the "condemned wing," on the upper floor that was the coldest, darkest, and oldest part of the jail. Although Markievicz's sentence was commuted, she was held in this wing, in a cell directly across the corridor from Michael Mallin's. She had one window of about one foot square, set high on the wall; it gave little light, even on a bright day. Copper piping ran across the back wall and passed under the window, so if she stood on the pipes, she could see into the bleak gravel yard that was adjacent to the stonebreaker's yard where the executions were carried out.

She was visited regularly by the Capuchin friar Fr. Albert Bibby, who brought great comfort to many of the rebels imprisoned in Kilmainham.[34] Markievicz wrote lines of poetry, aphorisms, and impressions on scraps of brown paper, which Bibby smuggled out and copied into a notebook before sending the originals to Eva in London.[35] Among these are lines from the play *Cathleen ni Houlihan* about the necessity of self-sacrifice, and attempts to justify and explain the deaths of her friends: "They gave themselves, they gave their all / This Vision in their eyes; / Nations live on though Empires fall / The future never dies, The future lives for Ireland now / Take it, we know you can— / I was born mid death and sacrifice / Through pain Life comes to men."[36] Of the eight pages that Bibby filled with her writing, only one quatrain gives a hint of anything less than optimism: "the world is staggered / Ireland reels back from the blow / with face grown pale & haggard / she faces her coward foe," but the poem then turns to an image of a proud nation and men whose God-given duty was to die for Ireland. Several of the

---

[32] Foy and Barton, *Easter Rising*, 307.

[33] Ibid.

[34] Bibby, from County Carlow, was a professor of philosophy and theology, a supporter of temperance, and fluent in the Irish language, and he became an important contact for Republicans during the Irish Civil War.

[35] "Copybook of the Writings of Countess Markievicz Whilst Imprisoned in Kilmainham Jail, May 1916," Lissadell Collection.

[36] Ibid.

poems convey her faith that the sun continues to shine outside, that summer commences, despite the "twilight in my dreary cell / so ugly, cold & bare. / a chilly twilight, towards the opaque windows stare // I put my eyes against the pane / a drab grey wall appears / Riddled with windows, just like mine / Entombing hopes & fears."[37]

She could see little, but the sounds were haunting. In a letter to Roger Casement's cousin, Gertrude Bannister, Markievicz described lying awake at daybreak each morning, listening "to the English murdering our leaders," clinging to a crucifix that was given to her by Bibby.[38] Families of the condemned men were permitted to visit the night before their execution, and she would have been able to hear their voices echoing through the corridor. Mallin and Colbert were executed on Monday, May 8. Both had grown even more mentally fragile in the days following their trials. Mallin, for example, demanded that his wife remain a widow for the rest of her life and that of their four children, two join the church and two follow in his footsteps, and that their unborn child be named after himself or named Mary for the mother of Jesus.[39] Under extreme stress, Markievicz's state of mind also became unstable. Although these cracks would appear later and beneath the surface, detectable only in her correspondence with Eva, the executions would have profound reverberations. The condemned men were led down the corridor to the entrance of the prison yard, where a white piece of paper was pinned above their hearts. They were blindfolded and their hands bound behind their backs before they were led into the stonebreaker's yard, which was farthest from the prison walls, where the firing squad stood.

Mercifully, Markievicz was transferred to Dublin's Mountjoy Prison before Connolly's execution. Eva, on her way to Ireland, worried how Connolly's death would affect Constance: "They have shot all her friends. . . . Did she know? Should I have to tell her?"[40] In fact, "She knew everything." Eva found Constance "calm and smiling"; "She talked very fast . . . asked a great many questions, and seemed only really puzzled by one thing. "Why on earth did they shoot Skeffy?"" Francis Sheehy Skeffington, a feminist and critic of the militarization of the Irish Volunteers, who had upheld the merits of pacifism in a debate with Markievicz about the First World War, had been arrested and taken to Portobello Barracks, where he was shot under orders

<hr/>

[37] Ibid.

[38] Constance Markievicz to Gertrude Bannister (n.d.), NLI, MS 13075 (1). Piaras Beaslai also remembered being awakened by shooting at daybreak; See Foy and Barton, *Easter Rising*, 308. When Markievicz was released from prison, she gave the crucifix to Bannister.

[39] Foy and Barton, *Easter Rising*, 314.

[40] Holograph account by Eva Gore-Booth of visit to Dublin.

from Captain J. C. Bowen Colthurst, who had a long career serving with the Irish Rifles in Dublin.[41] Colthurst mistakenly believed Sheehy Skeffington to be a "ringleader," when in fact he had been printing and distributing anti-looting leaflets and had attracted a small crowd because he was a well-known public persona. The shooting was a "slow-burning public relations disaster for the army" and was incomprehensible to the Dublin public, as well as to his friends.[42] Constance insisted, "He didn't believe in fighting," and implored, "What did it mean?" Sheehy-Skeffington's death was senseless, while the deaths of other friends—Colbert, Mallin, and Connolly—Markievicz understood to be part of the anti-imperialist struggle. She explained to Eva that Mallin had been compelled to take up arms "against England" after meeting Irishmen in South Africa.[43]

The sisters were permitted just twenty minutes to visit and on saying good-bye were separated for four months. Markievicz drew her strength from putting her affairs in order. As a convict, she lost all rights to property. Since Casimir's whereabouts were unknown—he was believed to have been "invalided from wounds" in the Carpathians—all her assets were passed to her brother Josslyn.[44] In a rambling letter to Josslyn at Lissadell, Constance vacillated between practicalities and idealism. Of principal concern to her was the return of her set of false teeth; although, she quipped, "I expect they would make no difference here, as I can duly eat slops." She expected, quite unreasonably, that Josslyn would have the inclination to help her locate cards that she had painted to sell as a fundraiser at the Sinn Féin convention. Percy Reynolds, a boy in the Fianna, had been looking after "the business part," but "he was arrested I know, for he was with us [at the College of Surgeons] at the end, but he was only a lad & a favourite in the Volunteers so he may be out & he may have seen about them."[45] She naively, perhaps maniacally, imagined

---

[41] For a thorough discussion of Sheehy Skeffington's arrest and execution, see Townshend, *Easter 1916*, 192–95; the degree of Sheehy Skeffington's pacifism has been interrogated; see O'Ceallaigh Ritschel, "Shaw, Connolly, and the Irish Citizen Army," 123–24.

[42] See Townshend, *Easter 1916*, 195. Diarmid Coffey recorded in his diary the "contradictory reports of why Sheehy Skeffington was shot, one that he made a speech against the British Empire the other that he was caught urging a Volunteer to shoot a soldier. The former the more likely"; "Account of the Rising by D. Coffey" (April 28, 1916), Coffey/Trench Papers, NLI, MS 46,315/4.

[43] Holograph account by Eva Gore-Booth of visit to Dublin. Although Mallin claimed never to have fought against fellow Irishmen in the Boer War, he served in India and South Africa; Barton, *Secret Court Martial Records*, 273; Laffan notes that comparisons between the Easter Rising and the Boer Revolt were almost immediate, with Britain's restrained response to the South Africa rising held up in stark contrast to the executions in Dublin; see *Resurrection of Ireland*, 51.

[44] Herbert Samuel to Chief Secretary's Office, NA, HO 144/1580/316818.

[45] Constance Markievicz to Josslyn Gore-Booth (June 22, 1916), PRONI D/4131/K/6A.

that she would "have heaps of money rolling in" from various investments and demanded of Josslyn, "*It must be invested in Ireland.*"

Josslyn turned his attention to Constance's most important asset, Surrey House. Susan Mitchell reported to him that it had "literally been sacked, furniture smashed & flung about, litter everywhere," the detritus of British soldiers' occupancy.[46] Several paintings had been left behind, including Casimir's triptych *Bread*, which George Russell valued at £50. The big portraits were worth much less (about £17), and the remaining paintings were worth a demeaning £4 each, which may suggest that the artist was Constance rather than Casimir.[47] Constance insisted that Josslyn should try to get everything back, including confiscated papers, assuring him disingenuously, "There was not a scrap of paper that had anything to say to a rebellion in it or even political. Some of Casi's letters, & the unfinished act of a Society play—a few poems. Nothing except personal things some photos, lace & scarves & flowers—just a few things I valued."[48]

Her thoughts turned frequently to her family, especially to Maeve, who was living with Constance's mother at Ardeevin near Lissadell. Constance wanted desperately to see her daughter but thought that she was too young to visit a prison, so she asked instead for a photograph of her to hang in her cell. She was also concerned for Casimir and Stanislaus and asked Josslyn to contact them: "I don't suppose any account of the rebellion was allowed into Russia & he & Stas wont know what has happened to me." She suggested that Josslyn only risk "one very vague *registered* letter" in order to evade the censor; "I believe very few of my letters ever got to him. I hardly ever heard from him." She thought the best way to get through might be for Josslyn to "shell him" with postcards and only write on one that Constance was "all right but unable to write & send my love."[49]

Despite their long separation, Maeve had kept in touch with her stepbrother and sent Josslyn Stanislaus's address at the Agency for the Russian Volunteer Fleet in Archangel.[50] Josslyn immediately received a reply from him, grateful for "some news of poor mother."[51] Like all the Gore-Booths except for Eva, Stanislaus regarded the Easter Rising as a "sad, stupid business," but he "suppose[d] it's no use crying over spilt-milk . . . it's a blessing that she cannot get into more trouble." Josslyn advised Stanislaus to contact Eva for

[46] Susan Mitchell to Josslyn Gore-Booth (June 28, 1916), ibid.
[47] Ibid. (Aug. 21, 1916).
[48] Constance Markievicz to Josslyn Gore-Booth (Oct. 17, 1916), PRONI, D/4131/K/5 (4).
[49] Ibid. (June 22, 1916), PRONI, D/4131/K/6A.
[50] Maeve Markievicz to Josslyn Gore-Booth (July 4, 1916), PRONI, D/4131/K/14.
[51] "Staskow" to Josslyn Gore-Booth (Aug. 17–30, 1916), PRONI, D/4131/K/13 (1).

further information on Constance, and he asked Stanislaus to pass on his best wishes to Casimir.[52]

It took six weeks for one of Josslyn's postcards to Casimir to reach him in Kiev. His reply was polite and cautious. Wary of the censor, he only briefly expressed his concern over "the sad events of the spring" and his pleasure at hearing that "Constance is well."[53] He asked for news of the whole family—Maeve and "Gaga," Molly and the children—and hoped that he might be permitted to write to Constance directly. Casimir's own health was not good: "typhus and effects of the shell bursting at very close distance have done their work & I am suffering from very severe headache & haven't yet recovered the use of my left arm." Despite the injury, Casimir had been able to return to portraiture, and he was also working again in the theater.

Kiev had a lively international theater scene. In 1916 the Polish- and German-language theaters were far more experimental than their Russian-language counterparts. Although Casimir had identified as a Russian artist in Paris—despite the strong reputation of modern Polish painters in the city—in Kiev, he joined the New Polish Theatre, which was using new acting and directing methods inspired by the radical advances of the Russian symbolist Nicolai Evreinov and the Austrian Max Reinhardt, who managed the Deutsches Theatre in Berlin.[54] Once again among the artistic avant-garde, Casimir lived in an apartment in the fashionable Khreshchatyk Boulevard and had a studio opposite the new Kiev Conservatory.[55] He boasted to Josslyn about his commissions for portraits but studiously avoided any discussion of the debts that he had left behind in Dublin.

The joy of hearing from Casimir was quickly tarnished by his financial irresponsibility. Constance told Josslyn that she had kept the creditors at bay for three years, but in prison there was no escaping them: "This is all rather like living to see yourself dead & your business all being wound up & 'Amen' being said."[56] The censors prevented Constance and Casimir from writing directly to each other.[57] In light of her indignation, this was probably a blessing. She told Josslyn that now that they had ascertained Casimir's whereabouts, Josslyn could "send *him* the receipt" for bills paid on his behalf: eighteen

[52] (Draft) Josslyn Gore-Booth to Staskow, ibid. (2).

[53] Copy, Casimir Markievicz to Josslyn Gore-Booth (Sept. 13, 1916), PRONI, D/4131/K/12. Casimir's address was Kreszezatuk 25 L. 164, spelled elsewhere as Kzeszczatick.

[54] For Reinhardt's technical developments, see Esslin, "Max Reinhardt."

[55] The Kiev Conservatory was founded in 1913 and renamed the P. Tchaikovsky National Music Academy of Ukraine. The building was destroyed in the Second World War and rebuilt in 1955.

[56] Constance Markievicz to Josslyn Gore-Booth (Oct. 17, 1916), PRONI, D/4131/K/5 (4).

[57] For the difficulty of Casimir and Constance's correspondence reaching each other, see Esther Roper to Josslyn Gore-Booth (Sept. 28, 1916), PRONI, D/4131/K/6A.

shillings owed for frames and mounts, over a pound to the wine merchants, and more than six shillings to Henry Lyons for a new suit and hat.[58] These debts had to be covered by Josslyn. Constance had sunk all her money into the Fianna and Liberty Hall, and just one of her remaining investments was showing a return: a little over a pound a year in dividends from her shares in the Cavan & Leitrim railway.[59] She apologized: "I always wished Casi had been a financial expert who would have seen [to] the house & given me so much a week pocket money. Anyhow here I have no expenses."[60]

Under the direction of General Maxwell, Markievicz was transferred from Mountjoy to Aylesbury Jail in England, in an attempt to prevent information about her being leaked. Maxwell suspected that the visiting justices to Mountjoy, who had been elected by Dublin Corporation, had "Sinn Fein sympathies," but in fact it was Eva who had been smuggling messages to Constance's friends outside.[61] In his own way, Josslyn was also working on Constance's behalf. He lobbied his friends to insist on Constance's exoneration, but he found little sympathy. Their mother, Georgina Gore-Booth, wrote blithely from Maltby Hall in Yorkshire, where she was visiting friends: "I'm sorry Con has gone to England—so much more lonely for her. This is quite a nice little place if it wasn't for coal fires—Mordaunt very busy in his garden planning out vegetables etc."[62] Some of the Gore-Booths' acquaintances even wrote to the commander of forces in Ireland, General Friend, to say that Markievicz should be kept locked up; one family friend judged, "It would be an appalling calamity if she got loose."[63] Despite the rest of their family's indifference, Eva encouraged Josslyn to continue to support Constance's case and to consider her actions as no "different to what soldiers get praised for & called heroes for."[64] Even so, he was plagued by the rumors that Constance had shot a policeman in cold blood. Eva attempted to pacify him by

---

[58] PRONI D/4131/K/12.

[59] Ibid.

[60] Constance Markievicz to Josslyn Gore-Booth (Oct. 17, 1916), PRONI, D/4131/K/5 (4).

[61] NA, HO 144/1580/316818 (3); and E. W. Sharp to the Governor (Sept. 6, 1916), NA, HO 144/1580/316818 (9).

[62] Lady Gore-Booth to Josslyn Gore-Booth (n.d. [received Aug. 20, 1916]), PRONI, D/4131/K/6A.

[63] G Ball to [General Friend] (Aug. 1, 1916), PRONI D/4131/K/5/1. By contrast, J. F. Cunningham, a barrister in London and member of the Irish Literary Society, misguidedly believed that releasing "this lady" would be "acknowledged throughout Ireland as an act of leniency and good will" and that it would increase recruiting and help to fill "the gaps in the Irish Divisions at the [western] front." He argued that "the Countess is not a bit more crazy than Annie Kenny, or Mrs Pankhurst." NA, WO 35/207.

[64] Eva Gore-Booth to Josslyn Gore-Booth (n.d. [received Nov. 23, 1916]), PRONI, D/4131/K/5 (13).

recounting how Constance had "volunteered" the story of holding "a revolver at a policeman's chest but [she] *could* not shoot when it came to the point" because "she recognised him & had known him before," and another occasion when she may have "hit one in the arm as he jumped."[65] Eva found the stories, and Josslyn's attitude, exasperating: "Really the worst crime they seemed to have proved against her was that she shot a *brick* at the Shelbourne! And I don't suppose the Brick is the much worse for it!"[66]

By Christmas 1916 Josslyn and Eva began to give up hope that the British government would ever consent to Constance's release, so they lobbied instead for her better treatment. Markievicz had been granted visitation rights and could write and receive correspondence. However, because she had been sentenced to life imprisonment, she was held in a different part of the prison than her comrades who had also been sent to Aylesbury: Winifred Carney, Helena Molony, and Ellen O'Ryan. O'Ryan was released in September 1916, and Carney and Molony were released at Christmas 1916.[67] While the other women were allowed to associate with one another, Markievicz was held separately, and after December 1916 she was alone. As the only political prisoner left at Aylesbury, she had no hope of availing of the right of association that was granted to male prisoners from the Rising.[68] The loneliness taxed her physical health. Always thin, when she was transferred from Kilmainham to Mountjoy on May 7, she weighed 136 pounds; after a month in Aylesbury, that fell to 120 pounds.[69] In the first weeks her letters maintained the chirpy banter for which she had been known in the worst days at the College of Surgeons:

> Send my love to all my friends in the Transport Union & the Co-op. Tell them I'm often with them in spirit and have nothing but pleasant happy busy memories of them. . . . Don't worry about me. I am quite happy & it is in nobody's power to make me unhappy. I am not afraid either of the future or of myself. You know well how little comforts or luxuries ever mattered to me. So at the worst I am only bored.[70]

---

[65] Ibid.

[66] Ibid. (n.d. [received Dec. 24, 1916]) (16).

[67] Matthews, *Renegades*, 157.

[68] Murphy notes that Markievicz was held at Mountjoy longer than her male counterparts and that her sex (while saving her life) was a "disadvantage" at Aylesbury; see *Political Imprisonment*, 62–63.

[69] Report of Prison Commission, encl. copy of weights; NA, HO 144/1580/316818 (16).

[70] Esther Roper (copy), Constance Markievicz to Eva Gore-Booth (Sept. 15, 1916), PRONI, D/4131/K/9 (126).

She longed for views of the Dublin Mountains: "The soft twilights & the harvest moon or cornfields. I must write a poem about cornfields."[71]

Markievicz's conversion to Catholicism was manifested in her drawings and in the language she used to frame her thoughts. In one letter, she quoted lines from Yeats and Gregory's play, *Cathleen ni Houlihan*, remarking that it "was a sort of gospel to me."[72] On one of Eva's visits, the prison matron overheard Constance tell her sister to give Marie Perolz one of her dresses—probably the one worn to Limerick—because it was "Elijah's Mantle."[73] In these early days at Aylesbury, it may have been easier for Markievicz to see herself as taken up, denied execution but nonetheless gone, with only a few garments and paintings left behind for "all rebels & felons, comrades & friends" to whom she sent her love.[74]

Surprisingly, Constance, Eva, and Esther (who often visited too) were allowed to talk about politics, but this seeming permissiveness actually enabled the prison matron to record their conversations. They mostly reminisced about old friends, including the society hostess Lady Ottoline Morrell and the Annesleys of Castlewellen Castle.[75] Constance's political allegiances had estranged her from most of the family, but Eva empathized with Constance's militant republicanism, though she refused to share it. She thought that Constance's spirits might be lifted by working on a new project, so she invited her to illustrate her new verse play, *The Death of Fionavar*.

Eva believed that the Easter Rising was a great tragedy, and she rewrote the final acts of her earlier play, *The Triumph of Maeve* (1905), to respond to the event. Her preface was addressed to "Poets, Utopians, bravest of the brave," naming "Pearse and MacDonagh, Plunkett and Connolly, / Dreamers turned fighters but to find a grave." Eva believed that by conceiving of the Rising as a visionary event, Constance ("my own sister") who suffered "wild hours of pain, / Whilst murderous bombs were blotting out the stars" could have her grief transformed into something "sublime." The poem concludes with the wish that Markievicz had "dreamed the gentler dream of Maeve," the high queen who was depicted in Eva's earlier poetry as explicitly

---

[71] Ibid. Poem and ballad writing was also common among male detainees; see Laffan, *Resurrection of Ireland*, 65.

[72] Ibid. Constance attributes the play solely to Yeats, but Gregory and Yeats's co-authorship is now firmly established.

[73] Report form Sharp to Governor (Sept. 6, 1916), NA, HO 144/1580/316818.

[74] Esther Roper (copy), Constance Markievicz to Eva Gore-Booth (Sept. 15, 1916), PRONI, D/4131/K/9 (126).

[75] Constance recalled that she never met the suffragist (and later Labour Party candidate) Clare Annesley but remembered her mother, "very beautiful & I used to love looking at her." Ibid.

pacifist.[76] In *The Death of Fionavar*, Eva imagines a utopian, pacifist future for Constance in her story of Maeve abandoning her kingdoms and possessions "to meditate and live austerely under the hazel boughs in an island on the Shannon," where she finds "the way to her own soul."[77]

Constance illustrated the volume with simple line drawings of Rosicrucian images, Arabian lamps, winged horses, and symbols of transformation, such as a repeated motif of larvae, caterpillars, butterflies, and moths. These images complemented the pacifist, utopian values encoded in Eva's text, but they can also be read as a counternarrative of the Rising as a transformative defeat, changing the very essence of the Irish nation. Images of seagulls also recur in Markievicz's illustrations for *The Death of Fionavar*; these have a private symbolism connected to a poem, "Seagull," that Markievicz wrote in Kilmainham, in which she shares the seagull's ability to fly to another world: "We'll rise on the wind with a joyous leap."[78] These codes were inaccessible, or ignored, by the *Guardian's* reviewer, who used the book as an occasion to disparage Irish separatism and to draw a distinction between Constance and Eva. Markievicz's drawings were described as "breaking out, at every hint of an occasion, into the mystic symbolism and visionary scenes of the Celt; just as Miss Gore-Booth herself is content to set sail for her Celtic faery-lands in ships framed of Saxon vocables to the rule of English rhythm and rhyme."[79] It was hoped, the reviewer commented, that the book would "serve the cause of peace in Ireland" and should "help to convince the English people that the Irish movement was not in essence revolutionary." By contrast, the *New York Times* interpreted the book as "ironical," with illustrations by "the woman with the sword, who with her little band of fighting men helped hold the streets of Dublin for days and nights against the British machine guns."[80]

Despite Eva's hopes, the work on the volume and the time that the sisters spent meditating in order to maintain their psychic connection were not enough to prevent Markievicz's mental health from deteriorating. Malnutrition may have been as much to blame as the trauma and isolation of imprisonment. Markievicz's diet consisted mostly of dry bread with a little rice added for dinner, since she refused to eat the fish that the prisoners were served. Much to the disgust of Rosamond Jacob, Markievicz had never

[76] This was a revision of Maeve's depiction in Irish mythological texts, such as the *Táin Bó Cúailnge*.
[77] Gore-Booth, *The Death of Fionavar*, 15.
[78] "Seagull," a poem by Constance Markievicz written while imprisoned in Kilmainham," Lissadell Collection.
[79] C.H.H., "New Books: 'The Death of Fionavar,'" *Manchester Guardian*, Oct. 9, 1916, 3.
[80] "Irish Rebel Illustrates Nonresistance Play," *New York Times*, Sept. 10, 1916, SF 2.

succumbed to the fashion for vegetarianism that was common among the Dublin avant-garde; rather, she refused to eat the fish because she puzzlingly claimed that it was a "big fish which lived off human bodies."[81] The prison governor would later deny the validity of Markievicz's protests, but in his study of political imprisonment, Murphy notes that internees in other prisons suffered from "wartime conditions"; in Knutsford in Cheshire, internees were driven to eat " 'lime out of the wall,' salt, grass, and dandelion leaves" because of food shortages.[82]

In letters to her mother, Markievicz maintained a stoic disposition—"I am quite well and cheerful so don't worry about me. I am a scullery maid and work much harder than any you ever had, and I write poetry in my spare time."[83] But to Eva and others, she complained of being "starved," "slave driven," and having "to mix with prostitutes & baby-killers it's the atmosphere of a brothel."[84] This is a stark change in attitude to the sympathy with which Markievicz had written in the *Irish Citizen* about Dublin women forced into prostitution by poverty. The volte-face may have been instigated by her mental instability, her sustained proximity to women of a lower class, or her ideas about herself as being of a different caliber of prisoner—political, not criminal. There was also political value in contrasting Irish women, imprisoned for their courage in fighting the empire, with ordinary (English) convicts. Murphy notes that the idea that Irishwomen were degraded by their association with other prisoners became "a common propaganda trope."[85]

Friends of the Gore-Booths and Eva's and Constance's political associates launched a campaign to grant Constance the freedom of association that was enjoyed by the male political prisoners held at other camps in England and Wales.[86] Many of these, including appeals from Jack White (formerly of the ICA) and Louie Bennett from the Irishwomen's International League, referred to the impropriety of a woman of Markievicz's class being held with "the dregs of the population."[87] C. P. Scott, editor of the *Manchester Guardian*, wrote to the new British prime minister, David Lloyd George, to plea for intervention; Scott remarked candidly to Eva, "Why were not steps taken

---

[81] E. D. Sharp to the Governor, Aylesbury Prison (Jan. 27, 1917), NA, HO 144/1580/316818.

[82] Conditions in Wakefield, Wandsworth, and Stafford were also described as "appalling"; Murphy, *Political Imprisonment*, 58.

[83] Sharp to Governor, Aylesbury (Jan. 27, 1917), NA, HO 144/1580/316818.

[84] Susan Mitchell to Josslyn Gore-Booth (Jan. 31, 1917), PRONI, D/4131/K/5 (33).

[85] Murphy, *Political Imprisonment*, 61.

[86] Frongoch, one such camp, was established as a place to house German prisoners of war until the Easter Rising, at which point the German inmates were moved to make room for nearly two thousand Irish internees.

[87] NA, HO 144/1580/316818.

long ago to get your sister out of that ghetto?"[88] Several of the Gore-Booths' friends in the political establishment were afraid to come out publically in support of Markievicz. Novelist Katherine Tynan Hinkson wrote to Eva that she had to be "unnecessarily careful" since her husband was a resident magistrate in Ireland; similarly the Irish peer Lord Muncaster said that he was sad to hear the news about Constance but felt he could be of no use.[89]

Prompted by letters in support of Markievicz, the Home Office inquired into conditions at Aylesbury. The prison governor, S. F. Fox, submitted a report on Markievicz's health in which he stated that she had been given unsweetened tea on her request; when she "lost a few pounds" (nearly ten) in September, it was recommended that she be sent to hospital for extra food, but Markievicz had asked "to continue her kitchen work." Fox claimed that she had never returned food that she had been given, despite complaining of the fish "which fed on human beings" to her visitors. Fox also compiled a report of all the "star class" prisoners with whom Markievicz worked in the kitchens, giving their names, offences, and sentences and noting "Any history of Prostitution."[90] He insisted, "There is no direct evidence of any one of them having been a prostitute though eight have had illegitimate children." Thirteen of the twenty women were imprisoned for "wilful murder," most of whom were incarcerated for "murder of an illegitimate child." The others were committed for various offenses: three for manslaughter, one for "wounding," one for "attempted murder," one for "embezzlement," and one woman, L. Wertheim, for passing "information to enemy." Markievicz's offense was listed as "taking part in Rebellion."[91]

When Irish Party MP Alfie Byrne raised a question in Parliament, the home secretary replied that the government had been informed that Markievicz was in good health and no modification of her treatment was necessary. Even so, Byrne's question helped to raise awareness of Markievicz's condition and instigated further enquiries into her well-being. J. Flemingham, a lawyer at Grays Inn, posed the rather improbable argument that leniency in Markievicz's case would help the recruiting effort and demonstrate the "good intentions of the Government":

> I know she has been tried and sentenced, and all that, but the idea of her being a blood thirsty revolutionist is preposterous. See how she

[88] C. P. Scott to Eva Gore-Booth (Dec. 17, 1916), PRONI, D/4131/K/7 (11).
[89] Katherine Tynan Hinkson to Eva Gore-Booth (Dec. 16, 1916), and Muncaster to Eva Gore-Booth (December 1916), PRONI, D/4131/K/7 (11).
[90] S. F. Fox, Governor, H. M. Prison, Aylesbury (Dec. 21, 1916), Lissadell Collection.
[91] Ibid.

apologized to those whom she inconvenienced at St Stephens Green. All the other women have been released. What is the use of pretending that these women are a danger to the Empire. The Countess is not a bit more crazy than [the suffragists] Annie Kenny, or Mrs Pankhurst.

He made the perilous offer to "go security for her future good behaviour. She will be a little noisy for a while, but it will mean nothing serious."[92] Unsurprisingly, the government did not take him up on it.

Some concessions were granted to Markievicz. From late January 1917 she was allowed to receive daily visits, but her release remained unforeseeable.[93] As the anniversary of the Rising passed, public sympathy in Ireland generated by the executions of the previous year reached critical mass. The change has been explained as an "emotional reaction" and an "almost instinctive anti-British backlash by Irish nationalists" that was "compounded by the failure of the home rule negotiations, by separatist propaganda, by the efforts of newspapers such as the *Irish Independent* and the *Irishman*, by the Prisoners' Aid Society."[94] The government's awareness of the change in public opinion was compounded by concerns that free association among male prisoners had the effect of turning British penitentiaries into universities of revolution. As Laffan writes in his history of Sinn Féin, "Dedicated revolutionaries could not yet inspire nationalist Ireland with their ideas and enthusiasms, but they could at least inspire or instruct their fellow-detainees."[95] Out of the misguided belief that the detainees would be more dangerous in prison than out of it, Lloyd George granted amnesty to the men held at on Frongoch on Christmas Eve, 1916. This did nothing to stem public protests for the recognition as prisoners of war of the Irish revolutionaries who were still interned in England.[96]

On June 15, 1917, a general amnesty was granted to all remaining Irish prisoners from the Easter Rising. Before traveling home, Markievicz spent a few days resting with Eva and Esther in London. An *Irish Times* correspondent reported spotting the sisters on the terrace of the House of Commons, "eating strawberries and cream," discrediting accounts of Markievicz's poor health. But to anyone who actually saw her, it was clear that the year of imprisonment had been corrosive. She seemed to have aged two decades. Her

---

[92] NA, WO 35/207.

[93] Sharp to the Governor of Aylesbury (Jan. 27, 1917), NA, HO 144/1580/316818.

[94] Laffan, *Resurrection of Ireland*, 75–76.

[95] Ibid., 65.

[96] "Imprisoned Nationalists: The Question of Their Treatment," *Weekly Irish Times*, May 26, 1917, 5.

hair was more gray than brown; her eyes were now marked by deep shad-ows, and her teeth were in worse condition than ever. Contrary to the *Irish Times*'s presumptions, Markievicz was now effectively homeless and bank-rupt. On her release, she was given £500 charity from the Irish National Aid Association and Volunteers Dependents' Fund, which had been organized in August 1916 to support the families of the participants in the Rising.[97] The fund had profited from sales of picture postcards, one of which was of Markievicz dressed in a ball gown, taken in 1903.[98] Even so, £500 was an ex-traordinary amount, matching the fund's donations to Éamon de Valera and William Cosgrave, who would both go on to serve as heads of state.

Eva accompanied Constance back to Ireland. When they arrived in Kingstown on June 21 aboard the mail boat *Leinster*, they were met by a cheering crowd. Before Markievicz could even step foot on the pier, she was showered with flowers, including a bouquet of highly symbolic Easter lilies tied with "Sinn Féin ribbons." People scrambled to accompany her on the train into Dublin, where she was welcomed at Westland Row by a group that the *Irish Times* described as "A body of men in civilian attire [march-ing] up to the platform in military order." A pipers' band from Liberty Hall assembled opposite the station and flanked Kathleen Lynn's car as the three women drove to ITGWU headquarters. The hollow shell of Liberty Hall was hung with "Sinn Fein bunting," and "women stood in the paneless windows waving what are called the republican colours."[99] Constance, Eva, and Kathleen Lynn lingered at Liberty Hall for an hour before going on to Lynn's house, but the crowd refused to leave them. A parade of two thousand people cheered them on as they drove to the southern suburb of Rathmines. The *Irish Times* reported riotous conditions with the explosion of fog sig-nals on tramway lines and a large force of police on the streets, in contrast to wholly positive coverage in the *New York Times*: "There was much singing of Irish songs and a great deal of cheering, but there were no signs of disorder."[100]

Contrary to Constance's expectations, the Russian newspaper *Russkoye Slovo* covered the Easter Rising extensively and noted the arrest of "Count-ess Markievicz," "a member of Irish high society, a daughter of an Irish bar-onet."[101] The paper's pan-Slavic agenda came through strongly: "[She] lived in Russia for a long time, at her husband's homestead [*kutor*] in Lipovetskiy

---

[97] The fund was created through merging the Irish Volunteer Dependants' Fund and the Irish National Aid Association; see Matthews, *Irish Citizen Army*, 148, 153.

[98] Ibid., 149.

[99] "Madame Markievicz in Dublin: Scenes in the Streets," *Irish Times*, June 22, 1917, 6.

[100] "Dublin Greets Released Rebels," *New York Times*, June 19, 1917, 3.

[101] *Russkoye Slovo* 90, April 10 [May 3], 1916, 2.

district, Kievskaya province, where according to the local Polish, she enjoyed universal esteem. Markievicz was very far from politics, from Sinn Fein at that time; nobody even knew that she was Irish, everybody thought she was pure English."[102] She and Casimir were presumed to have lived "in a castle near Dublin," where she had "nothing to do with ultra-national parties" until 1914, by which time Casimir was, of course, long gone.

In an interview with *Russkoye Slovo*, Casimir disavowed involvement in any revolutionary activity in Dublin, although he took some pleasure in relating his proximity to the Rising's martyrs:

> I knew personally many of the executed rebels. Pearse was the director of the model Irish school, Plunkett was an outstanding poet. . . . These people were far from politics at that time, just as my wife was; they were interested in pure art and even when they engaged in the Irish problem, it touched a narrow area of Irish national art only. . . . It continued this way until 1908, when the attitudes of my wife suddenly changed and she became engaged in the Irish nationalist movement, started delivering speeches in the assemblies and meetings . . . [advocating] an independent Irish republic.[103]

Casimir completely elided his falling out with the Dublin Repertory Theatre in 1913, when he had defended Constance and demanded that it was the theater's responsibility to be involved in Dublin's political life. He now complained that Constance "began running to extremes, [and] wanted to make our theatre purely nationalist. . . . I refused to take part in the theatre any more, and estrangement began between us."[104] By proclaiming that he was "a Russian subject interested in art only," Casimir underlines his allegiance to moderate pro-imperial nationalism, not the blood sacrifice and national insurrection that were preached by the Polish socialist Josef Piłsudski.[105] White-collar Galicians supported Piłsudski, but the Polish gentry in western Ukraine favored Roman Dmowski of the National Democratic Party, whose legacy would be marred by ideas of ethnic purity.[106]

In the short term, the landed class's allegiance to the Russian Empire seemed to bear fruit. During the February Revolution of 1917, the Petrograd Soviet declared that Poland deserved complete independence and

[102] Ibid. 93, April 23 [May 6], 1916, 3.
[103] "Ireland: Constance Markievicz," *Russkoye Slovo* 95, April 26 [May 9], 1916, 2.
[104] Ibid.
[105] Leslie, *History of Poland since 1863*, 17.
[106] Dmowski would later take a strongly anti-Jewish position, and he would seek to create a Polish state that excluded all minorities from its borders.

self-determination. This was followed in March by the Russian provisional government's promise of an independent Polish state that would be allied against the Germans and would comprise "all territories with Polish majorities," linked by a free military union to Russia.[107] Markievicz and his colleague at the Polish Theatre in Kiev, Arnold Szyfman, saw an opportunity to profit from Russian interest in Poland, and they opened a Polish theater on Br. Shapskiego in Moscow.

In Moscow, Markievicz became reacquainted with Alexander F. Salikowski, with whom he had gone to school as a boy.[108] Salikowski was part of a group of intellectuals who published a series of pamphlets, "The Freedom and Brotherhood of Peoples," which seized on the opportunity created by the February Revolution to advocate Russia's policy of self-determination for small nations. Each pamphlet addressed a different country within the Russian Empire. The only "peoples" outside of eastern Europe to be addressed were in a treatise on Belgium and one on Ireland, which was written by Casimir Markievicz.

Irlandiya was simultaneously a case for Irish and for Polish sovereignty. In his pamphlet, Markievicz describes the geography of Ireland and the history of the country in such a way as to exaggerate its similarities to Poland. He begins by asserting that "the independence of Poland has ceased to be a dream just as the question of the full political autonomy, if not the independence of Ireland, has become one."[109] He expands on his ambitions for the two countries in his conclusion:

> May their age-long struggle for freedom and the democratization of peoples at the moment of world war be crowned with success. May the Liberal leaders of the English parliament grant to Ireland freedom of political life on an unlimited democratic basis. May they find a way out of the conflict created by the protest of Ulster against Irish autonomy. Then emigration will cease and then the Irish, languishing in distant lands, will return to a free homeland. Then, at the same time as the re-establishment of an independent and united Poland, her younger sister in bondage, Ireland, will be rewarded for a much-suffering past.
>
> May the sun of Russian freedom, illuminating the whole world, warm even this distant island, the victim of the historical errors of the cultured English people.[110]

[107] Roos, *A History of Modern Poland*, 23–24.
[108] Quigley describes Salikowski as a "Ukrainian Revolutionary"; *Polish Irishman*, 170.
[109] MacWhite, "A Russian Pamphlet on Ireland," 98.
[110] Ibid., 110.

Irlandiya qualifies Markievicz's simplistic statements to *Russkoye Slovo* about his lack of political involvement. The pamphlet makes clear that there can be no doubt about his concern for Irish independence, but his goal was devolved autonomy—home rule—not complete separation.

Markievicz's twinning of Polish and Irish history can also be seen in his choice of plays for the New Polish Theatre in Moscow; for example, he produced *The Memory of the Dead* alongside Stanislaw Wyspianksi's *November Night*. Wyspianski's play is set at the start of the November Insurrection of 1830, when Young Poles attempted to assassinate Grand Duke Constantine, the brother of the czar and the governor of Warsaw.[111] *November Night* had a history of popularity amongst anti-Russian Poles, but it was given a new inflection after the abdication of Nicholas II in March 1917. Dmowski's party now sat in the Duma, and Markievicz and his fellow moderates working for "the Freedom and Brotherhood of Peoples" were optimistic about Poland's place in the Russian Empire.

At the beginning of June 1917, Casimir wrote to Josslyn, anxious about Constance's well-being and also hoping that it would now be possible "to try to do something for her through our new government" in Russia.[112] But the tide of politics was changing swiftly. His contract at the New Polish Theatre in Moscow expired in late June, so he returned to Kiev just as the Central Rada—a council formed of Ukrainian nationalist leaders—issued a declaration proclaiming that Ukraine was an autonomous land within a federated Russia. This was a short-lived victory for Casimir's political allies. Petrograd responded by casting the Rada's stance as a betrayal of the revolution, which prompted a second declaration in which the Ukrainian Rada reached a compromise with the Russian Provisional Government. This was followed by the organization of a Congress of Minority Peoples in Kiev in an attempt to lobby the Provisional Government. For a short time Casimir was able to live undisturbed by the political change. He lectured at the Polish School of Fine Arts (a post secured for him by his brother, who taught there), exhibited his own work, and worked at the Polish Theatre in Kiev.[113]

When the Bolsheviks overthrew the Provisional Government in Petrograd that autumn, the Central Rada tried to find footing by issuing a third declaration, which included a call for the seizure of land owned by the nobility and the church. Markievicz now found himself on the wrong side of all politics. He wrote to Josslyn, complaining of

[111] Bartelik, *Unity in Multiplicity*, 40.
[112] Casimir Markievicz to Josslyn Gore-Booth (June 4, 1917), PRONI, D4131/K/12 (5).
[113] Quigley, *Polish Irishman*, 173.

the very distressfull [*sic*] position of the land-owners of Russia. All our property is taken from us. . . . With the abolition of class distinction and titles people who used to have them now have not a slightest chance to get any employment under new system of government. One hardly can expect to do anything out of art or literature during such state of affairs. My position is simply desperate. The fact of my serving in the army as a voluntary and my birth are totally against my getting an intelligent employment.

He then asked to borrow "three hundert pounds" ("on the % you choose to settle").[114]

Casimir's impetuousness knew no bounds. Since it was difficult to move funds in or out of Russia, he suggested that Josslyn liaise with his friend, Count Emmanuel Malynski, who was living the high life of the exiled bourgeoisie in the Carlton Hotel, Pall Mall.[115] From London, Malynski would soon publish his treatise *A Short Cut to a Splendid Peace* (1918), which is an unambiguously antidemocratic and anti-Jewish manifesto. In considering the composition of what was in his view an oversized Ukraine, he declared: "Almost illiterate peasants have absolutely no ideas of patriotism or national identity; their aspiration and, so to speak, their motto is to have plenty of brandy, plenty of land on condition that they may leave it untilled or in a deplorable state through their horror of work." In his view, the only worthy element in Ukraine society was the Polish nobility, which, he argued,

practically constitute, besides the half-educated, half-alien, money-worshipping Jews, the almost only thinking, educated element; but belonging mostly to the upper or upper-middle classes, they are as such consequently taboo. . . . There remain some dreamers, chiefly imported from Galicia, who may possibly sincerely desire this independence, this democracy.[116]

Malynski's description of middle- and upper-class Polish nationalism as the stuff of "dreamers" approximates Markievicz's own estimation of the leaders of the Easter Rising. He told *Russkoye Slovo*: "I want to stress that the majority of people killed at the barricades in Ireland, prosecuted and already convicted, are not participants in some political adventure, but victims of

[114] Casimir Markievicz to Josslyn Gore-Booth (Nov. 19, 1917), PRONI, D/4131/K/12.
[115] Ibid.; and Emmanuel Malynski to Josslyn Gore-Booth (Mar. 5, 1918), PRONI, D/4131/K/12, and (Mar. 22, 1918), PRONI, D/4131/K/12.
[116] Malynski, *Short Cut to a Splendid Peace*, 11.

purely idealistic aspiration for national independence."[117] Constance's and Casimir's politics were now unambiguously divided. When a letter from Casimir finally reached her, she goaded Josslyn: "He says he wrote a book about Ireland when he heard I was released & that it made a 'great row.' All the nobilities privileges have been taken from them—(time too!)"[118]

[117] "Ireland: Constance Markievicz," *Russkoye Slovo* 95, April 26 [May 9], 1916, 2.
[118] Constance Markievicz to Josslyn Gore-Booth (n.d. [received Dec. 28, 1917]), PRONI, D/4131/K/6A.

Figure 9. Constance Markievicz arrives in O'Connell Street, Dublin, to address a meeting following her election victory in 1918. (Kilmainham Jail, 18PC-1A25–25.)

12

———

Victory behind Bars

SINN FÉIN AS A POLITICAL ENTITY WAS IN TRANSITION IN the second half of 1916, as a more radical set of principles replaced the inclusivity that had formerly characterized the organization. The party won a landmark victory when George Plunkett, a papal count who had three sons who fought in the Rising, won the County Roscommon by-election in February 1917. After Plunkett accepted his seat, he announced his intention to abstain from Westminster. The party, invigorated by Plunkett's victory, established new Sinn Féin clubs across the country, almost all of which were affiliated with a central branch in Dublin. These clubs were essential to organizing and campaigning for an important series of by-elections that were held across Ireland that summer, when formerly imprisoned leaders of the Rising contested—and won—seats at Westminster. The most important of these was the by-election in East Clare, won by Éamon de Valera, who had been sentenced to penal servitude for life but was released from Frongoch Prison Camp just two days before his election.[1]

Constance Markievicz was one of the few leaders of the Rising who survived. As a result, the attitude of the majority of nationalists toward her changed drastically. Previously subjected to ridicule and rumor, she was now offered the Freedom of the City of Kilkenny and of her native Sligo. On both occasions she urged the crowd to support Sinn Féin candidates in the forthcoming elections. She spent the summer of 1917 touring the country with other veterans of the Rising. In Sligo, guarded by men armed with

---

[1] Laffan, *Resurrection of Ireland*, 77–121.

hurling sticks, she declared that it was her mission to ensure "no Irishman crossed to Westminster to help England to govern Ireland."[2] In July she spoke at the Mansion House in Dublin alongside Thomas Ashe, who had commanded the Fingal division of the Irish Volunteers. She told the crowd that there was "one thing in her life that she looked back upon with absolutely unmixed pride and happiness—that she had worked by the side of James Connolly, and that, at any rate, she was the friend of the rest of the men who had died."[3] In just a few short months, Ashe was among their number. Imprisoned after a seditious speech, he went on hunger strike to demand prisoner-of-war status and was killed in the process of force-feeding.[4] At his funeral—the largest since the death of Charles Stewart Parnell—Markievicz paraded with the Citizen Army, but she wore a Volunteer uniform, signifying her camaraderie with Ashe and her place in the united Irish Republican Army that fought in 1916.[5]

In advance of the Sinn Féin convention in October, Markievicz used her celebrity to support the party's transition, as it attempted to win over the remaining adherents to the Irish Parliamentary Party, now in its death throes but holding out in important constituencies including Waterford and South Armagh. Speaking in Cork in August, Markievicz argued that in its use of physical and moral force, the Easter Rising had conjoined "the policy of Wolfe Tone and Parnell."[6] Alongside W. T. Cosgrave (future president of the Executive Council of the Irish Free State) and Tom Kelly, she addressed a meeting of farmers in Trim, County Meath, where she evoked Connolly's campaign against economic conscription. Markievicz argued that an Irish Republic could be established only through embracing Sinn Féin policy: the farmers must not sell their cattle, no matter the cost; they should hold the harvest and not thresh the oats. England might once more attempt to enforce famine on Ireland in order to implement "hunger conscription," and Ireland must be ready to survive on its own reserves.[7] This was not isolated

---

[2] "Sligo and Sinn Fein: Madame Markievicz's Visit," *Irish Times*, July 23, 1917, 6.

[3] "The Rebellion: Demand for Bodies of Executed Men," ibid., July 17, 1917, 5.

[4] See William Murphy, " 'Hunger Strike Mania': Ireland, June 1917–June 1918," in *Political Imprisonment*, 80–107.

[5] "Funeral of Thomas Ashe: Sin Fein Demonstration in Dublin," *Weekly Irish Times*, Oct. 6, 1917, 1.

[6] *Cork Examiner*, August 13, 1917, quoted in Oikarinen, *A Dream of Liberty*, 107.

[7] "Madame Markievicz and Food Exportation," *Weekly Irish Times*, Sept. 15, 1917, 4; Townshend cites a leaflet issued by the Women's Delegates Committee invoking the Land War of 1847, demanding "Remember '47" and "Hold the Harvest"; see Townshend, *The Republic*, 25.

propaganda but a widespread concern, especially in the west of Ireland with its history of famine.[8]

At the party conference in October, de Valera usurped Arthur Griffith as president of Sinn Féin. Griffith, aware that his time was up, stepped down privately and was immediately elected vice president of the party, publically and popularly.[9] At the conference, the aims and structure of the party were ratified; it would be governed by an executive, and its goal would be a republic. Although the republican aim was agreed on, de Valera acknowledged dissenting opinion but asserted that they "would agree to differ afterwards."[10] Differences were nonetheless palpable. Markievicz, Kathleen Clarke, and Helena Molony all attacked Eoin MacNeill, whom Markievicz blamed for the failure of the Rising.[11] Against de Valera's advice that an attack on MacNeill at the convention was inappropriate, she gave an impassioned speech, hurling his English name at him like a slur: "the proclamation had to be reprinted on Sunday in Liberty Hall in order to take John MacNeill's name off." Clarke was astonished at the "angry cries at [Markievicz] to shut up, sit down" since Markievicz "had gone out in the fight and done a man's part in it" while MacNeill, "no matter what anyone may say to the contrary, acted a coward at Easter 1916."[12] The newspapers merely reported a "piquant discussion," although Liam de Róiste noted in his diary that Markievicz had simply said aloud what many men had said privately but did not have the courage to say in public.[13]

Sinn Féin openly resolved "to deny the right and oppose the will of the British Crown and Parliament" and "to make use of any and every means available to render impotent the power of England to hold Ireland in subjection by military force or otherwise." It was effectively a declaration of war and turned Sinn Féin from an ephemeral idea into a real political force. In response to the convention, the chief secretary for Ireland, Henry Duke, advocated immediate imprisonment of a dozen of the party's leaders, including de Valera and Markievicz.[14] Yet there was widespread concern within the

---

[8] Campbell, *Land and Revolution*, 241–42.

[9] Laffan, *Resurrection of Ireland*, 117.

[10] Ibid., 117–19. Laffan notes that there were at least 1,700 delegates present at the convention, mostly young men between eighteen and forty years of age.

[11] "Sinn Fein Convention," *Manchester Guardian*, Oct. 27, 1917, 4; and "Sinn Fein Convention in Dublin: Constitution Adopted," *Weekly Irish Times*, Nov. 3, 1917, 1.

[12] Kathleen Clarke's report on the Sinn Féin Convention of 1917, Tom and Kathleen Clarke Papers, NLI, MS 49,356/2, quoted in Pašeta, *Irish Nationalist Women*, 230.

[13] For de Róiste, see Laffan, *Resurrection of Ireland*, 120.

[14] Chief Secretary, "The Situation in Ireland," War Cabinet Papers, NA, CAB/24/30.

British government that more arrests would further incite the general population. And in light of Ashe's death, if arrests were made, how would the inevitable hunger strikes be handled?

The delay gave Markievicz time to reorganize the Fianna. She published a propagandistic broadside, *Heroes and Martyrs*, which pleaded to a new generation, "For Ireland's sake take up the gun / That fell from our dying hand."[15] Six hundred boys marched to Glasnevin Cemetery in November to decorate the graves of Irish martyrs from 1848 to 1916, while the Dublin Metropolitan Police looked on impotently.[16] The next week she traveled to Belfast to speak at a commemoration of the Manchester Martyrs, three IRB men who had been executed in 1867.[17] Although Markievicz had been spared execution, she declared to her audience that her willingness to die in 1916 proved the righteousness of Republicanism, implicitly making a case for her own credibility as a leader.[18] She asked her Belfast audience "why [Carson] sent his poor boys out to die and did not go with them to lead them."[19] A few days later two Fianna were caught in Belfast carrying a portmanteau full of bombs that they had smuggled from Scotland, evidence that the armed struggle was imminent.[20]

Despite these frequent public appearances, Markievicz was not under the Dublin Metropolitan Police's surveillance of "local and provincial extremists" in the spring of 1918. However, when Lloyd George included Ireland in a Military Service Bill that permitted conscription in the country—and Sinn Féin gained even wider support—the DMP began to note her presence at party meetings. As one of four women elected to the Sinn Féin executive, she attended an important meeting on May 6 and another, larger one ten days

---

[15] Constance de Markievicz, I.R.A., *Heroes and Martyrs* (Nov. 23, 1917), NLI, ILB 300 P6 (Item 46). Markievicz's use of the suffix IRA on this broadside demonstrates the way that she continued to identify with a diversity of groups, which she believed were part of the same campaign for a Republic; while Markievicz was imprisoned in 1918, Hanna Sheehy Skeffington and Jennie Wyse Power would debate the role of Cumann na mBan, of which Markievicz was still the president. Wyse Power argued that "mobilising for funerals" was not "one of our main objects"; for their debate, see Pašeta, *Irish Nationalist Women*, 263.

[16] "Dublin and District," *Irish Times*, Nov. 26, 1917, 4.

[17] Markievicz's poem, "The Manchester Martyrs" emphasizes that these men were not "heroes" but "simple, common men, / Just rank and file of Ireland's Fenian breed"; Lissadell Collection.

[18] Jason Knirck argues that the rhetoric of sacrifice was a way for women to gain "political credibility" that was otherwise unavailable; see Knirck, "Women's Political Rhetoric."

[19] "News of the Week in Ireland," *Weekly Irish Times*, Dec. 1, 1917, 3.

[20] "Seize Bombs in Ireland," *New York Times*, Dec. 4, 1917, 3.

later.[21] On May 17, along with most of the Sinn Féin leadership, Markievicz was arrested and charged with conspiring to enter, and having entered, "into treasonable communication with the German enemy."[22] The same charge was applied to de Valera, Griffith, Cosgrave, Darrell Figgis, Sean Milroy, Count Plunkett, Maud Gonne, and Kathleen Clarke. Markievicz was taken to Ship Street barracks and deported from Kingstown (Dun Laoghaire) with seventy-three other party members. The men were sent to Frongoch, and Gonne and Markievicz to Holloway Jail in Islington, north London. At Holyhead, where they parted company from their male comrades, Markievicz was observed as looking neither "careworn nor anxious in appearance" and "walking along the pier with a light step."[23]

Although she missed having a Catholic chapel, Markievicz's impression of Holloway Jail was that it was better run than Aylesbury.[24] In fact, prison conditions were much better in 1918 than after the Rising. All Irish internees were allowed to associate, to exercise, to send and receive three letters per week, to receive money and parcels, and, after June 1918, even to read Irish newspapers.[25] Markievicz wrote to the chaplain at Mountjoy, "Very boring but after being a convict for a year it's not too bad, & mercifully I'm not a Sybarite."[26] At the very least, she thought that prison meals would be a change from the pea soup that constituted her three-penny dinners at Liberty Hall, and she believed that the arrests would be good propaganda for Ireland. The trumped-up charge of a German plot led her to ask, "What is the meaning of it all? We wonder more and more. Is it political or military?"[27] Had she been arrested because of the political threat that Sinn Féin posed? Or were the arrests an attempt to ease British plans to extend conscription in Ireland? Unbeknownst to Markievicz, it was the latter. In March the British commander-in-chief in Ireland had advised that in advance of the imposition of conscription in the country, all known opponents of conscription

---

[21] NA, CAB 24/59. In addition to Markievicz, Kathleen Lynn, Kathleen Clarke, and Josephine Plunkett were elected; Pašeta notes that the election of four women to a twenty-four-person executive was a "significant result" for the campaign to have the rights accorded in the 1916 proclamation enacted in the Sinn Féin Party; see *Irish Nationalist Women*, 230.

[22] "Sinn Fein Leaders Seized," *New York Times*, May 18, 1918, 1.

[23] "The Prisoners at Holyhead," *Irish Times*, May 20, 1918, 3.

[24] Murphy discusses how the practice of Catholicism in prison was a signifier of difference; *Political Imprisonment*, 114–15.

[25] Ibid., 111.

[26] Constance Markievicz to Fr. McMahon [Catholic Chaplain at Mountjoy], c/o Chief Postal Censor (n.d.), Sligo County Library BIO 118.

[27] Constance Markievicz to Eva Gore-Booth (June 8, 1918), in *Prison Letters*, 179.

should be removed.[28] Some members of the Sinn Féin executive were aware of the plot, having been informed by Michael Collins, and they had decided that the arrests would have greater political impact than attempting to evade the police.[29] Yet Markievicz was not privy to this information, and the arrest took her by complete surprise.

In candid letters to Eva, she compared the British idea of a German conspiracy with the sensational Billing trial that filled the pages of the English press. Actress Maud Allen had sued Noel Pemberton Billing—the MP for Hertford—for libel after he published an article "The Cult of the Clitoris," in which he accused Allen of being a lesbian. In the course of his defense, Billing expounded his theory that the Germans were plotting to eradicate British manhood and to deflower British children by luring them into homosexual acts. Billing's acquittal—after supporting testimony from Oscar Wilde's former lover, Lord Alfred Douglas—was proof to Markievicz of the absurdities of the British justice system: "What a show-up for England! What a judge, what a jury and what a crowd! I wonder what a 'competent authority' would think of the merits of that and of our 'German Conspiracy'?"[30] The Sinn Féin arrests seemed to her to be no more than a "comic opera."

Markievicz, Maud Gonne, Hanna Sheehy Skeffington, and Kathleen Clarke—who had been transported to Holloway separately—were uneasy jail mates. Early on, they disagreed about whether to go on a hunger strike. Markievicz thought that a strike would only give the government an opportunity to kill them through forcible feeding, as Thomas Ashe had been killed, and she also believed that Hanna Sheehy Skeffington was too mentally and physically fragile to undertake a strike. In a rare sarcastic aside, Constance described her to Eva as "One of your ideal mothers."[31] Antagonisms and resentments built up quickly. After just one month together, Constance was complaining that "Mrs. G. has been very tiresome and odd"; the prison censor reported Markievicz's assessment of Gonne as "all nerves and fancies but there is nothing physically wrong with her."[32] It was easier for her to be closer to Clarke, who seemed needy. She gave Clarke her only pair of warm stockings and made puddings for her from "spare bread" and marmalade that

---

[28] Laffan, *Resurrection of Ireland*, 142–43. The administration of Dublin Castle was also changed, to eliminate political "moderates."

[29] The negative consequences of the arrests were greater than the executive expected; see ibid., 144–45.

[30] Constance Markievicz to Eva Gore-Booth (June 8, 1918), in *Prison Letters*, 179.

[31] Ibid.

[32] Ibid. (July 31, 1918), 183; extract from Report on the Correspondence of 97 Irish Internees, July–Oct. 1918, NA, CO 904/164.

had been left at the prison gates as a gift.[33] ("If you come across a pot of raspberry jam do send me one."[34])

Sheehy Skeffington was released after a short hunger strike not long after her arrival, and Gonne was released due to ill health in October 1918.[35] This left Clarke and Markievicz alone to support each other. At times Clarke was too ill to leave bed, so Markievicz would visit her cell to keep her company and paint. Clarke found this incredibly annoying—"throwing her cigarette ashes around and flicking the paint and water off her brush"—but nonetheless diverting. To amuse Clarke, Markievicz drew a "beautiful caricature" that Clarke bragged about to her son, Daly: "it will make you split your sides laughing, when you see it. I have several chins."[36] Against all appearances, Markievicz was trying to be sensitive; she told Eva that she had been working in watercolors out of consideration for Clarke's "very delicate state": "I did not like to even suggest inflicting the smell of oil on her."[37] She also reached out to Clarke's family, using some of her carefully rationed stationery to reassure Madge, Kathleen's sister, that although Kathleen had been very ill, "She is now singing little songs and I have to restrain her from dancing jig steps. You know her wonderful spirit—she never loses heart."[38]

For the first three months of their internment, the political prisoners at Holloway were not allowed to receive visitors. Eva applied repeatedly for permission and was finally granted a pass in mid-August. Again, the sisters were permitted to discuss politics, as long as a prison officer was present to take notes. Consequently, their first conversation was about "how the dog Poppet was taught to hate everything English on the journey over," the allowance of larger sheets of writing paper to male prisoners, and the vileness of the postal censorship.[39] The privilege was soon revoked. When Eva arranged a visit for September, she was told that they must not discuss politics or prison matters. She complained in an angry letter to the Home Office:

---

[33] Constance Markievicz to Eva Gore-Booth (June 22, 1918) and (Oct. 18, 1918), in *Prison Letters*, 180, 186. Cumann na mBan advertised appeals for parcels of "home-made bread and cakes, jam, tobacco, chocolates, sweets, fruit, and biscuits" to be sent to prisoners; Murphy notes that de Valera was "uncomfortable" with the intiative to send "food out of Ireland at a time of scarcity and worried that it smacked of begging." See *Political Imprisonment*, 118.

[34] Constance Markievicz to Eva Gore-Booth (October 18, 1918), in *Prison Letters*, 186.

[35] Ward, *Hanna Sheehy Skeffington*, 216; Seán MacBride wrote letters appealing for his mother's release and threatening that Gonne would hunger strike; see nic Dháibhéid, *Seán MacBride*, 25.

[36] Kathleen Clarke to Daly (Nov. 29, 1918, NLI, MS 49,356/4.

[37] Constance Markievicz to Stanislaus Markievicz (n.d. [Autumn? 1924/25]), NLI, MS 13,778/1.

[38] Constance Markievicz to Madge Daly (n.d. [answ. Jan. 1, 1918]), Daly Papers, University of Limerick.

[39] (Aug. 14, 1918), NA, HO 144/1580/316818 (40); and (Aug. 20, 1918) (71).

On the one occasion I did see her she asked for news of her husband Casimir Dunin de Markievicz but was stopped at once by the officer as he is in Russia & to mention Russia was "politics" though I explained I know nothing of his political opinions since the Revolution. [A]s to the stipulation about not discussing the events that led up to her arrest, I can only suggest that as neither she nor I have ever been told what they are, we might speculate about them, but we could not possibly discuss them![40]

The new restrictions stipulated that Markievicz and Clarke sign an undertaking that they would not talk politics, and their visitors would not "carry messages or make reports."[41] Constance was as puzzled as Eva:

To-day life *is* "politics." Finance, economics, education, even the ever-popular (in England) subject of divorce is all mixed up with politics to-day. I can't invest my money, without politics; buy clothes without politics. Art is all political, music is battle tunes or hymns of hate or self-glorification, and I simply do not know what they mean when they say we must not talk politics.[42]

Rather than agree to the rules, Markievicz and Clarke refused visits, hoping "it will suddenly strike them that we are less powerful out than in, and then out we shall go!"[43]

They prepared for a hard winter in jail. Possibly drawing from donations from the Volunteer Dependents' Fund, Markievicz sent Eva a check to pay for fur coats for herself and Clarke. Her only stipulation was that they were not rabbit fur masquerading as "Coney seal," which she didn't "like anywhere, at all."[44] She also ordered Christmas cards from an Irish-language press and insisted on putting Clarke's name to several that she sent.[45] Her exuberance was both buoying and grating; Clarke wrote home, "Madame's tongue is . . . hung in the middle & its impossible to collect ones thoughts while she is knocking around."[46] Clarke was annoyed by what she perceived as Markievicz's sense of

[40] (Sept. 14, 1918), ibid. (73).

[41] Constance Markievicz to Eva Gore-Booth (Oct. 18, 1918), in *Prison Letters*, 187.

[42] Ibid. (n.d.), 208.

[43] (Sept. 19, 1918), NA, HO 144/1580/316818 (73); and Constance Markievicz to Eva Gore-Booth (Oct. 21, 1918), in *Prison Letters*, 188.

[44] Constance Markievicz to Eva Gore-Booth (Oct. 8, 1918), in *Prison Letters*, 185.

[45] Kathleen Clarke to Daly (Dec. 18, 1918), NLI, MS 49,356/4.

[46] Ibid.

superiority, and she cattily remarked on more than one occasion that it was not everyone's duty to go on platforms, "making speeches asking for arrest."[47]

Yet Markievicz's celebrity was not simply the product of self-promotion; as a result of a decade of activism, she had the support and affection of a wide range of people—suffragists and trade unionists, as well as Sinn Féin. When the Representation of the People Act came into effect, giving the right to vote to men of twenty-one and women who were householders (or married to householders) and over the age of thirty, Markievicz was immediately nominated to stand for election. In November Hanna Sheehy Skeffington received a letter informing her that Markievicz had been selected for candidacy but was yet to be informed.[48] By the end of the month, it was official: Constance Markievicz would stand for Dublin's St. Patrick's ward. Sinn Féin would continue its strategy of abstaining from taking up any seats at Westminster and therefore make visible by its absence the will of the majority of Irish people. Accepting her nomination, she replied, "Freedom has dawned in the East; the light that was lit by the Russian democracy has illuminated Central Europe,—is flowing Westward. Nations are being reborn, peoples are coming into their own and Ireland's day is coming. . . . There are many roads to freedom, to-day we may hope that our road to Freedom will be a peaceful and bloodless one."[49] To Albert Bibby, she wrote more candidly: "When we free our country I shall start a movement for the reformation of jails & jailers! I am so proud of being selected as a candidate. I wonder whether I should have a better chance of election in or out of jail!" She signed, "Love to you & Ireland & all dear rebels."[50]

It was a landmark election: the first in which women would vote, the first to take place on a single day throughout Great Britain and Ireland, and the first contest in which the votes would be securely counted en masse on an appointed date. The extension of the franchise also increased the electorate in Ireland from 31 percent of the population to 75 percent.[51] The younger electorate made political change all the more possible, and Ireland wielded extraordinarily disproportionate power; the country had 105 seats at Westminster in contrast to the 66 to which it was entitled based on its

[47] Litton, ed. *Kathleen Clarke*, 160.
[48] Anonymous to Hanna Sheehy Skeffington (Nov. 9, 1918), NLI, MS 22684.
[49] Extract from Second Report on the Correspondence of the Irish Prisoners, Nov. 1–10, 1918, NA, CO 904/164.
[50] Constance de Markievicz to Fr Albert Bibby (n.d.), Capuchin Archives IR/1/1/2/1.
[51] Laffan, *Resurrection of Ireland*, 151.

population.[52] Prompted by Cumann na mBan, Sinn Féin selected three women for candidacy: Winifred Carney, Hanna Sheehy Skeffington (who declined the nomination), and Markievicz.[53]

Markievicz, "a lady Sinn Fein candidate," as the *Irish Times* put it, stood against Dublin businessman and "Independent Nationalist" Alderman J. J. Kelly, and the incumbent Irish Parliamentary Party candidate William Field, who had held the seat since 1892.[54] The censorship of the Irish internees' post made it challenging for the prisoners to communicate their election addresses. Markievicz wrote to Jennie Wyse Power that the difficulty hardly mattered, "as the fact of them not getting through speaks for itself and our records and principles are so well known."[55] (In the same letter, she offered her "spare cash" to "any of our friends" who might be in need.) The copy of her address that passed through the censor on its way to Sinn Féin headquarters on Harcourt Street in Dublin opened by contextualizing Ireland's struggle in the midst of "world-chaos," when "Freedom is bursting her bonds, great tyrannies have fallen amidst seas of blood and horrors unthinkable." She drew comparisons between Ireland as a "Subject Nation" and Poland:

> When I was in Poland the Poles said to me "Ireland will be free her case is not hopeless like ours, she has not been partitioned and God himself has given her a boundary—the Sea. But Poland, poor Poland, what is she? Where are her frontiers? Partitioned and broken. She can never be reinstated, to win her Freedom three Empires must be swept away."

She declared that "To-day Poland is free," and Ireland must now seize its opportunity. Markievicz argued that the election was a choice between "complete and unlimited self-determination for Ireland" or "a limited and curtailed self determination 'Home Rule' within the Empire and probably Partition." To accept Home Rule, in her view, was to "deny Ireland's Nationhood" and to trust Ireland's future "to the Promises of English *Politicians*."[56]

The Irish Republic that Constance Markievicz envisaged was based on her interpretation of James Connolly's vision for a Republic, which he

---

[52] This disproportionate representation is a legacy of a declining population and the redrawing of electoral districts; ibid., 152.

[53] Helena Molony was nominated to stand for the Labour Party, but she declined the nomination, and the party subsequently decided not to contest the election; ibid., 154.

[54] "The General Election in Ireland," *Irish Times*, Dec. 14, 1918, 1; and "One Day General Election in Ireland," ibid., Dec. 21, 1918, 1.

[55] Postal Censorship, 4th Report, Dec. 1–15, 1918, NA, CO 904/164.

[56] Ibid.

wrote about, worked for and died for. Real *democratic* control with *economic and industrial* as well as political Freedom. To organise our new nation on just and equitable lines, avoiding the mistakes other Nations have made in allowing the powers of Government, law, force, education, foreign policy etc., to be the birthright of the moneyed classes to be used by them for the further accumulation of wealth and the building up of a class tyranny daily more subtle and more difficult to seize and overthrow.[57]

That these aims represented a minority view within Sinn Féin cannot be overstated.[58]

Just a year before, in a letter to Eva, Constance had expressed a sense of distrust in parliamentary methods: "I don't think Parliaments are much use anyhow. All authority in a country always seems to get into the hands of a clique and permanent officials. I think I am beginning to believe in anarchy. Laws work out as injustice, legalised by red tape."[59] These views would be tempered by the establishment of an independent Irish parliament, the Dáil, in 1919, but she believed that her candidacy in 1918 was a means of weakening Westminster and demonstrating the strength of popular support for an independent Irish republic.[60] That she would actually take her seat was never an option: "abstention is not only a Policy with me, it is a "principle.""[61]

Markievicz approached the "English election" with an attitude of amusement; the whole affair seemed to her like "Alice and Wonderland or a Gilbert and Sullivan Opera," with conspiracy theories about Sinn Féin so rampant in the British press that even the socialist-lite *Daily News* published spurious stories.[62] Markievicz found the misrepresentation of Irish Republicanism in the press tiresome, but as she wrote to Hanna Sheehy Skeffington, she believed that it had been "good for the country having no 'leaders,' they have *all* had a chance & learnt how to think & act. Leaders can be such a curse!"[63] She thanked Sheehy Skeffington for campaigning on her behalf and remarked, "One reason I'd love to win is that we could make St P's a rallying

[57] PRO, CO 904/164.

[58] Laffan, " 'Labour Must Wait.' "

[59] Constance Markievicz to Eva Gore-Booth (June 9, 1917), in *Prison Letters*, 175.

[60] Oikarinen notes that Markievicz's anarchical attitude is similar to those of the "cooperative nationalist Aodh de Blacam," who wrote in *Towards the Republic* (1918), in a chapter titled "Away with Parliaments," that Ireland "had no use for the corrupt inefficient and decivilising institution called Parliament"; Oikarinen, *A Dream of Liberty*, 118.

[61] NA, CO 904/164

[62] Constance Markievicz to Eva Gore-Booth (Dec. 4, 1918), in *Prison Letters*, 188.

[63] Constance Markievicz to Hanna Sheehy Skeffington (Dec. 12, 1918), NLI, MS 22,696 (iii).

ground for women, & a splendid centre for constructive work by women. I am full of schemes and ideas." Yet she was under no illusions that Sinn Féin would make the road for women smooth; she wrote to Jennie Wyse Power expressing dissatisfaction about the constituencies that the party had allotted to women: "Next time we will see that women get their share: we will be in a position to bargain."[64]

Seventeen female candidates stood in the 1918 election (importantly, the Irish Parliamentary Party had none), but Markievicz was the only woman to be victorious. Despite lackluster campaigning by Cumann na mBan, she won her seat by 5,083 votes—more than two to one over the incumbent.[65] Although Markievicz said that her election victory was "a foregone conclusion. I must know most of those who voted for me," Kathleen Clarke recalled that on hearing the news, "Madame got so excited she went yelling and dancing all over the place."[66] The British suffrage organization, the Women's Freedom League, held a banquet to honor the three candidates it had supported in the election, and the league sent a letter of congratulations to Markievicz, "the one successful candidate."[67] Number 10 Downing Street also sent a letter to her in Holloway, inviting her to attend the king's opening of Parliament on February 11. It began, "Dear Sir . . . I hope you may find it convenient to be in your place."

Markievicz's election strengthened the demands for her release. Kathleen Clarke had been released in February, leaving Markievicz alone in Holloway.[68] She wrote to Albert Bibby, asking him to "Tell Mrs T[om] C[larke] not to worry about me, my health is as tough as a Cabinet Ministers conscience, & bored is the worst that I am." She assured Bibby, "Im much better off than any other prisoners, & I hate to be singled out & meetings held about me. If they start petitioning I shall go off my head."[69] Markievicz was keenly aware that she was now a valuable commodity for Sinn Féin and had even more

---

[64] Ibid.

[65] Hanna Sheehy Skeffington and Nancy Wyse Power disagreed on political issues during the campaign; Margaret Connery of the Irish Women's Franchise League was asked to step in as manager. Connery wrote angrily to Sheehy Skeffington, "The very nerve of Sinn Féin sets my teeth on edge. The one woman that they have thrown as a sop to the women of the country has her interest neglected and what is one to say of Cumann na mBan. . . . They are too busy running after the men—the camp followers!!!" Quoted in Pašeta, *Irish Nationalist Women*, 263.

[66] Constance Markievicz to Eva Gore-Booth (Feb. 6, 1919), 193; and Litton, *Revolutionary Woman*, 164.

[67] The Women's Freedom League, cofounded by Charlotte Despard, supported Despard, Emily Phipps, and Edith How-Martyn in the election.

[68] Clarke was released on February 12, 1918, and stayed with Eva Gore-Booth until she was well enough to return to Ireland; McConville, *Irish Political Prisoners*, 637.

[69] Constance de Markievicz to Fr Albert Bibby (Mar. 4, 1919), CA/IR/1/1/2/1 (1–21).

power in prison than outside. At a meeting of over five hundred people on the South Circular Road in late February, her former fellow inmates Hanna Sheehy Skeffington and Maud Gonne, along with the labor leader William O'Brien, demanded the immediate release of "Madame Markievicz, M.P."[70] At another march in support of political prisoners, a member of the Irish Citizen Army declared that Markievicz had been "marked by the British Government" because of the English fear of socialism, which far outweighed the threat of Sinn Féin.[71] This was not Markievicz's own view. She believed that at Easter Week the aims of the ICA had been incorporated in the new Republican army and the reorganized Sinn Féin, and despite dissent within the party in 1918—and divisions that were soon to come—she remained firm in this perspective. She now signed her letters "Constance Markievicz, I.R.A.," sometimes adding "F. na É." to acknowledge her Fianna comrades.

The Irish Parliamentary Party was decimated by the 1918 general election. Sinn Féin was now in the majority, winning 48 percent of the Irish vote and 68 percent in the twenty-six counties that would become the Irish Free State.[72] Thirty-four Sinn Féin candidates were in English prisons during the 1918 election; of those, only three were defeated.[73] With political power at Westminster restricted to the party's conspicuous absence from its newly won seats, the leadership turned toward the wwinning Paris Peace Conference at which the map of postwar Europe would be redrawn.

Sinn Féin believed the conference was an opportunity to use Ireland's natural borders as a bid for sovereignty, riding the coattails of other small nations that had been subsumed in imperial aggression. Arthur Griffith, writing from Gloucester Prison where he was interned, suggested that the conference's consideration of the case of Poland should be used to justify Ireland's appeal. (He argued that Poland had actually become more prosperous under Russian rule, whereas Ireland had only suffered at the hands of the British.) Markievicz was skeptical about the chances of Irish success at the conference. She thought that the American president, Woodrow Wilson, was "a very dark horse," and she worried that when he visited England on his way to Paris he might lose sight of Ireland in the glamor of London, "los[ing] his head and his soul, wallowing in drawing-rooms and getting his eyes progged

---

[70] "Sinn Fein Meeting and Madam Markievicz," *Irish Times*, Feb. 24, 1919, 5.

[71] "Sinn Fein Prisoners," ibid., Jan. 6, 1919, 6.

[72] Townshend, *The Republic*, 61.

[73] Murphy, *Political Imprisonment*, 268. Éamon de Valera stood for four constituencies; he withdrew from the ballot for South Down, was defeated on the Falls (Belfast) ballot, but won seats for East Clare and East Mayo.

out with the spikes of crowns!"[74] Eva replied in agreement, lamenting, "Poor old world, it is indeed in the grip of a holy Alliance!!!"[75] The sisters were right in their estimation; as Townshend summarizes, Wilson was "in retreat from his commitment to self-determination," and by early June he delivered a crushing blow to the Irish American delegation that no delegations would be accepted at the conference without the unanimous consent of the United Kingdom, the United States, France, and Germany.[76] Ireland's hopes for the peace conference would come to nothing.

Alone in prison, Markievicz set herself on a course of intensive reading. She asked Eva for books on "Imperialism and earlier Peace Conferences and anything about Empire building and theories about internal construction of a State. I would buy any good books that might be useful to pass on. I want to get together a little library of Economics and Welt-Politik."[77] Markievicz had recently read J. A. Hobson's "last book," probably *Democracy after the War*, in which he argued that the political structures of democracy were extant in countries such as Britain and France but that real, functioning democracy was impeded by abuses of power and the drive of capitalism. He urged that "the causes of peace, democracy and internationalism are one and indivisible" and that the attainment of this triumvirate would bring about "personal liberty, political and industrial, as well as spiritual."[78] Constance told Eva that she had met Hobson once before and "liked him so much"; she now hoped that they could meet again to talk politics: "It's all true what he says and I want to ask him a score of questions."[79] She was also fascinated by the work of H. N. Brailsford, a prominent member of the Union of Democratic Control, a pressure group that campaigned for transparent democratic agreements to govern international relations rather than foreign policy that was driven by secret alliances. Markievicz saw Brailsford as "a man after my own heart"; she vowed to "always stand against "secret diplomacy","," a belief that foreshadows her deep anger and sense of betrayal by the Anglo-Irish Treaty.[80] In December 1917 Markievicz read Brailsford's new edition of *The War of Steel and*

---

[74] Constance Markievicz to Eva Gore-Booth (Jan. 6, 1919), in *Prison Letters*, 190.

[75] Eva Gore-Booth to Constance Markievicz (Jan. 27, 1919), extract from Seventh Report on the Correspondence of the Irish Internees, Jan. 16–31, 1919, NA, CO 904/164.

[76] Townshend, *The Republic*, 68.

[77] Constance Markievicz to Eva Gore-Booth (Jan. 22, 1919), in *Prison Letters*, 191.

[78] Hobson, *Democracy after the War*, 7. Hobson's landmark study *Imperialism* was a dominant influence on Lenin's *Imperialism, the Highest State of Capitalism*; see Kruger, "Hobson, Lenin, and Schumpter."

[79] Constance Markievicz to Eva Gore-Booth (Jan. 6, 1919), in *Prison Letters*, 190.

[80] Ibid. (January 30, 1919), 192, and (n.d.), 209.

Gold, which included a postscript in which he argued that the questions of "nationality which deeply affect the daily life of some small fraction of the European masses . . . would probably not have been raised had not Imperial issues lain behind them."[81] (Later, in November 1919, Brailsford remarked in an article for *Nation* on the "first startling and then unspeakably impressive" way that Sinn Féin asserted its vision: "It has boldly declared that the Irish republic exists, and faith is realising this invisible State."[82]) Markievicz believed that Brailsford's writing reinforced James Connolly's anti-imperialist teachings, and she read more deeply into socialism. She began with the light-weight Fabianism of G.D.H. Cole and moved swiftly on to the hard-line doctrine of the Bolshevik Maxim Litvinov.[83]

Litvinov joined the Bolsheviks in 1903 and fled Russia when the state started cracking down on arrests in the wake of the events of 1905. He was captured by French police and deported to London, where he shared a house with Joseph Stalin. After the October Revolution of 1917, Lenin appointed him as the Soviet representative in Britain. Soon after, he was arrested by the British government and held as a hostage in return for the repatriation of the British spy Robert Lockhart, who had been arrested in Russia. After Litvinov's release, the British Socialist Party published his short book *The Bolshevik Revolution: Its Rise and Meaning.* Eva sent the book to Constance, which prompted her reply, "Poor Russia!"[84]

Litvinov's reflections on "The First Revolution" (1905) evoked the similarities that Casimir Markievicz had delineated between labor in Russia and the struggle in Dublin that culminated in Bloody Sunday 1913. However, the distinction between Casimir's politics and Bolshevik policy are clear in Litvinov's argument that the struggle in 1905 was not for a change of parties but a "change of *classes*" in power. Litvinov described the workers' protest in 1905 not as the desire for a "democratic republic" but for a "social republic" in which central and local power was in the hands of "direct delegates of the working class."[85] Similarly to Connolly's arguments that he set out in the *Irish Worker* and *Workers' Republic,* Litvinov claimed that the Great War had distracted revolutionaries from the working-class revolution that had begun before the war's onset: "the overwhelming majority of them sprang to the

---

[81] Brailsford, *The War of Steel and Gold,* 312.

[82] Townshend, *The Republic,* 85.

[83] She asked Eva to buy her "Cole's new book," probably the revised edition of *Self-Government in Industry.* See (Dec. 12 [1918]), in *Prison Letters,* 197.

[84] Constance Markievicz to Eva Gore-Booth (n.d.), in *Prison Letters,* 205.

[85] Litvinov, *Bolshevik Revolution,* 4–5.

side of their respective Governments, all pledges were forgotten, and the nationalist watchwords were caught up with extreme avidity."[86]

The importance of Litvinov's book to Constance Markievicz's political thought is abundantly clear in the speeches that she delivered immediately after her release from prison in March 1919.[87] She was again welcomed to Dublin by large rallies in which members of the Citizen Army, Cumann na mBan, the Irish Women's Franchise League, trade unions, and Sinn Féin stood side by side. A parade of four hundred Fianna led a procession through the city center.[88] In her speech to the crowd, she addressed the aim of the Paris Peace Conference, which in her view was not simply national sovereignty. Rather, she argued that the Sinn Féin leadership should establish a council of delegates "to help their workers take their proper place in the Irish republic." She declared herself "a servant of the workers, and she was prepared to carry their flag."[89]

While Markievicz was in jail, the first independent Irish parliament, Dáil Éireann, was organized. It comprised Sinn Féin's elected representatives to Westminster—most of whom, like Markievicz—were incarcerated, and it was structured along similar lines, although—importantly—the Dáil had only a single chamber (effectively, the Commons) and no upper house (the Lords). When Markievicz took up her post after her release from prison, she was insistent that legislation was in place to ensure that the Dáil did not become an elite body. She argued that Dáil deputies' expenses must be managed closely; public funds should cover only third-class railway fare, and no more than fifteen shillings (less than $70 in today's money) per diem should be permitted as a maintenance allowance.[90] On these points she was successful.

The Dáil was governed by British parliamentary procedure, but the leadership was still "military-minded." The rank-and-file was outright militaristic, with the Volunteer newspaper, *An tOglac*, proclaiming the Volunteers' duty as to "interpret the national will" and to implement political policy.[91] The conscription crisis of late 1918 fueled Republican militarism. (In *An tOglac*'s view, nationalism and Republicanism were now synonymous.[92]) There were

---

[86] Ibid., 11. Litvinov's reflections on the period "After the Revolution" forshadow Markievicz's experience of civil war in Ireland; he discusses the ostracism of Bolsheviks, a slur akin to the use of the word "irregulars" to refer to Irish Republicans.

[87] "Correspondence," *Manchester Guardian*, Mar. 3, 1919, 10.

[88] Minutes of Meeting of the Fianna, Mar. 5, 1919, and Mar. 19, 1919, NA, WO 35/210.

[89] "Released Sinn Fein Prisoners," *Irish Times*, Mar. 17, 1919, 6.

[90] "Ministerial Reports. Motion Re Payment of Deputies Expenses' (April 1, 1919), Dáil Éireann, vol. F, no. 3.

[91] Townshend, *The Republic*, 76–77.

[92] Ibid., 76.

also strong concerns among the Volunteer leadership that the Dáil's political commitment would force the suppression of a military campaign in favor of parliamentary methods, which would result in what IRA commander Seamus Robinson described as "a state of stalemate."[93] Therefore, prior to the Dáil's first meeting on January 21, 1919, Robinson organized an ambush of a Royal Irish Constabulary shipment of gelignite being delivered to Soloheadbeg in South Tipperary. It was a small-scale event with enormous consequences. Eight Volunteers killed two RIC constables, and the armed struggle had resumed. For most of 1919 this took form in individual attacks on Royal Irish Constabulary police, a strategy that was initially almost as controversial as Markievicz's shooting of a policeman during the Rising. And indeed, she did much to encourage these assaults.

Markievicz's belief that the police should be targeted as representatives and enforcers of British rule in Ireland was one of her more mainstream opinions. Far more marginal were her ideas about the structure of the Republic and its aims. She was in prison during most of the time that James Connolly's son, Roddy, was attempting to exert a communist influence over the Irish Citizen Army and the Irish Republican Army. Roddy Connolly became involved in communist organization in Scotland, and on his return to Ireland in early 1919 he published several articles on Bolshevism and Ireland in which he defended Bolshevik tactics as lenient.[94] During the Civil War Markievicz would make use of some of the same republican networks in Scotland, but from 1919 to 1921 her attitude toward Bolshevism seems to have developed independently, based on what she had learned of Marxism from James Connolly before the Rising and from her prison reading afterward. She would, however, develop a close friendship with Patrick McCartan, who attempted to forge a diplomatic relationship with the Soviet government.[95]

From Holloway Jail, Constance had followed the events in Russia closely. She was concerned for Casimir's personal safety while she simultaneously hoped for Bolshevik success. On reading the news of the Red Army's capture of Kiev, she wrote to Eva, "What's happened to C—? I wonder if the Censor will object to this?"[96] "Poor Casi hated wars, revolutions and politics: and there he is—or was—in Kiev, or in the Ukraine."[97] Alienated by the objectives

[93] Ibid., 78.

[94] McGuire, *Roddy Connolly*, 27.

[95] Roddy Connolly and McCartan shared a room at the Hotel Lux in Moscow in 1921; see ibid., 39–40. For the Comintern, the CPI, and the IRA, see O'Connor, "Communists, Russia, and the IRA."

[96] Constance Markievicz to Eva Gore-Booth (Feb. 26, 1919), in *Prison Letters*, 197.

[97] Ibid. (n.d.), 205.

of the October Revolution, Casimir had left Moscow for Warsaw, where he found work as legal and commercial adviser in the Foreign Office of the American Consulate-General, and he moonlighted as manager of the Polish Theatre.[98] Casimir fared much better than Stanislaus, who remained in Archangel after the dissolution of the Russian Navy and worked as a translator between the White Russian Army and the British Expeditionary Force that occupied the port. The British occupation of Archangel was ostensibly an attempt to prevent German encroachment, but in fact it served to facilitate the counter-revolution in Russia.

In addition to the Soviet war against the White Armies, territorial wars were being fought among the states that emerged from a dissolved Austria-Hungary at the end of the First World War. At the Paris Peace Conference, the two Polish leaders, the socialist Józef Piłsudski and the nationalist Roman Dmowski, were forced to cooperate, united by the fear that civil war in Poland would further compress the powder keg in the East.[99] Piłsudski prepared the Polish Army for war with the Soviets, telling a correspondent of *Le Petit Parisian* in no uncertain terms, "I know the Bolsheviks are concentrating large forces on our front. They are making a mistake, thinking they can frighten us and present us with an ultimatum."[100] Over the winter of 1919–20, the Red Army drove through Kiev, Rostov, and Odessa in an attempt to commandeer the lucrative wheat lands and coalfields of Ukraine.[101] In the course of the Reds' encroachment, the Markieviczes' estate, Zywotowka, was raided. Casimir wrote to Josslyn in March 1920, hopeful that the Polish Army would drive them back: "I am cut off from the government of Kiev, where our property Zywotowka & Rozyn are until now in the hands of Bolsheviks, but the line of our front is rapidly approaching the open & one may hope that in a few months I shall be able to get something out of the place, although houses & furniture are [illegible] destroyed and burnt."[102] Eastern Ukraine, where Zywotowka was located, remained contested territory, but on April 21 Piłsudski and the Ukrainian head of state, the nationalist Symon Petlura, made an alliance. On the basis that "each nation possesses the inalienable right of self-determination," they redrew the borders, agreeing that

---

[98] Quigley, *Polish Irishman*, 179; and telegraph, Casimir Markievicz to Josslyn Gore-Booth (July 13, 1919), PRONI, D/4131/K/12. Markievicz gave his address as Bracka 20, Warsaw, Poland.

[99] Dmowski's partner Paderewski was appointed prime minister and foreign minister, while Piłsudski was Polish chief of state. See Lundgreen-Nielsen, *The Polish Problem at the Paris Peace Conference*.

[100] Quoted in Davies, *White Eagle, Red Star*, 98. The interview was published on Mar. 5, 1920.

[101] Ibid., 101–2.

[102] Casimir Markievicz to Josslyn Gore-Booth (March 25, 1920), PRONI, D/4131/K/12.

territories west of the River Zbrucz (eastern Galicia) would be returned to Poland, and Poland would possess lands that it would wrest from Russia up to the prepartition boundaries of 1772.[103] In exchange, Polish and Ukrainian national armies would stand together against the Reds.[104]

Casimir capitalized on the plight of Zywotowka in a bid for a loan of £100 from Josslyn. He instructed that the cash could be sent conveniently in an envelope to his address at the Polish Theatre, Warsaw; his guarantee was hardly reassuring: "Directly Ukraine is occupied by our army I shall pay you back with great gratitude." Casimir unself-consciously complained, "It is a damn hard job to live at present in Poland especially in Warsaw after long years of absence abroad & to earn one's living as a 'intellectual being.'" (Having seen Constance's name in the paper "from time to time," he "presumed that she is alright.")[105] He was persistent in his appeal to Josslyn and played on an exaggerated sense of rapport between two gentlemen. Writing again in April, Casimir explained why he needed the money so desperately: "I left most of my garde-robe behind in Dublin & the rest at home in Zywotowka when flying for life from the Bolsheviks." Josslyn knew, of course, that he had also left Dublin without paying for his new wardrobe. In case sending £100 in an envelope seemed too risky, Casimir offered Josslyn the option of wiring it to Lloyd's Bank in London with an order that it be forwarded to Banque de l'Est a Warsovic. Thanking Josslyn "in anticipation," he added, "I would never bore you with such a request if not to avoid parading in the streets of Warsaw practically naked."[106]

Stanislaus's problems were more serious. After the defeat of the White Russians and the withdrawal of the Allies from Archangel, he left for Moscow, where he hoped to secure approval to leave Russia for Poland. Stanislaus was now married to a Russian woman, Alexandra Ivanova Zimina, whose father had managed a timber mill in Archangel.[107] Because their marriage had been in an Orthodox church and the Bolsheviks only recognized civil unions, Alexandra was denied Polish identity papers. The couple suffered a hard winter in Moscow, where they lost their newborn baby to typhus.[108] The spring brought little relief. In June the Bolsheviks took Stanislaus prisoner

---

[103] For a transcript of the agreement, see Davies, *White Eagle, Red Star*, 102–3.

[104] The Polish-Soviet War lasted another year, ending in a stalemate in January 1921. The Treaty of Riga, signed on March 18, 1921, resulted in a return to the borders of Oct. 12, 1920, leaving Zywotowka within the borders of Ukraine.

[105] Casimir Markievicz to Josslyn Gore-Booth (Mar. 25, 1920), PRONI, D/4131/K/12.

[106] Ibid. (April 7 [1920]).

[107] Quigley, *Polish Irishman*, 176.

[108] Ibid., 181.

for his counterrevolutionary activities, and he was held captive for twenty-five months.[109] He was interned in Butyrka Prison in Moscow in January 1921 before being transferred to a prison camp at Kojochowo six months later.[110] While Stanislaus was still at Butyrka, Alexandra came to stay nearby, but when she learned that his release was not imminent, she left. Their relationship had broken down over the course of their suffering and separation, and the problems had been compounded by misunderstandings "about money affairs." Stanislaus privately hoped she would initiate a divorce under Soviet law.

From prison, Stanislaus read news of his father's new fame in Warsaw, where Casimir had starred in the role of the baron in Alexsander Hertz's silent film *Córka pani X* (1920) and had written the script for Hertz's *Powrót* (The Homecoming), a talkie released a few months later.[111] Stanislaus scribbled an angry letter on a scrap of linen, which was smuggled out of the camp inside the collar of his friend Victor Buchwitz when Buchwitz was released.[112] He was incensed at Casimir's "silence and apparent indifference" while his son was "in great need of fat & sugar foodstuffs," had "no clothes or footwear & even no blanket," and "had to go to work to earn a little bread." He asked his father for an encouraging note, as a reminder that Stanislaus had "somebody to go to when I [move to] Warsaw with my wife homeless and penniless."[113] If Casimir replied, the letters did not make it through. Stanislaus wrote persistently, frustrated at the continual appearance of his father's name in the newspapers; he was confused why Casimir, with his "large circle of acquaintances and good connections," could not secure his release, and he complained continually about "working 8–9 hours to make 1 punt of awful black bread."[114]

In December Stanislaus was transferred to Novospassky, a fortified fourteenth-century monastery in Moscow that the Soviet government turned into a prison camp. There, a parcel of warm clothes and sweets from Casimir finally reached him. He was relieved to have "proof" that Casimir still cared for him, but this gratitude quickly turned to greed. Heedless of the famine afflicting an area the size of England in the Volga region of Russia and

[109] Stanislaus Markievicz, "Life of Constance Markievicz" (Part 2), NLI, MS 44,619, 148.

[110] Quigley, *Polish Irishman*, 185. In his unpublished memoirs, Stanislaus writes that Mabel Gore-Booth's in-laws, the Fosters, even tried to adopt him to secure his release; see Stanislaus Markievicz, "Life of Constance Markievicz" (Part 2), NLI, MS 44,619, 148.

[111] Quigley, *Polish Irishman*, 183. Neither *Córka pani X* nor *Powrót* is extant.

[112] PRONI MIC 590/3.

[113] Stanislaus to Casimir (July 8, 1921), letter on linen, PRONI, D4131/K/8.

[114] Ibid. (June 22, 1921).

eastern Ukraine, Stanislaus wrote, "I can't say that we are starving—but I'm sure you will be interested to know that I've hardly tasted a drop of real tea coffee or cocoa."[115] He asked Casimir to send some of each and also "some *white flour* or *biscuits*." Casimir did his best to indulge him and sent an encouraging letter along with some cash, which remarkably made it through. Stanislaus responded with a letter of thanks and a request for fifty grams of Thiocol, which was used to treat pneumonia, five hundred grams of cod liver oil, "more money and some *real* tea, coffee & cocoa also some biscuits and white flour."[116] He wrote again in early March with a request for more money, "cocoa and condensed milk."[117]

Twelve days later Stanislaus joined a hunger strike to demand release. He wrote a letter of farewell in case he did not survive; in the event that he did, he asked Casimir to use his connections in the American Consulate in Warsaw to ensure that the American Relief Administration in Moscow immediately supplied him with $10 a month of provisions; "Send me money please . . . and also some cocoa & tinned milk. Good bye, dear Father—I may never worry you again."[118] In fact, Constance was more useful than Casimir in ensuring Stanislaus's good treatment and release. Through her relationships with an international network of socialists, she received reports about his condition, which she then forwarded to Jim Larkin, who was imprisoned in Sing Sing. Larkin promised "to try & get certain Bolshie friends of his" to arrange for Stanislaus's release.[119] He was set free on March 24 and arrived in Warsaw four days later.[120]

Constance was unsentimental about her family's hardships and held fast to an idealized vision of a socialist republic. When she finally took her seat in Dáil Éireann at the beginning of April 1919, she was one of its most radical members. She was appointed secretary for labor on the Dáil's executive, and as the executive's only female member, she was the second female cabinet minister in Europe.[121] The efficacy of the cabinet early on was limited by the severe restrictions on the Dáil's meetings; they met in secret at different locations, and meetings were brief in an attempt to evade police raids on the

---

[115] Ibid. (Jan. 7 [1922]).

[116] Ibid. (Jan. 16, 1922).

[117] Ibid. (Mar. 6, 1922).

[118] Ibid. (Mar. 18, 1922). For the diplomacy of famine relief, see Weissman, *Herbert Hoover and Famine Relief*.

[119] Constance Markievicz to Stanislaus Markievicz (n.d.), NLI, MS 13,778/1.

[120] Quigley, *Polish Irishman*, 187.

[121] Oikarinen notes that the Social Democrat Hilja Pärssinen was Minister for Social Affairs in "the short-lived [Finnish] revolutionary cabinet of 1918"; Oikarinen, *A Dream of Liberty*, 120.

assembly. Because of her sex and her strident interpretation of Republicanism, it was in the Dáil that Markievicz would face some of her most bitter antagonists: first Eoin MacNeill (secretary for industries) and later Michael Collins (secretary for finance), with whom she would have personal, vitriolic disputes over the Anglo-Irish Treaty. Yet Markievicz had allies as well. Laurence Ginnell, with whom she had campaigned in early 1918, served as head of the department for propaganda, and Markievicz spent a great deal of time in his office, where she made a memorable impression sitting "for hours on a corner of a table smoking cigarette after cigarette and discussing in her musical voice the most varied and fascinating topics."[122]

One of Markievicz's earliest political concerns was radical land reform, for which she and Ginnell lobbied. Landownership was paramount to the idea of the national struggle, but there were sharp divisions among separatists over the legitimacy and nature of private ownership. Some delegates interpreted the 1916 proclamation's declaration of "the right of the people of Ireland to the ownership of Ireland" as a socialist policy rather than an ephemeral ideal. In a Sinn Féin pamphlet in 1917, Ginnell had called for aggressive reforms that would be similar to the Ranch War: "immediate restoration of all evicted tenants and descendants of such still unprovided for; compulsory sale of all land remaining unsold; distribution of all ranches; amelioration of the condition of agricultural labourers; [and the] drainage of flooded areas."[123] The threat that these ideas posed to the social order were noted in Dublin Castle's surveillance file on Ginnell, which reports his opposition to the Irish Parliamentary Party's land purchase scheme, his support for "evicted men, landless young men, etc.," and his advocacy of cattle driving as an agitational practice.[124] Ginnell's views were shared among the rank-and-file of Sinn Féin in the west of Ireland, whereas the party's leadership, including Arthur Griffith, was committed to conciliation and averse to taking direct action.[125]

Markievicz's commitment to aggressive reform sprang from her study of James Connolly's writing, her interpretation of the Bolshevik Revolution, and her familiarity with the landscape and tenants in the west of Ireland. In April 1919 she seconded South Sligo delegate Alexander McCabe's motion that vacant lands and ranches should be redistributed among the people and that the Dáil should refuse to sanction any purchases of nonresidential land

---

[122] Kathleen McKenna quoted in Mitchell, *Revolutionary Government in Ireland*, 161.
[123] Quoted in Campbell, *Land and Revolution*, 240.
[124] Lawrence [*recte* Laurence] Ginnell, Castle File no. 356, PRO, WO 35/207.
[125] Campbell, *Land and Revolution*, 246.

by private individuals that had occurred since Easter Monday 1916. He argued that this would be "a warning to those who have recently availed themselves of the crisis in National affairs to annex large tracts of land against the will and interests of the people."[126] The land issue was so divisive that the discussion of McCabe's motion was not documented; his resolution was withdrawn, and land policy was delegated to a committee that included McCabe and Ginnell but not Markievicz.

Markievicz strove to maintain unity in the Dáil and was reluctant to disagree with de Valera, who was chief of the executive and príomh aire, or president, of the Dáil. When he called for the assembly to support the League of Nations, a number of delegates were openly skeptical. Seán MacEntee went so far as to call Woodrow Wilson "the Machiavelli of the new world," and he speculated that Wilson harbored "a deep and secret purpose . . . to make smooth and easy the subjection of small peoples at the hands of a huge commercial empire."[127] Alexander McCabe and several other Dáil delegates argued that the Dáil should instead support the International Socialist Commission, which sought to resurrect at Berne the Second International of 1889. Despite Markievicz's strong support for international socialism, she was not drawn into the debate. Instead, she simply pledged her support for de Valera. On the matter of Wilson, she argued, "They were judging in the dark."[128]

Outside the Dáil, Markievicz was more forthcoming. In Sligo at the end of April, she declared, "Whether they succeeded at the Peace Conference or not, Ireland's cause would go on under Sinn Féin. What they wanted was not a League of Nations, but a league of people, on the lines laid down at the Conference in Berne."[129] In Bray she wagered that "Ireland's two chances were Wilson and Bolshevism," and she preferred the latter: "If Bolshevism fired France, it would then fire England. When it fired England, Ireland would be free. They were for a workers' Republic, for which Connolly died."[130] The relationship between Irish labor and international socialism had been at the heart of the founding of the Irish Citizen Army, but to achieve solidarity in the ICA, the most radical socialist views had been cast aside. Support for the International at Berne now provoked divisions between nationalist trade unionists and socialists, and it took the British administration by surprise.

[126] "Distribution of Vacant Land" (April 4, 1919), *Dáil Éireann Debate*, vol. F, no. 5.
[127] Dáil Éireann, vol. 1 (April 11, 1919), http://debates.oireachtas.ie/dail/1919/04/11/00003 .asp (accessed Jan. 21, 2013).
[128] Ibid.
[129] "Madame Markievicz and Proportional Representation," *Irish Times*, April 23, 1919, 6.
[130] "Ireland's Two Chances," *Observer*, April 27, 1919, 12.

The viceroy, Lord French, reported in May 1919 that "a Bolshevistic element" had developed and these "extremists" had joined forces with militant Sinn Féin.[131]

Markievicz's speeches in Sligo and Bray laid the foundations for Sylvia Pankhurst's visit to Ireland in mid-May. Pankhurst believed that the First World War was merely a means of furthering capitalist interests, and she split from the Women's Social and Political Union (which had supported Britain in the war) and founded the Workers' Socialist Federation (WSF), which supported the Easter Rising through its newspaper, the *Workers' Dreadnought*.[132] Pankhurst was "very much impressed by the way people managed the strike" in Limerick, when the public rejected the imposition of what was believed to be martial law and set up an independent city government that issued its own laws and even printed its own currency.[133] Pankhurst spoke on the subject of "Russia To-day" at the Trades Hall on Capel Street in Dublin on May 12, and Markievicz chaired the session.[134] In her speech, Pankhurst warned against emerging similarities between the English Parliament and the new Dáil Éireann. She urged Irish people to consider the Soviet system as an alternative model in which "the whole management of the country was carried on by councils, which was self-government carried to a very fine point." Pankhurst had shared a platform with James Connolly at a rally in the Royal Albert Hall to agitate for James Larkin's release in 1913, but this appears to be the first time that Markievicz met her in person. She was impressed by Pankhurst's performance and wrote to Eva afterward, "She's a sport, and brave as brave."[135]

One week after Pankhurst's lecture, the police raided Kathleen Clarke's house, where Markievicz was staying. Michael Collins arrived in the early hours of the morning to warn them that the police were on the way. Clarke remembered, "Madame got into a wild state of excitement, rushing here and there and asking what she would do. I suggested she should first get

---

[131] (May 15, 1919), NA, CAB 24/79.

[132] The *Dreadnought* had the "scoop" on the Easter Rising, with firsthand reporting from one of its members, Patricia Lynch; see Davis, *Sylvia Pankhurst*, 57.

[133] Constance Markievicz to Madge Daly (n.d. [May 1919]), Daly Papers, UL; the strike, which lasted ten days in early April, became known as the Limerick Soviet; for a discussion of the impact on British fears about Ireland, see Townshend, *The Republic*, 100.

[134] "Miss Pankhurst on Soviet Government," *Irish Times*, May 13, 1919, 6.

[135] Constance Markievicz to Eva Gore-Booth (June 21, 1919), in *Prison Letters*, 224. She wrote similarly to Madge Daly, "S.P. is a great girl, she just came over to see for herself, knowing a few of us, & wanting to study our methods"; Constance Markievicz to Madge Daly (n.d.), UL.

dressed."[136] With a stern warning to "hide in the hedges if they saw a curfew car coming," Clarke sent her two sons over to Margaret Skinnider's house to tell her that Markievicz was on her way. In the rush, Markievicz forgot her glasses. Absurdly near-sighted, she could not see the number of Skinnider's house and wandered up and down the street, whispering, "Margaret, Margaret," until Skinnider finally heard her and ushered her inside. Markievicz was safe and the Clarke boys were back home in their beds before the police reached the house at six o'clock. Later that day Markievicz sent Clarke's sister, Madge Daly, a postcard: "House searched 6 a.m. 16 bullies on that alone—Kathleen does not seem to be the worse for it."[137]

The police were gearing up for another arrest. At the beginning of June Markievicz was taken into custody and sent to County Cork by train. The British government's anxieties about a Bolshevik threat were reflected in the charges against her: inciting traders to boycott the Royal Irish Constabulary and taking part in an unlawful assembly. The sentence was four months' imprisonment.[138] Markievicz responded to her accusers in Cork with the same insouciance she had displayed at her court martial, "by calling for cheers for 'the Irish Republic.'"[139] Her letters to family and friends were lighthearted. She wrote to Eva about the "Gilbertian" procession of an armored car and trucks filled with "several tons of soldiers and police" that followed her ("The only thing they hadn't got was an aeroplane"), and she described to Madge Daly how she spent her days, amusing "myself wondering how long it will take us to break up the Empire, & speculating on various policies."[140]

Reports of the arrest focused on Markievicz's campaign against the police. The *Irish Times* went so far as to suggest that her recent speeches—"treat the police as lepers . . . the money they earn is 'blood money'"—had incited the killing of RIC district inspector Hunt in Thurles, County Tipperary.[141] She strongly disavowed any responsibility for that or other murders, writing to Hanna Sheehy Skeffington, "Much as I dislike these spies and informers, I would never advocate a pogrom." "All" she wished was "that

---

[136] Litton, *Kathleen Clarke*, 167–68.

[137] Constance Markievicz to Madge Daly (n.d. [May 24, 1919], UL.

[138] "Arrest Countess Markievicz Again for Sinn Fein Work," *New York Times*, June 14, 1919; and "Madame Markievicz Sentenced," *Weekly Irish Times*, June 21, 1919, 4.

[139] "Countess Markievicz," *Manchester Guardian*, June 18, 1919, 6.

[140] Constance Markievicz to Eva Gore-Booth (June 21, 1919), in *Prison Letters*, 224–25; and Constance Markievicz to Madge Daly (July 13, 1919), UL.

[141] "The Case of Madame Markievicz," *Irish Times*, June 25, 1919, 5. Townshend notes that "no senior police officer had ever been shot down like this"; *The Republic*, 108.

people—by socially ostracising [the police] should render them harmless and prevent them getting information."[142] To Eva, she summarized her crimes as "advising girls not to walk out with the police and a few other remarks of that sort. The whole thing would make a very funny story for a magazine!"[143]

Instead, it made a somber story for the *Irish Citizen*. James Connolly's daughter, Nora, visited Markievicz in jail and described "Madame" as "looking very well." She was keeping busy and "improving her mind" with the study of "the social, political and religious history of Ireland."[144] In Cork, Markievicz resumed the program of radical reading that she had begun in Holloway. She now turned to Martin Haverty's *History of Ireland* (which she found in the prison library) and left-wing newspapers, including Sylvia Pankhurst's *Workers' Dreadnought* and the *Daily Herald*, which Hanna Sheehy Skeffington sent to her from Liberty Hall.[145]

Markievicz's Marxian underpinning is reflected in her focus on understanding the historical conditions necessary for revolution and her application of Lenin's political theory to Irish history up to Easter 1916. She tested out her ideas in her letters to Eva and began to construct a narrative of Irish history along the lines of James Connolly's *Labour in Irish History* (1910). Haverty begins his history with the ancient high king Brian Boru, whose reign was romanticized as unifying the island and freeing Ireland from Viking occupation. Markievicz inflected Haverty's depiction with her vision of just government. She argued that Brian had "never interfered with his under-King," a policy that she used to confirm her thesis that Ireland had never produced "a tyrant."[146] She believed that this was evidence of the Irish predisposition for " 'decentralisation' (modern 'soviets')."[147] Eva responded by joking that "true Blood and thunder conservative[s]" were "always the Herald of

[142] Constance de Markievicz to Hanna Sheehy Skeffington (June 26, 1919), NLI, MS 41,177 (31).

[143] Constance Markievicz to Eva Gore-Booth (June 14, 1919), in *Prison Letters*, 223.

[144] Nora Connolly, "In Jail with Madame de Markievicz," *Irish Citizen* (Sept. 1919): 28.

[145] Constance Markievicz to Madge Daly (July 13, 1919), Daly Papers, UL; Constance Markievicz to Hanna Sheehy Skeffington (June 26, 1919), (Aug. 21, 1919), (September 24 1919), NLI, MS 41,177 (31).

[146] Constance Markievicz to Eva Gore-Booth (Oct. 18, 1919), in *Prison Letters*, 246. Haverty writes, "The character of Brian is popularly described as faultless; and if the unprejudiced mind finds it difficult to acquit him altogether of ambition and usurpation, still the use to which he converted the power he acquired, and the benefits, though transitory, which redounded from it to his country, to religion, and to civilization, may palliate faults not very heinous in themselves, considering the spirit and circumstances of the age in which he lived"; Haverty, *History of Ireland*, 139–40.

[147] Constance Markievicz to Eva Gore-Booth (Oct. 18, 1919), in *Prison Letters*, 246.

Revolution! And they don't know it because they never read History. Conservatives always avoid history. I suppose because if you are much attached to the Past and wish to remain so, its well not to know too much about it."[148]

Markievicz was probably also reading John Mitchel's *Jail Journal*, the second edition of which had been published in Dublin in 1913, with a preface by Arthur Griffith. The journal exerted a powerful influence over Markievicz's generation.[149] She wrote extensively about Mitchel, who in her view was "certainly not a Bolshie, but that made it all the more wonderful that he took such risks and went in so whole-heartedly for the Revolution."[150] She conceded that his support for slavery in the southern United States was "queer," but she justified Mitchel's position in terms of his opposition to English abolitionism, which she believed had been motivated not by ethics but by capital: "slave labour, being unpaid, enabled the Americans to undersell the English tea-planters."[151] Markievicz's theories also hint at a Machiavellian influence, since she emphasizes policy as necessary to successful revolution: "I think [Young Ireland] all failed because they had no policy. They were all writers and theorists, but could neither organize nor frame a policy." However, she conceded that policy on its own was not enough: "I agree with Lenin that if the conditions are not there, no sort of propaganda will hasten or impede it."[152] Markievicz's prison reading provided the theoretical underpinning for understanding how the revolution should proceed after James Connolly. Despite the ongoing struggle for independence, she believed

[148] Eva Gore-Booth to Constance Markievicz, extract from Eighth Report on the Correspondence of the Irish Internees, Feb. 1–15, 1919, NA CO 904/164. The postal censor deemed another anti-British card from Eva Gore-Booth to be "undesirable"; on it was inscribed Eva's poem, "This Mighty Empire hath but feet of clay / If all its ancient chivalry and might / This little island is forsaken quite / Some enemy has stolen its crown of bay / And from its hills that voice hath passed away / Which spake of Freedom"; NA CO 904/164.

[149] John Mitchel (1915–1875) was a leader of Young Ireland, a writer for *The Nation*, and an advocate of passive resistance. Charged with treason and convicted, he was deported to Ireland Island in Bermuda and then to Van Diemen's Land, from which he escaped and settled in the United States. He defended slavery in racist depictions of "inferior" "negroes," returned to Ireland and was elected MP in 1875, but was denied his seat on the basis of a felony conviction. He published histories of Ireland, a life of Hugh O'Neill, and the poetry of Thomas Davis, in addition to his *Jail Journal* (1854), subsequently edited by Arthur Griffith (1913).

[150] Constance Markievicz to Eva Gore-Booth (July 9, 1919), in *Prison Letters*, 226.

[151] Ibid. In his preface, Griffith wrote, "His views on negro-slavery have been deprecatingly excused, as if excuse were needed for an Irish Nationalist declining to hold the negro his peer in right. When the Irish Nation needs explanation or apology for John Mitchel the Irish Nation will need its shroud. . . . His hatred of England was the legitimate child of the love of Ireland that glowed in the heart of the man"; Mitchel, *Jail Journal*, xiii–xiv.

[152] Constance Markievicz to Eva Gore-Booth (July 9, 1919), in *Prison Letters*, 226.

that the Easter Rising had been a success: "the organisation was there, and Connolly had the brain, so that when the moment came they were able to grasp it."[153]

From prison, Markievicz followed the newspapers closely in order to learn as much as possible about the revolution in Russia. She believed that the British strategy for suppressing the Russian Left would be valuable knowledge when planning Irish resistance to the counterrevolution. She was pleased that an outbreak of strikes by returning soldiers facing unemployment in Britain would make it difficult for British troops to supply the counterrevolution in Russia: "This may just save the Revolution."[154] Britain's naval blockade was contributing to famine in Russia, which Markievicz believed was analogous to Britain's Irish policy: "just the same policy was adopted over here as early as the time of Henry VIII. . . . They never stopped doing this till after Oliver Cromwell's day, and after that till quite lately they starved the people whenever they could by legislating so as to produce famines in Ireland."[155] During this period Markievicz returned to signing her letters "Constance de Markievicz I.C.A.," to express her allegiance to the organization of Irish workers. She was convinced that the majority of Irish Transport and General Workers' Union members embraced Sinn Féin policy, which she believed would help to strengthen the Sinn Féin Party, despite "some 'rotten' capitalists in it."[156]

Markievicz's political thought combined the ambitions of the Irish Revival, particularly the instructive vision of George Russell, with the Marxist teachings of Connolly, Litvinov, and Lenin. She imagined that one way Ireland might be protected from a British-imposed famine would be by returning to cooperative agriculture, which would reduce the country's reliance on imports.[157] She was not unique in this regard; Darrell Figgis and Aodh de Blacam, as well as AE, held fast to the idea of a cooperative economy that they believed was modeled on the ancient past.[158] Whereas AE sought this change at a grassroots level, Figgis, de Blacam, and Markievicz believed that state policy was integral to economic reform. As Constance wrote to Eva, "If a revolution comes it will be much worse than Russia, for people are so congested. There are no big open country districts, with stores of food. I don't fear a revolution here as many are so disciplined—not that silly compulsory thing which is automatic and breaks down—but disciplined voluntarily,

---

[153] Ibid., 226–27.
[154] Ibid. (Oct. 1, 1919), 243–44.
[155] Ibid.
[156] Ibid. (Aug. 17, 1919), 238.
[157] Nora Connolly, "In Jail with Madame de Markievicz," *Irish Citizen* (Sept. 1919): 28.
[158] Oikarinen, *A Dream of Liberty*, 127.

which is quite a different thing."[159] Markievicz believed that the biggest challenges to Ireland were the restrictions on trade and commerce that were imposed by the British government and the capitalist "gombeen" men at the
local level, who toed the British line out of self-interest. She argued that these
were counterrevolutionary collaborators who impeded the development of
education, manufacturing and other aspects of the country's infrastructure:
"Directly we get the Republic in working order we shall do a lot."[160]

[159] Constance Markievicz to Eva Gore-Booth (July 22, 1919), in *Prison Letters*, 232.
[160] Ibid. (Aug. 2, 1919), 234–35.

Figure 10. Constance Markievicz lays a wreath at Wolfe Tone's grave, Bodenstown, 1921. (Kilmainham Jail, 19PC-1A46–2.)

Figure 11. Constance Markievicz, "Free Staters in Action": "This courageous attack was launched against ladies, wives, mothers, & children of Republican prisoners, who were holding a meeting in O'Connell St. Mrs Despard is addressing the meeting, & Mme Gonne McBride stands by her. The ladies made an orderly retreat on Mountjoy, where they continued the meeting. They were [followed] by two Lancia cars and again attacked." (Lissadell Collection.)

Figure 12. Constance Markievicz, "The Voice of the People": "That one must have a job in the Free State. Would you look at her new coat!" (Lissadell Collection.)

Figure 13. Constance Markievicz, Eva Gore-Booth, and Maeve Markievicz. (Reproduced by the kind permission of the Deputy Keeper of Records, Public Record Office of Northern Ireland, D/4131/K/10/120.)

Figure 14. Casimir Markievicz's Polish passport. (Lissadell Papers, Public Record Office of Northern Ireland.)

Figure 15. Constance Markievicz, "Free Staters in Action": "Official Report. Glorious Victory over the two Miss O'Reed's. 2 Valuable bycycles captured." (Lissadell Collection.)

13

—

A Citizen of the Republic

LATE SUMMER 1919 SAW THE ESCALATION OF THE CON-
flict between the Irish Republican Army and the British government in Ireland. Constance Markievicz was released from Cork Jail on October 15. She
was now considered to be "a danger to the public peace" and "a leader of the
most extreme faction of Sinn Féin."[1] Immediately, the viceroy, Lord French,
sought to deport her from the United Kingdom, but his plans were complicated by questions regarding Markievicz's nationality. The issue had been
raised before. Prior to the Easter Rising, the chief secretary, Augustine Birrell,
had been asked in Parliament whether he was aware of Markievicz's inflam-
matory speeches, and he had deflected the question by answering that she
was, "by virtue of her marriage, a Russian subject. It is not in the public interest to say what, if any, restrictions will be imposed on her."[2] Now, the possibility of deportation was complicated by the lack of a precedent for expelling a
British-born national who had "become an alien by marriage." There was also
the recurring problem of Markievicz's sex. It was established practice that
no British-born woman should be forced to leave against her will, and even
if she were deported, "would the Poles accept her?" What would happen if
her husband could not be located? These problems were compounded by
the shifting national boundaries in the countries formerly belonging to the
Russian Empire.[3] The British government was uncertain whether Casimir
Markievicz should "be regarded as a Pole or Russian." The secretary of state
eventually ruled that deportation would be against Home Office practices;

[1] NA, HO 144/1580/316818.
[2] "Irish Questions," *Irish Times*, Mar. 16, 1916, 5. Also reported in "Disaffection in Ireland,"
Workers' Republic, Mar. 25, 1916, 5.
[3] (Nov. 10, 1919), NA, HO 144/1580/316818 (77)

furthermore, it "would without doubt cause a great outcry and might well give the lady and her sympathies a most undesirable advertisement."[4]

The "lady" went straight to work. Four days after leaving Cork Jail, she and Maud Gonne were evading the police, throwing Special Branch off the trail of the Cumann na mBan annual convention. All separatist organizations, including the Dáil, were now proscribed, but this only encouraged dissent. With the leaders of other prominent Irish women's organizations, Markievicz—who had been elected president of Cumann na mBan during her imprisonment in 1916—campaigned for the recognition of Irish internees as political prisoners and helped to draft a document to appeal to women's organizations in other countries to pledge their support for Irish prisoners.[5] Drawing from comparisons between Ireland and other small nations whose cases had been considered at the Paris Peace Conference, the women's coalition called for an international committee of inquiry to perform inspections of British prisons:

> Seeing that all liberty of the Press, all liberty of free speech, have been abolished under English military rule in Ireland, all our Republican and many other newspapers suppressed, and Public Meetings prohibited, we appeal to the civilised world to break down the wall of silence with which England seeks to surround Ireland, and to let the light into those prisons where England is trying to destroy the best and bravest of our race.

Their principal argument was that Britain's policy was the suppression of Irish democracy. Out of 105 Irish representatives who had been returned to the British Parliament in the 1918 general election, 78 were Republicans. The only female MP, Constance Markievicz, had been imprisoned for twenty-six months since Easter 1916. The appeal was also printed in the *Irish Bulletin*, issued by the Dáil's Propaganda Department and distributed not only within Ireland but also to press correspondents, politicians, religious leaders, and other important figures in several countries, including Egypt and India.[6]

Shortly after the appeal was printed, the Dublin Metropolitan Police issued an arrest warrant for Markievicz on the basis of her appearances at

---

[4] Ibid.

[5] She worked with Maud Gonne, Hanna Sheehy Skeffington of the Irishwomen's Franchise League, Helena Moloney of the Irish Women Workers' Union, Louie Bennett representing the Irish branch of the Women's International League for Peace and Freedom, and Kathleen Lynn of Cumann na dTeachtaire/the League of Women Delegation.

[6] *Irish Bulletin* (Jan. 1, 1919 [*recte* 1920]); for the *Bulletin*'s distribution, see Townshend, *The Republic*, 124.

proscribed meetings: "The Police on the spot must act firmly and promptly, as the Countess never remains at a meeting for more than a few minutes and may possibly be heavily veiled, and, therefore, difficult to recognise."[7] This was part of a large-scale program by the British Army to disrupt the activities of the Irish Volunteers, but it was hampered by the lack of solid intelligence and by a chaotic administrative structure.[8] Markievicz went on the run. She kept in close contact with Eva, never revealing her location but reporting several "very narrow shaves" with the police and the British Army as she risked arrest. She wrote dramatically about a meeting where she "wildly and blindly charged through a squad of armed police . . . and the crowd swallowed me up and got me away."[9] Another evening, she decided to follow "some of the Army of Occupation [her new byword for the police] round the streets" to document the atrocities committed against the Irish people. She was clearly enjoying herself: "It is awfully funny being 'on the run'! I don't know which I resemble most: the timid hare, the wily fox, or a fierce wild animal of the jungle!"[10]

These zealous letters do not entirely disguise Markievicz's profound fear for her life. The guerrilla tactics that the IRA used to plan ambushes and attacks on police barracks had sweeping consequences on British policy in Ireland.[11] The Royal Irish Constabulary (RIC) had been intimidated into inefficacy and was forced to rely on recruiting men from Britain to police Ireland. Owing to a shortage of RIC uniforms, the new recruits were dressed in a mix of the green RIC uniform and khaki British military dress, leading to the sobriquet "Black and Tans."[12] (In August another cohort of police, the RIC Auxiliary Division, recruited ex-British officers; these men wore full "military battledress and greatcoats" along with tam o' shanter hats that imitated the look of the British Army's Scottish regiments. The men "neither looked like police nor behaved like them."[13]) In late 1920 the Munster divisional commissioner of the RIC looked forward to receiving reinforcements from Britain who would help implement a new "policy" for suppressing the insurgents: "the stamping out of terrorism by secret murder."[14] The extent to

---

[7] Arrest Warrant for Countess Markievicz (Jan. 14, 1920), Sligo County Museum.

[8] Townshend, *The Republic*, 137–38.

[9] Constance Markievicz to Eva Gore-Booth (n.d.), in *Prison Letters*, 216.

[10] Ibid., 217.

[11] "The Irish Intelligence System and the Development of Guerrilla Warfare up to the Truce," in Hopkinson, *The Irish War of Independence*, 69–78.

[12] Townshend, *The Republic*, 157.

[13] Ibid., 158.

[14] Quoted in ibid., 155–56.

which assassinations of IRA men were directed by the British administration or were the consequences of isolated decision making is difficult to ascertain, but there is no doubt that such killings took place. Markievicz believed that the British government was attempting to provoke another rebellion, which would give them a reason to "murder a large number of intelligent and brave patriots."[15]

Markievicz spent the entire summer evading capture. On May 6 she wrote to an unidentified correspondent to apologize for not attending a meeting: "I was receiving a considerable amount of attention & once or twice had considerable difficulties in escaping from a too assiduous 'follower.'" She reported that she had just received "what is commonly called a 'Death notice from the Black Hand gang in the Police.'"[16] Showing up the huge gaps in RIC intelligence, she was able to clandestinely organize the annual Fianna convention—despite such meetings being forbidden. She used the commemoration of the Fianna martyrs of 1916 as an occasion to feature a cathartic attack on cardboard effigies: "It gives a boy a great sense of his own capabilities to sling sticks at a Peeler."[17] Evoking Larkin's appearance on Bloody Sunday 1913, on May 14 she staged a "theatrical reappearance" at an open-air meeting at the Gaelic football grounds, Croke Park, in Dublin, where—costumed in Michael Mallin's Citizen Army uniform—she addressed the crowd that had assembled to commemorate the executed leaders of the Rising.[18] In June she surfaced again, marching with her fellow Sinn Féin TDs on their annual pilgrimage to Bodenstown for the Wolfe Tone commemoration.[19]

In addition to brashly flaunting her disobedience of British law through these public appearances, Markievicz also worked privately in her capacity as minister for labor to expand Sinn Féin's alternative government, although she admitted that this work was slow to take hold, impeded not least by her imprisonments.[20] Markievicz helped to establish permanent conciliation boards to deal with industrial disputes over wages and working hours.[21] The Department of Labour also worked to find employment for men who

---

[15] Constance Markievicz to Eva Gore-Booth (n.d.), in *Prison Letters*, 214.

[16] Photocopy of two-page letter and accompanying six-page article, "An interlude," Gallagher Papers, NLI, MS 21,246.

[17] Ibid.

[18] "2,150 More Troops Landed in Ireland," *New York Times*, May 18, 1920, 1.

[19] "The Wolfe Tone Pilgrimage," *Irish Times*, June 21, 1920, 7.

[20] "Labour Ministry: The Settlement of Strikes and Disputes," Castle File 84, NA, WO 35/207.

[21] "Dublin Corporation and Dail Eireann," *Irish Times*, Sept. 14, 1920, 6. Markievicz still faced obstacles in local government; Farren, an ITGWU member of Dublin Corporation who had not embraced the ICA's amalgamation with the IRA, opposed her plans, but the corporation accepted her proposals without his support.

had resigned from the RIC and for unemployed Volunteers, in addition to overseeing a boycott of goods from Belfast. This was an attempt to pressure the northeast of the country into rejecting the partition of Ireland that was proposed in the legislation that would become the Better Government of Ireland Act, which was working its way belatedly through Westminster throughout 1920.[22]

The character of the war changed dramatically over the summer of 1920, as the British adopted a policy of reprisals for IRA raids, the assassinations of policemen by men in plainclothes in broad daylight, the failure of attempts at conciliation, and the impossibility of prosecuting the perpetrators.[23] The RIC's reprisals were not restricted to killing suspected members of the IRA. They also destroyed local infrastructures: decimating the cooperative creameries that were the nucleus of local agriculture, burning factories, and demolishing pubs.[24] The brutality of the undisciplined Auxiliaries exerted its own terror throughout the country; they were the perpetrators of vicious beatings, mock executions, sustained torture through the maiming and severing of body parts of suspects, and sexual violence against women.[25] Kathleen Clarke recalled one raid in which an Auxiliary policeman, "armed with a rifle . . . put the muzzle resting on my chest. He was so drunk it seemed as if he was keeping himself standing by holding on to the rifle resting on my chest . . . he kept on saying 'I'll teach you.'"[26]

Markievicz was arrested again at the end of September in what was for the police a stroke of good luck. She was traveling to Wicklow with Scán MacBride and Maurice Bourgeois, a French journalist whom MacBride was entertaining. Their car was stopped for a faulty taillight, and the policeman recognized the occupants. As Constance described it to Eva, "All the King's horses and all the king's men arrived with great pomp and many huge guns."[27]

---

[22] Mitchell, *Revolutionary Government*, 161–62; Townshend, *The Republic*, 140–41; "Interim Report of the Proceedings of the Department of Labour," *Dáil Éireann*, vol. 2 (Aug. 17, 1921), http://debates.oireachtas.ie/dail/1921/08/17/00010.asp (accessed Oct. 10, 2014).

[23] Hopkinson, *Irish War of Independence*, 81. Townshend notes that the title "IRA" was not consistently ("and never apparently officially") adopted and was instead referred to generally as "the Army"; *The Republic*, 181–82. IRA is nonetheless used here to distinguish the separatist Irish military force and the British Army.

[24] Hopkinson, *Irish War of Independence*, 79–80; and Townshend, *The Republic*, 161–71.

[25] Sexual violence is particularly difficult to document, although Lady Gregory records two cases in her journal, noting "the family of the girls violated by the Black and Tans wish it to be hushed up." Townshend, *The Republic*, 169–70.

[26] Quoted in ibid., 170.

[27] Constance Markievicz to Eva Gore-Booth (October 10, 1920), in *Prison Letters*, 251.

The three were taken to the Bridewell and then transferred to Mountjoy.[28] Despite the British secretary of state's advice, the Dublin Metropolitan Police considered deporting Markievicz and promptly began an inquiry into the validity of her marriage under Polish law and its implications for her nationality.[29] She was held for a week before she was charged, and another six weeks passed before she appeared in court. While she was waiting, she asked that her Irish grammar, left on her bedside table, be sent to her in jail, along with her needle book and silks, so she could continue to work on an outfit she was sewing for Kathleen Clarke.[30] Unaware of the policy inquiry, she wrote to Maud Gonne to say she was pleased that Maud's son, Seán, "got out all right": "I suppose someone is busy trying to concoct a charge against me. It takes a long time. I was wondering if anything would be planted in my bag!"[31]

The war took another turn while Markievicz was imprisoned in Mountjoy. In October Terence MacSwiney, lord mayor of Cork and a leader in the Volunteers, died after a seventy-three-day hunger strike in Cork Jail. His was the first death by hunger strike since the death of Thomas Ashe in 1918. MacSwiney's epic strike and his iconic public funeral were followed quickly by another martyrdom: the execution of eighteen-year-old Kevin Barry, who had been captured during an IRA ambush in Dublin. These deaths, and the almost inconceivable tragedy of the following month, were immortalized in popular memory.

On the morning of November 21, the IRA attempted to assassinate a team of undercover British agents known as the Cairo Gang, who were operating in Dublin. In a series of raids across the city, Michael Collins's squad of assassins killed twelve British Intelligence agents and two auxiliary policemen.[32] In reprisal, that afternoon the British Army opened fire on a crowd of civilians who were watching a Gaelic football match between Dublin and Tipperary at Croke Park, which the RIC believed that the assassins would attend. Markievicz heard the shooting from her cell. She wrote to Eva that it "lasted twenty minutes by my watch and there were machine-guns going. It felt like being back in the middle of Easter Week." The official inquiry

---

[28] Bourgeois was soon released; MacBride was held until October 8, while police sought incriminating evidence against him; nic Dháibhéid, *Seán MacBride*, 37. See also "Military Activity in Dublin: Madame Markievicz Arrested," Sept. 28, 1920, 6, and "Police Burn Town in County Meath," *New York Times*, Sept. 28, 1920, 1.

[29] J McGrath, Inspector (Sept. 30, 1920), NA, HO 144/1580/316818.

[30] (Copy) Constance Markievicz to Lily [?] (Oct. 13, 1920), NA, WO/35/211.

[31] Markievicz to "My Dearest M—" (Oct. 20, 1929), in *Prison Letters*, 253.

[32] Carey and de Búrca, "Bloody Sunday 1920"; and Dolan, "Killing and Bloody Sunday."

later determined that a military machine gun had fired 50 rounds, and the Auxiliaries had fired another 220 shots.[33] Twelve people were fatally shot, including a Tipperary footballer, and eleven others were injured. Markievicz believed that it was "a miracle that so few were killed."[34] The event became known as Bloody Sunday, forging a link with the police brutality of September 1913. This created a sense of historical continuity between the struggles of the labor Left under Larkin and Connolly in 1913 and the IRA campaign for independence in 1920–1921.

In Mountjoy, Markievicz's prison reading turned to biography. She read a life of Tolstoy (who seemed to her to be "unbalanced" and "like an English Trades Union Leader") and Hilaire Belloc's study of *Danton*, a French revolutionary leader and member of the first Committee on Public Safety.[35] Belloc's book influenced Markievicz's understanding of contemporary Russia. She was being kept abreast of Russian politics by "first-hand" reports, probably from Patrick McCartan, who was attempting to negotiate a Russo-Irish Treaty through his contact, Maxim Litvinov, now serving as a roving Soviet diplomat. Markievicz judged the mass executions of what came to be known as the Red Terror to be "nothing approaching the orgies of appalling murders that Robespierre indulged in."[36] She fully believed that the working class endorsed the total suppression of counterrevolution in Russia, since all accusations against suspected counterrevolutionaries "were proved, quite honestly." When Eva expressed concerns that Lenin's central government was autocracy by another name, Constance responded, "I haven't given up the Bolshies yet."[37] She was concerned that if Lenin slackened his policy of terror in dealing with counterrevolutionaries, then, like Danton, he would be usurped:

> Of course, they may go mad with the idea of Empire, and go out with their armies to force the world to come under their ideas and do awful things in the name of freedom, small nationalities, etc., but even so, they have done something. The French Revolution gave France new life, though all their fine ideas ended in horrors and bloodshed and

---

[33] Townshend, *The Republic*, 202.

[34] Constance Markievicz to Eva Gore-Booth (Dec. 6, 1920), in *Prison Letters*, 255.

[35] Danton played an important role in the execution of Louis XVI and was key to the development of the policy of Terror, until he fell victim to the guillotine owing to accusations of counterrevolutionary activity and financial corruption.

[36] Constance Markievicz to Eva Gore-Booth (Dec. 15, 1920), in *Prison Letters*, 260. For McCartan's negotiations with Russia in 1920, see Documents on Irish Foreign Policy, 1.31 and 1.33, hosted by Royal Irish Academy at http://www.difp.ie (accessed Jan. 20, 2013).

[37] Constance Markievicz to Eva Gore-Booth (Dec. 8, 1920), in *Prison Letters*, 257.

wars. The world too gained. Nothing else would have given courage to the underdog and put fear into the heart of the oppressor in the way it did.

I believe all the reforms at the beginning of the nineteenth century have their roots in the Terror. . . .

I have always used my influence towards decentralisation, and to make people think and act independently.[38]

Markievicz's sustained interest in Soviet Russia and revolutionary France built on her existing ideas about revolution in Ireland. The theoretical models and historical examples that she took from her prison reading were used as justification for her support of the guerrilla tactics that were used in the war for independence, the policy of assassinating the police as agents of the empire, and her later interpretation of the Irish Free State as a counterrevolutionary force.[39]

On December 2 Markievicz once more faced court martial for her revolutionary activities. She was tried under the Restoration of Order in Ireland Act, which replaced the Defence of the Realm Act that had expired at the conclusion of the First World War.[40] Alongside Eamon Martin, whom she had fostered through the Fianna, Markievicz was charged with "conspiracy to organize and promote a 'certain organization known as the Fianna Eireann (Boy Scouts) for the purpose of committing murders on his Majesty's military and police forces, unlawful drilling of men, unlawful carrying and using of arms, and furnishing and training of Irish Volunteers.' "[41] When asked to state her plea, she refused to acknowledge the authority of the court, which she asserted was not constituted by the will of the people but by "the armed force of enemies of the Irish Republic." The prosecution presented as evidence Fianna literature that had been seized in a raid several months before, and an officer who was present at her arrest in September testified that she had admitted murdering British soldiers and police in the past.

Markievicz cross-examined the witnesses herself. She was permitted to pursue an extraordinary line of questioning in which she challenged the ethics of the officer who testified against her, proclaimed the illegality of policing in Ireland, and described the affinity between the Irish and other

[38] Ibid. (Dec. 6, 1920), 256.
[39] For an historical survey of the reversal of revolutionary ideals through treaty politics, the Irish Civil War, and the establishment of Cumann na nGaedheal and Fianna Fáil, see Regan, *The Irish Counter-Revolution*.
[40] Townshend, *The Republic*, 151–52.
[41] "Countess Markievicz before Court-Martial," *New York Times*, Dec. 3, 1920, 17.

anti-imperialist struggles. She asked: would the witness like to see her treated "as you would wish your mother to be treated by a foreign army in England"; had the witness been drinking; was the witness aware of prisoners being tortured for information; had soldiers committed robberies during raids; and finally, "Did you tell me you had just got back from Mesopotamia, and that you were deeply interested in Sinn Fein?" In her closing remarks, she returned to the "shooting of Arabs at Mesopotamia" and asserted the "right of a small nation to fight for her freedom." The atmosphere of the courtroom was heated as she mounted her grievances. Ignoring interruptions from the judge advocate general, she rushed headlong through her defense and concluded by declaring: "The voice of the dead carries to the four ends of the earth, and the spiritual forces, and the noble words of our martyrs will overwhelm you and bring us freedom in the end. That is all I have to say."[42]

On Christmas Eve 1920, at forty-six years of age, Constance Markievicz was sentenced to two years' imprisonment with hard labor in Mountjoy.[43] Much of the work would entail gardening, which was no great hardship. In early spring she delighted in raising a successful crop of peas, which—she bragged—grew much faster than those planted by her fellow inmates. Surprisingly, the prison guards also allowed her to grow flowers: pink carnations and pansies, "all come out of a desert."[44] In summer, when the weather grew too dry for planting, a particularly "obliging warder" helped her gather stones to create an elaborate rock garden, with stairs, winding paths, and an obelisk at the center. All the while, gunfire sounded intermittently as the Anglo-Irish War was waged without her.

The cheerful tone that Markievicz adopted in her letters disguises an important change in her political thought. Her reference to "spiritual forces" during the trial marks a further turn away from a purely socialist discourse of class warfare to a language of spiritual struggle that was reflective of Irish republicanism more broadly. This was a gradual turn, not an abrupt change, and its causes are multifarious. First, separatist discourse after the Easter Rising was dominated by a Pearsean "spiritual emphasis" rather than a Connollyite language of economically determined history and class struggle.[45] A Marxian and even communist impulse remained within a small fragment of the movement, but the prevailing antimaterialist rhetoric was potent. Sec-

[42] "Trial of Madame Markievicz," *Irish Times*, Dec. 4, 1920, 6.
[43] "Madame Markievicz Sentenced," *Irish Times*, Dec. 29, 1920, 3; and NA, WO 35/133. The *Manchester Guardian* reported her age as thirty-six; see "Countess Markievicz Sentenced," Dec. 29, 1920, 3.
[44] Constance Markievicz to Eva Gore-Booth (June 8, 1921), in *Prison Letters*, 273.
[45] English, *Radicals and the Republic*, 14–18.

ond, Connolly's execution in 1916 deprived Markievicz—and Irish Republicanism generally—of a guiding influence. As her understanding of world events and her responses to her prison reading illustrate, when Connolly was killed, Markievicz's grounding in socialist economic and political theory was still shaky. Although her practice of Catholicism was far from orthodox, her conversion after the Rising must also be taken into account, not only because of the antimaterialist focus of Catholic doctrine but also because her newfound spiritualism revived the mysticism that she had exercised at the turn of the century. Finally, the deaths of friends and political comrades had a profound effect on her psyche; during her imprisonments, she reflected on these losses, and one way of combating depression was to focus on spiritual redemption. In November 1918, after her candidacy for Westminster was announced, Constance wrote to Eva justifying her endorsement of armed force: "I believe that we were right and justified in our actions, because the death of our heroes has freed the soul of Ireland, and we who remain are now the incarnation of the National Spirit of Ireland."[46]

Constance's letters to Eva convey a return to Revivalist principals, some of which she had missed out on the first time around. She described her efforts to learn Irish, which she had begun "as a duty, not as a pleasure," but, through the course of her study, she came to believe that the language contained something of an essential Irish quality. That there was no Irish verb for "to have" was to her an indication of the Irish "national character"; it "shows that we are not a covetous and aggressive race."[47] At the height of the Irish Revival, Markievicz had been preoccupied with painting, the theater, and spiritualism. In Mountjoy, she returned to Revivalist principles with a different perspective. Rereading W. B. Yeats's *The Celtic Twilight*, she was "surprised to find it so bad" and believed that it was nothing more than "egoistic and frothy bubble" and had nothing to do with the struggle for independence. She remembered George Russell prophesying at one of his theosophist meetings that an avatar would emerge from the mountains of Fermanagh to "lead Ireland to victory." At the time, "blood and flames [had] seemed incredible and of the Dark Ages," but the upheavals of war across Europe had made anything seem possible: "We'll hope the end will come true. . . . I believe myself that it is only a question of holding out, and that it is by sacrifice that we shall win."[48] Although she did not acknowledge it, there is an echo here of the

[46] Constance Markievicz to Eva Gore-Booth, Extract in Third Report on the Correspondence of the Irish Internees, Nov. 16–30, 1918, NA, CO 904/164.

[47] Constance Markievicz to Eva Gore-Booth (Dec. 30, 1920), in *Prison Letters*, 264.

[48] Ibid., 265.

hunger-striker Terence MacSwiney's famous statement, "It is not those who can inflict the most, but those who can suffer the most who will conquer," an aphorism that sums up the ideology of Republican martyrdom and the antimaterialist rhetoric that was common across the spectrum of republican politics.

Markievicz described the anti-imperialist struggle in antimaterialist terms, amalgamating mysticism, the Irish Revival, Catholicism, and Marxism. She asserted that empires were materialist by their nature, and "the spiritual must prevail over the material in the end."[49] Her reading of W. H. Prescott's *The History of the Conquest of Peru* (1847), a study of the "subjugation" of the Incan civilization by the Spanish, reinforced her belief in the cyclical nature of history.[50] She wrote, "It's so modern. . . . The only hopeful thing is that the Spaniards went down, and if corruption drags a nation down and breaks up an Empire, we ought soon to see a debacle such as has never been seen before!"[51] This curious mix of ideas is one variation of a blend of ideas that were typical of the revolutionary generation. In Tom Garvin's study of the political sentiments of activists of the period, he notes that "asceticism and dislike of commercial civilisation were common themes in Catholic social thought of the period, expressed well, for example in the writing of [Hillaire] Belloc."[52] Markievicz had read Belloc and her ideas reflect a wider Republican rhetoric that contrasted asceticism with "a materialistic and opportunistic careerism."[53] This is evident in Markievicz's denunciation of perceived collaborators with the British government in Ireland and, later, in her condemnation of supporters of the Anglo-Irish Treaty. The mystical strain in Markievicz's writing is also far from unique. For example, after Maud Gonne converted to Catholicism, she continued to believe in "witchcraft."[54]

Markievicz was released early from Mountjoy in May 1921 as the Government of Ireland Act (1920) came into force. The act had passed in Westminster in December by a narrow margin, receiving the approval of neither the Unionist MPs nor the few Home Rulers who remained in the British Parliament. The act was effectively a fourth Home Rule Bill, which partitioned

---

[49] Constance Markievicz to Eva Gore-Booth (April 1, 1921), in *Prison Letters*, 269.

[50] Prescott, *The History of the Conquest of Peru*.

[51] Constance Markievicz to Eva Gore-Booth (Dec. 20, 1920), in *Prison Letters*, 262.

[52] Garvin, "Great Hatred, Little Room," 107. The idea that the nation was a spiritual entity and not a material construct was a frequent theme in writers as different as W. B. Yeats and Patrick Pearse; Yeats's early poetry and his play *Cathleen ni Houlihan* had a strong impact on the formalization of this idea.

[53] Ibid.

[54] Ibid., 108.

Ireland into two states, north and south, each of which would be governed by a devolved parliament that would be subservient to the crown on matters of defense, trade, and foreign affairs.[55] Although these conditions contradicted Sinn Féin policy, the Dáil nonetheless chose to use the "election machinery" of the act.[56] De Valera was conflicted over whether Sinn Féin should contest the northern election; to participate would be an effective endorsement of partition but to refrain would give no option to northern nationalists but to cast their votes for another party. Sinn Féin's election manifesto ignored partition and instead declared simply Ireland's right to self-determination and a binary politics of "Ireland against England," "freedom against slavery," "right and justice against force and wrong."[57] (Nominations to the newly formulated Senate would not be acknowledged, since Sinn Féin did not regard the Senate as a democratic body.)

In the northern election, Sinn Féin won only 6 seats in contrast to 36 seats won by Unionists. By contrast, in the south, only 4 seats (belonging to Trinity College, "Dublin University") were contested. The party ran unopposed in elections for 124 seats, including 4 that were contested by women: Mary MacSwiney, sister to the martyred Terence; Margaret Pearse, Patrick Pearse's mother; Kathleen O'Callaghan (widow of the murdered Michael O'Callaghan); and Constance Markievicz. Markievicz's old constituency of St. Patrick's had been abolished, so she now represented Dublin South alongside her friend Tom Kelly, who had stood in as minister for labor during her internment. Without authority, but nonetheless unchallenged, de Valera dissolved parliament and reconstituted it as the Second Dáil. Later, in August 1921, he would reduce the executive to five posts: the secretary of foreign affairs (Arthur Griffith); secretary of home affairs (Austin Stack); secretary of national defence (Cathal Brugha); secretary of economic affairs (Robert Barton); and secretary of local government (William Cosgrave). Markievicz retained her position as minister for labor, but this post was relegated as outside the executive. Later in the summer, in the Dáil on August 23, Kathleen O'Callaghan and Mary MacSwiney both objected to the exclusion of Markievicz and recommended "a war cabinet of six," but de Valera refused.[58] A snide remark from Cathal Brugha suggested that misogyny might be one reason for her exclusion; he commented that since the ministerial posts had not been confirmed, "no one knew yet who was going to be on the new Cabinet.

[55] Laffan, *Resurrection of Ireland*, 333–35.

[56] Townshend, *The Republic*, 283–84.

[57] Quoted in ibid., 284; Laffan, *Resurrection of Ireland*, 335.

[58] Dáil Éireann, vol. 4 (Aug. 23, 1921), http://debates.oireachtas.ie/dail/1921/08/23/ (accessed Sept. 17, 2012).

It might all be ladies (laughter)." The possibility that de Valera's motivation was sexist is reinforced by his later comment to Kathleen Clarke that she must withdraw from the 1926 Senate election to allow Margaret Pearse to stand, since "the party would not support two women as they would only be able to elect five members."[59]

Another reason, perhaps, was Markievicz's strident and rather undiplomatic attitude.[60] At the end of June de Valera responded to an opportunity to negotiate a truce by inviting James Craig, the newly elected Northern Ireland premier, and Lord Midleton (leader of the Unionist Anti-Partition League) to Dublin to discuss terms. Craig declined the offer, but Lloyd George sent General Jan Smuts to Dublin as "unofficial intermediary," and he met de Valera, Robert Barton, Arthur Griffith, and Éamonn Duggan, a lawyer who worked in IRA intelligence but was not perceived as a militant. A truce was reached, but its terms were reported differently in Irish and British accounts.[61] Both sides agreed that the IRA should cease attacks and that the British Army would end "military manoeuvres, raids and searches," and the curfew was lifted.

The months between the truce and the Anglo-Irish Treaty were far from peaceful. Some units of the Volunteers began conscripting young men, training them for battle in the event that negotiations in London dissolved.[62] The Volunteer membership more than doubled between July and December 1921, but the RIC was powerless to do anything but watch.[63] A rift opened up between the central government of the Dáil and local governments, reinforcing what Laffan has described as "the tensions which had already emerged between democrats and bureaucrats on the one hand, and freedom-fighters on the other."[64]

In Mountjoy, Markievicz had expressed an idyllic vision of Sinn Féin's unity: "Great attempts have been made to divide us, but nobody differs about fundamentals, and everybody has their own ideas of policy, which they discuss quite amiably and openly. There is no jealousy, and no one is out for self."[65] The reality would prove to be very different. De Valera entered the treaty negotiations with an attitude of compromise. There is no record of

---

[59] Quoted in Ferriter, *Judging DeV*, 238.
[60] Townshend notes that the "remodelling of the inner cabinet" has been interpreted by some as "shifting the balance away from the fundamentalist republican wing"; *The Republic*, 324.
[61] Hopkinson, *Irish War of Independence*, 196.
[62] Laffan, *Resurrection of Ireland*, 302.
[63] Ibid.
[64] Ibid., 303.
[65] Constance Markievicz to Eva Gore-Booth (Dec. 24, 1920), in *Prison Letters*, 262–63.

his rejection of Lloyd George's insistence on dominion status; he was committed instead to an ephemeral idea of "external association."[66] "Conflicting messages" and a lack of linguistic precision enabled other members of Sinn Féin to believe that the Dáil remained committed to a republic and kept de Valera in a powerfully ambiguous position.[67] Although members of the Dáil had unanimously voted to grant plenipotentiary powers to the treaty delegates, the delegates were privately instructed to consult the cabinet in Dublin with any draft settlements.[68] (This discrepancy was revealed to the public only during the treaty split.) De Valera did not attend the treaty negotiations and instead sent a delegation led by Arthur Griffith and Michael Collins, who were supported by Robert Barton, Gavan Duffy, and Éamonn Duggan. These men were experienced but were no match for a British committee that included Prime Minister Lloyd George; Winston Churchill; Austin Chamberlain; and the British attorney general, Gordon Hewart.

The Anglo-Irish Treaty negotiations lasted a month, with Lloyd George issuing an ultimatum on December 6 to the effect that the delegates sign the treaty or else face the immediate resumption of war in Ireland. Without consulting the executive in Dublin, the Irish delegation agreed to the document. The treaty granted dominion status to southern Ireland under the name of the Irish Free State, a literal rendering of the Irish *saorstát*, itself a translation of the English "republic."[69] Members of the Dáil would be required to swear an oath of allegiance to the British monarch: to be "faithful to H.M. King George V., his heirs and successors by law."[70] As "citizens of the British Empire," the Irish Free State assumed partial liability for Britain's war debt, and until the Free State was capable of undertaking its "own coastal defence, the defence by sea of Great Britain and Ireland shall be undertaken by His Majesty's Imperial Forces." Furthermore, the treaty granted the British government control over specified ports, and "other such facilities as may from time to time be agreed." Ireland would be partitioned in accordance with the Government of Ireland Act, but the exact border would be determined by a boundary commission at a future date. Of all these conditions, the oath of allegiance and the semantics of dominion status versus "republic" would rankle most with the majority of Republicans whose commitments

[66] Laffan, *Resurrection of Ireland*, 347.
[67] Ferriter, *Judging DeV*, 65–69.
[68] Laffan, *Resurrection of Ireland*, 349.
[69] Ibid., 350.
[70] "Treaty between Great Britain and Ireland" (Dec. 6, 1921), NAI 2002/5/1, http://treaty.nationalarchives.ie/document-gallery/anglo-irish-treaty-6-december-1921/ (accessed Dec. 13, 2014).

have been described as "symbolic."[71] However, an important minority shared Markievicz's far-left vision for the government of Ireland and its social structure, and in her rejection of the treaty's terms, she emphasized the material consequences for the country.

If Markievicz's place as minister for labor had been retained on the cabinet, the votes on the treaty's ratification would have been equally divided. However, when the cabinet met—without her—on December 8, de Valera, Stack, and Brugha were the only dissenters. The Dáil opened a week later to debate the cabinet's recommendation to ratify the treaty. De Valera argued that the treaty delegation had neglected to present the alternative agreement that he had formulated in the event that treaty negotiations broke down. The agreement, known as Document No. 2, had asserted "that the legislative, executive and judicial authority of Ireland shall be derived solely from the people of Ireland" and was, he claimed, consistent with the Proclamation of the Republic.[72] He declared that the Provisional Government that had been created by the treaty should not be recognized since the Dáil was the elected government of the people and had not been disestablished. Furthermore, he argued that the Dáil represented the whole of Ireland, but no northern-based representative had been invited to the treaty negotiations. He pleaded for unity and urged the Dáil to accept Document No. 2. The Speaker of the Dáil, Eoin MacNeill (whom Markievicz had urged de Valera to expel from Sinn Féin because of the countermanding order that he had issued at the outset of the Easter Rising), argued that the substance of the documents was the same and that to substitute Document No. 2 for the treaty signed by the delegation would be to throw the country into further confusion. The meeting descended into a cacophony of blame. Kevin O'Higgins accused de Valera of "split[ting] the finest, the solidest political movement the world has ever seen from top to bottom."[73] Markievicz jumped immediately to de Valera's defense, arguing that the split had been evident when the treaty was first published; she said that she would not have ratified the agreement and neither would the people with whom she had spoken. She made it clear that on being asked to stand down from the cabinet, she had ascertained de Valera's exact position on Ireland's relationship to the British Empire, which was one of external association, not subordination.[74]

---

[71] Laffan, *Partition of Ireland*, 80.
[72] Dáil Éireann, vol. 4 (Dec. 15, 1921), http://debates.oireachtas.ie/dail/1921/12/15/00002 .asp (accessed Sept. 17, 2012).
[73] Ibid.
[74] Ibid.

When the Dáil resumed after a break over Christmas and the New Year, the battle lines were drawn. Each deputy was given the opportunity to speak just once in order to articulate his or her position on the treaty. As a demonstration of loyalty to the idea of the nation, Markievicz began by speaking in Irish, with an accent that the *Irish Times* mocked as reminiscent of "the Irish of Stratford-atte-Bowe."[75] She argued that the treaty was a sugarcoated Home Rule bill, which would disestablish the democratically elected Dáil. (These observations later prompted George Gilmore to claim that Markievicz was unique in her understanding of "the realities" of the agreement.[76]) She believed that the delegates who were in favor of the treaty, led by Arthur Griffith, were bound to give southern Unionists a disproportionate voice through the establishment of an upper house:

> And what do the Southern Unionists stand for? . . . First and foremost as the people who, in Southern Ireland, have been the English garrison against Ireland and the rights of Ireland. But in Ireland they stand for something bigger and still worse, something more malignant; for that class of capitalists who have been more crushing, cruel, and grinding on the people of the nation than any class of capitalists of whom I ever read in any other country.[77]

At her declaration of commitment to Connolly's vision of a workers' republic, she was interrupted with cries from the floor: "Soviet Republic." She rebutted, "co-operative commonwealth," before hurling a jibe at the "Cheap State Army," with which the English and the capitalists would be sure to replace the IRA. The mudslinging brings certain truths to light. During the Civil War of 1922–1923, the Provisional Government concentrated on establishing a centralized state infrastructure, clawing back the devolved power of the Republican courts of 1919–1921, which operated on a local level, and creating a strong local presence of centrally controlled military and police in order to "break the hold local brigades of the IRA had on the public's perception of events at the centre."[78] Markievicz's vision for Ireland could be derided as "Soviet," but she believed that devolved power overseen by a central government (the Dáil) was also an Irish way of doing things, applying the principles and structure of the cooperative movement more widely in the Republic.

[75] "Dail Discusses Treaty," *Irish Times*, Jan. 4, 1922, 5.

[76] For Gilmore's observation and Richard English's critique, see *Radicals and the Republic*, 37.

[77] Dáil Éireann, vol. 3 (Jan. 3, 1922), http://debates.oireachtas.ie/dail/1922/01/03/ (accessed Sept. 19, 2012).

[78] Kisssane, *The Politics of the Irish Civil War*, 166.

In these final days of the treaty debates, Markievicz brought anti-imperialist rhetoric back into play. She asked the Dáil how self-professed Republicans could consent to Ireland's endorsement of the British oppression of Egypt and India, which the country would be required to support under the oath of allegiance to the empire. Without flinching, she confronted her own controversial geneology: "Now you all know me, you know that my people came over here in Henry VIII's time, and by that bad black drop of English blood in me I know the English—that's the truth. I say it is because of that black drop in me that I know the English personally better perhaps than the people who went over on the delegation. (Laughter)."[79] Heckled, "Why didn't you go over?," she replied, "Why didn't you send me?"

As well as targeting MacNeill, Markievicz directed her attack toward Michael Collins, whom she accused of betraying "the Workers' Republic for which Connolly died," and she charged him with acting in the interest of the capitalists. She barbed her political arguments with rumor, telling the assembly that Collins was to be engaged to Princess Mary and would be appointed first governor of the Saorstát. The gloves were off. The *New York Times* published a sensational front-page report: "with knit lips and with one piercing glance," Collins replied,

> I do not come from the class that the Deputy of the Dublin division comes from. I come from the plain people of Ireland. The personal allusion to the lady whose name was mentioned may cause her pain and may cause pain to the lady betrothed to me [not Princess Mary, but Kitty Kiernan], and I will not allow it to go unchallenged by any Deputy in any assembly of any nation to insult anybody.[80]

Yet Collins was not above hurling insults himself. As the Dáil took a recess for lunch on January 10, he shouted across the floor at Markievicz and Daithí Ceannt, "Deserters all! . . . I now call upon the Irish people to rally to us, and we shall stand by them." "Traitors and cowards," Markievicz retorted. "Foreigners, traitors, and English," Collins returned, to which Ceannt yelled, "Long live the Republic!"[81]

When the vote was cast on January 7, sixty-four men voted in favor of the Anglo-Irish Treaty, and fifty-one men and six women voted against it. The Republicans continued to participate in the Dáil for another week, reiterat-

[79] Dáil Éireann, vol. 3 (Jan. 3, 1922), http://debates.oireachtas.ie/dail/1922/01/03/ (accessed Sept. 18, 2012).

[80] "Foes Powerless to Block Treaty," *New York Times*, Jan. 4, 1922, 1.

[81] "Exciting Exchanges: Mr De Valera Comes Back," *Irish Times*, Jan. 11, 1922, 5.

ing their argument that the people of Ireland had voted for a Republic, and the Republic could not be reconstituted as a Free State without the consent of the people. In one of her most eloquent speeches, Markievicz told the assembly that the protreaty government faced a "clear road" ahead: "They go over—they take up the negotiations, they form a Constitution and then go on. But I say why should our side be supposed to end our opposition to the destruction of the Republic?"[82] Supported unanimously by her fellow female TDs, Markievicz affirmed Cumann na mBan's rejection of the treaty, telling the Dáil that in all of Cumann na mBan, only one division had supported the treaty; six were against it.[83]

In fact, Markievicz and the female Republican members of the Dáil had declared Cumann na mBan's antitreaty stance without the consent of the majority. The figure of six in favor and one against that Markievicz quoted was merely an estimate of Cumann na mBan opinion. A convention would not be held until February 5, and then its purpose seemed predetermined: to ratify the Cumann na mBan executive's resolution, reaffirming "their allegiance to the Irish Republic" and declaring that on that basis, Cumann na mBan could not "support the Articles of [the] Treaty signed in London."[84] In advance of the convention, Jennie Wyse Power claimed that Markievicz "misappropriated some £200 of the organisation's funds in order to finance" antitreaty propaganda, drafted a circular without the executive's approval, and sent it out to Cumann na mBan branches across the country.[85]

Markievicz's arguments proved to be fruitless in changing majority opinion in the Dáil, but they were essential in the battle for public opinion. Inspired by the strong stance taken by most of the Cumann na mBan executive, members of the organization protested the treaty outside the Dáil during the debates. When the convention finally took place, the Republican stance won an overwhelming majority, with 419 delegates accepting the proposed resolution. Just 63 women voted in favor of Jenny Wyse Power's proposed amendment, which acknowledged that the treaty, "if accepted by the Irish people, [will] be a big step along the road to that end [the Republic], [and] we declare that we will not work obstructively against those who support the treaty."[86] This amendment would have restricted Cumann na mBan from continuing to protest if "the majority of the people accept[ed] the treaty

---

[82] Dáil Éireann, vol. 3 (Jan. 9, 1922), http://debates.oireachtas.ie/dail/1922/01/09/00003.asp (accessed Sept. 19, 2012).

[83] "Fair Play All Round," *Weekly Irish Times,* Jan. 14, 1922, 3.

[84] Quoted in McCarthy, *Cumann na mBan,* 177.

[85] Ibid.

[86] Quoted in ibid., 179.

at a general election."[87] Wyse Power also suggested that Cumann na mBan should refrain from taking a stance on the treaty until it was clear which direction the men of the IRA would choose. This subservience to a male organization did not sit well with women who, in Mary MacSwiney's words, had fought "for women's right to take their place in the councils of the nation."[88] After the rejection of Wyse Power's amendment, Margaret Pearse introduced a successful motion to prohibit branches or individual members of Cumann na mBan from assisting any candidates standing for the Irish Free State.[89]

Did the women at the Cumann na mBan convention represent the majority? In his study of Cumann na mBan, McCarthy notes that there were 702 Irish branches of the organization documented at the convention of 1921; in the vote at the 1922 convention, only 327 branches were represented. Some delegates from Munster, who were sure to have voted against the treaty, were prohibited from attending by a railway strike in the south of the country. However, other branches may have refrained from attending because the stance of the organization seemed predetermined by Constance Markievicz and Mary MacSwiney. Tactics like these reinforce historical judgments that assert that the "republican view of public opinion was and remained generally dismissive."[90]

In the first six months of 1922, the fight between pro- and antitreaty factions was a war for public opinion. Markievicz and her fellow Republican TDs established a new newspaper, *The Republic of Ireland: Poblacht na h-Éireann*, to gain a wider audience for the arguments that they voiced in the Dáil and to counter the unanimous protreaty opinion of the national press: the *Irish Times* and the *Freeman's Journal*.[91] The first issue of *Poblacht na h-Éireann* addressed the public's aversion to another war. Markievicz's front-page article, "Peace with Honour," was remarkably gentle in tone. She argued that England did not want a war any more than Ireland did, and Ireland could afford neither the financial cost nor the casualties that the attempt to suppress the Irish Republic would bring about. She was optimistic: "We too, are

[87] Ibid.
[88] Quoted in ibid., 180.
[89] "Women Sinn Feiners Oppose Treaty," *Manchester Guardian*, Feb. 6, 1922, 8. Margaret Pearse was the mother of the executed Patrick Pearse. Richard Mulcahy's wife was summarily expelled from Cumann na mBan, along with Markievicz's foe from the Irish Women's Franchise League, Jennie Wyse Power.
[90] Townshend, *The Republic*, 359.
[91] The editor of *Poblacht na h-Éireann* was the socialist republican Liam Mellows, with Frank Gallagher as assistant editor, Joseph McDonagh as manager, and a "Committee of Direction" composed of Cathal Brugha, Austin Stack, J. J. O'Kelly, Constance Markievicz, Mary MacSwiney, Sean Etchingham, Erskine Childers, Kathleen O'Callaghan, and Robert Brennan.

weary and shrink from the horrors of the foreign occupation. Therefore, we can meet on the common plane of Peace—a love for Peace."[92] Since the *Irish Times*, among others, habitually referred to the treaty as "the Peace Treaty," Markievicz and her fellow Republicans referred to it as the Articles of Association, emphasizing the bond that it forged between Ireland and Britain and its effective disestablishment of the Republic. Her interpretation was based on the treaty's establishment of a Provisional Government that was separate from the Dáil and would govern the country until an election could be held.

That the Republic had been proclaimed at Easter 1916 and had been established by the democratically elected First Dáil Éireann in 1919 were the historical facts on which the Republicans established their antitreaty policy. Coincidentally, a group of Irish Republicans in South Africa had organized the Irish Race Conference, an international meeting to commemorate the third anniversary of the Dáil in 1922, scheduled to take place in Paris in January. That group had not foreseen the treaty and had planned to use the conference to demand Irish independence and as a platform for organizing an international association to determine Irish social, cultural, and economic objectives in Ireland and abroad.[93] Instead, the conference became a battleground for pro- and antitreaty factions. A delegation from Ireland attended, with Eoin MacNeill, Michael Hayes, Douglas Hyde, Diarmid Coffey, and the lord mayor of Dublin, Laurence O'Neill, representing the Provisional Government, and Éamon de Valera, Constance Markievicz, Mary MacSwiney, Harry Boland, and the lord mayor of Cork, Donal O'Callaghan, representing the antitreaty side.[94] Giving women a strong diplomatic presence was a savvy maneuver to win the support of Irish women worldwide. And although the Republican contingent has been blamed with hijacking the proceedings, the delegates from the Provisional Government behaved equally divisively. In the end, the Republicans were more successful in winning public opinion during a conference that was unquestionably a "debacle" with no clear aims.[95]

The week after they returned from Paris, Republicans attempted to set out a policy that they hoped would give them a positive political identity, rather than have their position defined negatively as a rejection of the treaty. De Valera launched a new party, Cumann na Poblachta, and a new political program. At a monster meeting on O'Connell Street, which drew crowds that stretched half a kilometer from the Parnell Monument to Nelson's Pillar

---

[92] Constance de Markievicz, "Peace with Honour," *Poblacht na h-Éireann* 1, no. 1 (Jan. 3, 1922), 1.
[93] Keown, "The Irish Race Conference."
[94] Ibid., 367.
[95] Ibid., 375.

outside the GPO, Markievicz and Cathal Brugha declared that "all State authority in Ireland is derived solely from the People of Ireland" and that partition was "unconstitutional and illegal."[96] Opening with the issue of partition—an issue on which de Valera had been ambivalent—captured the attention of the audience and laid the groundwork for the economic questions that were more important to Markievicz. One of the terms of the treaty was that after a period of two years, the Irish Free State would be responsible for compensation to "members of Police Forces and other Public Servants who are discharged by it or who retire in consequence of the change of government."[97] Markievicz and Brugha implicitly referred to this condition when they demanded that Volunteers, prisoners, and their dependents "should be the object of the nation's first care" and should be given preference in employment. This focus also evoked Connolly's preoccupations in the *Irish Worker* and *Workers' Republic* at the onset of the First World War and put anti-imperialist rhetoric in real terms.

Republicans withdrew from their ministerial posts in the Dáil, including de Valera, who resigned from his place as príomh aire and was replaced by Arthur Griffith. Protreaty journalist Stephen Gwynn reported on the changeover in the *Observer*, caustically remarking that Markievicz had "been replaced by Mr. Joseph McGrath, whose speech in the Dáil showed a personality well fitted to deal with men."[98] Although they had stepped down from positions of leadership, de Valera, Markievicz, and other Republican TDs still participated in Dáil sessions. Markievicz continued to lobby for a strong labor policy, questioning McGrath's loyalty to strikers. Similarly, she and Daithí Ceannt pressed for large-scale land reform. Echoing Markievicz's work with Laurence Ginnell the previous year, she and Ceannt proposed that all land "evacuated by enemy forces," except for land being used as training grounds for the IRA, should "be divided into economic holdings, and distributed among landless men, preference being given to members of the I.R.A."[99] Land redistribution had been sanctioned in two Sinn Féin policy documents in 1917 and 1918 and at three Land Conferences in Mayo

---

[96] "Republicans Denounce the Peace Treaty," *Irish Times*, Feb. 13, 1922, 6.

[97] This did not apply to members of the Auxiliary Police Force or other police recruited in Britain for the RIC for the next two years. "Anglo-Irish Treaty," NAI, http://treaty.nationalarchives.ie/document-gallery/anglo-irish-treaty-6-december-1921/anglo-irish-treaty-6-december-1921-page-3/ (accessed Dec. 13, 2014).

[98] "The New Order in Ireland," *Observer*, Jan. 15, 1922, 13.

[99] "Republican Drum-Fire," *Irish Times*, Mar. 2, 1922, 7. Campbell argues that the characterization of Republicanism as "entirely conservative" must be revisited in light of conservative reactions to social radicalism advocated within Republican Sinn Féin; *Land and Revolution*, 282–83.

in 1920, but in 1922 conservatism, particularly from protreaty Sinn Féin, dominated.[100]

Opposition from protreaty delegates provided valuable ammunition for the Republican propaganda war. On the question of land reform, Richard Mulcahy (minister for defense) replied that it was not clear yet which land belonged to the British Government and which to private individuals. Such a politically naive response enabled Markievicz to declare at a hundreds-strong St. Patrick's Day meeting in Harold's Cross that "a few men had signed away the Republic and brought serfdom to the nation."[101] Conversely, the socialist discourse employed by Markievicz and several other Republicans was used to fuel mainstream support in Britain to suppress Irish Republicanism. At a meeting in England where Winston Churchill was heckled by one hundred members of the Communist Party, he said he was "encouraged" by recent speeches from Republicans, whom he believed were driven to violent rhetoric because they lacked majority support: "Mr De Valera and the Countess Markievicz" represent "the true spirit of madness . . . the true spirit of Bolshevist mania."[102]

At the beginning of April, Markievicz embarked on a tour of the United States to fundraise for the Republicans.[103] She was accompanied by Kathleen Barry, sister of Kevin Barry, who had been executed by hanging in 1920. Markievicz and Barry set sail from Southampton to New York aboard the *Aquitania*, a Cunard liner whose close quarters reminded Markievicz of the years she spent in prison:

> I find a ship the next worse thing to jail—and rather like it! Small, stuffy cabin and crowds of people around you that you don't want . . . I already wish that I was home again. It's awful not to be there at such a moment. The difficulties ahead are colossal, not the least being that for a very long time (perhaps never) we shall each and all of us be suspicious of everyone and everything. In fact, I sometimes wonder if the rank and file will ever trust a leader again. I wouldn't be surprised if the Army or some of it didn't start off doing things on its own.[104]

When the *Aquitania* docked and Markievicz disembarked, the *New York Evening World* flattered her with faint praise:

---

[100] Campbell, *Land and Revolution*, 283–84.
[101] "Why I.R.A. Convention Was Prohibited," *Manchester Guardian*, Mar. 18, 1922, 9.
[102] "Mr Churchill on the Coalition," *Observer*, Mar. 26, 1922, 15.
[103] For the context and history of tours like this one, see Eichacker, *Irish Republican Women in America*.
[104] Constance Markievicz to Eva Gore-Booth (n.d.), NLI, MS 21, 816.

Despite her martial achievements she is not a martial looking person—frail, rather and almost deprecatory except when she is talking about the Irish Republic. Very tall and slender she has the stoop characteristic of so many women of her height. Her soft, waving ash-brown hair is done in the quaint psyche knot at the crown of her head, her eyes behind the eye-glasses are clear blue and there is a dash of pink in her thin cheeks. Her smile is charming. Back of everything she says one feels emotion like a flame.[105]

At the pier she gave a brief interview to the *New York Times*, calling Griffith and Collins traitors and affirming her unstinting willingness to die for the Republic, before she was whisked off to the Waldorf Astoria by Austin Stack and Seán Ó Ceallaigh, who were also on tour.[106]

Irish Republicans were in a turf war with the Free State delegation, which had also launched a publicity campaign in the United States in advance of the general election that was scheduled for June. Republican efforts were focused on securing Irish American trust in de Valera's leadership. As Constance wrote to Eva:

> I believe that his influence, and his alone, has made it safe for the new domestic enemies to flaunt around, and I don't like to think of what might happen if they were ever able to get the People, more especially the Army, to distrust him and to disbelieve in his honesty, his brains and his courage. If they succeed in this, I am sorry for them, for their end will be swift and sure, more sure than his.[107]

They also had a hefty financial concern. The Free State was being supported by the British government, but the Republicans had to meet all their own costs—including funding for the IRA—through donations. They had an ambitious itinerary touring Republican clubs, many of which were named for recent martyrs, including Kevin Barry. In Philadelphia on Easter Sunday, Markievicz praised de Valera as "worthy to be a comrade of George Washington" and took in over $75,000 in cash and pledges. In Cleveland, Ohio, she appeared dressed in mourning and shouted to the audience: "I am a rebel and I hope there are many others here tonight." That evening, they brought in between $10,000 and $15,000.[108]

[105] Quoted in Eichacker, *Irish Republican Women in America*, 142.
[106] "Countess Markievicz, Irish Rebel, Arrives," *New York Times*, April 8, 1922, 6.
[107] Constance Markievicz to Eva Gore-Booth (n.d.), NLI, MS 21, 816.
[108] Eichacker, *Irish Republican Women in America*, 144–45.

In late April they arrived in St. Paul, "in the wilds of Minesota [*sic*]," where Markievicz was surprised to find a letter from Stanislaus waiting.[109] Although she was living more extravagantly than she had in a decade—she had bought Maeve presents of Hudson Bay furs in New York—a strong sense of frugality lingered. She saved the stationery from her stay at the Waldorf Astoria, on which she wrote a long reply to Stanislaus. She told him about how she had mobilized friends in Russia and the United States to effect his release, but she was unsentimental about Stanislaus's imprisonment. To her mind, Bolsheviks and Irish Republicans were part of the same struggle: "You rail against the Bolshies . . . but one thing I do know [is] that our people suffered far worse from the English." Having witnessed so much violence in Dublin, she was unsurprised by the burning of Zywotowka; it was another manifestation of the raiding and ransacking to which she had been subjected. She told Stanislaus flatly: "I have no house now." She continued, thinking of the split in the Dáil and what she believed was a second betrayal by Eoin MacNeill: "I begin to believe . . . all governments are the same, & that men in power use that power to get more power for themselves & are absolutely unscrupulous in their dealings with those who disagree with them."

Despite their political differences and her frustrations with Casimir's financial irresponsibility, she "hate[d] to think of him having to work a job" but then qualified, "Of course we are all frightfully poor just now, for money won't buy anything."[110] Her hardships were imperceptible to the midwesterners, who marveled at her "Oxford pronunciation" and her "zest . . . for 'the people' of Ireland," which created the impression of "a living paradox."[111] In contrast to the wealthy patrons of Republicanism in New York and Boston that she entertained, for these Americans, Irishness was synonymous with poverty. Stepping off the train in Butte, she wore a glamorous black dress trimmed in red braid, with a low-cut collar lined with red silk and pinned with American Beauty roses, which the press commented on at length. Yet her "nervous fingers" betrayed her intensity of purpose, and the incongruity of her appearance and her politics diminished as she won over the residents of Butte by her willingness to take part in their everyday life.[112] "Put up to things a bit by 'wicked' friends" in the International Workers of the World, she went down a copper mine, where she saw men at work with pick and

---

[109] Constance Markievicz to Stanislaus Markievicz (n.d.), NLI, MS 13,778/1.

[110] Ibid.

[111] Interview with the *Butte Miner* quoted in Eichacker, *Irish Republican Women in America*, 147.

[112] Ibid.

drill. She was outraged to observe a man drilling copper ore without water to dampen the dust, which would have prevented the toxic cloud from entering his lungs: "This is nothing but murder. . . . They tell us that few men live to be old in Butte Montana."[113]

Astutely conscious of the sympathies of her different audiences, she changed the focus of her speeches to make Republican policy relevant to local concerns. To Montana's miners, she discussed the importance of Ireland controlling its own commerce; she assured a meeting of Freemasons in Seattle that the women appointed to the Republican government were "honest," "fearless," and unselfish. In San Francisco, she avoided any references to Irish Republicanism's socialist underpinnings and instead regaled the audience with stories of the Easter Rising, when bullets flew around her like so many "bees buzzing."[114] The tour was exhausting: "hustle, hustle, hustle, from mutiny to trains, from trains to meetings, interviews & so on."[115]

She found time to write to Eva on the return journey across the North American continent. With most of the tour complete, she could now relax and allow the landscape to capture her imagination. Passing through the "waste Lands of Montana," she imagined that "each hummock might hide a scaly prehistoric monster, & each stagnant pool a water snake." She was impressed at the resilience of San Francisco ("one would never know that there had been a fire & an earthquake so short a time ago"), and marveled at the palm trees and aloe bushes "scattered like thistles" in the concrete in the tropics of Los Angeles. She reflected on the American suburbs, where "even the poor houses stood alone, among greenery"; here was an important lesson for Ireland and for England when it came to the state's provision for the working poor.[116]

While Markievicz was in the United States, the militant phase of the Irish Civil War began. The Irish Republican Brotherhood was still holding conferences on the treaty, but on April 14 two hundred antitreaty IRA men seized the Four Courts on the north bank of the Liffey. As nic Dháibhéid writes, "It was an incongruous location for a rebel fortress: amid the neoclassical flour-

---

[113] Constance Markievicz to Eva Gore-Booth (n.d.), NLI, MS 21,816.

[114] Eichacker, *Irish Republican Women in America*, 149–50. Anxieties in the American Irish Liberty League about Irish Republicans' close ties to Bolshevism are evinced in Shane Leslie's broadside "Repentant Peter Says Sinn Feiners Have Nothing in Common with Bolshevists" (American Irish Liberty League, 1920), the text of which derives from Leslie's articles in the *Boston Post* (reprinted in the *San Francisco Leader* and the *Los Angeles Examiner*): "[the] world will find in a free Sinn Fein Ireland the greatest breakwater and pledge against universal Bolshevism that is possible. The world may have to choose between recognizing the green flag or being swamped under the red."

[115] Constance Markievicz to Eva Gore-Booth (n.d.), NLI, MS 21,816.

[116] Ibid.

ishes of James Gandon's great dome, sandbags were piled to form barricades and legal tomes stacked against windows."[117] Arguably, the occupation was more of a symbolic "gesture than a military initiative."[118] Other public buildings were taken in the northern part of the city, including the Rotunda Hospital, where the future novelist Liam O'Flaherty raised the red flag. Their tactics seem to have been to provoke a response from the British military; an attack would, it was hoped, increase popular support for the Republican side. A similar awareness was behind the reluctance of the IRA officer commanding in Dublin, Oscar Traynor, to "resort . . . to Ambushes in the streets, as it would alienate public sympathy."[119]

There was a standoff for six days, before firing erupted across the city on the night of April 20. The garrison in the Four Courts denied responsibility for the shooting. On hearing reports of the fighting, Constance wrote to Eva: "Nobody likes the Freak State. They are trying to block us by pretending that *we*! are making civil war in Ireland, from whence I hear that they are opening 'Stunts' every night Firing vast quantities of ammunition at nothing & pretending that we are attacking them."[120] As she and her comrades prepared to return to Ireland, they organized a final rally for the Republican cause: a ticketed event at Madison Square Garden. When Markievicz took the stage, she was cheered for six minutes by a crowd of five thousand people.[121] Spontaneously, the cheering changed to the singing of "The Soldier's Song," before finally quieting so that Markievicz could deliver the most powerful speech of her entire tour. Discrediting the authority with which the delegates had signed the treaty, she said,

> When we read it we could not understand. We had trusted those men as we had trusted ourselves. . . . The so-called treaty is nothing but a surrender, and in signing it they attempted to subvert the Irish Republic and to place Ireland in a position she has never occupied before—that of deliberately sacrificing her nationhood and accepting the subordinate position of a British dominion.

Her use of the word "ourselves" is important, since it evoked Sinn Féin's "Ourselves Alone" and cast the treaty signatories as standing outside of Sinn Féin politics. She told the crowd that the question Ireland faced was not a

---

[117] nic Dháibhéid, *Seán MacBride*, 60.
[118] Townshend, *The Republic*, 397.
[119] Twomey to Lynch, quoted in ibid., 414.
[120] Constance Markievicz to Eva Gore-Booth (n.d.), NLI, MS 21,816.
[121] "Markievicz Tour Halted," *New York Times*, May 25, 1922, 2; and Eichacker, *Irish Republican Women in America*, 153.

"question of de Valera or Collins or Griffith"; it was one "of a republic such as America versus a miserable travesty of Canada's Constitution." She concluded by paraphrasing the well-known words of the hunger-strike martyr Terence MacSwiney: "To him who can endure the most victory will come."[122]

On May 30 Markievicz set sail for Southampton aboard the Cunard liner, the *Berengaria*. British Special Branch noted her arrival and expressed concern about her powerful influence in the forthcoming election, which would be the first since the signing of the treaty.[123] Privately, politicians on pro- and antitreaty sides of Sinn Féin had agreed on an "electoral pact," which essentially rigged the vote; they would divide the seats proportionally to reflect the treaty split in the Dáil: sixty-four in favor, fifty-seven against.[124] The emergence of the Labour Party, the Farmers' Party, and the Businessmen's Party broke Sinn Féin's monopoly, as the new parties looked for their share in the new state. To retain as much of the vote as possible, de Valera, leading antitreaty Sinn Féin, and Michael Collins, leading the protreaty faction, implausibly agreed to not make the treaty an issue in the election. Markievicz supported this unified front. The night before the poll, she campaigned beside pro- and antitreaty candidates at a rally in York Street, where she declared that Sinn Féin "wanted law and order in Ireland, they wanted to see the crops sown and work found for the unemployed, and they wanted to do something for the people starving in Mayo and Donegal, and even in [the Dublin suburb] Balrothery."[125]

The election of 1922 was the first time that proportional representation was used in Ireland, which—despite Sinn Féin's attempts to feign unity—allowed voters to express their treaty preferences.[126] In Markievicz's constituency, four seats were contested among seven candidates, three of whom represented parties other than Sinn Féin. The result was the election of two protreaty candidates and one each from labor and the independents. Despite receiving 3,951 first-preference votes and over 15 percent of the ballot, Markievicz was narrowly defeated by Tom Kelly, who supported the treaty.[127] She believed that her defeat was due to a " 'rotten' register," which had listed her name third on the ballot, whereas she had been listed first

---

[122] "5,000 Irish Cheer Sinn Fein Countess," *New York Times*, May 22, 1922, 3.

[123] "Mme Markievicz Returns," *Independent* , June 7, 1922, in Castle File 84, "Markievicz, Constance Georgina (Countess)," NA, WO 35/207.

[124] Townshend, *The Republic*, 398.

[125] "Last Words to the Electors," *Irish Times*, June 16, 1922, 6.

[126] Hopkinson, *Green against Green*, 110–11.

[127] Kelly received 4,344 first-preference votes and a 16.51 percent share of the ballot.

on the notice of poll.[128] However, her loss was in keeping with the wider electoral trend, which reflected a protreaty majority.[129] At the final count, protreaty candidates received 239,000 first-preference votes and won fifty-eight seats, whereas antitreaty candidates received 130,000 first-preference votes and won thirty-six seats. Even newly emerged labor was preferred over antitreaty Sinn Féin, receiving 132,000 first-preference votes and winning seventeen seats.[130] Protreaty Sinn Féin won 78 percent of the overall vote.

The British government urged Michael Collins, commander-in-chief of the new Free State, to suppress Republican dissent. The IRA after the treaty split represented approximately two-thirds of the majority; they were experienced fighters and also well armed, at least at first. These factors contributed to Collins's reticence to escalate the conflict. The assassination of First World War hero and Unionist politician Sir Henry Wilson by two IRA men in London on June 22 put further pressure on Collins. Winston Churchill declared in Parliament that if the "band of men styling themselves the Headquarters of the Republican Executive" was "not brought to an end and a speedy end ... we shall regard the Treaty as having been formally violated ... and we shall resume full liberty of action in any direction ... to any extent that may be necessary."[131] When an antitreaty IRA commander was captured in a raid in Lower Baggot Street on June 27, the Republicans captured in reprisal a prominent treaty supporter, Ginger O'Connell, and held him in the Four Courts garrison. This provided the necessary provocation for intervention. In the early hours of June 28, the Provisional Government issued an ultimatum to the Republican occupants of the Four Courts: evacuate or "the building will be taken by force."[132]

The Republicans held their ground, though tenuously, having failed to secure strategic outposts around the Four Courts and lacking in adequate arms and ammunition.[133] Although Collins was aware of the danger of alienating public opinion by using British weaponry, it proved necessary. The Republicans were ill equipped, but the Four Courts was "effectively a fortress" that would require artillery if it were to be breached. The British supplied

---

[128] The election agent Kenneth Reddin was charged with attempting to deceive the electorate in the South Dublin constituency; he placed an advertisement in the *Irish Times* on election day to apologize for the mistake. See "An Election Card," *Irish Times*, June 15, 1922, 7; "Display Ad 21," *Irish Times*, June 16, 1922, 7; "Republican Plans Affected," *Weekly Irish Times*, June 24, 1922, 1.

[129] Hopkinson, *Green against Green*, 110.

[130] Townshend, *The Republic*, 403.

[131] Quoted in ibid., 406.

[132] Ibid.

[133] nic Dháibhéid, *Seán MacBride*, 64.

two eighteen-pounder field guns but only twenty shells, so the Free State troops resorted to firing shrapnel to keep up the appearance of a sustained attack. Cumann na mBan mobilized to nurse the wounded, cook for the IRA, and carry dispatches. As in the Rising, Markievicz did not take part in this work but instead shouldered her weapon; this time she would fight with the IRA's Dublin Brigade.

The Irish Citizen Army agreed to be directed by the Dublin Brigade and to take orders from its commanding officer, Oscar Traynor. While the ICA had no guns to spare, it provided three thousand rounds of .303 ammunition to the IRA. ICA commandant John Hanratty, who had worked in the kitchens of Jacob's Biscuit Factory during the 1913 Lockout, took charge of the Citizen Army contingent at Barry's Hotel, and Markievicz once more served as second-in-command.[134] Situated on Great Denmark Street, off the northeast corner of Parnell Square, Hanratty and Markievicz were near the Republican forces that were concentrated on the east side of O'Connell Street. Just over a hundred meters north of the GPO, the Hammam Hotel—the windows and entrances barricaded with a few sandbags and luggage from the tramway offices nearby—served as Republican headquarters.

Traynor preferred to launch an urban guerrilla war, but the tactics of barricading buildings replicated some of the mistakes from the Easter Rising. Ernie O'Malley, who led the Four Courts garrison, described their position as "rats in a trap."[135] Mid-morning on June 30, the IRA munitions store at the Four Courts was hit by a shell and exploded. Traynor ordered the garrison to surrender on the basis that their surrender would enable the other garrisons to evacuate their positions voluntarily.[136] The ICA covered the IRA's retreat to other outposts throughout the north of the city, where they held out for another four days. On July 4 Free State troops had drawn close enough to begin firing on the IRA garrisons in the hotels along O'Connell Street. De Valera, Traynor, Stack, and Markievicz all left their posts, expecting the others to follow, and were surprised when many did not.[137] On July 5, with the buildings on fire, Traynor gave the order to retreat or surrender.

Although they had abandoned their headquarters in Dublin, the Republicans had not entirely given up the war. Liam Lynch, chief of staff of the IRA, established headquarters in Mallow, County Cork. Traynor was captured by

---

[134] Fox, *Citizen Army*, 218.

[135] Townshend, *The Republic*, 408.

[136] Ibid., 409.

[137] "Report by General Officer Commanding-in-Chief on the Situation in Ireland for Week Ending July 8th 1922" (July 11, 1922), NA, CAB/24/138.

Free State troops in Dublin on July 27, by which time Markievicz had escaped to Munster, where Lynch had established a defensive line stretching from Limerick to Waterford. With Free State troops being increased at the rate of three hundred per day, and artillery and armored cars supplied by the British, Republicans had little hope of holding the line.[138] At the end of July Markievicz surfaced in Carrick-on-Suir in South Tipperary, where she was spotted with Erskine Childers and Kathleen Lynn.[139] The region was a Republican stronghold, with the deposed de Valera serving as director of operations for the Second Southern Division of the IRA in Carrick-on-Suir and Clonmel.[140] Prior to Markievicz's arrival in the county, the Republicans had occupied the courthouse and the RIC barracks before they were set on fire. Similar to the IRA's occupation of the South Dublin Union in the Easter Rising, Carrick-on-Suir's hospital and workhouse were seized and used as headquarters.[141] On July 14 the Irish-American General J. T. Prout, who served in the U.S. infantry in France prior to joining the Tipperary Brigade, advanced on Carrick, leading six hundred troops armed with field artillery, machine guns, and trench mortars.[142] The Free State took the town on August 3, and the Republican forces fell back into the surrounding countryside.

Childers directed the IRA publicity department, which issued daily newspapers, *Poblacht na h-Éireann War News* and *Republican War Bulletin*, that attempted to keep up morale and turn public opinion away from support of the Free State. Markievicz had a hand in running both, publishing important and emotive—if not always effective—propaganda. She frequently designed the front pages and, like the editors of the Polish newspaper *Rzespospolita*, discussed below, adopted a system of dating that evokes the French revolutionary calendar; issues in 1922 were dated "Seventh Year of the Republic," taking Easter 1916 as the foundational event. On August 4 her anonymous article "A Prophecy" mourned the death of Harry Boland, who had been shot when Free State soldiers raided his room in the Grand Hotel at Skerries, in the north of County Dublin. She reported that Boland had told her at a Republican meeting, "I expect Mick will get me 'plugged.' I know too much about him."[143] Just three weeks later, Michael Collins was assassinated in an ambush in western County Cork. In *War News* on August 24, the

---

[138] Ward, *Unmanageable Revolutionaries*, 187.
[139] "Irregular Rule: Life in Carrick-on-Suir," *Irish Times*, Aug. 7, 1922, 6.
[140] Hopkinson, *Green against Green*, 167.
[141] "Irregular Rule: Life in Carrick-On-Suir." For the occupation of the South Dublin Union, see Arrington, "Socialist Republican Discourse."
[142] For Prout, see Townshend, *The Republic*, 421.
[143] "A Prophecy," *Poblacht na h-Éireann War News*, Aug. 4, 1922, 1.

Republicans "acknowledge[d] his bravery" but insisted that "the war in which he has fallen was of his own making" and "that it was he who declared with most emphasis that there would be no peace until the I.R.A. had laid down its arms."[144] Markievicz wrote privately to Joseph McGarrity, referring to the assassination of Collins and Arthur Griffith's death from natural causes:

> Our people have had a bitter lesson, every pact has been broken & no Free Staters word is sacred. The air is gradually clearing now, & the removal of their two cornerstones will help much. . . . The rank & file of the F.S. troops absolutely believe that M[ichael].C[ollins]. never intended to take the oath & that they are going on for the Republic! Some lads who raided us told me so—These boys will wake up some day & find out how they have been duped.[145]

Markievicz's cool tone was by no means unique; when Muriel MacSwiney (widow of the martyred Terence) was on a lecture tour in the United States in 1922, the *Washington Post* commented, "She mentions the deaths of Arthur Griffith and Michael Collins in the calm way one would speak of two pawns of an opposing chess-player swept from the board."[146]

Markievicz was equally frigid on the subject of Republican assassinations, kidnappings, and reprisals against the agents—and perceived agents—of the Free State.[147] Her ideas about the political uses of terror and the suppression of counterrevolution that had been sparked by her prison reading were not merely academic. The one person with whom Constance would have felt able to let her guard down about such topics was Eva, but it was hard to write letters on the run, and what correspondence survives between the sisters has been carefully curated.

In the September issue of the *Irish Republican War Bulletin*, Markievicz published a sketch titled "with the I.R.A. (somewhere in Ireland)," which—if it did not take its cue directly from Seán Keating's "Men of the South" (1921)—was working from similar principles of Socialist Realism. This was one of several of her large cartoons that regularly covered the front

[144] "Michael Collins," ibid., Aug. 24, 1922, 1.

[145] Constance Markievicz to Joseph McGarrity (n.d.), NLI, MS 17,627.

[146] Quoted in Foster, *Vivid Faces*, 317.

[147] Peter Hart's close analysis of regional studies is essential to the study of IRA violence in this period; see *The IRA and Its Enemies*. Hart controversially formulates the Irish Civil War as an "ethnic conflict" between Catholics and Protestants; Hart, *The I.R.A. at War 1916–1923*, 8; yet his formulation of "ethnicity" as constituted by race, religion, and language is complicated by individuals such as Constance Markievicz and Roger Casement, whose conversions were motivated by their rejection of the values of the social class into which they were born. When Markievicz converted to Catholicism, she did not consider herself to be a Protestant but an atheist.

page of the *War Bulletin*. The newspaper also used a sunburst motif for its banner, which was similar to the one that she had designed for *Bean na hÉireann*. Markievicz's drawings were an important component in the Republicans' propaganda machine: emotive, unambiguous, and immediate. A sketch published at the end of September referred to the abduction and murder of Timothy Kenefick, who had been taken from his home in Cork city and killed, his body dumped in Macroom. A grotesque portrait of Major General Ernest Dalton—who had been traveling with Collins but survived the raid—loomed above the damning caption:

> At an inquest held at Coachford, Co. Cork on Sept 21st, on the body of Captain Kenefick I.R.A., the jury found that he was wilfully murdered after arrest by imperial troops, and brought a verdict of wilful murder against the officer in charge of the imperial troop and Richard Mulcahy as Minister for Defence. General Dalton was the officer in charge of the Imperial Murder Gang.[148]

The next week's "Free Staters in Action" responded to the brutality of Free State Army raids on civilian homes in an attempt to flush out Republican fighters and humiliate their supporters; here, she depicts a "nervous elderly gent" trembling at gunpoint.

Markievicz signed most of the cartoons, situating herself as a direct witness in the midst of the action.[149] While she chose a militant role for herself, she also gave credibility to conventional gender roles. Her cartoon "At a Republican Home" is accompanied by a caption that evokes British recruitment propaganda from the First World War: "Kiss Daddy Goodbye, darling, he's going off to fight for the Republic."[150] The article that follows is written with Markievicz's characteristic rhetoric:

> In these terrible days a vast throng of our women watch sadly and wait for the passing of the dread clouds which have settled over our land. These pearless [*recte* peerless or fearless] women would no more barter their Freedom than they would their faith. But traitors have lied so effectively that all they can do is to raise their hands to Heaven in prayer.

She goes on to refer to Cumann na mBan's reaffirmation of allegiance to the Republic, the "noble, brave part played by Cumann na mBan in 1916," and the cooperation of women that was essential to the Anglo-Irish War 1920–

---

[148] *Republican War Bulletin*, Sept. 24, 1922, 1.
[149] Ibid., Oct. 1, 1922, 1.
[150] Ibid., Oct. 5, 1922, 1.

1921.[151] Invoking her previous columns for the *Irish Citizen*, she referred to a female hero from Robert Emmet's rising; now there were "hundreds of Anne Devlins": "Ireland's Republican women of 1922 have effectively co-operated with the boys in the hills: they have sheltered and caved the boys 'on the run.' They have proved themselves to be powerful auxiliaries of the I.R.A." Markievicz's classification of women as auxiliaries is a surprising retraction of her previous stance that women should be regarded as comrades and equals in battle. This choice of phrase demonstrates her awareness of her audience and plays to the trope of helpless women at the hands of brutal Free State troops that was common in Republican propaganda.[152] Importantly, Markievicz used these stereotypes self-consciously and did not relinquish her vision of women fighting as equals with men. In another article for *War Bulletin*, "Mere Utilitarianism Is No Sufficient Rule of Christian Citizenship," she returned to the image of Joan of Arc, contradicting the stereotype of women as auxiliaries, mothers, and wives.[153]

This reference to utilitarianism is also important. The concept was being used to justify the Free State's passing of the Public Safety Bill, which echoed the British government's "draconian" Restoration of Order in Ireland Act of 1920, which had instituted martial law.[154] If the state protected the people through legislation and policing, then—in a utilitarian view—it was in the people's interest to support the state.[155] The new legislation made the possession of firearms a crime punishable by death, which would provide legal justification for the Free State's policy of executions. Markievicz responded to the bill by evoking past martyrs with renewed vigor. On the anniversary of Terence MacSwiney's death, she published a sketch of him in his prison cell, with the words "Republican War Bulletin" floating dreamily above the window.[156] The implication was that the Provisional Government had simply replaced the British in the same state structure, with the same policy of suppressing Republican aspirations.

In an enigmatic cartoon for the Scottish edition of *Poblacht na hÉireann*, Markievicz seems to be claiming a classical model for the communist

[151] Women's activities during the war of 1920–1921 are difficult to trace. Ernest Blythe later declared that Cumann na mBan was not a military organization, but testimony from male and female participants describes the young girls in Cumann na mBan working in the same way as the Fianna, taking "serious risks" by carrying dispatches, administering first aid, and carrying arms; see Townshend, *The Republic*, 250–52.

[152] Ibid., 252.

[153] *Republican War Bulletin*, Oct. 13, 1922, 1.

[154] Jackson, *Ireland 1798–1998*, 267.

[155] See Kissane, *Politics of the Irish Civil War*, 171.

[156] *Republican War Bulletin*, n.d. [c. Oct. 25, 1922], 1.

republicanism that she envisaged. Her cartoon "The Branded Arm of James O'Reilly" shows a man's forearm tattooed with the letters P and Q, suggesting the SPQR that was the emblem of the Roman Republic and the declaration of ownership by the people.[157] The Irish Republican clubs in Scotland were important bases of support for the far Left, including communists Roddy Connolly and Sean McLoughlin, who had returned to Ireland during the Civil War and presented the IRA commander-in-chief Liam Lynch with a social and economic program that included "nationalization of industry and finance; confiscation and re-distribution of ranch land; abolition of all rents and mortgages; a shorter working day; municipalisation and free use of all public services; and the arming of the workers."[158] Connolly and McLoughlin believed that Lynch was sympathetic to their aims, although his first priority was to organize a military defeat of the Free State; in fact, Lynch was skeptical of the "views and opinions of political people."[159] After the meeting, Connolly traveled to Germany and Moscow to try to organize arms for the IRA, and McLoughlin joined the IRA to promote communist ideas from within. They published their program in the *Workers' Republic* and gained a few supporters. The social and economic program was attractive to Liam Mellows, the Republican defense minister, but by the time the Dáil met in secret in October to restore a form of government, Mellows was imprisoned in Mountjoy, and de Valera was anxious about "get[ting] the allegiance of the men who are fighting" since their visions for peace and the future of the state were "unlikely to be the same."[160]

Although there is no proof of their meeting, it is probable that Markievicz met Connolly or McLoughlin while she was in Munster, since she soon left Ireland to go to Scotland to deliver lectures to the Republican organizations there. Her commitment to a radical social program was balanced with the Republican campaign to gain control of the state. In Glasgow at the end of January 1923, she spoke to the communist Irish Republican Organisation in Scotland and declared that "she was a Communist but their first duty was to clear the British out of Ireland, then they could have any form of Republic they liked," echoing James Connolly's stance in the months prior to the Easter Rising.[161] On the whole, Markievicz was unrestrained in her support for Bolshevism during her Scottish tour. British Special Branch followed

---

[157] *Poblacht na hÉireann* (Scottish edition), Oct. 7, 1922, n.p.
[158] McGuire, *Sean McLoughlin*, 94.
[159] Ibid., 94; Lynch quoted in Townshend, *The Republic*, 440.
[160] Quoted in Townshend, *The Republic*, 441.
[161] Report on Revolutionary Organisations in the United Kingdom (Feb. 1, 1923), NA, CAB 24/158b, 18.

her movements closely, although they never attempted an arrest, perhaps because, as their surveillance reports noted, the "attendance [was] very poor."[162] They took careful note of her support for the Republican policy of arson, which Markievicz believed had a model in the Bolsheviks' burning of large estates, including Zywotowka: "The burning of houses belonging to those high in authority against the Republic was, she said, a means of making them feel a sense of their responsibilities."[163] She believed that "Capitalist property" should be destroyed and that spies should be shot, but that the execution of prisoners of war was unacceptable. Throughout her visit, she supported the Republican clubs' resolutions condemning the Free State's executions of Republican prisoners. Two recent executions, of Rory O'Connor and Liam Mellows in Mountjoy, were ostensibly in reprisal for the assassination of Free State TD Seán Hales. However, many Republicans suspected that Mellows and O'Connor were selected for reprisal because of Mellows's support for the emergent Communist Party of Ireland.[164] Markievicz stayed longer in Scotland than she initially planned, attending a meeting of the Irish Self-Determination League in Glasgow and rendezvousing with Joe Robinson—officer in command of the IRA in Glasgow—in an attempt to unite Communists and Irish Republicans in Scotland.[165]

The relationship between Irish republicanism and communism was fraught with dissension. Roddy Connolly cofounded the Communist Party of Ireland (CPI) in 1921 but failed to win the support of Ireland's socialists, evidenced by the ICA's joining up with the Dublin Brigade of the IRA in 1922. (The CPI's Red Guard joined the IRA in July 1922 but comprised just a dozen people so its effect was negligible.[166]) From the CPI's earliest days, Roddy Connolly was seen as something of a loose cannon, and Markievicz had little to do with him.[167] Sylvia Pankhurst warned her in October 1922 that "several of the heads of the movement in this country [England] are not in accord with the tactics of [Roddy] Connolly, who is best left to himself."[168] The Communist Workers' Party in Britain, founded by Pankhurst, publi-

---

[162] NA, WO 35/207.

[163] (Feb. 15, 1923), NA, CAB 24/159, 16. For a discussion of arson as a tactic, see Clark, *Everyday Violence in the Irish Civil War*.

[164] Report on Revolutionary Organisations in the United Kingdom (January 25, 1923), NA, CAB 24/158, 12. See O'Connor, *Reds and the Green*, 71–74.

[165] NA, CAB/24/159.

[166] O'Connor, *Reds and the Green*, 66.

[167] Comintern would dissolve the CPI in 1924.

[168] Special Branch Report on Revolutionary Organisations in the United Kingdom (Oct. 12, 1922), NA, CAB/24/139.

cized Irish Republican propaganda but denounced Connolly *fils*.[169] In the *Workers' Dreadnought*, Pankhurst published a long article, "Communism versus Reforms: Mistakes of the Communist Party of Ireland," to correct the "non-communist programme of the Irish C.P.."[170] Her principal grievance was the CPI's recognition of Dáil Éireann, which she argued should be dissolved and replaced by soviets (workers councils).

On this point, Markievicz and Pankhurst disagreed. Although Markievicz had discussed the adoption of a soviet model for Irish government, she was also faithful to the Dáil, which she believed had been founded on the will of the people. A Republican Dáil—in Markievicz's view, the true Dáil—was a step toward an Irish state that would reflect the principles of the Comintern. At a meeting in Burnley in Lancashire, she declared: "Republicans were idealists. . . . She claimed they had worked for the ideals of service and their aim had been gradually to supplant the industrialism of modern civilisation by the intellectual qualities of art, poetry, and religion of the old Gaelic order, with its emphasis on cooperation and equal opportunities for all."[171] Markievicz's rhetoric self-consciously built on a Revivalist discourse that combined utopianism and rural cooperation. In so doing, she attempted to create a sense of continuity of vision in the Irish struggle, which would render the principles of international socialism acceptable to a majority that was schooled in a local, national paradigm. The myth of Gaelic renewal was widely used across the spectrum of pre–Civil War republican thought, including the work of (protreaty) Michael Collins and (antitreaty) Ernie O'Malley, who emphasized "race, racial qualities, racial similarities and differences."[172] The language of race is far less prevalent in Markievicz's writing than in O'Malley's; when she chooses to use it, "race" takes on an inclusive tone that denotes a spiritual and cultural difference rather than essential physical characteristics.

With the Free State officially recognized by Westminster in December 1922 and legitimacy granted to the protreaty army's raids and executions by the Public Safety Bill, the Irish Civil War entered its final stage. In autumn 1922 the Free State government carried out a series of executions, including the killing of Erskine Childers on what was believed to be a "trumped-up charge," since Childers had on him a miniature pistol, which Michael Collins

---

[169] Ibid. This was a small group, which Pankhurst founded after she was expelled from the Communist Party of Great Britain for refusing to hand over her newspaper, *The Workers' Dreadnought*.

[170] Pankhurst and Pannekoek, *Communism versus Reforms*.

[171] "Countess Markievicz at Burnley: Free State 'Founded on Trick and Fraud,'" *Manchester Guardian*, Mar. 14, 1923, 10.

[172] English, *Ernie O'Malley*, 94–95.

had given him as a gift.[173] Consequently, the IRA issued a threat to members of the Provisional Government, declaring that they were all "equally guilty" in the "murder of soldiers."[174] Protreaty TD Seán Hales was assassinated by the IRA in Dublin, and four Republican leaders of the Four Courts garrison were sentenced to death in retaliation. In the name of "counterterrorism," executions continued apace, with the extrajudicial shooting of Republican fighters after surrender and the killing of Free State troops by booby trap in reprisal.[175]

Several civilian organizations campaigned for peace throughout the autumn of 1922, urging—at the very least—a temporary ceasefire. A group that styled itself the Neutral IRA, organized by former IRA men in Cork, called for an end to the war and held a convention in February 1923 that was attended by over 150 delegates.[176] Liam Lynch, chief of staff of the Republican IRA, was firmly committed to continuing the fight, but his subordinates were almost in consensus about the futility of continuing the war. At the end of March the Republican executive met, and for the first time since the onset of the war, de Valera was invited to the proceedings, suggesting that the Republican leadership was at least glancing toward a return to political methods. No agreement could be reached, however, and the executive adjourned to deliberate and reconvene in April.

In Britain, Scotland Yard worked closely with the Free State to conduct raids that targeted known members of the Irish Self-Determination League, which was under close surveillance by Special Branch. In mid-February Markievicz left Glasgow for London, where she spoke to a meeting of the Central Branch of the Irish Self-Determination League at the Minerva Café in Holborn.[177] Her prominence at meetings was noted in the international press, which reported her claim that "the Irish Republic's chance was imminent and that the support of many other countries could be expected." She continued to place Ireland in a wider imperial context, arguing that troubles in India and Egypt were "aiding the Irish Republican aspirations."[178] Scotland Yard launched a concerted effort to arrest and deport suppliers of munitions, but the police allowed Markievicz freedom to travel unimpeded, perhaps in the hope that she would lead them to an even bigger catch.

---

[173] Townshend, *The Republic*, 441.
[174] Quoted in ibid., 442.
[175] Ibid., 443.
[176] Ibid., 445.
[177] NA, CAB/24/159.
[178] "Fear More Raids in England," *New York Times*, Mar. 14, 1923, 6.

In early April Markievicz returned to Dublin via the Liverpool boat, arriving in Clonmel, Tipperary, on April 10, where she joined her fellow Republican leaders to discuss what newspaper reports speculated would be "the abandonment of the so-called war."[179] The Free State Army ambushed the meeting and shot and captured Liam Lynch, but de Valera and Markievicz were among those who were able to escape.[180] Frank Aiken, one of the IRA officers in attendance, later commented that those who could get away were forced to abandon Lynch, since "the papers we carried must be saved and brought through at any cost."[181] The *New York Times* published an erroneous report that Markievicz was subsequently captured along with Mary MacSwiney on their way to Lynch's funeral.[182] In fact, she had escaped back to Scotland. From Glasgow down to Burnley in the northwest of England, she toured Republican clubs and petitioned the British Labour Party to support Irish Republicans, capitalizing on the British Conservative and Unionist Party's support for the Provisional Government.[183] She argued, "In reality the Free State was an attempt to build up English civilization in Ireland, and to get the capitalist system firmly rooted there, for it was a happy hunting-ground for the makers of fortunes."[184] In late March she returned to Ireland, where the Republic had vanished from the realms of possibility.

[179] "Free State Takes More Rebel Chiefs," *New York Times*, April 13, 1923, 19.
[180] "Irish Rebel Chief Dies after Fight," ibid., April 11, 1923, 1.
[181] Townshend, *The Republic*, 447.
[182] "Free State Takes More Rebel Chiefs," 19.
[183] "Republican Demonstrations in Scotland: What Madame Said," *Éire: The Irish Nation*, Feb. 24, 1923, 7; "Miss MacSwiney on the Deportations," *Manchester Guardian*, Mar. 14, 1923, 10.
[184] "Manchester to Dublin Service," *Manchester Guardian*, Mar. 15, 1923, 10.

14

===

Counterrevolution

IN SUMMER 1923 CASIMIR TRAVELED TO DUBLIN FOR THE first time in a decade. The details of his visit are unclear, but on his way, he arranged to meet Maeve in London. He was surprised to discover that she seemed neither Polish nor Irish but "English *pur sang*."[1] She still harbored a strong resentment toward her mother for being "permanently in prison," and she expressed a profound hatred toward all politics. Surprisingly, Casimir stood in Constance's defense, telling Maeve that her mother should be respected as a "woman willing to sacrifice everything—her family, her social standing, her personal freedom." When he arrived in Dublin, according to O'Faolain's jovial account, Casimir spent almost the entire time in his old haunt, Neary's pub, catching up on the city's gossip. He also arranged to see Constance, with whom, he wrote, "despite the geographical distance," he felt "connected by a true friendship."[2] As a memento, she gave him a signed photograph from her tour to the United States the previous year. Unusually for a posed photograph from this period, she does not wear a uniform but is dressed in a richly brocaded jacket with a satin collar, and she signed the picture simply, Constance de Markievicz.[3]

When he returned to Warsaw, Casimir contributed a long series of articles to the Polish newspaper *Rzeczpospolita*, "the Republic." This "Republic" refers to the Second Polish Republic, established in November 1918 and imagined as a partial restoration of the Polish-Lithuanian Commonwealth of the late eighteenth century, which had been retrospectively claimed as the First

[1] PRONI, D4131/K/10 (part 2).
[2] Casimir Markievicz, "Letters from Ireland," *Rzeczpospolita* (n.d. [1923]), n.p.
[3] PRONI, D4131/K/10 (part 2).

Republic. Evoking the French revolutionary calendar, *Rzeczpospolita* marked the first year of the republic as Year One and dated each subsequent issue accordingly. In Casimir's series, "Letters from Ireland," the differences between Polish and Irish Republican identities—principally the difference between his politics and Constance's—come to the fore. In London, Casimir had told Maeve that he had "sympathies with Ireland," but in *Rzeczpospolita*, the extent of his sympathies and the limits of his understanding are revealed. He writes, "Green Erin has recently been accused of Bolshevik tendencies, but it is not really drawn in that direction"; rather, Ireland's difference was "based on the distinctiveness of Celtic culture and race."[4]

Casimir's emphasis on "race" reflects a sharp turn of his politics to the right in the aftermath of the Bolshevik Revolution. Whereas his earlier pamphlet for the Freedom and Brotherhood of Peoples, *Irlandiya*, had imagined Poland as a constituent in the Russian Empire, the tone of his writing in 1923 is distinctly nationalist. His ideas strongly reflect the influence of Roman Dmowski's political program in the National Democratic Party. Dmowski advocated Polonization and reified the "folk," whom he believed, as Snyder writes, were "in fierce competition with wily Jews and disciplined Germans."[5] Markievicz attempted to characterize himself as one of the folk, describing himself as an average farmer rather than an upper-class landowner. He also insisted that he was different from the Irish landlords, who were the "backbone and garrison" of the English presence in Ireland.[6]

For Dmowski, language and religion were the distinguishing characteristics of Polish nationality, and these are the focal points of Markievicz's series. Perhaps drawing from Constance's newfound enthusiasm for the Irish language, Casimir described the proliferation of Irish literary culture in English: "the language of Erin's most hated oppressor; the language of the invader." He asked his readers, "Can you imagine Mickiewicz writing *Pan Tadeusz* in German, Krasiński writing *Nie-boska komedia* in Russian, or Słowacki writing *Kordian* in Jewish? That's what makes the Polish situation fundamentally different from the Irish."[7] He may easily have said instead, that's what makes the Polish situation superior.

"Letters from Ireland" is full of references to Jews as a foreign corrupting influence in Ireland. In his first letter, Casimir indicts the Warsaw press for ignoring the Irish war for independence and for calling "President de Valera a

---

[4] Kazimierz Dunin Markiewicz, "Letters from Ireland," *Rzeczpospolita*, year 5, no. 208 (n.d. [1923]), n.p.

[5] Snyder, *The Reconstruction of Nations*, 58.

[6] "Letters from Ireland," *Rzeczpospolita*, year 5, no. 208 (n.d. [1923]), n.p.

[7] Ibid., no. 192 (n.d. [1923]), n.p.

Jew." He goes on to extol the virtues of presumed racial purity: Ireland's "natives" are described as "truly Aryan Celts"; shopkeepers on Grafton Street are sarcastically described as "the chosen people" who "tempt goys with antiques or expensive jewelry"; popular music halls that detract from Dublin's literary theaters are described as staging "filthy Anglo-Saxon foolery brought to Erin directly from London by various Frohmans and other Jews."[8] In the last installment of his series, Markievicz writes that W. B. Yeats has married "an English woman and has two children with her," and he hopes that in spite of this, Yeats's "talent for poetry is inherited."[9] This assertion hauntingly intuits Yeats's own developing notions about the importance of pure bloodlines to high art, and it unknowingly suggests the way in which the far Right in Ireland would manipulate the Revivalist discourse that focused on the purity of Irish culture.

Although anti-Jewish attitudes were prevalent among the Sinn Féin leadership, including Maud Gonne, Arthur Griffith, and J. J. O'Kelly, Constance never endorsed those opinions.[10] Her resilience to such nefarious ideas probably stemmed from her reading of James Connolly, who wrote in his pamphlet *Labour, Nationality, and Religion* (1910), "The day has passed for patching up the capitalist system; it must go. And in the work of abolishing it the Catholic and the Protestant, the Catholic and the Jew, the Catholic and the Free-thinker, the Catholic and the Buddhist, the Catholic and the Mahometan will co-operate together."[11] In an article for the Republican newspaper *Éire*, Markievicz commented that in the early days of the fight for independence, "nobody minded" a person's origin because "everyone realized that Robert Emmet, Wolf Tone, and many another Gael, whose lives had been given for Ireland, were of foreign origin."[12] The idea that one could be a foreigner and a "Gael" contradicts the ideas of racial purity that are at the forefront of Casimir's essays. Rather than seek essential physical qualities of "race" in ancient Ireland, Constance Markievicz represents the past as a historical model of an egalitarian society that could inspire a modern "co-operative commonwealth." In a lecture she delivered in the Lancashire mill town of Burnley, outside Manchester, she described how the Republic would "supplant the industrialism of modern civilization by the intellectual quali-

---

[8] Ibid., nos. 180 and 271 (n.d. [1923]).

[9] Ibid., no. 271 (n.d. [1923]), n.p.

[10] Gonne's point of view was bred among the "right-wing French circles" in which she moved at the turn of the century; for Gonne, Griffith, and O'Kelly, see Garvin, "Revolutionary Activists," 108.

[11] Quoted in Ellis, *James Connolly*, 117.

[12] Quoted in Oikarinen, *A Dream of Liberty*, 34.

ties of art, poetry, and religion of the old Gaelic order."[13] Constance and Eva shared this vision of the Irish past, which was romantic but also politically expedient.[14] To the urban working class, it was a utopian vision; to the rural poor in Ireland, it differentiated the Republican program from the interests of the ranchers who supported the Provisional Government and their new political party, Cumann na nGaedheal.

There is also an absence of "whiteness" from Constance Markievicz's political discourse. After the First World War, campaigns for self-determination argued that national sovereignty was the "right for white men the world over," an idea that was particularly prominent in Erskine Childers's propaganda.[15] This language was adopted by de Valera, who in 1920 proclaimed that Ireland was "the last white nation that is deprived of its liberty."[16] In the interest of diplomacy, de Valera referred to nonwhite nations, but these occasional references lacked the sustained presence that countries including Egypt and India have in Constance Markievicz's anti-imperialist speeches and writing.[17] She discusses a mutual battle for equality rather than structuring her arguments as a complaint about Ireland's status as the last oppressed "white nation."

For example, Markievicz saw in Britain's recognition of Egypt as a sovereign state the model for Irish Republican victory.[18] Britain had declared Egypt a protectorate at the outbreak of the First World War and implemented martial law; Zaghlul Pasha, the leader of the Egyptian People's Party, was arrested in March 1919 and deported to Malta. This only increased his popularity when he was released during the Paris Peace Conference. In 1921 Zaghlul rejected the treaty with Britain that had been negotiated by a political rival and would only grant partial independence.[19] The Unilateral Declaration of Egyptian Independence and the Anglo-Irish Treaty are similar; they both protected British interests in foreign relations and allowed a continued military presence in a nominally free state, and both agreements were equally unsatisfactory to radicals who demanded complete independence from the

---

[13] "Miss MacSwiney on the Deportations," *Manchester Guardian*, Mar. 14, 1923, 10.

[14] For Eva Gore-Booth's representation of the equality of the sexes in ancient Irish society, see Arrington, "Liberté, Egalité, Sororité."

[15] Nelson, *Irish Nationalists*, 148–77.

[16] Ibid., 212.

[17] For de Valera's speech to the Friends of Freedom for India when he was on a lecture tour to the United States, see ibid., 230–31.

[18] "Fear More Raids in England," *New York Times*, Mar. 14, 1923, 6.

[19] For the British imposition of martial law and media censorship, see Botman, "Occupation and Nationalist Response," in *Egypt from Independence to Revolution*, 25–54; for a contemporary expression of Egyptian nationalists' lack of confidence in the treaty negotiations, see Ebeid, *Complete Independence*.

British Empire.[20] In a similar measure to the Free State's Public Safety Bill, the Egyptian high commissioner had instituted a policy of martial law and had arrested, imprisoned, or exiled the country's revolutionary political leaders, including Zaghlul, who was deported to the Seychelles. Zaghlul's supporters conducted a series of attacks against British institutions and British people and successfully provoked the government into returning their leader, who organized the Wafd Party that would sweep the elections in late 1923 and would result in an independent Egyptian parliament. Speaking in March 1923, Constance Markievicz argued that Irish Republicans, like the Egyptian people, "had been compelled to resort to guerilla warfare."[21]

Markievicz also hoped that her formulation of Ireland and Egypt as analogous would appeal to the socialist Independent Labour Party (ILP) in Britain, the most radical members of which had supported the Bolshevik Revolution and called for the independence of Ireland, Egypt, and India. She published an open letter to the ILP in which she urged the party to put pressure on the government to "cease financing the Free State Junta" and to allow the "people [to] vote free from threats and coercion in a free election."[22] Irish Republicans officially laid down their arms in the spring of 1923, and despite the internment of much of the leadership, they prepared to contest the forthcoming general election. Members of the Provisional Government organized a new political party, Cumann na nGaedheal, with William T. Cosgrave, chairman of the Provisional Government, at its head. Antitreaty Sinn Féin, organized by de Valera and Austin Stack, applied its policy of parliamentary abstention to what was perceived to be a government in which Britain remained the authority. Nonetheless, Republicans who followed de Valera believed that the election would demonstrate that their ambitions represented the will of the people.

In advance of the election, Markievicz renewed her Republican propaganda campaign, publishing a series of articles for the Republican newspaper *Éire* in which she argued that Kevin O'Higgins, the Free State minister for justice and orchestrator of the Public Safety Bill, violated the democratic mandates of the 1918, 1920, 1921, and 1922 elections in Ireland and that the Civil War had been launched as a last resort, instigated by the Free State's unwillingness to risk the judgment of the people on the treaty.[23] In a series of darkly comic drawings, she caricatured members of the government and their

---

[20] For the terms of the Egyptian agreement, see Vatikiotis, *The History of Modern Egypt*, 264.

[21] "Miss MacSwiney on the Deportations," *Manchester Guardian*, Mar. 14, 1923, 10.

[22] Constance de Markievicz, "An Open Letter to the Independent Labour Party," *Éire*, April 28, 1923, 3.

[23] "Madame Markievicz Challenges O'Higgins," *Éire*, July 7, 1923, 2.

supposedly revolutionary credentials. "Free State Freaks No. 1" was Seán O'Muirthile, "I.R.B." and " "Gaolic" Leaguer" whose present headquarters was " "Kill-and-maim-em" Gaol."[24] She also sketched a smirking Desmond Fitzgerald in coat and tie, the "Liar in Chief to Publicity Department Slave-State"; another drawing cast Andrew Cope, the assistant undersecretary to Dublin Castle, as a ringmaster wielding a whip and a harness of monkeys, one of whom—dressed in an army coat and wielding a rifle—is undoubtedly Kevin O'Higgins.[25]

Markievicz published a series of articles, "Memories," in *Éire* from which much erroneous biographical detail has been drawn. It is here that she relays the story of her conversion to Republicanism, which would be seized on by her first biographer, Seán O'Faolain, and parroted by many biographers since. She describes finding a bundle of old copies of *The Peasant* and *Sinn Féin* and being immediately captivated by the image of Robert Emmet, "whose face was familiar to me as I had often seen it on cottage walls . . . like a flash, I made up my mind I must join up."[26] This was an ingenious presentation of the genesis of contemporary Republicanism in an individual who was a Protestant and a revolutionary. It was also an implicit argument for the importance of radical newspapers to the movement, especially in light of the overwhelming support for the protreaty government in the national daily newspapers.[27]

"Memories" makes a thinly veiled attack on the Catholic hierarchy. Many local priests, such as the Capuchin friar Albert Bibby, supported Irish Republicanism, but Irish bishops had used their powerful influence on members of the Dáil and on wider public opinion to secure support for the treaty and the Irish Free State. The October Pastoral of 1922, issued by the bishops at Maynooth, declared that Republicans who were in contravention of the bishops' edicts would "not be absolved in Confession, nor admitted to Holy Communion, if they purpose to persevere in such evil courses."[28] Markievicz's essays can be seen as a counterclaim for Republicans' spiritual authority in the new state.[29] She describes Cathal Brugha as "Pierced with 17 wounds in Easter

---

[24] Free State Freaks No. 1, NLI, Prints & Drawings.

[25] "Free State Freaks No. 2" and "Free State Freaks: Cope the power behind the Freaks—but de Valera & our army chiefs can 'cope' with him,'," NLI, Prints & Drawings.

[26] Constance Markievicz, "Memories," *Eire*, Aug. 18, 1923, 3.

[27] Kissane, *Politics of the Irish Civil War*, 187.

[28] Quoted in Murray, *Oracles of God*, 76; Murray discusses the "honoured place" of the Capuchins in "Republican folklore" for the highly publicized activities of Fr. Albert and Fr. Dominic, although other members of the order were also extensively, though less obviously, Republican supporters; *Oracles of God*, 169.

[29] McCabe, *For God and Ireland*.

Week" and Tom Clarke as betrayed by "men who had been at one with him in 1916, [who] to-day desecrate the graves in which lie the martyred comrades whose cause they have surrendered." These men were "Apostates, whose lips are soiled with [a] false oath, whose hands are red with patriots' blood."[30]

She challenged the Church's position on Republicanism more overtly in her pamphlet *James Connolly's Policy and Catholic Doctrine*, which she presented as a scholarly work, even including a bibliography that listed books on Irish and British labor movements, the encyclical of Pope Leo XIII, an essay by Rev. P. Coffee (PhD Maynooth) from the *Catholic Bulletin*, and a pamphlet *The Social Teachings of James Connolly*, written by a Jesuit priest and published by the ultraconservative Catholic Truth Society.[31] Here, she presents a very different portrait of James Connolly in which she distances him from the radical left-wing politics that she espouses elsewhere: "Some people would try and label [Connolly] a disciple of Marx, but in reality he was no man's disciple; he studied and appreciated Marx, just as he studied and appreciated the thoughts and lives of all men who had worked for the betterment of the world."[32] She argued that Connolly had not sought to attack the institution of the Church in *Labour and Irish History* but rather had meant to target the clergy: "the question of how far an individual priest or a hierarchy is justified in taking political action has often been discussed with bated breath."[33] Campaigning for the Republican party in County Mayo, she was even more simplistic in her remarks. Objecting to the bishop of Meath's support for a government that "include[s] in its machinery a Senate which contains thirty Freemasons," she argued, "for Freemasons, as every Catholic knows, are under the ban of our Holy Father the Pope."[34]

Markievicz was keenly aware that the discourse of international socialism would only further isolate Republicanism from the majority of public opinion in Ireland, so in *James Connolly's Policy*, she described Marxist late capitalism in spiritual terms. Imperialism, she argued, bred "luxury, ignorance and vice," "the germs" that would result ultimately in the dissolution of "each empire when it has reached its climax amidst desolation and untold sufferings." She described "the internationalism of Connolly" not as socialism but

[30] Constance Markievicz, "Tom Clarke and the First Day of the Republic," *Éire*, May 26, 1923, 3.

[31] Markievicz, *James Connolly's Policy*.

[32] Ibid., 7.

[33] Ibid., 10–11; for a discussion of the Church in Ireland's attitude toward the Irish labor movement from 1910 to 1914, see Larkin, "Socialism and Catholicism in Ireland."

[34] "County Mayo," *Irish Times*, Aug. 14, 1923, 6. This is echoed in Seán Lemass's speech in Dublin in February 1925: "Ireland today is ruled by a British garrison, organized by the Masonic lodges, speaking through the Free State parliament, and playing the cards of England all the time"; quoted in Dunphy, *The Making of Fianna Fáil Power*, 65.

as the carrying out of the ideals of "the early Church at its noblest and best." Marxist language only appears in the pamphlet in places where those well schooled in theory would spot it, such as in her use of the words "weak and backward" to describe the "nations" that were forced by their conquerors to join an empire. She argued that the Church in its "Holy Alliance" functioned similarly to the League of Nations: "smoke screens of high sounding ideals, behind which the Juggernaut car of Imperialism advances."[35]

The "Juggernaut car" was a literal and metaphorical force. Republican rallies were closely policed, since the party posed a real political threat to the Free State government after its successes at the general election in August. Cumann na nGaedheal won the majority of the vote, at 72.5 percent, but antitreaty Sinn Féin still managed to secure 27.5 percent, winning forty-four seats.[36] De Valera won an important victory in Clare, and Markievicz won her seat in Dublin City (South) with the second-highest number of votes, coming second to Philip Cosgrave, the governor of Mountjoy Prison and the brother of the Free State's president.[37] On the night of September 2 a mass meeting was held in Sackville Street to celebrate the election's successes. Markievicz declared that results showed the objection of the Irish people to the treatment of political prisoners and their belief that the Public Safety Bill was "an outrage on civilization." As she spoke, two officers drove a motorcar "slowly through the crowd," causing panic, a stampede, and injuries to the otherwise peaceful assembly.[38]

The purpose of the meeting was also to reaffirm the goals of the Republican party: to achieve international recognition of the Republic and the approval of the political and economic programs of "Sinn Fein." However, the party's actual political programs were still largely undefined, since the party had to negotiate the vast differences between the minority social radicalism endorsed by figures such as Markievicz and Mellows and the social and economic conservatism that dominated the majority.[39] Markievicz was determined to refute Cumann na nGaedheal's assertion that Republicans had no practical policy. She went to work campaigning with Maud Gonne for the release of Republican political prisoners and condemning their maltreatment.[40] With Madeline Ffrench Mullen and Helena Molony, she worked to improve

---

[35] Markievicz, *James Connolly's Policy*, 43.

[36] Regan, *Counter-Revolution*, 148.

[37] Cosgrave won 34.7 percent of the votes and 12.6 percent went to Markievicz.

[38] "Republicans in Dublin," *Irish Times*, Sept. 3, 1923, 6.

[39] Ibid.; Dunphy, *Fianna Fáil Power*, 36.

[40] "County Mayo," *Irish Times*, Aug. 14, 1923, 6; and "The Release of the Prisoners," ibid., Sept. 24, 1923, 6.

the welfare of the city's children. At a meeting at the Bleeding Horse pub on Camden Street, near the old Fianna Hall, they spoke out against child labor and formulated plans to build a playground in a vacant lot near Charlemont Street that would provide a safe recreational space for the poor.[41]

Markievicz expanded the Republican program to include care for the elderly; this was a particularly savvy maneuver: just two months later, Ernest Blythe, Cumann na nGaedheal's minister for finance, announced that the government intended to reduce the old-age pension by one shilling.[42] This represented some of her most effective work. She also continued to advocate an agricultural economy that would be organized on "co-operative and progressive lines," in the hope of expanding antitreaty Sinn Féin's rural support base, which was principally constituted by the rural poor and small farmers.[43] The new, conservative Farmers Party represented the interests of larger landholders and won a remarkable 12.1 percent in the August 1923 general election.[44] Yet, again, she was unable to formulate or implement a workable economic program, and her vision of a "cooperative commonwealth" remained propaganda only.

The summer of 1923 was marked by extreme industrial unrest following cuts in wages of all blue-collar industries, including agricultural laborers, dockers, carters, trades workers, and manufacturing workers.[45] Cumann na nGaedheal made it a policy to keep wages down and did not see it as the responsibility of the government to create employment. Families were unable to pay their debts, a crisis to which Markievicz's nemesis Kevin O'Higgins responded by saying, "The ceasing of the bailiff to function is the first sign of a crumbling civilisation."[46] Markievicz attacked Cumann na nGaedheal's policy in a series of articles for the Glasgow socialist newspaper *Forward*, which were reprinted as *What Irish Republicans Stand For* by the Marxist Glasgow Civic Press. Her articles give a more slightly more nuanced analysis than a simple restatement of the ideology that Britain was the source of all of Ireland's ills. Rather, she argued that the Free State imposed British economic and social systems that were "devised by the British Cabinet of Imperialists and Capitalists and accepted by their would-be counterparts in Ireland, whom they supply with money, arms, and men for the purpose of

[41] "Republican Meeting in Camden Street," ibid., Oct. 1, 1923, 9.
[42] Regan, *Counter-Revolution*, 158.
[43] "South Dublin Election," *Irish Times*, Oct. 18, 1923, 7.
[44] Dunphy, *Fianna Fáil*, 39.
[45] Ibid., 54.
[46] Quoted in ibid.

breaking up the growing movement."[47] More superficially, she argued that the government's use of the word Saorstát (literally, free-state) was fraudulent, since it was intended to refer to the Republic; similarly, the government had co-opted the Republican flag (the tricolor), and used the green uniform of the IRA for the Free State Army. She believed that this was a masquerade, amounting to a sinister trickery of the Irish people.[48] These claims are indicative of the idea that the Irish people had been defrauded into supporting the treaty and voting for Cumann na nGaedheal, which was foundational to the establishment of Fianna Fáil, "the Republican party," in 1926.[49]

In October 1923 Republican prisoners interned by the Free State Army undertook a hunger strike to demand release.[50] The strike began in Mountjoy Jail on October 14, spread to at least ten prisons and internment camps, and at its height included eight thousand strikers.[51] As the days wore on, Markievicz launched a series of lightning-fast meetings across her constituency in support, speaking from the back of a truck so she could move swiftly should the police or Free State Army attempt to intervene.[52] On November 20 hunger striker Denis Barry died at the Curragh Prison hospital, where he had been taken from the Republican prison camp at Newbridge. Markievicz spent the day distributing leaflets and collecting signatures in protest; how long would the public allow Republicans to die?[53] On her way to another meeting, she was surrounded by detectives in Aungier Street and was arrested along with several "young girls" who were with her.[54] Hanna Sheehy Skeffington, who was also on the truck with Markievicz, told the press that the "detectives used revolvers" and "there was a 'scene.'" They had arrested Markievicz without charge, but Sheehy Skeffington believed that the eventual charge would be "causing obstruction in the public thoroughfare."[55] Markievicz was held for the night in College Street Police Barracks, where she informed the police— with "the sort of shrinking that one has before taking a header into a cold sea"—that she had joined her friends on hunger strike. She felt, she later told Eva, "a want of faith in the unknown but that was all."[56]

---

[47] Markievicz, *What Irish Republicans Stand For*.

[48] "The Bitter Fraud: An Interview Given by Constance de Markievicz," *Eire*, Oct. 13, 1923, 4.

[49] Kissane, *Politics of the Irish Civil War*, 177–91.

[50] Between two thousand and eight thousand prisoners took part in strikes at Mountjoy, Kilmainham, the North Dublin Union, Cork, Gormanstown, Newbridge, the Curragh, Tintown, Dundalk, and Kilkenny. They refused all food and any drink except for water.

[51] Healy, "Civil War Hunger-Strike," 213.

[52] "Madame Markievicz in Custody," *Irish Times*, Nov. 21, 1923, 5.

[53] "Hunger Striker Dies in Irish Prison Camp," *New York Times*, Nov. 21, 1923, 3.

[54] "Madame Markievicz in Custody," *Irish Times*, Nov. 21, 1923, 5.

[55] Ibid.; and "Hunger Striker Dies in Irish Prison Camp."

[56] Constance Markievicz to Eva Gore-Booth (n.d.), in *Prison Letters*, 303.

Markievicz was transferred to the North Dublin Union, where forty-nine fellow Republicans were also on strike. She described to Eva how she passed the time sleeping, having "lovely dreams," and feeling surprisingly comfortable since one of the unexpected effects of hunger was the disappearance of her rheumatism. Other women at the North Dublin Union told a different story. Baby Bohen from Ballymote was on hunger strike for over a month; she remembered Markievicz cooking for her, sitting at her bedside, keeping her warm with the heat of her body, and giving her own mittens—as she had given Kathleen Clarke her tights in Aylesbury—as a small measure of comfort against the intense cold.[57] Markievicz's strike was brief; three days after her imprisonment, the leaders called for its end.[58] Markievicz remained in the NDU, which seemed to her "a vast and gloomy place, haunted by the ghosts of broken-hearted paupers."[59] She continued to be held solely on the charge of "impeding the traffic," but she knew she had been arrested because of the power of her "tongue and voice. My real democratic principles, I expect!"[60]

Markievicz maintained that all her political work was in full public view, not clandestine, and that her "activities were passivist and within the law."[61] This was the official antitreaty party line since de Valera had called an end to armed struggle in the spring. However, not all Republicans were marching in step. On the morning of the general election in August, there had been bursts of gunfire in the north of Dublin city, and the *Irish Times* published a report of attacks on Mountjoy Jail, the King's Inns, and the North Dublin Union. Shots had also been fired at sentries posted outside Collins and Arbour Hill Barracks.[62] The Free State Army did not give an official response to the Republican violence, and there was widespread silence in the press with just one article appearing in the *Irish Times*. There was similar silence in response to a series of fires at the North Dublin Union that winter. Constance wrote to Eva of a fire in the censor's office that occurred in late November:

> It was a glorious blaze. We enjoyed it enormously—far better than the pictures! The red shirts and brass helmets of the firemen on the roof, in and out of the smoke and the orange flames, made a dramatic note, and suggested thrills and romance and heroines and the nethermost

[57] For Baby Bohen's memory, see Norman, *Terrible Beauty*, 256.
[58] Healy, "Civil War Hunger-Strike." There was no immediate release of prisoners, and the success or failure of the strike has attracted little debate.
[59] Constance Markievicz to Eva Gore-Booth (n.d.), in *Prison Letters*, 281.
[60] Ibid., 282.
[61] (n.d.), in *Prison Letters*, 303.
[62] "Election Morning in Dublin: Heavy Rifle and Revolver Fire," *Irish Times*, Aug. 28, 1923, 5.

pit. But all that was burnt was beds and boots and an apple pie of mine and other rather valueless property![63]

In fact, the fire had also destroyed a single-story building that the Military Police used as a billet at the NDU.[64] In late December another fire was discovered in a second-floor dormitory that the British military had recently evacuated and was being used to billet Free State troops.[65] These may have been coincidental accidents, but they may also be the work of a dissident faction within Irish Republicanism that refused to obey the ceasefire.

On Christmas Eve 1923 Markievicz was released along with 165 other prisoners. Nearly 2,000 Republicans remained in custody, including de Valera, who had been imprisoned since August. Markievicz's typical conviviality was marred by a deep disillusionment. She was profoundly depressed by the changes that she saw in the city of Dublin, which was congested with motorcars, afflicted by extreme poverty, and suffering from a severe housing shortage.[66] Cumann na nGaedheal's answer to the crisis was private enterprise. The government issued grants to private builders to construct housing, but the unsurprising result was that houses were built only for people who could afford them.[67] At first Markievicz was unable to find a place to live in her own constituency; she was eventually taken in by the Coughlan family, who lived at 1 Frankfort Terrace in the South Dublin suburb of Rathgar.

The depression into which Constance sank after her release from the North Dublin Union was evident to the friends who met her. Mary Colum, the wife of the poet Padraic, remembered seeing her one evening at George Russell's house. Markievicz sat in her usual seat on the couch in the corner, but to Colum she looked "haggard and old, dressed in ancient demoded clothes; the outline of her face was the same, but the expression was different; the familiar eyes that blinked at me from behind glasses were bereft of the old fire and eagerness; she gave me her limp hand."[68] Colum's dramatized recollection is corroborated by the dark mood of Constance's letters to Eva. In response to Eva's mystical exegesis, *A Psychological and Poetic Approach to the Study of Christ in the Fourth Gospel*, Constance remarked, "every church and every sect is but an organization of thoughtless and well-meaning people trained in thought and controlled by juntas of priests and clergy who are used to doing all the things that Christ would most have disliked." Her

---

[63] (n.d.), in *Prison Letters*, 282.

[64] "Fire in Dublin Barracks," *Irish Times*, Nov. 29, 1923, 8.

[65] "Two Soldiers Injured in Dublin Workhouse Fire," *Weekly Irish Times*, Dec. 23, 1922, 4.

[66] (n.d.), in *Prison Letters*, 303.

[67] Dunphy, *Fianna Fáil*, 59.

[68] Quoted in James, *Gore-Booths*, 186.

anger and resentment extended to "all organisations," which seemed "in the end to go the same road: and if it does not go in for graft and power it just fizzles out."[69]

Markievicz was not only bitter toward her former Sinn Féin colleagues who she believed had betrayed the Republic. The Irish Transport and General Workers' Union had also split between members who supported Jim Larkin's militant tactics and those who preferred a conservative approach to negotiations. As Greaves later concluded, "The most difficult task for any general is to maintain the morale of a retreating army," and William O'Brien was not up to the task.[70] When Jim Larkin, released from Sing Sing, returned to Dublin at the end of April 1923, he preached peace but held fast to an unmistakably antitreaty stance. He gave impassioned speeches, embarked on costly court cases, and riled up a strike on which he failed to follow through; "from then on the key sections of the Dublin working class went down like ninepins."[71] The leadership of the Labour Party was equally weak-willed; Thomas Johnson bowed to pressure to be "constructive rather than revolutionary" in government, further alienating the radical parts of the ITGWU.[72] Sinn Féin also seemed to be fizzling out. The year 1923 saw a rapid rise in Sinn Féin clubs across the country, increasing from just 16 to 729 in the space of six months.[73] However, in the attempt to extend the wide base of support for the party, there was a concomitant neglect of firm policy and no clear direction.

The admission of the Irish Free State into the League of Nations in late September, though expected, was a great blow to Markievicz's utopian aspiration for a "free federation" of nations. The league as constituted in 1923 did not include the United States, Germany, or the Soviet Union, which led Markievicz to believe that the only effect of the organization was to give more power to secret diplomacy. She was right, at least in terms of the league's initial phase: in January 1923 France—one of the league's heavyweights—occupied the Ruhr; in August Mussolini bombarded Corfu, but interference from the league was inhibited by France's fears that its occupation of Germany would be challenged. Furthermore, because of its dominion status, the Irish Free State was represented in the league not as an independent

[69] (n.d.), in *Prison Letters*, 303.
[70] Greaves, *International Transport and General Workers' Union*, 315.
[71] Ibid., 320.
[72] *Irish Independent*, July 13, 1923, quoted in Dunphy, *Fianna Fáil*, 55.
[73] Laffan, *Resurrection of Ireland*, 439. Building on the work of Peter Pyne, Laffan refers to post–Civil War antitreaty Sinn Féin as the "Third Sinn Féin," which he argues "violated the [party's] constitution" of 1917 because it ignored the "officer board and its (pro-treaty) standing committee" (436); Pyne, "The New Irish State," 37.

entity but collectively as part of "the British Empire."[74] Constance wrote to Eva, "What the world has got to think out is some scheme by which power can be evenly distributed over every person in the world and by which the foolish and uneducated can no longer be grouped in unthinking battalions dependent on the few pushers, self-seekers and crooks and made slaves of and exploited."[75] Her attitude was paternalistic, but she was equally unable to formulate a large-scale political solution.

Instead, Markievicz attempted to enact her core principal of the "cooperative commonwealth" in her work for local government. As a member of Rathmines Urban Council, she helped secure a motion to build public baths and a washhouse for the suburb's forty thousand residents who were without sanitary facilities.[76] She worked closely with Kathleen Lynn to reform council legislation so that the urban poor could keep small numbers of livestock for subsistence.[77] Unable to effect political change on a national level, she focused on the individual; at one council meeting, she campaigned for improved working conditions of a single window-washer.[78] These small gestures were incapable of offsetting the rapid decline of the Republican party, but they endeared her to the working class in her constituency and would go a long way in shaping her positive legacy in public memory, despite the violence and bloodshed that she advocated in her propaganda.

By no means had the rhetoric of blood sacrifice run dry. During the Anglo-Irish and the Irish Civil Wars, Markievicz's propaganda had been connected to a political program. Her language was now dangerously simplistic and abstract. Despite the withdrawal of the IRA's support for the Republican government in November 1925, the ratification of partition on December 3, and the dire state of the party that put an end to Republican cabinet members' salaries that same month, she continued to preach the doctrine of self-sacrifice for the Republic. In "A Christmas Message to the Fianna," published in the Republican weekly newspaper *An Phoblacht*, she reminded Irish children of the examples set by Jesus, by Thomas Ashe, "our first hunger strike martyr," and by the Fianna's "first martyrs," Con Colbert and Sean Heuston.[79] After reminding her readers of how so many of the Fianna had been "tortured and battered . . . cruelly and secretly murdered . . . [and] faced

[74] Keatinge, "Ireland and the League of Nations."

[75] n.d., in *Prison Letters*, 303.

[76] "Public Baths for Rathmines," *Irish Times*, Oct. 8, 1925, 11.

[77] "Pigs in Rathmines," ibid.

[78] "Dublin and the Provinces," ibid., 1.

[79] Madame Markievicz, TD, "A Christmas Message to the Fianna," *An Phoblacht*, Dec. 18, 1925, 10.

the firing squad," she encouraged the nation's children to be merry on their feast day and pray with all their hearts for " 'A Happy Christmas' in a free and Gaelic Ireland."

As part of her propaganda campaign, Markievicz organized a new theater company, the Republican Players, which was explicitly violent in its aims. She wrote two plays, *Blood Money* and *The Invincible Mother*, which were performed at the Abbey Theatre on March 1, 1925.[80] In flagrant contravention of the Treasonable Offences Act, which prohibited any incitement of war against the Free State, the performance was advertised in the popular and mainstream *Evening Herald* as a "Mobilization" with an accompanying order that "All Republicans Parade at the Abbey Theatre Tomorrow (Sun) Night."[81]

Blood Money is a thinly plotted allegory that nonetheless uses history quite skillfully. Set during 1798, the play does not directly refer to the Rising until the end, which creates a temporal ambiguity that facilitates Markievicz's didacticism. Two Irishmen have joined the "British Army of occupation" and have captured a fellow countryman; at the end of the play, the captive gives a rousing speech about Judas's betrayal of Christ and declares, "The man who sells his country for the one piece of silver will burn in hell with him."[82] *The Invincible Mother*, which followed, is better executed and is similar in tone and structure to one of the Abbey's most popular plays, Lady Gregory's one-act comedy *Spreading the News*. In Markievicz's play, the mother-figure is taken to Mountjoy for questioning about men who have been observed visiting her house; the police attempt to coerce her into informing, but she evades them through her use of a simplistic idiom and recounts her family's esteemed history of dying "true," with martyrs stretching back to 1798. *The Invincible Mother*'s conservative gender politics are offset by the far more radical *Broken Dreams*, which expresses Constance's disillusionment with the Republican movement, particularly the repression of women within it. Yet *Broken Dreams* was produced only posthumously, when its title took on a different significance.[83]

[80] Bonnie K. Scott, intro. to Constance Markievicz, *The Invincible Mother, Journal of Irish Literature* 6, no. 2 (May 1977): 119.

[81] Advertisement, *Saturday Herald (Evening Herald)*, Feb. 28, 1925, 4; the Republican Players hired the Abbey for the performance, and the theater—desperate for revenue—was willing to oblige.

[82] TS, *Blood Money*, O'Mullane Papers, NLI, MS 22,636.

[83] The script is unpublished but came into the possession of Hanna Sheehy Skeffington, as indicated in an autograph note on the typescript, which is held in the Sheehy Skeffington Papers, NLI, MS 24185. For the posthumous performance of *Broken Dreams* by the Republican Players on Dec. 11, 1927, see Caulfied, " 'The Woman with a Garden.' "

Markievicz's loyalty to Éamon de Valera was not unwavering. Privately, she expressed strong resistance to his decision to abandon abstention and create a new party, Fianna Fáil, which billed itself as "the Republican party," despite the schism that the decision created within what remained of Sinn Féin. Of forty-seven Republican deputies, fewer than half followed him into Fianna Fáil.[84] To admit that Sinn Féin was defunct would be political suicide, so de Valera focused on persuading his followers that it would be possible to join the Dáil without taking the Oath of Allegiance and that they might thereby begin to instigate a return to Republican principals. Constance confided to Eva that she believed that "the oath of allegiance made it absolutely impossible for an honorable person who was a Republican, to go in," and if the oath were removed, it would be mere policy without principle.[85] However, she conceded what de Valera was unwilling to admit publically: the new party would reflect the opinion of "the ordinary man and woman in the street," and the "howling" protests of the intransigents within Sinn Féin were "unlogical." Yet joining parliamentary politics would not come without compromise. Markievicz would be forced to abdicate the presidency of Cumann na mBan, which maintained a strict policy of nonparticipation.[86] Even more significantly, her support for the socially conservative Fianna Fáil would contribute to historical appraisals of her politics as "confused' and "woolly thinking."[87]

[84] Pyne notes that twenty-one followed de Valera; twenty-two opposed the abandonment of abstention; "and the attitude of the remainder is not clear"; see "New Irish State," 63.

[85] (n.d.), in *Prison Letters*, 303.

[86] Bluebird, "Round the World and Home," *Weekly Irish Times*, April 17, 1926, 3. Markievicz was succeeded by Eithne Coyle O'Donnell, who held the post until 1941. Like Markievicz, O'Donnell was a charismatic character, holding up a train in order to seize and burn copies of Belfast newspapers, going on a hunger strike in Ballyshannon and Mountjoy, and escaping from the North Dublin Union internment camp in 1923. (She was captured the following day.)

[87] English, *Radicals and the Republic*, 37–38.

15

Reconciliation

AFTER TEN YEARS SPENT ON THE CAMPAIGN TRAIL, FIGHT-
ing, in prison, or evading arrest, Constance was suddenly struck by a sense
of time passing. She did her best to resist it, bobbing her hair and wearing it
"smooth and straight as a rule"; she told Stanislaus that she saw no reason
"why old women should not be as comfortable as the young."[1] In one of her
most personal letters to him, she marveled at how the "thin and fragile" boy
with "the most pathetic little face" could now be in his thirties.[2] All her fa-
milial relationships except for her friendship with Eva had disintegrated. She
never saw Josslyn—"and never want[ed] to see him"—and was alienated
from her siblings Mordaunt and Mabel, as well as the other Gore-Booths
in England. She harbored no ill will toward these more distant relations; if
she happened to "blow across them," she resolved to be "quite amiable to
any of them" since they were "no worse than anyone else." Demonstrating
her at times acute lack of self-awareness, she wrote to her stepson how she
could understand that it might be "very embarrassing [for the Gore-Booths]
to have a relation that gets into jail and fights in revolutions that you are not
in sympathy with."[3]

She was determined to revive her relationship with her children and
signed her letters to Stanislaus "Mother," instead of the flourish of "Constance de Markievicz" that ended most of her correspondence to him. When
a friend of his visited and relayed Stanislaus's request for books in English
that might help with his writing, she sent him a remarkably sophisticated

[1] (n.d.), in *Prison Letters*, 308; and Constance Markievicz to Stanislaus Markievicz (n.d. [Jan-
uary 14, 1926]), NLI, MS 13778.
[2] Constance Markievicz to Stanislaus Markievicz (n.d. [Autumn? 1924/1925]), ibid.
[3] Ibid. (n.d. [Jan. 14, 1926]).

selection: *The Romantic* by May Sinclair ("rather nasty" but "awfully interesting as a character study.... Its very modern"), four novels by Joseph Conrad, and *When Winter Comes to Main Street*, a selection of essays by Grant Overton with chapters on Rebecca West, Somerset Maugham, and Stephen McKenna ("good as a novel natural and sincere and well written").[4] Constance was equally committed to becoming reacquainted with Maeve. Maeve met her in London and visited her in Dublin, where the two bonded over mechanic work on Markievicz's old Tin Lizzy. She bragged to Stanislaus about how his sister "loves machinery and is so very clever at it. She is very tall and pretty, and full of life and charm."[5]

Many of these efforts came too late. Busy with Dublin politics, Constance neglected her letters to Eva and put off traveling to London to see her.[6] Suddenly, "the only real relation" she had left was gone.[7] A letter from Esther brought the news of Eva's death, leaving Constance feeling "vague and stupid" and thrusting her into another deep depression. Eva had been the benchmark against which Constance measured herself. Every sketch she made, she wondered what Eva would think of it; each time she saw beauty in the world, she wished Eva were also there to observe it. She told Esther that it was Eva's influence that had prevented her from becoming "very brutal" over the years, even claiming "I once held out and stopped a man being shot because of her." Despite Eva's physical death, Constance believed that the sisters' spiritual connection remained: "When I'm painting she seems to look up at me and help me from the clouds. I wake suddenly and it is just as if she was there. Last Sunday at mass, when I wasn't thinking of her at all, she suddenly seemed to smile at me from behind the priest, and I know it is real and that she, the real Eva, is somewhere very near."[8] In her grief, Constance was unwilling to confront her estranged family. She "simply could not face" the funeral, where she might have been able to speak to their mother for the last time. Eva was followed closely in death by Georgina, whose funeral Constance also felt unable to attend. She wrote to Josslyn afterward, hoping that their differences would not stand in the way of her visiting Lissadell to pay her respects. She added, "I think its best to be quite frank, that I've always felt you had something against me, & was prepared if I met you to take my

---

[4] Ibid. Constance may have read these books on Eva's recommendation; according to Esther Roper, Eva's poem "The Secret Sharer" was "written in deep appreciation of Joseph Conrad's wonderful story"; see Roper's introduction to Gore-Booth, *Poems of Eva Gore-Booth*, 29.

[5] Ibid.

[6] "Fianna Eireann," *An Phoblacht*, May 7, 1926, 6; and Constance Markievicz to Eva Gore-Booth (n.d. [May or June 1926]), in *Prison Letters*, 306.

[7] Constance Markievicz to Stanislaus Markievicz (n.d. [Jan. 14, 1926]), NLI, MS 13778.

[8] Constance Markievicz to Esther Roper (n.d. [1926]), in *Prison Letters*, 311.

cue from you; I would have been glad if you'd been pleased to see me."[9] She signed her name coldly, "Constance de Markievicz."

Through public political commemorations, Markievicz articulated her private sense of loss. In December 1926 she unveiled a wayside cross to the memory of two Fianna boys, Alf Colley and Sean Cole, who had been captured and killed during the Civil War. To the eight hundred people gathered at the memorial, she spoke about the crucifixion and likened the "two little lads . . . who were tortured and cruelly murdered by grown men" to the martyrdom of Christ. She asked the crowd to "march on" and look forward to the time when they would "look into the happy, boyish faces of our comrades waiting to greet us at the Starry Gates of Heaven, beyond earth's clouds and shadows, its sorrows, its wrongs, its sufferings."[10] Her emotive rhetoric had lost its fire and now rang hollow and nostalgic. Resurrecting the Republican antirecruitment campaigns of the last decade, Markievicz spoke alongside Maud Gonne, Charlotte Despard, and Tom Kelly at an anti–Remembrance Day rally on November 11, where she repeated many of her old arguments while the Fianna ran around "plucking Flanders poppies from the coats of pedestrians." Afterward she led a crowd of "several hundreds" to the La Scala Theatre, which was showing the British film *Mademoiselle from Armentieres*, where the protestors threw a smoke bombs into the theater.[11]

Markievicz's campaigns for Fianna Fáil conveyed a similar fatigue and lack of political imagination. Abandoning the Marxist language of capitalism and imperialism, at a rally in February 1927, she said simply "that Governments were much like the managing directors of big business, and in their hands lay the prosperity or misery of the people under their control or rule."[12] In her local government work, her most impassioned speeches pertained to old battles. She encouraged "the citizens of Dublin and its suburbs" to "take control of their tramway system," which was coming up for sale: the same trams owned and operated by William Martin Murphy who led the Lockout in 1913. Another meeting provided the opportunity to come to heads with her nemesis Kevin O'Higgins, who supported the government's proposed Electricity Supply Bill. Markievicz proclaimed that the bill was unjust, since it would take power out of the hands of the local government and give a monopoly to a private body appointed by Cumann na nGaedheal. At the meeting, O'Higgins was drowned out by shouts of "Up, De Valera" and "Up Russia." Markievicz—whose dog "ran around the hall barking"—rose from

[9] (n.d. [received Jan. 22, 1927]), PRONI, D/4131/K/3.

[10] "Memorial Wayside Cross Unveiled by Madame Markievicz," *An Phoblacht*, Dec. 17, 1926, 3.

[11] "A Meeting of Protest," *Irish Times*, Nov. 11, 1926, 8.

[12] "Fianna Fail: Views on Defence Problem," *Irish Times*, Feb. 19, 1927, 8.

her seat in the gallery to make a speech but was commanded by the chairman to "sit down." Her retort, "I am afraid of no man," was met with a dismissive, "No one says you are." In a scene reminiscent of the *Playboy* riots, the crowd battled out their political differences in the uproarious singing of "God Save the King" and "The Red Flag."[13] This was the last great political performance in which she would take part.

Markievicz stood for Fianna Fáil in the 1927 general election as a relic of the quickly receding past. Her biography of candidature in the *Irish Times* focused on events no more recent than the previous decade: "Came into prominence in Dublin labour troubles in 1911 to 1913. Took an active part in Irish Volunteer Movement, and fought in 1916 Rebellion. Death sentence was commuted. First woman elected to the British House of Commons (in 1918), but never took her seat. Elected for South Dublin City in all elections since 1918."[14] She polled just over four thousand votes from her constituency, in contrast to the over eight thousand that were awarded to the up-and-coming Fianna Fáil TD and future taoiseach, Seán Lemass.[15] For two years Lemass had been campaigning for a new departure in Sinn Féin that would rid the party of the inhibiting influence of older hangers-on. In the Republican newspaper *An Phoblacht*, he criticized "a large number of middle-aged men and women, who have given valuable service to the Movement in the past and who, because of that, are invariably elected to fill the most important positions."[16] He argued that these people were "so tied up with precedents and experiences, that they are incapable of giving an active lead." What was needed was a generational coup. People who were born in the twentieth century, who were committed to "useful action," must overthrow the "incompetent leadership" if Sinn Féin was to "achieve a revolution in Ireland by the methods of a mutual benefit society."[17] Although Lemass wrote about revolution and the protection of the "common Irish people" from oppression by "private or by public interests," the extent of his social radicalism was free education, university scholarships for the poor, and the "protection of industries" through the imposition of tariffs.[18] As the 1927 election made clear, this was what the Irish people wanted: a centrist party, not a radical Republicanism.

[13] "Ministers Shouted Down: Stormy Meeting in Rathmines," ibid., April 13, 1927, 4.

[14] "Other 9—No Title," ibid., June 9, 1927, 3.

[15] "Other 13—No Title," ibid., June 13, 1927, 5.

[16] Seán Lemass, "Sinn Féin in Dublin: What Is Wrong with It?," *An Phoblacht*, Sept. 18, 1925, quoted in Garvin, *Judging Lemass*, 84.

[17] Seán Lemass, "New Leaders for Sinn Féin: The Coming Year," *An Phoblacht*, Oct. 9, 1925, quoted in Garvin, *Judging Lemass*, 86–87.

[18] Garvin, *Judging Lemass*, 79–80.

Two weeks after the election, Constance suddenly fell ill. Kathleen Lynn diagnosed appendicitis and had her admitted to St. Patrick Dun's Hospital, where she underwent an operation on July 1. De Valera visited a few days later, and on July 6 the *Irish Times* published a report announcing Markievicz's hospitalization.[19] Her condition deteriorated rapidly; the next day she underwent a second operation to remove an obstruction in her abdomen. Lynn was notified of the emergency procedure by telegraph and lamented in her diary, "There is little hope in that case. I think she was just tired of life, poor dear Madam."[20] That night the BBC broadcast a message calling "Maeve, daughter of Countess Markievicz, believed to be in the South of England, [to] come at once to Sir Patrick Dun's Hospital, Grand Canal Street, Dublin, where her mother is lying seriously ill."[21] Maeve arrived in Dun Laoghaire the next day and was the only visitor that the doctors allowed. Markievicz was restless, vomiting, and suffering acute pain from complete intestinal paralysis. Lynn expected her to die in the night.[22] On July 10 Lynn noted in her diary, "Kevin O'Higgins [was] shot dead with awful brutality. Madam improved."[23] O'Higgins had been assassinated by three IRA men on his way to Sunday mass in reprisal for the executions that O'Higgins had sanctioned during the Civil War. That news—and the arrival of Casimir and Stanislaus from Poland—gave Markievicz the energy for a final rally. Lynn met them at the hospital, exclaiming, "Life is rejoiced!"[24]

The Gore-Booth family was reconnected by expressions of love and concern—some more enthusiastic than others. Constance asked the hospital matron to send news to Lissadell: she "had a good night and has been quite bright today. . . . She said to give you her dear love & to tell you she was thinking of the beautiful sunshine, flowers & sea." Josslyn contacted Mabel, who replied warmly and with regret that she was so far away.[25] Mordaunt seemed less concerned, writing to Josslyn, "I don't know if you have heard that Constance is in the Thomas [*sic*] Dunne Hospital in Dublin with appendicitis. I gather she has been operated on & is in a poorish way. Those O & C [Oxford and Cambridge] tickets were most useful. Oxford are not a good side."[26] Joss-

---

[19] "Madame Markievicz's Illness," *Irish Times*, July 6, 1927, 9.

[20] Lynn Diary (July 8, 1927), Royal College of Physicians in Ireland (RCPI).

[21] "Illness of Madame Markievicz: Broadcast Message to Her Daughter," *Irish Times*, July 8, 1927, 7.

[22] Lynn Diary (July 9, 1927), RCPI.

[23] Ibid. (July 10, 1927).

[24] Quigley, *Polish Irishman*, 202; "Madame Markievicz," *Irish Times*, July 14, 1927, 8; Lynn Diary (July 10–13, 1927), RCPI.

[25] Mabel to Josslyn Gore-Booth (July 12, 1927), PRONI, D4131/K/9.

[26] PRONI, D4131/K/8/1.

lyn, Constance's only sibling still living in Ireland, kept in close contact with the hospital matron until he was able to arrange a visit; it was then that the siblings made their final peace. Constance Markievicz died in the early hours of Friday, July 14, surrounded by friends and family: Casimir and Stanislaus, Hanna Sheehy Skeffington, the Coughlans, and Kathleen Lynn, with de Valera arriving soon afterward.

Markievicz's coffin was draped in the tricolor, and her remains were taken from St. Patrick Dun's Hospital to St. Andrew's, a Catholic church on Westland Row. Her remains were immediately claimed as a political commodity for Fianna Fáil. Josslyn wrote to his son Brian, "Uncle Casi said that it was the wish of the family that the funeral should be private [but] they insisted on having it public & they took her to lie in state in the Rotunda & the funeral started from there ab 12.30 today. Their idea appears to have been to have a bigger funeral than Kevin O'Higgins for political reasons."[27] The coffin was placed in the Rotunda Concert Hall because Dublin Corporation refused permission for Markievicz to lie in state at City Hall or at the Mansion House, in an attempt to subvert the power that her death would lend to Fianna Fáil.

Josslyn was angry at the politicians' insistence on "mak[ing] a show of what should be a reverent occasion." He was so out of touch with Irish political life that he was unable to recognize that crowds of people wished to express their support and affection for his sister: "Being a very fine Sunday the inhabitants lined the streets everywhere with their families but most of them appeared to have been there from idle curiosity and it was all most sad & depressing."[28] Accounts in the press give a very different story, telling how "several thousands lined the route" from the Rotunda to Glasnevin Cemetery. An honor guard of Fianna boys in uniform led the procession, followed by the Irish National Forresters' brass band and a contingent of the Citizen Army. Members of the (Republican) 1916 Club carried a floral cross inscribed "In Loving Memory of our old Comrade," followed by the Fintan Lalor Pipers' Band, another group of Fianna, and several members of the clergy who preceded the coffin. Casimir and Stanislaus were in the first mourning coach, followed by Josslyn and his wife, who shared what must have been an awkward journey with the Republican George Plunkett, brother of the 1916 martyr Joseph. Eight cars followed, conveying wreaths sent from friends and comrades, and a host of mourners followed on foot: de Valera and Sean T. O'Kelly, Maud Gonne, Charlotte Despard, and representatives

---

[27] Josslyn Gore-Booth to Brian Gore-Booth, PRONI, D4131/K/8 (32–35).
[28] Ibid.

from Cumann na mBan. Jim Larkin and members of the Workers' Union of Ireland carried a red banner bearing a slogan in Russian; "This emblem was said to have been presented to the Irish workers by the workers of Moscow."[29] This last contingent caused great offense to Casimir, who—the *New York Times* reported—was "indignant" that Larkin was permitted to march with a "Bolsheviki" flag.[30]

It took three hours for the procession to cover the route to Glasnevin Cemetery, where "about a thousand people" had already gathered at the graveside. They were overseen by a hundred Free State soldiers armed with rifles that Lynn believed were ready "to fire on us should there be [a] volley over the grave."[31] The Fianna stood guard around the Republican plot as the wreaths were laid. While the crowd waited, Casimir, de Valera, Patrick Rutledge, and the chief of staff of the IRA, Frank Aiken, quietly carried Markievicz's coffin to the mortuary chapel, where the rosary was recited in Irish and de Valera delivered a short oration:

> Madame Markiewicz is gone from us. Madame, the friend of the toiler, the lover of the poor. Ease and station she put aside and took the hard way of service with the weak and down-trodden. Sacrifice, misunderstanding and scorn lay on the road she adopted, but she trod it unflinchingly. She now lies at rest with her fellow champions of the right—mourned by the people whose liberties she fought for, blessed by the loving prayers of the poor she tried so hard to befriend.
>
> They would know her only as a soldier of Ireland, but we knew her as a colleague and comrade. We knew the friendliness, the great woman's heart of her, the great Irish soul of her, and we know the loss we have suffered is not to be repaired. It is sadly we take our leave, but we pray [to] High Heaven that all she longed and worked for may one day be achieved.[32]

After the crowd waited for nearly an hour, it was announced that Markievicz's burial would be delayed. Was this simply in respect of the fact that "the grave-diggers did not work on Sundays," as Fianna Fáil later stated?[33] Or was it a means of avoiding an outbreak of violence, in the wake of heightened tensions following O'Higgins's assassination? One correspondent for the *Manchester Guardian* wrote, "To-day's tribute was partly a political dem-

---

[29] "Funeral of Madame Markiewicz," *Irish Times*, July 18, 1927, 5.
[30] "Article 1—No Title," *New York Times*, July 18, 1927, 5.
[31] "Funeral of Madame Markiewicz"; Lynn Diary (July 18, 1927), RCPI.
[32] "Funeral of Madame Markiewicz."
[33] Ibid.

onstration by Republicans, but it was also still more a tribute of love by the poor. . . . It being Sunday the actual interment in the Republican plot could not take place, and there could be no question of a firing-party discharging a volley over the grave. This fact probably averted some trouble."[34] A large cohort of soldiers, police, and detectives were at the ready the following morning. They began to arrive at eight o'clock, and by the time of the burial at nine-thirty, there were 150 armed representatives of the state standing guard just one hundred yards from the gravesite.[35] Far fewer people were in attendance as Casimir, Stanislaus, de Valera, and other "Fianna Fáil and Republican deputies" oversaw the opening of the vault. Five boys from the Fianna led the procession to the grave, and as the coffin was lowered into the ground, the green Citizen Army uniform that Markievicz had worn during the Rising was placed over it. "A small crowd of women," a contingent from Cumann na mBan, stayed at the graveside, guarded by four boys from the Fianna. They were watched closely by the police and the military, who finally withdrew around noon.

After Constance's funeral, suppressed resentments rose to the surface. Maeve, jealous to discover that her mother had sustained an intimate correspondence with Eva during the long periods of absence from her own life, ripped up the entire cache of letters from Eva that Constance had lovingly preserved and threw every single one of them into the fire. Esther lamented the loss to Hanna Sheehy Skeffington: "A priceless treasure destroyed. . . . Maeve is most generous with material things, but with the more precious things—ruthless."[36] She was a little ruthless with material things too, grasping for a physical connection to her mother that might in some way compensate for the relationship that had come so late and so fleetingly. She saw four lawyers in an attempt to claim what remained of Constance's furniture and books from Sheehy Skeffington and the Coughlans. Casimir fought Maeve for his share of the spoils and left Dublin on very bad terms with his daughter. He wrote to Josslyn on his return journey through Holyhead to say that he had "put everything in good order," but the silver was still missing, and he suspected that Maeve had filched it.[37] The next year, when Maeve sold her grandmother's house to buy a house in Kent, she coldly informed Hanna Sheehy Skeffington, the executor of Constance's will, that she would be taking the paintings that Casimir had left behind in Dublin: "I am sure he will

[34] "Funeral of Madame Markievicz: Three-Mile Long Procession," *Manchester Guardian*, July 18, 1927, 12.

[35] "Burial of Madame Markievicz," *Irish Times*, July 19, 1927, 5.

[36] Roper to Sheehy Skeffington (July 29, 1927), quoted in Quigley, *Polish Irishman*, 209.

[37] Casimir Markievicz to Josslyn Gore-Booth (Sept. 28, 1927), PRONI, D/4131/K/12/25.

never send for them and as my house has big rooms they will look very nice on the walls."[38]

The only claim that Stanislaus sought to exact was the right to Constance's biography. After the funeral, he returned to Warsaw where he worked for the Polish Timber Company. He kept up an amiable correspondence with the Gore-Booths, exchanging affectionate letters with Josslyn's wife, Molly, who always remembered Stanislaus and Casimir with small gifts at Christmas.[39] In his letters he lobbied the family for their support of a biography that would give "a true and authoritative account" of Constance's life, "her work and her sacrifice." His perspective was deeply entrenched in his own experience of revolution in Europe:

> It was from father I had it that Lissadell was spared owing to Constance. He says almost all mansions in Ireland were burnt . . . he gives as example Hollywood, Templehouse, etc. I myself would call it characteristic of civil war that you *were not* spared . . . for the gangs and bands would probably not know of the connection, even if they were admirers and sympathizers of Mother's! In Russia, when Bolshevism began, our own peasants did not touch us, in fact they gave refuge to some members of the family; it was the roaming bands who burnt, killed, and pilfered! Of course the struggle in Ireland was political, whereas in Russia it was a class war.

For most of her political career, Constance believed that the national struggle and the class war were indivisible, although Stanislaus's summation is nearer the mark when it comes to the actuality of Irish politics. Even so, his focus was the result of a personal grudge rather than political acuity. Thinking of the red banners unfurled at her funeral procession, he wrote:

> I can tell you in spite of Larkin and Connolly I am not giving the Bolsheviks or their methods any quarter in my book! Perhaps it is non consistent of me, for she associated herself with such "extreme" elements (do you recall her triumphant visits to the Clyde, the very heart of communism in England) I can't help it, that's against *my convictions*. I don't mind "extreme" sentiments on nationality, but the Bolsheviks are anti-national, i.e. international!![40]

---

[38] Maeve Markievicz to Hanna Sheehy Skeffington (June 25, 1928), NLI, MS 33606; quoted in Quigley, *Polish Irishman*, 215.

[39] Stanislaus Markievicz to Lady Gore-Booth (Dec. 28, 1928), PRONI, D/4131/K/13/11.

[40] Ibid. (July 21, 1931), (29).

His total rejection of anti-imperialist thought is further belied by the plan, when he lost his job with the Polish Timber Company in late 1930, to make a new start on a cocoa plantation in French Cameroon. He was ever eager to distance himself from his father, but in fact the nut fell near the tree: he asked Josslyn for the loan of £350 as a nest egg and offered his life insurance policy as security.[41] Josslyn, unsurprisingly, ignored the request.

Stanislaus became more obstinate in his claim of authority over Constance's life when he discovered that Maeve also intended to write a book. He wrote to Molly of "our méchant Maeve" and relayed Hanna Sheehy Skeffington's "most indignant" response that it was "just monstrous of Maeve to be butting in like this."[42] He also claimed that Casimir was upset at the prospect, "for without looking at it from a moral or ethical point of view, the subject is too serious and sacred (or rather should be) to risk having our name laid open to ridicule, for without a doubt we will be the laughing-stock of all serious people if within a few months of each other both children try and wrote [sic] biographies!"[43] In the end, Maeve's ambition proved to be mere sibling rivalry, and Stanislaus's book never amounted to anything more than a series of sentimental memories published in the Dublin newspapers, recounting well-worn anecdotes and wholly avoiding the events of the Irish Revolution.

Casimir was more prolific. He published a novel, *Przemoc Krwi* (The Power of Flesh and Blood), in 1928, which is partly set during the Easter Rising. His protagonist, Annie O'Rourke, grows up an orphan in a convent, attempts to rescue her mother from her profession as a prostitute, and in the process "falls into the clutches of an evil tavern keeper [who is] in league with white slavers."[44] The novel was puffed in the newspapers *Kurjer Poznanski* and *Swiat*, which invited comparisons to Dumas and Hugo, despite Casimir having paid scant attention to the Irish political landscape. After Constance's funeral, Casimir returned to his middle-class existence in Warsaw, but he refused to relinquish his aristocratic pretensions. He wrote nostalgic letters to Josslyn about the Gore-Booth "plantations," still lamenting the loss of the estates on "the eastern front of Poland" to the Bolsheviks.[45] He had given up hope of earning a living solely as an artist and took up work for the American Consular Service. The stability of his finances improved his relationship with

---

[41] Stanislaus Markievicz to Josslyn Gore-Booth (Dec. 14, 1930), PRONI D/4131/K/13 (14).
[42] Stanislaus Markievicz to Lady Gore-Booth (July 21, 1931), ibid. (29); and (Feb. 17, 1932) (41).
[43] Ibid. (Jan. 31, 1932) (39).
[44] As summarized in Quigley, *Polish Irishman*, 212.
[45] Casimir Markievicz to Josslyn Gore-Booth (Jan. 28, 1929), PRONI, D/4131/K/12 (32).

his in-laws, and he and Josslyn exchanged chatty letters, mostly about their hunting expeditions.

In his correspondence with the Gore-Booths, Casimir never hints at his relationship with Roza, the lover in whom he took great comfort as his health began to fail. In the winter of 1931–32 he suffered a pulmonary embolism, and, with his leave at the consulate exhausted, he was forced to go without pay. Josslyn sent money to assist with the doctor's bill, and Casimir replied with a long letter of thanks and a vivid description of the landscape where he had last hunted.[46] A series of hospitalizations followed, until at last Maeve and Stanislaus were summoned to their father's side. The contrast with Constance's death could not have been starker; the mayor of Warsaw insisted that such a notable painter be given a private room and a private nurse.[47] Maeve and Casimir were finally reconciled, and the siblings also made their peace before saying good-bye to their father for the last time on December 2, 1932.

Even at the time of his death, there was confusion about the details of Casimir's life and work. His obituary in the Warsaw newspapers gave his age as a year younger than he was and made no reference to a title, although this omission may be a reflection of the contemporary political temper. It was announced that Casimir would be buried in Warsaw's principal cemetery, Powaski, but the funeral and burial both took place outside of Kutno, a village west of Warsaw and north of Lodz. He was laid to rest beside his friend, the artist Wojciech Piechowski. Another friend and collaborator from the Warsaw theater, Fijałkowski, gave the oration in which he described Casimir as

> exceptionally gifted in painting and literature but first of all in life. He loved life and knew how to live. Although he would generously share his thoughts and visions on paper and canvas he believed that even the most beautiful love story was not able to compensate for real love. He would rather love than write about love and he would rather live than picture life.[48]

In Ireland and the United States, Casimir's death was an occasion to reflect on Constance's life. There was a great deal of speculation about their relationship, with the New York Times placing the blame for its failure squarely on Constance: "The increasing political activities of the Countess led to a separation. The husband joined the Russian Army; the wife became the brilliant and romantic leader of the Sinn Fein."[49]

[46] Ibid. (Mar. 5, 1931 [recte 1932]) (40).
[47] Quigley, Polish Irishman, 219.
[48] Radiogram, scrapbook, PRONI, D4131/K/8,
[49] "Count C. D. Markievicz, Journalist, Is Dead," New York Times, Dec. 3, 1932, 17.

This pronouncement has been repeated in accounts of the Markieviczes' lives ever since. Such judgments impose a rigid set of expectations regarding marital relations and women's roles in public life, which are not the values that either of the Markieviczes shared. Constance and Casimir met in the sexually liberal atmosphere of fin de siècle Paris, and he was probably still married when they began their romantic relationship. Their years in Dublin were characterized by a sheer joie de vivre, an acceptance of their differences, and a mutual support of their individual ambitions. This openness may have even extended to Constance's acceptance of Casimir's sexual relationships outside of their marriage; there is no indication that she had extramarital affairs, but neither is there any evidence of jealousy. When disputes did arise, they were over money, not politics. Casimir was always at the fringes of the Irish national movement while Constance moved toward its center, but their political differences did not become acute until after Casimir left Dublin for the Balkans in late 1913. His decision to enlist in the Russian Imperial Army and her commitment to an anti-imperialist pathway to national independence set the course for the rest of their lives and put an end to the possibility that they might ever live together again. Yet Constance and Casimir remained in sympathy with each other, on a human if not on a political plane.

16

———

Legacies

AFTER THE EASTER RISING, CONSTANCE MARKIEVICZ CEDED
her identity to political commodification. She served as a Republican icon
on her lecture tours and in her campaign speeches, a figurative role that was
rendered literally in the picture postcards of her image that were sold as part
of Republican fundraising initiatives. After her death, different organizations in which she was involved competed to control her legacy. Fianna Fáil,
Irish labor, feminists, and militant Republicans made claims on her life and
work in their attempts to shape the course of Irish politics. The divergence in
these interpretations sharply increased as Fianna Fáil gained power, Catholic and antifeminist ideology was instituted in the state apparatus, and the
IRA's border campaign ensued. Given the stark divisions that arose between
these different groups in the final years of her life, it is surprising that Fianna
Fáil, labor, and Republicans put aside their differences in a joint commemoration on the first anniversary of her death, as they marched together from
St. Stephen's Green to Glasnevin Cemetery to lay wreaths at her grave.[1] The
demonstration is all the more remarkable in light of the controversies that
marked national commemorations of the events that are now described as
the Irish Revolution.[2] The importance of Constance Markievicz to these

---

[1] "The Late Madame Markievicz," *Irish Times*, July 16, 1928, 5.
[2] For example, in 1924 Republicans boycotted the first official ceremony to commemorate
the Easter Rising. The Cumann na nGaedheal–sponsored ceremony the next year was closed to
the public, and Republicans held alternative commemorations as a mark of protest. De Valera's
first commemoration of the Easter Rising as taoiseach in 1932 was a variation on the tune; the
public were admitted for the first time, and "the relatives of those who were killed or executed from
1916 to 1923" were invited—a tacit acknowledgment of the Civil War—but these relatives were
excluded from the procession. See Fitzpatrick, "Commemoration in the Irish Free State." 196–97.

vastly different groups helped to cement her place in the Irish pantheon, even though the lineaments of her character remain subject to dispute.

One of the most influential sculptors of Markievicz's legacy was de Valera, who sought to forge a narrative of a continuous Irish past of which Fianna Fáil was the inheritor and guardian. This required excising most of Constance Markievicz's political thought and revising the history and nature of socialism in Ireland. On July 3, 1932, the year of the party's landmark election victory, he unveiled at St. Stephen's Green a memorial bust of Markievicz by Albert Power. In his dedicatory speech, de Valera praised Markievicz's devotion to the poor: "Her heart was with the people and her desires were the same as [James] Connolly's."[3] However, those desires as described by de Valera are far more conservative than the ideas that Markievicz or Connolly expressed during their lifetimes. For example, de Valera declared that Markievicz had stepped "down from the class to which she belonged . . . into the life of the plain people."[4] "The plain people," a phrase common to de Valera's rhetoric, homogenized the poor, the working class, and the middle class and pandered to the kind of mythical national identity that was propagated in the most conservative aesthetics of the Irish Revival. The idea of the "plain people" enabled him to sidestep the wider issue of social class in modern Ireland and to avoid particular problems, such as the matter of the democratic program, which had been adopted by the First Dáil (1919) and made, among other things, a commitment to public ownership ("all right to private property must be subordinated to the public right and welfare").[5] At the unveiling, de Valera claimed that for Markievicz, "freedom won would have meant very little unless it had brought with it real freedom for the individual."[6] Similarly, he corrupted the radical gender politics that Markievicz had advocated. She had fought for women's freedom to participate in national life in whichever way they saw fit, but de Valera now decreed, "To many she was simply a strange figure following a path of her own and not the accustomed paths, but she did that because she was truly a woman."[7] In the same way, he credited her as "Chief Scout and foundress" of the Fianna, using a

---

[3] "Mr. De Valera at Rathfarnham: Madame Markievicz Commemoration," *Irish Times*, July 20, 1931, 8; and "The Markievicz Memorial," ibid., July 4, 1932, 3.

[4] "The Markievicz Memorial."

[5] "Democratic Programme" (Jan. 21, 1919), Dáil Éireann Debate, vol. 5, no. 1, http://oireacht asdebates.oireachtas.ie/debates%20authoring/debateswebpack.nsf/takes/dail1919012100016 ?opendocument (accessed Sept. 10, 2013).

[6] "Mr. De Valera at Rathfarnham."

[7] "The Markievicz Memorial."

gender-specific term that is at odds with Markievicz's gender-neutral vocabulary of comradeship and her title as president of the Fianna.[8]

The memorial bust that was unveiled in 1932 depicted Markievicz in Fianna uniform, but the inscription identified her solely with the ICA: "Constance Gore-Booth, Countess de Markievicz, T.D., 1868–1927, Major in the Irish Citizen Army." The description presented a politically inclusive image, distancing her from the IRA that rejected Fianna Fáil's legitimacy and buttressing Fianna Fáil's lobby for votes from Irish labor. An important presence at the unveiling was the Gujarati politician Vithalbhai Patel, whose arrival interrupted de Valera's speech when the crowd gave him "a tumultuous welcome."[9] Patel was the founder of the Swaraj Party, which sought independence from the Raj through the policy of civil disobedience. He had withdrawn from the Indian National Congress after the end of the nonviolent Salt March in early 1930, and he rejected Mahatma Gandhi's pact with the British viceroy, allying himself instead with the radical nationalist Subhas Chandras Bose. Early on, Patel and Bose looked for support from Ireland and founded the Indian-Irish Independence League, a cross-national solidarity movement that sought complete independence from the British Empire.[10] Despite this rich history of affinity between Irish and Indian anti-imperialist movements, de Valera averred from any mention of Patel's transnational anti-imperialist politics and instead introduced him to the crowd as "a man who is fighting for the freedom of his country from outside interference."[11] This was an early indication of the isolationist nationalist rhetoric that de Valera would continue to propagate within the party and is another example of how a major facet of Markievicz's political thought was suppressed in public memory.

In April 1956, on the fortieth anniversary of the Rising, the president of Ireland, Seán T. Ó Ceallaigh, unveiled a second memorial bust to Markievicz to replace the bust that had been defaced in 1945 and 1947. Whether the defacement was politically motivated or was simply a random act of vandalism is unclear; when questions were raised in the Dáil about the damage, Ó Ceallaigh replied that it was possible that it was accidental.[12] The new bust, by the sculptor Seamus Murphy, was sponsored by the Madame Markievicz Memorial Committee, of which Nora Connolly O'Brien was one of the chief organizers. The bust depicted Markievicz in Citizen Army uniform,

---

[8] Ibid.
[9] "Unveils Markievicz Bust," *New York Times*, July 4, 1932, 3.
[10] Bose would later seek support from the Axis Powers during the Second World War.
[11] "Unveils Markievicz Bust," *New York Times*, July 4, 1932, 3.
[12] Dáil Éireann Debate, vol. 95, no. 17, http://debates.oireachtas.ie/dail/1945/02/07/00010 .asp (accessed Sept. 10, 2013).

reflecting the interests of the committee and also perhaps distancing Markievicz from the Fianna, which continued the armed struggle and would play a
prominent role in the IRA's guerilla war against partition that began later the
same year. Nora Connolly O'Brien introduced Ó Ceallaigh and spoke briefly
and affectionately about "Madame," the respectful term of endearment by
which Markievicz was known. Ó Ceallaigh gave a slightly fuller portrait of
Markievicz's career than de Valera had in 1932; he mentioned, for example,
her work for the Daughters of Ireland, but on the whole his speech replicated
de Valera's in its tone and in its judgments. Ó Ceallaigh pronounced that
St. Stephen's Green marked the place where "Constance Markievicz reached
the culmination of her pilgrimage from the big house to a dwelling-place
in the hearts of the Irish people, where she and her memory have ever since
abided and will continue to abide."[13] He surmised, "without ceasing to be a
woman of charm and grace, she became a soldier."

The perceived feminine virtues to which Ó Ceallaigh referred are reflected
in more recent commemorative statues. Elizabeth McLaughlin's statue (1998)
that stands on Tara Street in Dublin was commissioned by Treasury Holdings and depicts Markievicz without any hint of militancy, dressed in a non-
descript long skirt and long-sleeved blouse and standing beside her dog,
Poppet. A statue by John Coll (2003) in Rathcormac, County Sligo, shows
her as a freedom fighter, breaking through prison gates ahead of a poverty-
stricken man, woman, and young girl. Here, Markievicz wears her characteristic feathered hat and a military-style tunic, but rather than the trousers and
puttees that she wore during the Rising, she is shown in a long skirt typical of
the Cumann na mBan uniform. These representations illustrate attempts to
reconcile Markievicz's sex with the nature of her political activism, which are
still perceived as at odds. Whether de Valera shot anyone during the Easter
Rising is never a matter for public debate, whereas the singular occasion of
Markievicz's shooting of the constable at St. Stephen's Green continues to
plague the Irish public imagination.

David Fitzpatrick has noted the "multiple connections between ceremo-
nial and literary commemoration," an interrelationship that is certainly true
of the way that major writers including W. B. Yeats, Sean O'Casey, and Sean
O'Faolain have served as the architects of Constance Markievicz's legacy.[14]
Yeats wrote three poems in which Markievicz features: "Easter, 1916" and
"On a Political Prisoner" from *Michael Robartes and the Dancer* (1921) and
"In Memory of Eva Gore-Booth and Con Markiewicz," which opens *The*

[13] "Memorial to Madame Markievicz Unveiled by President," *Irish Times*, April 3, 1956, 7.
[14] Fitzpatrick, "Commemoration in the Irish Free State," 185.

Winding Stair and Other Poems (1933). In "Easter 1916," she is described scathingly as "That woman":

> That woman's days were spent
> In ignorant good-will,
> Her nights in argument
> Until her voice grew shrill.
> What voice more sweet than hers
> When, young and beautiful,
> She rode to harriers?

In Yeats's aesthetic formulation, the Anglo-Irish ascendancy is associated with sweetness, fecundity, intelligence, and beauty. Since Markievicz rejected her social class, in Yeats's mind, she could no longer personify those virtues and is instead depicted as coarse and hardened: "Too long a sacrifice / Can make a stone of the heart."[15] She is the only person featured in "Easter, 1916" who survived the Rising and its aftermath and as a result goes unnamed, unlike "MacDonagh and MacBride / And Connolly and Pearse," who are immortalized near the poem's end.

Markievicz is also unnamed in "On a Political Prisoner," where the female figure might at first be interpreted as Maud Gonne.[16] The poem begins, "She that but little patience knew, / From childhood on, had now so much / A grey gull lost its fear and flew / Down to her cell and there alit." Seabirds feature frequently in Yeats's work, but the gull here also evokes Markievicz's illustrations for Eva Gore-Booth's *The Death of Fionavar and the Triumph of Maeve*, which she drew in prison after the Rising. "On a Political Prisoner" builds on Yeats's characterization of Markievicz in "Easter, 1916." Here, he asserts that

> her mind
> Became a bitter, an abstract thing,
> Her thought some popular enmity:

[15] The image of the stone also appears in Yeats's writing about Maud Gonne's revolutionary activities; he writes in *Autobiographies*, "To women opinions becomes as their children or their sweethearts, and the greater their emotional capacity the more they forget all other things. They grow cruel, as if in defense of lover or child, and all this is done for 'something other than human life.' At last the opinion is so much identified with their nature that it seems a part of their flesh, becomes stone and passes out of life"; W. B. Yeats, *Autobiographies*, 429.

[16] In a section of his *Autobiography* written after the 1916 Rising, Yeats acknowledged the resemblance between Constance Markievicz and Maud Gonne in their youth, especially their "very exact resemblance in voice." He qualified that "in later years her voice became shrill and high, but at the time I write of it was low and soft. I was perhaps the first to give her any detailed account of one [Gonne] in imitation of whom, perhaps, she was to earn the life-sentence she is now serving"; Yeats, *Memoirs*, 78.

Blind and leader of the blind
Drinking the foul ditch where they lie.

Again, her years in Sligo provide a contrast to the later politics of which Yeats disapproves; the words "youth," "beauty," "wildness," and "clean and sweet" describe her early life and exemplify his antidemocratic aesthetics. The gull, coming to the prisoner's window, provides a link to her past, and the poem concludes with an image of the bird suspended between "the cloudy canopy" and "the hollows of the sea," or between the eternal and fractured time.[17]

These images are important for interpreting "In Memory of Eva Gore-Booth and Con Markiewicz," with its famous refrain, "Two girls in silk kimonos, both / Beautiful, one a gazelle."[18] Yeats's elegy softens the judgments he makes in his previous poems; the word "ignorant" still appears, but in the later poem it is attributed to the people with whom she conspires rather than to Markievicz herself. Yeats presumes that the sisters, now "shadows," are finally able to see "All the folly of a fight / With a common wrong or right," with "common" suggesting something shared as well as signifying the lowly or vulgar. The tone of the earlier poems is accusatory, but here Markievicz's agency is stripped from her, as Yeats asserts "The innocent and the beautiful / Have no enemy but time." By conceptualizing Markievicz's transformation as a product of a historical cycle and not of personal choice, Yeats is able to reconcile the Constance Gore-Booth that he knew at Lissadell with the Madame Markievicz that she became in Dublin.

Casimir Markievicz's legacy is almost nonexistent, despite the important role he played in the campaign for a municipal gallery in Dublin and his contribution of the phrase "Bloody Sunday" to Irish political discourse. His paintings have begun to draw some critical attention, and 2012 saw the publication of a full-scale biography that focuses on the years he spent in Ireland.[19] Owing to rapid changes in the political landscape of eastern Europe, from the two world wars through the rise and fall of the Soviet Union, his political activities—his work with the Freedom and Brotherhood of Peoples and his service in the First World War—as well as his artistic contributions have been obscured. This marginalization is exacerbated by the inclination to ignore the scope of Demowskiite politics in Poland in the wake of the atrocities of the Second World War. Yet, in addition to enlightening scholarship on the amateur and professional theaters of early twentieth-century Dublin, Casimir Markievicz's life and work inform our understanding of how

[17] Albright notes that "the sea partly signifies tumultuous historical process, as is explicit in 'A Prayer for My Daughter'"; Yeats, *The Poems*, 612–13.

[18] For a discussion of the afterlife of this poem, see Chandran, "Auden's Allusion."

[19] Ryan-Smolin, "Casimir Dunin Markievicz Painter and Playwright."

nationalism and class functioned historically in Russia, Poland, and Ukraine, where the same questions of national identity continue to be bloodily contested.

The subtleties of Casimir's Polish nationalist politics and the importance of the avant-garde in Dublin in provoking them were disregarded in Sean O'Faolain's 1934 biography, which was the first of Constance Markievicz. Originally published with a biting addendum, *Constance Markievicz: Or, the Average Revolutionary*, the subtitle was dropped for the 1967 edition and all subsequent editions. Every biography since has taken O'Faolain's book as its starting point, lured in by his tantalizing anecdotes and eminently quotable vitriol. The book began as a plan for a series of articles for the *Sunday Chronicle*, for which O'Faolain hoped to commission articles from Stanislaus Markievicz, Hanna Sheehy Skeffington, Jack White, and Sean O'Casey. When O'Casey was asked, he flatly refused: "I've no reverence for the de mortuis nonsense. To launch an attack on the living is much more dangerous than to launch an attack on the dead, and I did this on M. de Markievicz, when she was living when she was popular, and when those who were greater and higher than I was then, were afraid to say boo to the goose."[20] When his other commissions also fell through, O'Faolain decided to undertake a full-length biography himself. In his attempts to persuade O'Casey, O'Faolain had specified that the work "should not insult the intelligence of the Irish artisan and farmer by doing the rotten stuff that is needed to stir the jaded palettes of Newcastle-on-Tyne."[21] Instead, the biography that emerged soothed the jaded palettes of a country that was eager to forget about the Civil War and its most extreme elements.

Throughout his biography, O'Faolain's tone undermines any seriousness in Constance or Casimir's artistic or political endeavors:

> He was full of life and she was full of energy; he joked a good deal, and she loved practical jokes; he had been reared in the country and she loved the country; they were both extremely boyish; he loved the theatre and she loved the limelight; he craved the society of women, and was an excellent boon-companion for men—she enjoyed the society of men. Like enough to be a perfect match, not different enough to find out how different until it was too late. The truth is—as time was to show—they made perfect friends. The main difference was that in her

[20] Sean O'Casey to Sean O'Faolain (Aug. 10, 1932), Jonathan Cape Archive. My thanks to Niall Carson.

[21] O'Faolain to O'Casey (Mar. 4, 1932), Cape Archive.

there lurked a fundamental earnestness, while he was a born dilettante; yet even there they came near to one another, for he was serious about the most superficial things and she was superficial about the most serious things. Worst of all, she was, it is clear, sexually cold. These, alas, were things that nobody could then have realized.[22]

Casting Casimir and Constance as foils for each other, O'Faolain disguised the extent of their political affinities during the early years of their marriage, just as he disparaged the quality of their theatrical and artistic collaborations. Privately, O'Faolain expressed a more positive opinion of Constance; he wrote to Edward Garnet that he "admire[d] her greatly for a warm, passionate, active woman. You couldn't but admire a woman who told her [daughter's] governess she was 'a blighted bloody Sasenach' and cleaned her car, *quite naturally*, in her red knickers in the middle of Rathmines Rd!!"[23] To Stanislaus, now living in Dublin, the book was an "awful parody" that had only been published "owing to my not doing it, nor Maeve."[24]

Most infuriating for Constance's friends was O'Faolain's misrepresentation of her activism and her militant engagements. Cathal O'Shannon, trade unionist leader and cofounder with James Connolly of the Socialist Party of Ireland, was enraged by O'Faolain's novelistic approach to Irish history and his total omission of the Civil War from his narrative.[25] O'Shannon wrote angrily to James Connolly's daughter, Nora Connolly O'Brien, who scathingly commented that the biography was "up to the author's usual standard."[26] O'Shannon and Connolly O'Brien worked together to compile a list of factual inaccuracies in the biography, while also complaining of points of interpretive difference. O'Faolain had worked as director of publicity for the Republicans in Cork during the Irish Civil War, where—according to Connolly O'Brien—"he spent most of his time in the 'Examiner' smoking innumerable cigarettes or reading French novels." She told O'Shannon that she intended to published her own account of the revolution in order "to give the lie to the filth that is O'Faolain & Frank O'Connors. I am not at all narrow minded

---

[22] O'Faolain, *Constance Markievicz*, 39.

[23] Sean O'Faolain to Edward Garnett (n.d. [Dec. 13, 1932]). My thanks to Frank Shovlin.

[24] Stanislaus Markievicz to Lady Gore-Booth (Dec. 4, 1935), PRONI, D/4131/K/13 (65).

[25] ILHS/MSS18/COS 76. O'Shannon (1893–1969) was mobilized with the Volunteers in County Tyrone in 1916 but did not fight owing to Eoin MacNeill's countermanding order. He was subjected to several arrests, undertook a hunger strike, and fought as a member of the IRA during the Anglo-Irish War; a supporter of the treaty, he served briefly as a Labour Party TD in 1922 and afterward edited *The Voice of Labour* and *The Watchword* from 1930 to 1932; he was secretary of the Irish Trade Union Congress and the Congress of Irish Unions.

[26] Nora Connolly O'Brien to Cathal O'Shannon (Sept. 17, 1934), Irish Labour History Society Museum and Archive (ILHS), MSS 13/COS 76.

about things but . . . it seems tragic that those of us who were actually the ultimate friends of the lads who really did the work are silent while these outsiders are so busy defaming them." She believed that O'Faolain's "idea [was] to blacken everyone & so please England [and] sell his muck in England & make money." Refusing to buy a copy, she pledged to "wait until Boots have it on their secondhand list [so] that sale wont help him."[27]

Connolly O'Brien was not far off the mark; as the Cape archive shows, the biographies that O'Faolain published in this period were financially motivated, and his politics were fickle. In addition to the biography of Markievicz, O'Faolain published *The Life Story of Eamon de Valera* (1933), *King of the Beggars* (1938) about Daniel O'Connell, and lives of Hugh O'Neill (1942) and Cardinal Newman (1953). In his study of O'Faolain's biographies, historian F.S.L. Lyons describes the de Valera biography as "overwritten, under-documented, hagiographical rather than historical" and goes so far as to call it "the ugly duckling among O'Faoláin's works," an opinion that O'Faolain himself expressed about the book in an article for *The Bell* in 1945.[28] Because Lyons shared O'Faolain's opinions about Constance Markievicz, he claims that "no one who reads that book will doubt that the oral legend helped rather than hindered him in attaining, if not the cold truth, then the psychological truth about 'the Countess' which is its principal achievement."[29] This truth, as Lyons has it, is the story of a woman's "love for mankind in general and her disastrous personal relations with her family, her husband and the unfortunate daughter whom she virtually abandoned to the care of the child's grandmother," and Lyons goes so far as to quote Yeats in his summation of the "bitterness, and perhaps even the barrenness of those lonely later years [that Markievicz] spent 'conspiring among the ignorant.'"[30]

The two major biographies that were written at the fiftieth anniversary of the Rising, Jacqueline van Vorris's *Constance de Markievicz: In the Cause of Ireland* and Anne Marreco's *The Rebel Countess: The Life and Times of Constance Markievicz*, are kinder in tone but still rely on O'Faolain for their detail. Somewhat oddly given the occasion of their publication, neither devotes much attention to Markievicz's role in the Easter Rising. Marreco's book is highly influenced by Stanislaus's opinions as well, as she acknowledges in her preface.[31] Diana Norman's *Terrible Beauty: A Life of Constance Markievicz* (1987) is sympathetic—and at times sycophantic—when it comes to Con-

---

[27] Nora Connolly O'Brien to Cathal O'Shannon (Oct. 25, 1934), ibid.
[28] Lyons, "Seán O'Faoláin as Biographer," 95–96.
[29] Ibid., 97.
[30] Ibid., 98.
[31] Marreco, *The Rebel Countess*, xii.

stance's character, but Norman merely paraphrases O'Faolain on the subject of Casimir: "He did everything well and nothing seriously. . . . That it [Dublin] did not fit him later was because he owed it no allegiance and because, unlike Con, he did not pursue anything to its depth."[32]

Esther Roper's edition of the *Prison Letters of Countess Markievicz* (1934) stands as a quiet riposte to O'Faolain and Yeats. Roper writes, "Some of those who never really knew Constance and Eva regret that what might, in a worldly sense, have been 'successful lives' were spent, so they suggest, in Eva's case, in the pursuit of 'a vague Utopia,' and in Constance's case, in 'conspiring among the ignorant.'"[33] The book begins with a biographical sketch that incorporates historical sources, including the Proclamation of the Republic, documents from Markievicz's court martial, and letters to Eva from Constance's friends and compatriots, such as Fr. Albert Bibby and Jim Larkin. The detail in the prison letters offers insight into Constance's love for Casimir, Stanislaus, and Maeve, as well as the intricacies of her prison reading, which undermine assumptions that her politics were vacuous, lacking grounding in any theoretical basis. By the same token, the letters give glimpses of some of her most vulnerable moments: the erratic nature of her thoughts when she was under the most severe mental and physical strain, episodes of depression, and candid discussions of her spiritual life. De Valera contributed a preface to the volume in which he commented that the book "was necessary to correct misrepresentation of Madame's character to which opponents of the causes she espoused had given some currency during her lifetime." Somewhat incredibly he writes that "a woman in public life has a double gauntlet of criticism to run" and that "she gloried in" the "Declaration of Independence by Dail Eireann" of 1919 because "it was coupled with the Democratic Programme," all values to which de Valera showed little actual political commitment.[34] In fact, it seems unlikely that he read the full text of the letters, or perhaps he simply hoped that most readers would ignore the unambiguous support for Bolshevism and Lenin that Markievicz expresses in them.

On the whole, the historiography of modern Ireland reflects Lyons's—and thereby O'Faolain and Yeats's—opinion rather than the facts of the Markieviczes' lives and thought. The reasons for this are multifarious. One interpretive hindrance has been the armed struggle in Northern Ireland. The Easter Rising and even more so the Irish Civil War were the genesis of the late twentieth-century permutations of the IRA, leading some historians to

---

[32] Norman, *Terrible Beauty*, 34.
[33] Roper, *Prison Letters*, 122.
[34] Ibid., vii.

dismiss early Republicans as enamored with violence for its own sake. As Seamus Deane sums up in his critique of Irish historiography, "the biggest threat to democracy is that outlandishly retarded form of nationalist violence that Easter 1916 spawned and the IRA inherited."[35]

This inclination is fueled by scintillating caricatures by some of Constance Markievicz's most bitter antagonists. In *Drums under the Window* (1945), O'Casey depicts the presentation of the Starry Plough, the flag of the Citizen Army, to Liberty Hall: "All pressed back to have a good look at it, and a murmur of reverent approval gave the flag a grave salute—all except the Countess, who returned to the oiling of her automatic with the remark that the flag bears no republican message to anyone."[36] In Liam O'Flaherty's novel *The Martyr* (1933), a satire on the Irish Civil War, Markievicz appears as the thinly veiled character of Angela Fitzgibbon, a vampiric Cathleen ni Houlihan: mystical, sexual, and above all bored:

> Her face was very beautiful. Great yellow eyes slanted upwards slightly towards her temples and her cheek-bones were high as if she had Mongolian blood. The expression of her eyes was sleepy and mysterious, passionate, yet cold and cruel, in the irresponsible way that the eyes of a tigress are cruel; it merely being their nature to devour. . . . She moved towards Crosbie suddenly, swinging her long flanks and thighs; exactly like the walk of a long, lazy tigress. She called his name in a bird-like voice that was strangely out of keeping with her size and majesty. It was the voice of a spoilt child.[37]

Over the course of the novel, Fitzgibbon's energy fades into political and sexual malaise: "Each love had given way to a feeling of disgust, almost of hatred for the lover; until at last the very idea of physical intimacy with men had become repulsive to her." In her darkest moments, she insults her comrades by calling them "peasants," and she is afflicted by a loneliness "at being cut off from her own class." Her life force is channeled into a death wish: "She halted in the middle of the room and blew a cloud of cigarette smoke towards the ceiling, thinking that perhaps the sensation of death was the only one left now that was able to satisfy her . . . in any case, it would be exciting to try."[38] These caricatures took such a strong hold in the popular imagination that

---

[35] Deane, "Wherever Green Is Read," 99.

[36] O'Casey, *Drums under the Window*, 314.

[37] O'Flaherty, *The Martyr*, 62–63. The novel was banned under the Censorship of Publicans Act since it not only dealt with a taboo subject but lambasted national heroes, many of whom were still living.

[38] Ibid.

when T. H. White was formulating the character of Morgause for his Arthurian series, *The Once and Future King*, he sketched her as "beautiful . . . an unchaste woman. At seventy she was seducing a boy of twenty . . . possessive . . . Clytemnestra, Cleopatra (Shakespeare's) . . . the witch from Snow White . . . a fanatical anti-Norman, a Countess Marcewitz."[39]

The opposing, hagiographical views of Constance Markievicz are equally flawed. In R. M. Fox's book of martyrs, *Rebel Irishwomen* (1935), he claimed that Markievicz and Gonne were "two of the most representative Irishwomen of their generation."[40] In fact, they are two of the most exceptional. Fox describes Markievicz as a woman of "epic quality" with an "aristocratic spirit" who wished to create "a nation of aristocrats," a drastic misinterpretation of Markievicz's socialism.[41] Dorothy MacArdle's *The Irish Republic* (1937) is a swashbuckling narrative of an unbroken tradition of Irish Republicanism that exaggerates some of Markievicz's contributions, for example, presenting her as sole founder of the Fianna and blatantly shunning Hobson.[42] Similarly, MacArdle's account of Markievicz's time at Aylesbury ignores her protests at being housed with prostitutes and murderers; rather, MacArdle has her "enduring the same conditions as the ordinary women convicts and taking a profound interest in their cases and the stories of their lives."[43]

The archive poses another significant barrier to writing the lives of the Markieviczes, and to writing about the nuances of Irish Republicanism and Polish nationalism in this period. As Steele and other feminist critics have noted, official archives are heavily gendered, and the Bureau of Military History, which houses witness statements from the Irish Revolution, is no exception. That archive was compiled "during two critical epochs: after the political fallout from the Civil War, when political women in Ireland were widely maligned by the Free State, and in the late 1940s—1950s, when interviews of political witnesses were gathered."[44] While the upheavals of the revolutionary period facilitated the flexibility of women's activities in public life, the process of state formation stymied the fluidity of gender roles.[45] This conservatism is reflected in the structure of the archive. Socialist, trade unionist, and Republican documents are similarly marginalized. National newspapers,

---

[39] T. H. White Diary (1939–41), Harry Ransome Centre, Box 27 (1). My thanks to Anne Thompson.

[40] Fox, *Rebel Irishwomen*, 35.

[41] Ibid., 26.

[42] MacArdle, *The Irish Republic*, 68.

[43] Ibid., 202.

[44] Steele, "Gender and the Postcolonial Archive," 58.

[45] Valiulis, "Politics of Gender in the Irish Free State," 570.

such as the *Irish Times* and the *Freeman's Journal*, which represent upper-class and majority middle-class opinion, have been digitized and are easily accessible. By contrast, the *Irish Worker* and *Workers' Republic*, and the many Republican newspapers that were published during the Civil War, are available only in crumbling hard copy or on poor-quality microfilm, which is difficult to access and is rapidly degrading. Furthermore, the ad hoc nature of the Republican publications, many of which are mimeographed rather than professionally printed, often affects the level of credibility that researchers are willing to attribute to them. This bias either reinforces the status quo or results in an outright neglect of the sources. The reorganization of archives that occurs during processes of regime change, as in the case of Russia, creates further impediments, as much material simply disappears; it was impossible to trace, for example, Casimir Markievicz's service record in the Russian Army. Constance's and Casimir's lives illustrate the necessity of continuing to interrogate the archive and of adopting an inclusive methodology.

Extreme visibility poses other problems, as accepted views become crystallized through the process of memorial. Ireland now murmurs Constance Markievicz's name alongside MacDonagh and MacBride, Connolly and Pearse. As the American poet Louise Bogan wrote to Edmund Wilson about her visit to Ireland in April 1937: "It's not a country, it's a neurosis. . . . Did I mention the 1916 collection in the National Museum of Dublin? That's something. All the grisly memtoes [*sic*] of those heroic but gruesome days: farewell letters . . . ; death masks . . . ; uniforms; photographs . . . ; guns; autographed prison biscuits. . . . There's a photo of the Countess, in uniform, looking very beautiful with a drawn pistol in her hand, that slew me. I tell you, it gets you. For it's still going on, and will never end."[46]

<hr>

[46] Quoted in Smith, "The Countess and the Poets," 51.

Selected Bibliography

Archives

Capuchin Archives, Dublin
Documents on Irish Foreign Policy, hosted by Royal Irish Academy
Irish Labour History Society Museum and Archive
Lissadell Collection, Lissadell House
National Archives (UK)
National Archives of Ireland
National Library of Ireland
National Museum of Ireland
Public Record Office of Northern Ireland
Royal College of Physicians in Ireland
Sligo County Library
Sligo County Museum
University of Limerick

Contemporary Periodicals

Bean na hÉireann
Catholic Bulletin
Éire: The Irish Nation
Fianna Handbook
Freeman's Journal
Irish Bulletin
Irish Citizen
Irish Independent
Irish Nation and the Irish Peasant
Irish Press
Irish Times
Irish Worker
Kerryman
Manchester Guardian
New York Times

Observer
An Phoblacht
Poblacht na h-Éireann
Poblacht na h-Éireann (Scottish edition)
Poblacht na h-Éireann War News
Republican War Bulletin
Russkoye Slovo
Rzeczpospolita
Sinn Féin
Sligo Champion
Sligo Independent
Votes for Women
Workers' Republic

Works Published before 1932

Brailsford, Henry Noel. *The War of Steel and Gold: A Story of the Armed Peace.* 10th rev. ed. London: Bell, 1918.

Brussilov, A. A. *A Soldier's Note-book 1914–1918.* London: Macmillan, 1930.

Connolly, James. *Labour and Irish History.* New York: Donnelly Press, 1919.

Craig, E. T. *The Irish Land & Labour Question Illustrated in the History of Ralahine and Co-operative Farming.* London: Trübner, 1882.

Crofts, Joseph M. arr. *A Battle Hymn, Words by Constance de Markievicz.* Dublin: Art Depot, 1918.

Douglass, Frederick. "Men of Color, to Arms!" Rochester, March 21, 1863.

Ebeid, W. Makram. *Complete Independence versus the Milner Scheme.* London: W. Makram Ebeid, 1921.

Gore-Booth, Eva. *The Death of Fionavar from the Triumph of Maeve.* London: Longmans, 1916.

———. *The Egyptian Pillar.* Dublin: Maunsel, 1907.

———. *Poems of Eva Gore-Booth: Complete Edition.* Edited by Esther Roper. London: Longmans, 1929.

———. *Unseen Kings.* London: Longmans, 1904.

Griffith, Arthur. *The Resurrection of Hungary.* Dublin: James Duffy, 1904.

Haverty, Martin. *The History of Ireland: Ancient and Modern.* Dublin: James Duffy, 1867.

Hobson, J. A. *Democracy after the War.* New York: Allen & Unwin, 1918.

Lalor, James Fintan. *The Writings of James Fintan Lalor.* Edited by John O'Leary. Dublin: T. G. O'Donoghue, 1895.

Litvinov, Maxim. *The Bolshevik Revolution: Its Rise and Meaning.* 3rd ed. London: British Socialist Party, 1919.

Malynski, Emmanuel. *A Short Cut to a Splendid Peace*. London: P. S. King & Son, 1918.

Markievicz, Casimir. *The Memory of the Dead: A Romantic Drama of '98 in Three Acts*. Dublin: Tower Press, 1910.

Markievicz, Constance. *Heroes and Martyrs: Dedicated to na Fianna Éireann*. Dublin: [n.p.], 1917.

———. *James Connolly's Policy and Catholic Doctrine*. N.p., n.d.

———. *What Irish Republicans Stand For*. Glasgow: Civic Press, n.d.

———. *Women, Ideals and the Nation: A Lecture Delivered to the Students' National Literary Society, Dublin*. Dublin: Inghinidhe na hÉireann, 1909.

Martyn, Edward. *Grangecolman: A Domestic Drama in Three Acts*. Dublin: Maunsel, 1912.

Mitchel, John, *Jail Journal*. Edited by Arthur Griffith. Dublin: M. H. Gill, 1913.

Myers, Frederic. "On Indications of Continued Terrene Knowledge on the Part of Phantasms of the Dead." *Proceedings of the Society for Psychical Research* 8 (1892): 170–252.

Ostrovsky, Alexander. *The Storm*. London: Allen & Unwin, 1930.

Pankhurst, Sylvia, and Anton Pannekoek. *Communism versus Reforms: Two Articles Reprinted from the* Workers' Dreadnought, *1922*. Birkenhead: Workers' Voice, 1922.

Prescott, W. H. *The History of the Conquest of Peru*. London: Richard Bentley, 1847.

Yeats, W. B. *Autobiographies: Reveries over Childhood and Youth and The Trembling of the Veil*. London: Macmillan, 1927.

Works Published after 1932

Anderson, W. K. *James Connolly and the Irish Left*. Dublin: Irish Academic Press, 1994.

Arrington, Lauren. "Liberté, Egalité, Sororité: The Poetics of Suffrage in the Work of Eva Gore-Booth and Constance Markievicz." In *Advancing the Cause of Liberty: Irish Women's Writing 1878–1922*. Edited by Whitney Standlee and Anna Pilz. Manchester: Manchester University Press, forthcoming.

———. "Socialist Republican Discourse and the 1916 Easter Rising: The Occupation of Jacob's Biscuit Factory and the South Dublin Union Explained. *Journal of British Studies* 53, no. 4 (October 2014): 992–1010.

Ascher, Abraham. *The Revolution of 1905: A Short History*. Stanford: Stanford University Press, 2004.

Bartelik, Marek. *Unity in Multiplicity: Early Polish Modern Art*. Manchester: Manchester University Press, 2005.

Barton, Brian. *The Secret Court Martial Records of the Easter Rising*. Stroud: History Press, 2010.

Beasley, Ina. "The Art of Ostrovsky." *Slavonic and East European Review* 6, no. 18 (March 1928): 603–17.

Beaumont, Matthew. "Socialism and Occultism at the *Fin de Siècle*: Elective Affinities." *Victorian Review* 36, no. 1 (Spring 2010): 217–32.

Botman, Selma. *Egypt from Independence to Revolution, 1919–1952.* Syracuse: Syracuse University Press, 1991.

Boylan, Patricia. *All Cultivated People: A History of the United Arts Club, Dublin.* Gerrards Cross: Colin Smythe, 1988.

Campbell, Fergus. *Land and Revolution: Nationalist Politics in the West of Ireland, 1891–1921.* Oxford: Oxford University Press, 2007.

Carey, Tim, and Marcus de Búrca. "Bloody Sunday 1920: New Evidence." *History Ireland* 11, no. 2 (Summer 2003): 10–16.

Caulfield, Mary. "'The Woman with a Garden': Unearthing the Artistry and Activism of Constance Markievicz 1908–1927." PhD thesis, Trinity College Dublin, 2011.

Cavanaugh, Jan. *Out Looking In: Early Modern Polish Art, 1890–1918.* Berkeley: University of California Press, 2000.

Chandran, K. Narayana. "Auden's Allusion to 'In Memory of Eva Gore-Booth and Con Markieivicz' in 'In Memory of W. B. Yeats,'" *ANQ* 7, no. 2 (1994): 82–84.

Charazinska, Elzbieta, and Lukasz Kossowski, eds. *Fin de Siècle Polish Art 1890–1914.* Translated by Robert Kirkland. Warsaw: Muzeum Narodowe w Warszawie, 1996.

Clark, Gemma. *Everyday Violence in the Irish Civil War.* Cambridge: Cambridge University Press, 2014.

Clarke, Frances. "Máire nic Shuibhlaigh." In *Dictionary of Irish National Biography,* 6:922–24. Cambridge: Cambridge University Press, 2009.

Connolly, James. *Collected Works.* Volume 1. Dublin: New Books, 1987.

Cottington, David. "The Formation of the Avant-Garde in Paris and London, c. 1880 . . . 1915." *Art History* 35, no. 3 (June 2012): 596–621.

Cronin, Mike. *Sport and Nationalism in Ireland: Gaelic Games, Soccer and Irish Identity since 1870.* Dublin: Four Courts, 1999.

Cullen, Fintan. "The Lane Bequest: Giving Art to Dublin." *Field Day Review* 4 (2008): 186–201.

Davies, Norman. *God's Playground: A History of Poland in Two Volumes.* Oxford: Oxford University Press, 1982.

———. *White Eagle, Red Star: The Polish-Soviet War, 1919–1920 and "the Miracle on the Vistula."* London: Pimlico, 2003.

Davis, Mary. *Sylvia Pankhurst: A Life in Radical Politics.* London: Pluto, 1999.

Deane, Seamus. "Wherever Green Is Read." In *Revising the Rising.* Edited by Máirín ní Dhonnchadha and Theo Dorgan, 91–105. Derry: Field Day, 1991.

Denson, Alan, ed. *Letters from AE.* London: Abelard-Schuman, 1961.

nic Dháibhéid, Caoimhe. *Seán MacBride: A Republican Life.* Liverpool: Liverpool University Press, 2011.

Dixon, Joy. *Divine Feminism: Theosophy and Feminism in England*. Baltimore: Johns Hopkins University Press, 2001.

Dolan, Anne. "Killing and Bloody Sunday, November 1920." *Historical Journal* 49, no. 3 (September 2006): 789–810.

Dunphy, Richard. *The Making of Fianna Fáil Power in Ireland, 1923–1948*. Oxford: Clarendon, 1995.

Eichacker, Joanne Mooney. *Irish Republican Women in America: Lecture Tours 1916–1925*. Dublin: Irish Academic Press, 2003.

Ellis, Peter Beresford. *James Connolly: Selected Writings*. London: Pluto, 1997.

English, Richard. *Ernie O'Malley: IRA Intellectual*. Oxford: Oxford University Press, 1998.

———. *Radicals and the Republic: Socialist Republicanism in the Irish Free State 1925–37*. Oxford: Clarendon, 1994.

Esslin, Martin. "Max Reinhardt: 'High Priest of Theatricality.'" *The Drama Review* 21, no. 1 (June 1977): 3–24.

Fehrer, Catherine. "Women at the Académie Julian in Paris." *Burlington Magazine* 136, no. 1100 (November 1994): 752–57.

Ferriter, Diarmaid. *Judging DeV: A Reassessment of the Life and Legacy of Eamon de Valera*. Dublin: Royal Irish Academy, 2007.

Fitzpatrick, David. "Commemoration in the Irish Free State: A Chronicle of Embarrassment." In *History and Memory in Modern Ireland*. Edited by Ian McBride, 184–203. Cambridge: Cambridge University Press, 2001.

Fletcher, Ian. "Poet and Designer; W. B. Yeats and Althea Gyles." *Yeats Studies* 1 (1971): 42–79.

Foster, R. F. *Modern Ireland 1600–1972*. London: Penguin, 1988.

———. *Vivid Faces: The Revolutionary Generation in Ireland, 1890–1923*. London: Allen Lane, 2014.

———. *W. B. Yeats: A Life*. Volume 1. Oxford: Oxford University Press, 1997.

Fox, R. M. *The History of the Irish Citizen Army*. Dublin: J. Duffy, 1944.

———. *Rebel Irishwomen*. Dublin: Talbot, 1935.

Foy, Michael T., and Brian Barton. *The Easter Rising*. Stroud: History Press, 2011.

Frazier, Adrian. *George Moore, 1852–1933*. New Haven: Yale University Press, 2000.

Garvin, Tom. "Great Hatred, Little Room: Social Background and Political Sentiment among Revolutionary Activists in Ireland, 1890–1922." In *The Revolution in Ireland, 1879–1923*. Edited by D. George Boyce, 91–114. London, Macmillan Educaton, 1988.

———. *Judging Lemass: The Measure of the Man*. Dublin: Royal Irish Academy, 2009.

Greaves, C. Desmond. *The Irish Transport and General Workers' Union: The Formative Years 1909–1923*. Dublin: Gill & Macmillan, 1982.

Greger, René. *The Russian Fleet, 1914–1917*. Translated by Jill Gearing. London: Ian Allen, 1972.

Hall, Richard C. *The Balkan Wars 1912–1913: Prelude to the First World War*. London: Routledge, 2000.

Harper, George Mills. *Yeats's Golden Dawn*. London: Macmillan, 1974.

Hart, Peter. "The Fenians and the International Revolutionary Tradition." In *The Black Hand of Republicanism: Fenianism in Modern Ireland*. Edited by Fearghal McGarry and James McConnel. Dublin: Irish Academic Press, 2009.

———. *The IRA and Its Enemies: Violence and Community in Cork 1916–1923*. Oxford: Oxford University Press, 1998.

———. *The I.R.A. at War 1916–1923*. Oxford: Oxford University Press, 2003.

Haverty, Anne. *Constance Markievicz: An Independent Life*. London: Pandora, 1988.

Hay, Marnie. *Bulmer Hobson and the Nationalist Movement in Twentieth-Century Ireland*. Manchester: Manchester University Press, 2009.

———. "The Foundation and Development of Na Fianna Éireann, 1909–16." *Irish Historical Studies* 36, no. 141 (May 2008): 53–71.

Hayes, Alan, ed. *The Years Flew By: The Recollections of Madame Sidney Gifford Czira*. Galway: Arlen House, 2000.

Healy, James. "The Civil War Hunger-Strike: October 1923." *Studies* 71, no. 283 (Autumn 1982): 213–26.

Henry, Paul. *An Irish Portrait*. London: B. T. Batsford, 1951.

Hogan, Robert, Richard Burnham, and Daniel P. Poteet: *The Rise of the Realists, 1910–1915*. Dublin: Dolmen, 1979.

Holroyd, Michael. *Bernard Shaw: The Search for Love, 1856–1898*. London: Chatto & Windus, 1988.

Hone, Joseph, ed. *J. B. Yeats: Letters to His Son W. B. Yeats and Others 1869–1922*. London: Faber, 1944.

Hopkinson, Michael. *Green against Green: The Irish Civil War*. Dublin: Gill & Macmillan, 1988.

———. *The Irish War of Independence*. Montreal: McGill-Queen's University Press, 2002.

House, John. "Framing the Landscape." In *Critical Readings in Impressionism and Post-Impressionism: An Anthology*. Edited by Mary Tompkins Lewis, 77–99. Berkeley: University of California Press, 2007.

Hughes, Brian. *Michael Mallin*. Dublin: O'Brien, 2012.

Hutchinson, John. "Sir Hugh Lane and the Gift of the Prince of Wales to the Municipal Gallery of Modern Art, Dublin." *Studies* 68, no. 272 (Winter 1979): 277–87.

Hryniuk, Stella. "Polish Lords and Ukrainian Peasants: Conflict, Deference, and Accommodation in Eastern Galicia in the Late Nineteenth Century." *Austrian History Yearbook* 24 (1993): 119–32.

Jackson, Alvin. *Ireland 1798–1998: Politics and War*. Oxford: Oxford University Press, 1999.

James, Dermot. *The Gore-Booths of Lissadell*. Dublin: Woodfield, 2004.

Keatinge, Patrick. "Ireland and the League of Nations." *Studies* 59, no. 234 (Summer 1970): 133–47.

Kelly, Matthew. *The Fenian Ideal and Irish Nationalism, 1862–1916.* Woodbridge: Boydell and Brewer, 2006.

———. "Irish Nationalist Opinion and the British Empire in the 1850s and 1860s." *Past and Present* 204 (August 2009): 127–54.

Keown, Gerard. "The Irish Race Conference, 1922, Reconsidered." *Irish Historical Studies* 32, no. 127 (May 2001): 365–76.

Kissane, Bill. *The Politics of the Irish Civil War.* Oxford: Oxford University Press, 2005.

Knirck, Jason. "Women's Political Rhetoric and the Irish Revolution." In *Turning Points in Twentieth-Century Irish History.* Edited by Thomas E. Hachey, 39–56. Dublin: Irish Academic Press, 2011.

Kruger, Daniel H. "Hobson, Lenin, and Schumpter on Imperialism." *Journal of the History of Ideas* 16, no. 2 (April 1955): 252–59.

Laffan, Michael. "'Labour Must Wait': Ireland's Conservative Revolution." *Irish Historical Studies* 15 (1985): 203–22.

———. *The Partition of Ireland 1911–1925.* Dundalk: Dundalgan, 1983.

———. *The Resurrection of Ireland: The Sinn Féin Party, 1916–1923.* Cambridge: Cambridge University Press, 1999.

Larkin, Emmet. "Socialism and Catholicism in Ireland." *Church History* 33, no. 4 (December 1964): 462–83.

Leslie, R. F. *The History of Poland since 1863.* Cambridge: Cambridge University Press, 1980.

Lewis, David D. *The Public Image of Henry Ford: An American Folk Hero and His Company.* Detroit: Wayne State University Press, 1976.

Litton, Helen, ed. *Kathleen Clarke: Revolutionary Woman.* Dublin: O'Brien, 2008.

Lundgreen-Nielsen, Kay. *The Polish Problem at the Paris Peace Conference: A Study of the Politics of the Great Powers and the Poles, 1918–1919.* Odense: Odense University Press, 1979.

Lyons, F.S.L. *Culture and Anarchy in Ireland, 1890–1939.* Oxford: Oxford University Press, 1979.

———. *Ireland since the Famine.* 2nd ed. rev. London: Fontana, 1973.

———. "Seán O'Faoláin as Biographer." *Irish University Review* 6, no.1 (Spring 1976): 95–109.

MacArdle, Dorothy. *The Irish Republic: A Documented Chronicle of the Anglo-Irish Conflict and the Partitioning of Ireland, with a Detailed Account of the Period 1916–1923.* London: Gollancz, 1937.

MacWhite, Eóin. "A Russian Pamphlet on Ireland by Count Markievicz." *Irish University Review* 1 (Autumn 1970): 98–110.

Mandle, W. F. "The I.R.B. and the Beginnings of the Gaelic Athletic Association." *Irish Historical Studies* 20, no. 80 (September 1977): 418–38.

Marreco, Anne. *The Rebel Countess: The Life and Times of Constance Markievicz.* New York: Chilton, 1967.

Martin, F. X., ed. *The Howth Gun-Running and the Kilcoole Gun-Running*. Dublin: Browne & Nolan, 1964.

Matthews, Ann. *The Irish Citizen Army*. Dublin: Mercier, 2014.

———. *Renegades: Irish Republican Women 1900–1922*. Cork: Mercier, 2010.

McCabe, Michael. *For God and Ireland: The Fight for Moral Superiority in Ireland 1922–1932*. Sallins: Irish Academic Press, 2012.

McCarthy, Cal. *Cumann na mBan and the Irish Revolution*. Cork: Collins, 2007.

McConnel, James. *The Irish Parliamentary Party and the Third Home Rule Crisis*. Dublin: Four Courts, 2013.

McConville, Seán. *Irish Political Prisoners, 1848–1922: Theatres of War*. London: Routledge, 2003.

McDiarmid, Lucy. *The Irish Art of Controversy*. Ithaca: Cornell University Press, 2005.

McGarry, Fearghal. *The Rising: Easter 1916*. Oxford: Oxford University Press, 2011.

McGuire, Charlie. *Roddy Connolly and the Struggle for Socialism in Ireland*. Cork: Cork University Press, 2008.

———. *Sean McLoughlin: Ireland's Forgotten Revolutionary*. Pontypool: Merlin, 2011.

McHugh, Roger. *Dublin 1916*. London: Arlington, 1966.

Mitchell, Arthur. *Revolutionary Government in Ireland: Dáil Éireann, 1919–1922*. Dublin: Gill & Macmillan, 1995.

Moore, George. *Hail and Farewell!* Edited by Richard Allen Cave. Gerrards Cross: Colin Smythe, 1985.

Morrow, Ann. *Picnic in a Foreign Land: The Eccentric Lives of the Anglo-Irish*. London: Grafton, 1989.

Mulligan, Adrian N. "'By a Thousand Ingenious Feminine Devices': The Ladies' Land League and the Development of Irish Nationalism." *Historical Geography* 37 (2009): 159–77.

Murphy, Rose. *Ella Young, Irish Mystic and Rebel*. Dublin: Liffey Press, 2008.

Murphy, William. *Political Imprisonment and the Irish, 1912–1921*. Oxford: Oxford University Press, 2014.

Murphy, William M. "John Butler Yeats: The Artist and the Man." In *The Drawings of John Butler Yeats*. Edited by Fintan Cullen, 11–16. Albany: Albany Institute of History of Art, 1987.

Murray, Patrick. *Oracles of God: The Roman Catholic Church and Irish Politics 1922–37*. Dublin: University College Dublin, 2000.

Nelson, Bruce. *Irish Nationalists and the Making of the Irish Race*. Princeton: Princeton University Press, 2012.

Nevin, Donal, ed. *1913: Jim Larkin and the Dublin Lock-Out*. Dublin: Workers' Union of Ireland, 1964.

Nolan, Jerry. "Edward Martyn's Struggle for an Irish National Theater, 1899–1920." *New Hibernia Review* 7, no. 2 (Summer 2003): 88–105.

Norman, Diana. *Terrible Beauty: A Life of Constance Markievicz*. Dublin: Poolbeg, 1988 [Hodder and Stoughton, 1987].

O'Brien, Nora Connolly. *James Connolly: Portrait of a Rebel Father*. Reprint. Dublin: Four Masters, 1975 [Talbot Press, 1935].

ÓBroin, León. *W. E. Wylie and the Irish Revolution*. Dublin: Gill & Macmillan, 1989.

O'Byrne, Robert. *Hugh Lane 1875–1915*. Dublin: Lilliput, 2000.

O'Casey, Sean. *Drums under the Window*. London: Macmillan, 1980 [1945].

Ó Cathasaigh, Aindrias, ed. *James Connolly: Lost Writings*. Dublin: Pluto, 1997.

Ó Ceallaigh Ritschel, Nelson. "James Connolly's *Under Which Flag*, 1916." *New Hibernia Review/ Irish Éireannach Nua* 2, no. 4 (Winter 1998): 54–68.

———. "Shaw, Connolly, and the Irish Citizen Army." *Shaw* 27 (2007): 118–34.

O'Connor, Emmet. "Communists, Russia, and the IRA, 1920–1923." *Historical Journal* 46, no. 1 (March 2003): 115–31.

———. *Reds and the Green: Ireland, Russia and the Communist Internationals, 1919–43*. Dublin: University College Dublin Press, 2004.

O'Faolain, Sean. *Constance Markievicz*. Reprint. London: Cresset Women's Voices, 1987 [Jonathan Cape, 1934].

O'Flaherty, Liam. *The Martyr*. London: Gollancz, 1934 [1933].

O'Kelly, Seumas. *Lustre*. Edited by George Brandon Saul. *Éire/Ireland* 2, no. 4 (Winter 1967): 53–71.

O'Neill, Marie. *From Parnell to de Valera: A Biography of Jennie Wyse Power*. Dublin: Blackwater, 1991.

Ó Síocháin, Seamus. *Roger Casement: Imperialist, Rebel, Revolutionary*. Dublin: Lilliput, 2008.

Oikarinen, Sari. *"A Dream of Liberty": Constance Markievicz's Vision of Ireland, 1908–1927*. Helsinki: Suomen Historiallinen Suera, 1998.

Oppenheim, Janet. *The Other World: Spiritualism and Psychical Research in England, 1850–1914*. Cambridge: Cambridge University Press, 1985.

Owens, Rosemary Cullen. *A Social History of Women in Ireland, 1870–1970*. Dublin: Gill & Macmillan, 2005.

Pašeta, Senia. *Irish Nationalist Women, 1900–1918*. Cambridge: Cambridge University Press, 2013.

Pyne, Peter. "The New Irish State and the Decline of the Republican Sinn Féin Party, 1923–1926." *Éire-Ireland* 11, no. 3 (1976): 33–65.

Quigley, Patrick. *The Polish Irishman: The Life and Times of Count Casimir Markievicz*. Dublin: Liffey Press, 2012.

Quinlan, Carmel. *Genteel Revolutionaries: Anna and Thomas Haslam and the Irish Women's Movement*. Cork: Cork University Press, 2002.

Raine, Kathleen. *Yeats, the Tarot and the Golden Dawn*. 2nd ed. rev. Dublin: Dolmen, 1976.

Regan, John. *The Irish Counter-Revolution 1921–1936*. New York: St. Martin's Press, 1999.

Roos, Hans. *A History of Modern Poland: From the Foundation of the State in the First World War to the Present Fay*. Translated by J. R. Foster. 2nd ed. London: Eyre & Spottiswoode, 1966.

Roper, Esther, ed. *The Prison Letters of Countess Markievicz, Constance Gore-Booth*. London: Longmans, 1934.

Ryan-Smolin, Wanda. "Casimir Dunin Markievicz Painter and Playwright." *Irish Arts Review Yearbook* 11 (1995): 180–84.

Saul, George Brandon. *Seumas O'Kelly*. Lewisberg: Bucknell University Press, 1971.

Scoular, Clive. *Maeve de Markievicz: Daughter of Constance* (Killeyleagh Co. Down: Clive Scoular, 2003).

Smith, D. J. "The Countess and the Poets: Constance Gore-Booth Markievicz in the Work of Irish Writers." *Journal of Irish Literature* 12, no. 1 (January 1982): 3–63.

Smythe, Colin, ed. *Seventy Years: Being the Autobiography of Lady Gregory*. Gerrards Cross: Colin Smythe, 1974.

Snoddy, Theo, ed. *Dictionary of Irish Artists*. Dublin: Merlin, 2002.

Snyder, Timothy. *The Reconstruction of Nations: Poland, Ukraine, Lithuania, Belarus, 1569–1999*. New Haven: Yale University Press, 2003.

Standlee, Whitney. *"Power to Observe": Irish Women Novelists in Britain, 1890–1916*. Oxford: Peter Lang, 2014.

Starr, Kevin. *Golden Dreams: California in an Age of Abundance, 1950–1963*. Oxford: Oxford University Press, 2009.

Steele, Karen. "Gender and the Postcolonial Archive." *CR: The New Centennial Review* 10, no. 1 (2010): 55–62.

Swanson, Vern G. *Soviet Impressionist Painting*. 2nd rev. ed. Woodbridge: Antique Collectors' Club, 2008.

Tiernan, Sonja. *Eva Gore-Booth: An Image of Such Politics*. Manchester: Manchester University Press, 2012.

Trotter, Mary. *Ireland's National Theaters: Political Performances and the Origins of the Irish Dramatic Movement*. Syracuse: Syracuse University Press, 2001.

Townshend, Charles. *Easter 1916: The Irish Rebellion*. London: Allen Lane, 2006.

———. *The Republic: The Fight for Irish Independence, 1918–1923*. London: Allen Lane, 2013.

Valiulis, Maryann Gialanella. "The Politics of Gender in the Irish Free State, 1922–1937." *Women's History Review* 20, no. 4 (September 2011): 569–78.

Van Voris, Jacqueline. *Constance Markievicz in the Cause of Ireland*. Amherst: University of Massachusetts Press, 1967.

Vatikiotis, P. J. *The History of Modern Egypt*. Baltimore: Johns Hopkins University Press, 1991.

Ward, Margaret. "Gendering the Union: Imperial Feminism and the Ladies' Land League." *Women's History Review* 10, no. 1 (2001): 71–92.

———. *Hanna Sheehy Skeffington: A Life*. Cork: Attic Press, 1997.

———. *In Their Own Voice: Women and Irish Nationalism*. Cork: Attic Press, 1995.

———. *Maud Gonne: A Life*. 2nd ed. London: Pandora, 1990.

———. *Unmanageable Revolutionaries: Women and Irish Nationalism* (London: Pluto, 1989).

Warner, Marina. *Joan of Arc: The Image of Female Heroism*. London: Penguin, 1981.

Warner, Sylvia Townshend. "Countess Markievicz: Women of Yesterday No. 4." *Women Today* (September 1937). In *With the Hunted: Selected Writings*. Edited by Peter Tollhurst, 124–29. Norwich: Black Dog, 2012.

Weihman, Lisa. "National Treasures and Nationalist Gardens: Unlocking the Archival Mysteries of Bean na h-Éireann." *Tulsa Studies in Women's Literature* 27, no. 2 (Fall 2008): 355–64.

Weissman, Benjamin M. *Herbert Hoover and Famine Relief to Soviet Russia, 1921–23*. Stanford: Stanford University Press, 1974.

White, James. *John Butler Yeats and the Irish Renaissance*. Dublin: Dolmen, 1972.

Yeates, Pádraig. *Lockout: Dublin 1913*. Dublin: Gill & Macmillan, 2001.

Yeats, W. B. *Collected Letters of W. B. Yeats*. Edited by John Kelly. Oxford: Oxford University Press (Intelex Electronic Edition).

———. *The Collected Letters of W. B. Yeats*. Volume 1: *1865–1895*. Edited by John Kelly and Eric Domville. Oxford: Oxford University Press, 1986.

———. *The Collected Letters of W. B. Yeats*. Volume 3: *1901–1904*. Edited by John Kelly and Ronald Schuchard. Oxford: Oxford University Press, 1986.

———. *The Collected Works of W. B. Yeats*. Volume 8: *The Irish Dramatic Movement*. Edited by Mary Fitzgerald and Richard J. Finneran. New York: Scribner, 2003.

———. *The Collected Works of W. B. Yeats*. Volume 9: *Early Articles and Reviews*. Edited by John P. Frayne, and Madeleine Marchaterre. New York: Scribner, 2004.

———. *Memoirs: Autobiography [and] First Draft Journal*. Edited by Denis Donoghue. London: Macmillan, 1972.

———. *The Poems*. Edited by Daniel Albright. London: Everyman, 1994.

Index

Leabharlanna Poibli Chathair Bhaile Átha Cliath
Dublin City Public Libraries